MANAUS

SUNY Series in Anthropological Studies of Contemporary Issues
Jack R. Rollwagen, Editor

MANAUS

Social Life and Work in Brazil's Free Trade Zone

Leo A. Despres

State University of New York Press

HD
8290
M362
D47
1991

Published by
State University of New York Press, Albany

For information, address State University of New York
Press, State University Plaza, Albany, N.Y., 12246

Production by Diane Ganeles
Marketing by Dana Yanulavich

Library of Congress Cataloging-in-Publication Data

Despres, Leo A.
   Manaus: social life and work in Brazil's free trade zone / Leo A. Despres.
   p. cm.—(SUNY series in anthropological studies of contemporary issues)
   Includes bibliographical references.
   ISBN 0-7914-0536-2 (alk. paper).—ISBN 0-7914-0537-0 (pbk.: alk. paper)
   1. Manaus (Brazil)—Economic conditions. 2. Manaus (Brazil)—Social conditions. 3.
Employees—Brazil—Manaus. 4. Free ports and zones—Brazil—Manaus. 5. House-
holds—Brazil—Manaus. 6. Household surveys—Brazil—Manaus. I. Title. II. Series.
HC189.M28D47 1991
306'.0981'13—dc20   90-35150
                                                                                    CIP

10 9 8 7 6 5 4 3 2 1

For Loretta, my wife and field companion.
And John W. Bennett.

Contents

List of Tables

List of Acronyms

BASA
: Banco da Amazônia
Bank of Amazônia, South America

BNH
: Banco Nacional da Habitação
National Bank of Housing

CEBRAP
: Centro Brasileiro de Pesquisas e Planejamento (São Paulo)
Brazilian Center for Research and Planning

CEDEC
: Centro de Estudos de Cultura Contemporanea (São Paulo)
Center for the Study of Contemporary Culture

CEPA
: Comissão Estadual de Planejamento Agrícola
State Commission for Agricultural Planning

CIPA
: Comissões Internal de Prevenção de Acidentes
Internal Commissions for the Prevention of Accidents

CNPq
: Centro Nacional de Pesquisa
National Center for Research

CODEAMA
: Comissão de Desenvolvimento do Estado do Amazonas
Development Commission for the State of Amazonas

COHAB-AM   Comissão de Habitação do Amazonas
            Housing Commission for the State of Amazonas

CPRM   Companhia de Pesquisa de Recursos Minerais
            Research Company for Mineral Resources

EMBRAPA   Empresa Brasileira de Pesquisa Agricultura
            Brazilian Company for Agricultural Research

EMBRATUR   Empresa Brasileira de Turismo
            Brazilian Company for Tourism

FAMASA   Fábrica de Artefatos de Madeira da Amazônia S/A
            Factory for the Manufacture of Artifacts of Wood in
            the Amazon

FGTS   Fundo de Garantia por Tempo de Serviço
            Guaranteed Fund for Time of Service

IBGE   Instituto Brasileiro de Geografia e Estatística
            Brazilian Institute of Geography and Statistics

INAMPS   Instituto Nacional de Assistência Médica e
            Previdência Social
            National Institute for Medical and Social Assistance

INCRA   Instituto Nacional de Colonização e Reforma Agrária
            National Institute for Colonization and Agrarian
            Reform

INPA   Instituto Nacional de Pesquisa da Amazônia
            National Institute for Research in the Amazon

INPS   Instituto Nacional da Previdência Social
            National Institute for Social Assistance
            (INPS has been replaced by INAMPS.)

IPCM   Indice de Preços ao Consumidor de Manaus
            Index of Consumer Prices for Manaus

IPI   Imposto sobre Produtos Industrializados
            Manufacturers Sales Tax

IUPERJ	Instituto Universitário de Pesquisas do Rio de Janeiro University Research Institute of Rio de Janeiro
MOBRAL	Movimento Brasileira de Alfabetização Brazilian Literacy Movement
NAEA	Núcleo de Altos Estudos Amazônicos, Universidade Federal do Pará Nucleus for Advanced Amazonian Studies
PDAM III	Plano de Desenvolvimento da Amazônia Third Plan for the Development of Amazônia
PDS	Partido Democrático Social Social Democratic Party
PIN	Programa da Integração Nacional National Integration Program
PMDB	Partido do Movimento Democrático Party of the Brazilian Democratic Movement
PROTERRA	Programa de Redistribuição de Terras Land Redistribution Program
SENAI	Serviço Nacional de Aprendizagem National Service for Industrial Training
SEPLAN	Secretária de Coordenação do Planejamento do Amazonas Secretary for the Coordination of Planning for Amazonas
SESI	Serviço Social da Indústria Social Service for Industrial Workers
SETRAS	Secretária do Estado de Trabalha e Serviços Sociais Secretary of State for Work and Services
SHAM	Sociedade de Habitação do Estado Amazonas Housing Society for the State of Amazonas

SPVEA   Superintendência do Plano de Valorização
             Econômica da Amazônia
             Superintendency for the Amazon Economic
             Valorization Plan

SUDAM   Superintendência do Desenvolvimento da Amazônia
             Superintendency for the Development of Amazônia

SUFRAMA   Superintendência da Zona Franca de Manaus
             Superintendency for the Free Trade Zone of
             Manaus

ZFM   Zona Franca da Manaus
             Free Trade Zone of Manaus

Acknowledgments

The research reported here was supported principally by a grant from the National Science Foundation (BNS 83, 17543). Supplementary support was provided by the University of Notre Dame's Helen Kellogg Institute for International Studies and the Institute for Scholarship in the Liberal Arts. Thanks to the assistance of Drs. Sergio Abranches, Paulo J. Krischke, and Regis S. De Castro Andrade, my work in Brazil was conducted in cooperation with the Instituto Universitario de Pesquisas do Rio de Janneiro (IUPERJ) and the Centro de Estudos de Cultura Contemporânea (CEDEC) in São Paulo.

I sincerely regret not being able to name all who have contributed to this work. The initial construction of the project began with a graduate seminar relating to theories, problems, and processes of developmental change and jointly conducted by myself and three colleagues at Notre Dame, Professors Fabio Da Silva, Denis Goulet, and David Lewis. I am grateful for the insights they provided me during the course of these discussions. In 1980, thanks to the Rev. Theodore Hesburgh, Dr. David C. Legee, and the university's Center for the Study of Contemporary Society, I was able to spend the better part of a sabbatical year in Brazil laying the groundwork for the project. For the assistance I received during this phase of the project's construction, I particularly want to thank Drs. Octavio Ianni, Geraldo Müller, and Vilmar Faria of CEBRAP (Centro Brasileiro de Pesquisas e Planejamento), Dr. J. V. Freitas Marcondes of the União Cultural Brasileiro e Os Estados Unidos, and Dr. Aneas Salati of INPA (Instituto Nacional de Pesquisas da Amazônia).

My fieldwork in Manaus was a pleasurable experience and, in almost every respect, it brought home to me the true meaning of Brazilian hospitality. I am grateful to "Father Paulino" of Nossa Senhora do Carmo for easing our way into the neighborhoods of Bairro Raiz and for the contacts he helped us establish in other bairros. The families that were drawn into the project were confronted with long and sometimes tedious interview sessions. I cannot thank them enough for their hospitality, their patience, and their assistance.

Mention must be made of others who also facilitated our work in Manaus. Vera Moura Bananeira, Directora Técnica at CODEAMA (Comissão de Desenvolvimento do Estado do Amazonas), was most helpful in directing our attention to various studies and reports issued by CODEAMA and SEPLAN (Secretaria de Estado de Coordenação do Planejamento do Amazonas). Rosalvo Machado Bentes of CODEAMA and the Federal University of Amazonas graciously made available his research concerning the migratory flow of population in relationship to the the ZFM. Dr. J. A. Luc Mougeot, at NAEA (Núcleo de Altos Estudos do Amazônicos), brought to our attention the data that he and his colleagues had collected with reference to migratory flows in the Amazon. In addition, Dr. Mougeot helped us locate and reproduce the raw data that Bentes had collected in Raiz, the bairro in which we intended to concentrate our investigation of working-class neighborhoods in Manaus. Edila Arnaud Ferreira Moura, Professor of Sociology (Federal University of Amazonas), allowed us to xerox some of the unpublished data she had collected in a study of female participation in the industrial labor force in Manaus. I want to thank all of these good people for their assistance. I also want to thank the directors and various functionaries of SUFRAMA, SUDAM, SHAM, SESI, CEPA, the Sindicato dos Trabalhadores Nas Indústrias Metalúrgicas, Mecánicas e de Materiais Elétricos de Manaus, the Sindicato dos Trabalhadores de Madeira, and the officers and/or proprietors of the various small- and large-scale enterprises that we included in the research.

With reference to fieldwork, I especially want to thank Ricardo Araújo, a Brazilian student of economics who took time out from his studies at Notre Dame to assist me in Manaus. Together, Ricardo and I conducted and recorded all of the initial interviews that were made with workers and various members of their families. To follow-up these interviews for the purpose of collecting additional information or clarifying ambiguous responses, it was necessary that these recordings be transcribed and typed while in the field. Without Ricardo's assistance this task could not have been accomplished. I also want to thank my wife, Loretta, who surveyed newspapers and kept everything else order for Ricardo and me.

Beyond our work in the field, I am indebted to Drs. Paulo J. Krischke, Regis S. de Castro Andrade, and others at CEDEC who contributed their thoughts to the analysis of data. I also wish to thank my colleagues at Notre Dame, specifically Drs. Fabio Da Silva, Kenneth Jameson, and Michael Zalkin, for the benefit of their comments on various sections of the analysis. Antônio Luiz Paixão, a Professor of Sociology from the Federal University of Minas Gerais, graciously gave of his valuable time and read the entire manuscript while a Residential Fellow at the Kellogg Institute. I am most grateful for his comments and corrections.

I want to reserve my most sincere thanks for Jasiel César. I first met Jasiel in Manaus, where he was employed by EMBRAPA. After many long discussions relating to developments in Brazil and the Zona Franca, I persuaded him to come to Notre Dame where he subsequently earned his Ph.D. in sociology. Jasiel not only followed my work in Manaus, but while working on his Ph.D. he carefully and critically scrutinized several drafts of this work. Although I must assume full responsibility for what is to follow, I have benefitted immensely from his comments, suggestions, and editorial suggestions. I am grateful both for his friendship and his help.

Finally, I want to thank the staff at the Kellogg Institute, particularly Albert H. LeMay, Caroline Domingo, and Daphne Shutts, for their assistance in the preparation of this manuscript.

Introduction

> More than one million televisions produced in only twelve months...
> Only this mark—fantastic, but still little known—is sufficient to
> demonstrate the dynamics of Manaus' Zona Franca in the electronics
> sector. Today, besides the almost 200 industries implanted, 46 others
> are already planned, and soon they also will be producing. All this is
> happening in the interior of the country, restoring to Manaus the
> enthusiasm to give leadership to the growth of the Amazon, now on a
> more realistic base than in the so-called 'cycle of rubber.'[1]

Thus the editor of *Interior,* a publication of the Ministry of the
Interior, described the progress of economic development in 1982 in
Manaus, an old port city and the capital of the State of Amazonas. The
frame in which this picture is drawn is peculiar to the city. It recalls
another era of development, a glittering moment when Manaus
acquired great wealth and considerable influence as the center for trade
in rubber, and thereby presented itself as the gateway to that vast and
empty El Dorado called the Upper Amazon. Generations of Brazilians
have held fast to the belief in El Dorado. They have confidently argued
that the Amazon contained the resources necessary to propel the nation
to a commanding position in the world economy. If access to these
resources was denied in the past, many Brazilians believe, it was mainly
for lack of political will, capital, technology, and the scarcity of population. Indeed, President Getúlio Vargas had said as much in a famous
speech delivered in Manaus in 1940. And then, in 1982, history seemed
to have proven Vargas correct. Only fifteen years after the ZFM (Zona
Franca de Manaus) was created by an act of political will and provided
with a powerful set of fiscal incentives with which to attract capital,
Manaus had once again become the major entrepôt for the industrial
and commercial development of the region.

1

This book presents an analysis of data relating these developments to the social and cultural lives of a select sample of approximately
100 working-class families that became the focus of an anthropological
field study. The study was conducted over a period of almost seven
months in 1984. The presentation and analysis of these data will perhaps proceed more meaningfully for the reader if, by way of introduction, I briefly summarize the experiences that prompted me to under-
take this research and the substantive and theoretical considerations
that informed the construction of the project.

To begin, I first heard of these developments in Manaus during
the course of a Fulbright teaching and research fellowship at the University of Guyana in 1970. The Amazon rain forest extends northward
over the Guyanas to the mouth of the Orinoco and, like the Brazilians,
the Guyanese also hold fast to a belief in El Dorado. In Guyana, it was
the dream of the Burnham Government to expand the country's economy by moving population from the coastlands to open the interior for
development. To accomplish this, an army of volunteers was organized
in the 1970s for the construction of a road into the interior of Essequi-
bo. According to plan, the road was to extend to the Roraima border
with Brazil and eventually connect the port of Georgetown to Boa Vista
and the Free Port of Manaus. Thus, in Guyana, there was much talk of
Manaus and its industrial development. As an anthropologist interested
in the social and cultural dimensions of economic and political change,
and observing the somewhat ludicrous self-help effort by which the
Burnham Government was proposing to extend Guyanese society into
the interior in the hopes of forming some type of economic pact with
Brazil, I was somewhat curious about what was happening on the other
side of the Guyana highlands in the Brazilian Amazon. However, at the
time, other commitments precluded pursuing the matter further.

The University of Notre Dame presented me and two departmental colleagues with an opportunity to spend a month working in Manaus. The purpose of our visit to Manaus was to learn more specifically
of the large-scale development programs that were being implemented
by the Brazilian government in the Amazon region and to explore the
research interests and priorities of INPA (Instituto Nacional de
Pesquisas da Amazônia) regarding these programs. More specifically,
we wanted to determine whether or not linkages might be established
with INPA for the purpose of conducting research in the region.

What I observed in Manaus during the course of this visit rekin-
dled my interest in developments there. Clearly, the city was in the
midst of an economic boom. Among other things, during the decade
that followed the creation of the the Free Trade Zone, SUFRAMA

(Superintendency for the Development of the Free Trade Zone of Manaus) completed the reconstruction of the city's port and the construction of a large Industrial Park. More than 100 new industries, most of which were of the assemblage type, had already been implanted in the ZFM. The city's commercial district bustled with a seemingly endless flow of Brazilian tourists on a shopping spree in the Free Trade Zone. In fact, the complex of shops marketing television sets, sound equipment, watches, tape recorders, radios, and other products assembled in Manaus reminded me of a large K-Mart or factory outlet of the type one sees in the U.S.

From discussions with Brazilian colleagues and public officials, there seemed to be little evidence of unemployment in 1978. In the new urban economy, there seemed to be a job for everyone who desired to work. However, there was much talk of the "Zona Fraca" (weak or poor trade zone), low wages, poverty, job insecurity, high prices, unmanageable urban growth, and a multitude of related problems. And, for anyone who would visit the bairros and neighborhoods of the city, there existed a great deal of visible evidence that many people were not living very well in Manaus. In the midst of all that was happening to restore in the city the enthusiasm and the leadership aspirations of a former age, physically, much of Manaus appeared (to me and to many Brazilians with whom I spoke) to have taken on the characteristics of a huge favela or slum.

Specifically, in almost every bairro one could find numerous neighborhoods in which the housing was strikingly poor and physically inadequate. In some places, homes were constructed over open drainage systems. In others, they were strung along a seemingly endless maze of unpaved streets in which rodents were usually pawing over uncollected garbage. There appeared to exist few parks or special recreational spaces. In many areas sewerage ran into the streets, filling the humid tropical air with its odious smell. Even the downtown commercial district, perforated by narrow streets that were often littered with the uncollected rubbish of shops, restaurants, and street vendors, was in many places stinking and unsightly. And, every day it seemed, the newspapers complained of problems—problems of inadequate schools, inadequate medical facilities, unfinished public works projects, electrical blackouts, the interruption of potable water to one or another bairro, street crime, and the like.

I did not find all of this too surprising. After all, within the span of a decade, by centralized planning and fiat the federal government had almost completely restructured the economy of Manaus and the state of Amazonas. During this period, the city's population exploded (from

134,000 to 635,000) well beyond the capacity or the will of the public
and private sectors to cope with the problems of growth. On the surface
it appeared to me questionable what this planned intervention by the
federal and state governments had wrought in the material, social, and
cultural lives of the working-class families who contributed the overwhelming majority to the city's population.

I was convinced by my brief visit that, depending on the research
of others, Manaus might present anthropologists with an unusual
opportunity to investigate problems relating to urban-based industrial
change (and in an area one would have thought most unlikely for this
type of change to occur). I decided to explore whether or not such a
project might be substantively and theoretically justified.

Substantive Considerations

Following my return to Notre Dame, I initiated an exhaustive
review of the social science literature relating to Brazil, the Amazon,
and studies of development and underdevelopment in Latin America.[2]
From this study of secondary sources, it became apparent to me that an
anthropological field project in Manaus could make a worthwhile contribution to our substantive knowledge and theoretical understanding of
developments in the Brazilian Amazon. Moreover, appropriately conceptualized, such a project might also make a worthwhile contribution to
discussions concerning theories of development and underdevelopment. The substantive and theoretical considerations that informed the
construction of the study that was subsequently made may be briefly
summarized as follows:

Since 1964, the political and economic adventures of various military regimes in the Amazon have been well documented, discussed, and
criticized.[3] However, except for Araújo's (1974) general and relatively
unfocussed survey of Manaus, there exists surprisingly little research
relating to urban-based working-class populations in the region. The
focus, instead, has been largely on rural populations and agrarian developments.[4] This is in contrast to the extensive research relating to working-class populations in the industrial cities of the South.[5] Perhaps this
lack of attention to urban developments is attributable to the somewhat
mythic reputation that the Amazon has acquired as a mysterious and relatively unknown tropical forest. Or, alternatively, perhaps it is related to
the fact that the region's sparse population has been largely distributed
in rural hamlets and small *cidades* (mostly the administrative seats of
county-like districts or municipalities).

In recent years the urban character and composition of the Amazon has changed extensively (Cardoso and Müller 1977: 53–59). As various Brazilian researchers have shown, there has been a substantial movement of people originating mainly in the small cidades and rural areas of the Amazon to cities within the region with populations of 50,000 or more inhabitants.[6] As we shall see in chapter 2, in Manaus the overwhelming majority of working-class households are headed by men (and in some cases women) who came to the city from the rural interior of Amazonas and neighboring areas. This datum assumes research significance. The social and cultural characteristics of these rural and semi-rural populations, referred to in the literature as *Caboclos,* has been profiled in a surprising number of ethnographic studies.[7] Collectively, these studies provide perhaps the best historical baseline available for assessing the social and cultural changes associated with urban-industrial developments and working-class culture in Manaus.

Still, as previously noted, with reference to Manaus and other large cities within the region, there exist hardly any data relating to economic developments and their impact on the social and cultural life of workers and their families. We do not know, for example, how "core" and "peripheral" industries (both types of which have been established with the fiscal incentives provided in the Zona Franca) relate to the social and cultural profiles of workers (i.e., their rural or urban origins, education, occupational experience, sexual identity, etc.). We do not know how rural migrants enter the labor force or what determines their position within it. Nor do we know how this affects their personal sense of worth. We do not know how occupation and sector of employment relate to household economies, or how they position workers in relationship to family, kin, and neighbors. We also do not know the extent to which urban-based industrial developments have affected the beliefs, values, ideological proclivities, collective identities, and political consciousness of working-class populations. Thus, an exploratory field project giving research focus to these substantive concerns seemed to be very much in order. The conceptual construction and organization of the project, however, was another matter; it necessitated disassembling some rather sticky issues relating to theories of developmental change in Latin America and Brazil.

Theoretical Issues

Roberts (1978: 60–87) has proclaimed that during the 1960s and 1970s, urban-based industrialization became the dominant economic force in Latin America. Brazil was no exception. Since the military coup of 1964, the prevailing developmental policy of the Federal Government was one that generally promoted urban-based industrialization, resulting in an increasing concentration of population in urban centers and non-agricultural employment. However, as far as the industrially employed and other sectors of the working class are concerned, it is not at all clear what social, cultural, and political forces these changes set in motion in Brazil or elsewhere in Latin America. Both data and theory seem to be somewhat divided in this regard.

The forces of urban industrialization seem as difficult to interpret theoretically as they are to track empirically. Two problems of political economy in particular have drawn considerable attention. One has to do with the meaning and significance of capitalism for understanding the dynamics of developmental change. The other concerns the impact of industrial development on the labor process and its consequences for the social and cultural organization of working-class populations; i.e., the marginalization problem.

Since the end of World War II, a seemingly endless theoretical debate has existed among social scientists concerning these problems. The nature and history of this debate have been thoroughly outlined by others.[8] It suffices here to note that much of the discussion concerning development and underdevelopment has revolved around the question as to whether their causes are best understood in reference to processes external or internal to particular societies. Modernization theorists have generally attributed underdevelopment to the regional or local persistence of traditional cultural values, institutions, and associated patterns of economic behavior. Dependency theorists have countered this thesis by suggesting that the causes of underdevelopment are to be found in the global system of unequal exchange that emerged with the economic hegemony of the advanced capitalist societies. Various Marxist scholars have criticized both these positions by insisting on the infrastructural primacy of local modes of production and specific class structures. Despite these and related differences, all three approaches treat as problematic the social position, material well-being, and political influence of working-class populations in relationship to the evolution or historical development of capitalist economies.

To underscore this convergence, it is well known that modernization theorists consider poverty the result of certain populations remaining at the "margin" of integration in the market and other institutions of society. From a very different perspective, Cardoso (1973) has emphasized the dynamics of "associated-dependent" development which, in effect, entails urbanization, industrialization, and widespread penetration by multinationals. He further associates this pattern of development with a regressive profile of income distribution, an emphasis on luxury consumer durables as opposed to basic necessities, and the "social marginality" of large sectors of the working class. Quijano (1974), perhaps more firmly than Cardoso, draws a linkage between dependent industrial development and marginality. Similarly, Evans (1979: 28–29) has argued that capital intensive technologies and dependent development "marginalize" the mass of the population both as producers and consumers, and that social and cultural exclusion follow from economic exclusion. And, moving beyond the concept of dependency, de Janvry (1985) associates disarticulated economic growth patterns with increasing inequality in the distribution of income and repressive forms of government that render large sectors of the working class marginal or unimportant.

While the dependent-development-marginality thesis has received some empirical support (e.g., Lopes 1964; Rodrigues 1966, 1970; Berlinck 1973, 1975), the majority of studies seem to question its validity. For example, in several studies relating to Rio, Leeds (1969; 1974; and Leeds 1970; 1976) has shown that the underemployed inhabitants of favelas are very much a part of the urban industrial system. Morse (1971: 162–64) has suggested that the marginality thesis is of limited relevance to the case of São Paulo. Based on his analysis of the importance of cheap labor for industrialization, de Oliveira (1972) is inclined to agree with Morse. Wells (1976) has shown that in São Paulo the poorest segments of the urban working class form an important market for durable consumer goods and, thus, are very much a part of the urban-industrial economy. Epstein (1972; 1973), in reference to squatter settlements in Brasília, and Perlman (1976), based on her research in Rio, both question the validity of the marginality thesis. And, in a more general context, Faria (1978) has presented data suggesting that marginality theory seriously underestimates the extent to which dependent industrial development generates employment opportunities.[9]

What seems to be at issue in these contradictory studies is not so much the social position of working-class populations but rather the manner in which their position is to be described and interpreted. If they are marginalized, in what sense are they marginalized? Is their marginality to be construed with reference to traditional institutions and modes of economic organization and, thus, offered up as the cause of their underdevelopment or of the underdevelopment of certain economic sectors? Or, alternatively, is their marginality an expression of the inequalities and social class divisions inevitably associated with the "development" or evolution of capitalist social formations? It follows that one might assume the posture of modernization theory, dependency theory, or Marxist theory without rejecting the concept of marginality. A case in point is Colin Henfrey (1981) who, in a Marxist frame, rejects modernization theory while acknowledging the existence of a "marginal sector" of the working class in Bahia.

The point of all this is to suggest that however one disassembles these theories of development, the relationship between urban-based capitalist industrialization and the marginalization of working-class populations remains problematical.[10] Perhaps the problem needs to be rephrased. As some observers have argued (e.g., Quijano 1974; Friedman 1977; Godelier 1977: 63–69; Burawoy 1979; Henfrey 1981), we cannot assume that a particular society will not combine different forms of capitalism (e.g., commercial mercantilist, industrial laissez-faire, monopoly, finance, etc.) and their associated modes of production. Nor, I would add, can we assume that different sectors of the working class in a particular society will be more or less marginalized according to whether they are employed in externally capitalized hegemonic industries or internally capitalized enterprises of a more peripheral nature.

Ultimately, the question of marginalization entails an analysis of the social and cultural differentiation of working-class populations in relationship to the processes of economic change that are occurring within a *real* social formation. As Alba Zaluar (1985) has recently illustrated by her research in Cidade de Deus, a public housing project in Rio de Janeiro, we cannot subordinate data to grand theoretical abstractions (e.g., modernization, dependency, modes of production, and the like) and simply ignore the social and cultural complexity of the social formation under consideration.[11] Accordingly, I am inclined to agree with Chilcote (1974: 20) who has suggested that what is needed to advance the discussion of these and related theoretical issues are substantive case studies conducted from an "ethnological" point of view.[12]

It was in light of these substantive and theoretical considerations that the field study in Manaus was structured. Eighty-eight working-class households were selected for in-depth study.[13] This purposive sample was drawn with reference to 16 workers who were identified as being self-employed, 20 who were employed as clerks or lower echelon service workers of some type in the white collar sector, 20 who were employed by one of two firms (sawmills) selected for study in the traditional industrial sector, and 32 who were employed by one of two firms (electronics) selected for study in the new industrial sector. As these 88 households contained an additional 117 economically active persons, a total of 205 individual workers were included in the study.

Both structured and unstructured interviews were conducted with these workers, with representatives from firms and enterprises, labor unions, community organizations, and the like. With regard to households, the data collection process was initiated by a structured interview with the workers originally selected in reference to the previously noted sectors of employment. All of these interviews were tape-recorded and immediately transcribed for preliminary analysis and follow-up. Proceeding from this preliminary analysis, extensive data were then collected concerning the educational, occupational, and employment history of all persons residing in the household and other members of the family living nearby. Data were also collected in respect to household economy, food consumption, the possession of consumer durables, domestic organization, associational ties, neighborhood and community involvement, friendship networks, church affiliation and participation, and attitudes to labor unions, political parties, the state and national governments, and problems thought to be critical in regard to improving the well-being of workers and their families.

Outline of Chapters

In chapter 1, I summarize historical data relating to cultural formations in the Amazon and the creation of the Zona Franca. The demographic effects of the Zona Franca are discussed. The chapter concludes by showing the extent to which the Zona Franca has transformed the urban economy and redistributed its gainfully employed population.

In chapter 2, I describe and analyze the labor process characteristic of new and traditional industrial firms and enterprises operating in the new or hegemonic and the peripheral (traditional) industrial sectors, the commercial and public (white collar) sectors, and the so-called informal sector. The chapter concludes with a brief comparative analysis of work in these four sectors.

Chapter 3 presents an analysis of sectors of employment in relationship to workers. The chapter opens with a consideration of the cultural factors affecting the selectivity or recruitment of workers in the new and traditional industrial sectors, the white collar sector, and the informal sector. The status mobility of these workers relative to their fathers and the status inequalities that exist among the workers themselves by sector of employment are then considered. It emerges from this that the educational and occupational mobility of workers relative to their fathers does not enjoin a significant improvement in their economic status within the Zona Franca. In addition, employment in the new industries has contributed less to the economic mobility of workers than employment in other sectors. The chapter concludes with an analysis of living work in the formal and informal sectors based on the biography of selected cases.

In chapter 4, an analysis of household economies is presented. The analysis begins by focussing on the income characteristics of households with reference to their composition and the number of economically active workers they contain. I then consider household consumption patterns in respect to food items and consumer durables (e.g., housing, automobiles, television sets, and the like) with reference to household incomes and sector of employment. It is concluded from these data that households reporting less than three minimum salaries, and to a somewhat lesser degree those reporting up to five, have derived very little benefit from the industrialization of Manaus.

In chapter 5, the analysis turns to factors affecting the formation of households and family units. The chapter begins with a consideration of factors affecting the organization of family units, including the Brazilian parentela or extended families. It is suggested that to the extent that "modified extended families" persist, they do not appear to arise out circumstances affecting the economies of households. More critical for the economic status of households than family type is whether or not they form multiple income units. At this juncture, the focus shifts to the relationship between domestic status and gainful employment and how the latter seems to affect the authority structure within the domain of domestic relations.

In chapter 6, I deal with the relationship between work and social life in the city and the bairros and vizinhanças (neighborhoods) in which data were collected. The analysis begins with the impact of the Zona Franca on the material and cultural dimensions of city life in Manaus. I then move to a series of sections in which I briefly describe the social and cultural dimensions of life in the working-class bairros and neighborhoods in which lived most of the families included in the study.

While doing research in Manaus, the author, his wife, and research assistant found it necessary to sublet a small and partially furnished apartment in a very small but distinctly middle-class housing conjunto or condominium. The conjunto was centrally located in Raiz, the working-class bairro wherein lived 56 of the 88 families included in the study. Formal interview data were not collected within this middle-class housing conjunto. However, we soon learned that many working-class families in Raiz viewed viewed the "good life" as the life lived in this conjunto. Thus, for purposes of general comparison, observations based on our participation in the social life of this conjunto were systematically recorded. Based on these data, chapter 6 concludes with a brief description of social life in this small middle-class neighborhood.

In the conclusion, drawing together materials presented in previous chapters, I summarize the impact of developmental change in Manaus on the city, the organization of work, and on the economic, social, and cultural lives of workers and their families. Proceeding from this summary, I take up the theoretical issue concerning the relationship between urban-based capitalist industrialization and the extent to which this has ordered the marginalization of workers and their families in this particular context. The chapter concludes with a discussion of the applicability of macrotheories of development and underdevelopment to the analysis of the microcontexts in which real social formations are embedded.

CHAPTER 1

Cultural Formations and the Zona Franca

Amazônia, 4.9 million square kilometers, constitutes 60 percent of the total area of Brazil. Legally, the area (see Map, p. 15) includes the states of Acre, Amazonas, Pará, and Rondônia, the territories of Amapá and Roraima, the state of Mato Grosso, and the state of Goiás (divided into the states of Goiás and Tocantins by the 1988 Constitution) to the north of the 13th parallel, and the state of Maranhão to the west of the 44th meridian. All of this vast and relatively uninhabited area did not become officially recognized as a region of Brazil until the Treaty of Madrid in 1750. The Treaty of Madrid came more than a century after the earliest efforts made by the Portuguese to explore and colonize the region. These colonizing attempts have continued sporadically into the present. Although Amazônia is better known and better understood today than ever in its past, its full developmental potential and its economic integration remains that of a frontier region (Katzman 1976, 1977).

Prior to the rubber boom (1850–1910), Amazônia made only a small and insignificant contribution to the Brazilian economy. During the boom, the region became the dynamic center of economic activity. However, the impact of the boom on most of Amazônia was shallow and transitory (Wagley 1971: 53–62). As Furtado (1968: 162) has noted, the multiplier effect of investment in rubber was low, if not negative, and a substantial part of the profits made was consumed by imports. Still, the rubber boom occasioned a great deal of interest, exploration, and settlement in the region. As Amazônia became more populated, a loosely organized regional economy was formed. It combined the production of foodstuffs for subsistence and distribution in internal markets with the extraction of forest products, mainly rubber, for external markets. This traditional system of Amazônian trade, in which goods are advanced on credit along a line of middlemen who are repaid with agricultural or extractive products, is locally known as *aviamento*.[1] Within the context of the aviamento system, two interdependent and relatively different cultural formations emerged.[2] For convenience, these are labeled (1) the *Caboclo* and (2) the *Urban*. Even today in many areas, the persistence of these cultural formations is related to the relative stability and isolation of the environments to which nineteenth century populations became culturally adapted.

The character and relationship that obtained between these cultural formations underscores the problem of structure that now exists throughout much of Amazônia. As development programs restructure local environments for new modes of production, they give issue to social arrangements that have never existed among the local populations of the region. Moreover, as these new modes of production articulate more firmly with the national and international economies, they impose a much more tightly integrated system of regional relationships than has ever existed before. In sum, given the regional origin of Manaus' current population, the cultural formations associated with extraction and the aviamento system of credit provide an historical glimpse of the social and cultural life that generally existed in the area before the Zona Franca.

The Caboclo Formation

The term Caboclo is not always used with precise reference in the literature (Freyre 1936) but, in general, it calls attention to peasants, mainly descendants of Luso-Brazilians and Indians, who have occupied widely scattered settlements along the banks of the rivers and *igarapés* (narrow streams or creeks) of the Amazon Valley at least since the early decades of the seventeenth century.[3] The culture characteristic of these populations was forged of Indian and Iberian elements during the colonial period when an extractive economy and a mercantilist form of capitalism was imposed upon the indigenous populations of the region.

During the early colonial period, Indian labor was appropriated from among the relatively dense riverine populations of the floodplains (*várzeas*) by slave-raids in order to establish colonies, extend the commercial exploitation of forest products, and secure Portugal's claims to the region. As the commercial and demographic transformation of the Valley progressed, riverine cultures were destroyed, their populations were either dispersed and driven upstream or away from the main rivers, or they were enslaved. Many of the survivors were brought under the protective control of *aldeiamentos* (Catholic mission villages), which were established at strategic points along the Amazon River and its main tributaries and where, as Wagley notes (1953: 34–40), they

MAP 1

BRAZIL'S
DEVELOPMENT
AGENCIES

were transformed into 'Jesuit Indians.' Practices laid down by Jesuit priests, Christan dogmas and Catholic ceremonies, including those relating to marriages, quickly replaced many traditional elements of the native cultures. Although Indians achieved some degree of protection under the ecclesiastical control of the Jesuits, in the aldeias their labor was made available for use by soldiers, colonists, merchants, and the Church to propel boats, construct buildings, supply food, and collect forest products for trade.

This process of cultural transformation deepened in 1767 when, to advance the development of the region, the Marquis of Pombal, brother of the Governor-General of Pará, issued a series of laws aimed at the incorporation of Indians into colonial life. The Jesuits were expelled from Brazil and missionaries were stripped of all temporal powers over Indian populations. Mission stations were transformed into towns and villages; the Portuguese language was substituted for Tupí (at that time the *língua geral* in the Amazon); and Portuguese males were offered special inducements in the form of land grants, free tools, tax exemptions, and sometimes political posts, if they would marry native women. As Ross (1978) has emphasized, these laws promoted a shift away from the exclusive exploitation of natural resources in the floodplain of the várzea for purposes of subsistence, to the commercial exploitation of forest products, mainly in the less productive lands located above the floodplain on the *terra firme,* in combination with subsistence activities. The economy as well as the relationship of Indian populations to the ecology of the Valley was wholly restructured.[4]

By 1822, when Brazil acquired its independence from Portugal, the population of the Amazon Valley was mainly mestizo. While the way of life of the majority was essentially Portuguese, its culture was strongly influenced by the unique Amazônian environment and by the Indian cultures that had preceded it (Wagley 1953: 38–42). Thus, as previously noted, well before the rubber boom the Caboclo formation was firmly rooted in subsistence activities as well as the extractive economy of the region. However, before the rubber boom, the extractive economy of the Amazon was not particularly lucrative and, compared to the sugar-producing areas of the Northeast, its contribution to the national economy was truly insignificant. Still, a migratory trickle of explorers and landless peasants from other regions continued to flow into the area in search of land and independence.

The number of Caboclos is not easily estimated before 1872, when the first official census for Brazil appeared. In that year, 330,000 people are listed for the area (Katzman 1976: 447). However, between 1870 and 1910, when rubber dominated Brazil's export economy (Diégues 1960; Furtado 1963: 141–48; Katzman 1976: 446–48), the population of the Valley assumed more significant proportions. During this period, the economy of the region reached its highest level of prosperity and its population increased by the addition of more than 500,000 migrants, mainly from the drought-stricken state of Ceará. By 1900, there were more than 700,000 inhabitants in the region and this number continued to grow until 1920, when it reached 1.1 million. Following the rubber boom, Amazônia quickly reverted to its former state of almost complete economic inactivity in relationship to the national economy. Except for Henry Ford's unsuccessful effort to revive rubber production in the 1920s, the area attracted the attention of neither politicians nor entrepreneurs. These circumstances persisted until World War II when, under the Washington accords of 1942, Brazil agreed to supply the Allied Forces with strategic raw materials. A major effort was made to revive the production of rubber. However, as Mahar (1979: 1–5) has noted, relative to costs, the results of this program were quite modest. Failing in this, the population of the region stabilized again until the 1960s when the Brazilian government initiated large-scale interventions throughout the region. As a consequence of the latter, by 1980, Amazônia contained more than 7.5 million people (Anuário 1983: 78–9) and perhaps one-third or more of this population could be classified as Caboclo.[5]

Practically every feature of Caboclo culture can be traced to the fusion of Iberian and Indian elements, to variations in micro-environments that dictated the principal economic activity chosen—i.e, whether it be farming, fishing, rubber collecting, the cutting of timber, the cultivation of jute, the collection of Brazil nuts, the planting of peppers, or the raising of cattle (Moran 1974: 139–52)—and, above all, to the aviamento system in which subsistence and related activities were embedded (Wagley 1953: 91–100).

In terms of work, the Caboclo does not have an occupation in the sense of a relatively stable status identity. He may be a horticulturalist, a rubber collector, a hired hand, a canoe-paddler, a wood cutter, or a fisherman. He generally earns a living from more than one of these pursuits simultaneously. None of these activities are considered a lifelong commitment. As Wagley (1953: 90) notes, if he is attracted or forced into rubber collecting, it is only with the hope of making a quick profit and moving on to a more favorable situation. His debts dictate the character of this movement and engender a 'strike-it-rich' attitude. Thus, if he accepts wage employment, it is considered temporary in order to remove debts or because more favorable work is unavailable or out-of-season. This pattern of economic activity is persistent. The Caboclo cannot produce all that he needs (e.g., clothing, condiments, lamps, fuel, tools, etc.); he is dependent upon markets. At the same time, the amount he earns from wages or the production of commodities for trade is always insufficient to remove his debts and provision himself and his family. Thus, bound by debts, the Caboclo is always 'moving on' and never getting anywhere. He, and as many members of his family as possible, must combine a multiplicity of activities, including the cultivation of crops and the collection of foodstuffs, in order to secure their basic necessities.

Many of these activities are seasonal but they also oscillate in response to markets for the export of forest products. During the rubber boom, for example, the market value of rubber and the unavailability of labor for collecting it were such that *seringalistas* (the owners or lessees of extraction areas) prohibited *seringueiros* (rubber tappers) from engaging in subsistence cultivation in the *seringais* (rubber plantations) that they controlled. Seringalistas as well as seringueiros became almost completely dependent upon imported foods. The withdrawal of population from the production of food provisions contributed to such dietary deficiencies and high mortality rates that the government of the State of Pará attempted to induce European farmers to settle in the Zona Bragantina, an area close to Belém (see Sawyer 1979 and Bunker 1985: 65–72).

As the rubber boom terminated, the percentage of the economically active population tied to extractive activities in the primary sector, relative to the population engaged in agricultural or subsistence activities, declined. By 1950, almost half the Caboclo population of Amazonas was involved in some form of food production and the percentage was even higher for Acre (73.5), a major source of rubber in the Upper Amazon. Still, in both the Upper and Lower Amazon regions, farming and the collecting of forest products remained the two principal activities and individuals moved in and out of these seasonally and in response to favorable export markets.

As many observers have noted (e.g. Meggers 1950; Wagley 1953; Ianni 1979; Martins 1981), this pattern of economic activity, and the 'debt peonage' (Cunha 1913) which reinforced it, is itself determined by the credit (aviamento) and land tenure systems that developed mainly out of the rubber-collecting industry. Throughout the history of the region, legal titles to vast areas—whether issued by government or privately purchased—have been confused and precarious. Ownership was secured by effective occupation and, if necessary, by the force of arms rather than legal instruments.

The import-export companies (*aviadores*) of Belém and Manaus established trading posts (*barracões*) run by seringalistas who leased or claimed estates in the uplands along the rivers. These small scale entrepreneurs, the *regatões* (hucksters) who plied the rivers for trade, and the *comerciantes* (merchants) who operated collecting posts, were extended credit in the form of imported goods. They, in turn, extended credit on these goods to seringueiros (collectors) who repaid them in kind with rubber and other forest products. Each determined the terms of trade and each was in debt to the next, the collector to the trader, the trader to the import-export firm, and the latter to banks and rubber exporters in Brazil or elsewhere.

The force of the aviamento system has declined since the passing of the rubber boom. As trade has become more monetarized and the production of foodstuffs and related products more closely tied to local and regional markets, producers have gained more freedom of choice in their dealings and the dependency relationships engendered by the aviamento system have loosened somewhat. However, the system's fundamental structure has persisted throughout the region (Cardoso and Müller 1977: 31). It is particularly characteristic of the jute industry (first introduced by Japanese in the 1920s) in which monopoly control of the terms of trade is exercised by the *Instituto de Fibras da Amazônia* in Belém. And for small agricultural producers and collectors who have great difficulty securing credit against their crops from banks, the comerciantes and regatões continue to exercise considerable control of the terms of trade by providing the credit needed to finance productive activities.

Thus, Wagley (1953: 95–100) found that even as late as the midtwentieth century in the farming community of Itá, a small town in the Lower Amazon, the aviamento system remained intact. The rural neighborhood was formed by a trader and his collector-customers who lived scattered near the rubber trails and who came periodically to the trading post that is the center of the neighborhood. The relationship between seringalistas and seringueiros was a patron-client relationship and it was often reinforced by extending to the client the status of fictive kinsmen: as when the patron of a collector became godparent (*padrinho*) to the collector's children. In the farming area of the community, a similar pattern obtained between the agriculturalists and the local traders and storekeepers. The same was observed between the latter and their suppliers in Belém.

The settlement patterns that characterize Caboclo communities reflected micro-environmental adjustments within the constraints imposed by the extractive economy that developed within the region (Cardoso and Müller 1977: 32; Bunker 1977: 58–76). As Moran (1974: 142–44) notes, *municípios* (official county-like subdivisions) in the Amazon are much too large to form natural communities, but each município contains a *cidade* (small city, which is generally the seat of government) and several hamlets or *vilas*. The Cablocos generally live in rural neighborhoods that are within range of these units by walking or by boat. Vilas located in the terra firme, where manioc and other food crops are cultivated, are more concentrated and they seem to evince a somewhat greater degree of solidarity than those in the várzea, where people tend to live more isolated from one another. The shifting cultivator and the rubber collector lead isolated lives and their involvement in communal activities, except for trade and perhaps participation in several annual saint's festivals, is relatively limited.

The family structure among Cablocos reflects the conditions and constraints of economic dependence and the social and physical isolation it entailed in the backlands of the Amazon. When at home, the Cabloco's household consisted of one nuclear family: the collector, his wife, and their children. The father was ideally the absolute head but, probably because of his collecting activities, women in fact tended to assume a significant position of influence and leadership within the household. In Itá, Wagley (1953: 145–86) tells us, people of all social classes shared the Brazilian ideal of a large and united family group, called the *parentela*. The parentela is characteristically a diffuse network of relatives by descent and marriage. It almost never forms a residential unit or household. The unity of the parentela, as Wagley seems to suggest, is more a function of favorable social position and the availability of economic resources, the result of circumstances that position relatives to assist and do favors for one another.

The collector in Itá was generally a man with few, if any, relatives. Hoping to escape debt, he was always looking for more favorable opportunities; thus, his habits were inclined to be nomadic and he often left his relatives behind. To the extent that kinship ties were extended, they were as much extended fictively by baptism and similar rituals as they were extended by marriage. However, these fictive kinship ties were preferred between individuals of different economic and social status, and the strength and degree of intimacy involved in them depended not only on personal inclinations and the continuity of association but also upon their instrumentality for economic or political purposes.

In Brazil marriage is a civil ceremony that is ideally followed by a church celebration. Among the Cabloco town dwellers interviewed by Wagley (1953: 169), less than 25 percent claimed both civil and religious rites at marriage; 42 percent were married only in Church; 25 percent admitted to consensual unions; and the remainder reported a civil union. Only as long as a woman was a virgin could she hope for marriage according to the ideal pattern. According to Wagley (p. 172), in Itá people claimed that three-fourths of the marriages among farmers and collectors took place 'by the police;' i.e., they were forced. The economic instability of lower-class townsmen, of the farmer, and especially of the rubber collector, contributed significantly to marital instability (Wagley 1953: 175). Thus, in the Cabloco formation, women are often heads of households formed by consensual unions that have been dissolved. It also is not uncommon for men to 'walk out' of unions that have been civilly contracted or 'sanctified' in Church. Neither of these rites are perceived to be sufficiently binding to preclude the formation of a consensual union in another community.

Religion among Caboclos is a form of folk Catholicism that combines Iberian and Indian beliefs and practices (Galvão 1952; Wagley 1953: 187–256; Moran 1974: 148–53). Magical and religious beliefs of Indian origin that are integrated into Caboclo folk beliefs include, for example, the belief in *mães-do-bicho* and *Curupira*. The former, literally 'mothers of the animals,' are supernaturals who protect the animals of each species by stealing the 'shadow' of hunters and fishermen who take too many of them. Curupira is a small manlike creature whose feet are turned backward and who protects the forests from hunters by attracting them more deeply into it until they become lost. There is also *Anhaná*, a demon who hunts people in the forests, and who may appear as an *inhambu*, a magically malignant bird. The *boto*, freshwater dolphin, is believed to be enchanted and, as Wagley (1953: 238–9) reports, almost the entire body of the dolphin may be used for some magical or medicinal purpose. Still another aboriginal belief is *panema*, a magical concept extended to cover all sorts of bad luck (Moran 1974: 148). Panema can be contracted from the touch of a menstruating woman, by not sharing a catch with needy neighbors, or by mutilating the carcass of a game animal.

In the context of these and other folk beliefs, and of the Amazônian environment itself, it is not surprising that Caboclos are unusually preoccupied with the dangers of pregnancy and childbirth, disease, and with health in general. Wagley (1953: 241–52) reports that the people of Itá spent a large proportion of their incomes on patent medicines. He also describes a variety of herbal remedies, taboos, and magico-religious practices employed by individuals and by different categories of folk practitioners (including *pajés* or shamen) to cure or protect against diseases and physical accidents, and to free individuals and objects from panema. Many of these beliefs and practices have been carried over into cities like Manaus and Belém, where shops specializing in folk medicines and magico-religious paraphernalia do a thriving business alongside pharmacies. In some instances, these beliefs and practices form the basis for spiritist cults which prescribe medicinal baths, herbal teas, and cleansing fumigations to remove evil influences from their subjects.[6]

Besides these beliefs and practices of Indian origin, there exist those associated with folk Catholicism as well as those attached more formally to the official Church. Throughout Brazil, particular saints are thought to have special attributes and powers. These beliefs engender personal devotions—in the form of *promessas* (vows) and *novenas* (prayers) as well as public ceremonies and festivals. Cities, towns, neighborhoods, rural hamlets, often even families, have patron saints to whom they are dedicated. This cult of saints enjoins an annual cycle of celebrations and festivals. In Itá, for example, Wagley (1953: 188–209) found that between June 13, St. Anthony's Day, and December 27, when the festivities for St. Benedict ended, more than fourteen religious festivals were regularly celebrated. All but three of these were celebrated in rural neighborhoods, away from the town, and only two (St. Anthony's and St. Benedict's) were officially recognized by the Church. The festivals of June—St. Anthony's (June 12), St. John's (June 24), and St. Peter's (June 28)—are celebrated almost everywhere in Brazil. In the Amazon and Northeast regions, however, St. John's is the most festive of these celebrations and it engages the widest communal participation, including fireworks when affordable, bonfires around which families and friends gather to eat, public dances, and the like.[7] In fact, by comparison to the feast days celebrating St. Anthony and St. Peter, the celebrations in honor of St. John assume more the character of a public holiday than a religious festival.

What is particularly of interest is the organization of these festivals rather than their ritual detail. To celebrate these feast days, brotherhoods (irmandades) were created. These brotherhoods are corporately organized with elected offices, including the procurador (attorney for the saint), the tesoureiro (treasurer), the secretário (secretary), the zelador (keeper of the image), mestre sala (master of ceremonies), and the andador (official in charge of the saint's errands). As described by Wagley (1953: 188–89) and Galvão (1952), these brotherhoods were not merely an association of devotees of a particular saint. The officers, which may include both males and females, were generally individuals of highest prestige and the leaders of the community. Apart from these brotherhoods and the festivals they organized, and apart from the cooperative work arrangements (mutirões) which came into being from time to time, there existed in the Caboclo formation a relatively weak sense of community.[8]

The Caboclo formation is rooted in a subsistence economy that attaches the production of foodstuffs and the collection of forest products to a complicated network of commodity markets in which forest resources are exported in exchange for necessities that are not locally produced. Traditionally, this extractive economy was integrated by a credit system that sustained a pattern of dependent, rather than interdependent, relations from top to bottom. At various levels of the system individuals were not afforded the possibility of independent decisions in respect to economic pursuits or the production and expropriation of particular natural resources relative to prevailing market values. At the bottom of the system, horticulturists and collectors followed an essentially pre-industrial mode of production. Bound by what amounted to debt peonage, they were dependent upon patrons for their livelihood. Some Caboclos could not even move from one locality to another without the permission and support of the patron to whom they were indebted.

The colonial origins of this extractive economy, the environmental adjustments that it required, and the social and physical isolation that it imposed, all served to create and sustain among the populations it enjoined a relatively distinct cultural profile. In its institutional dimensions, Caboclo social life was largely determined by the material constraints of subsistence production or, alternatively, the collection of forest products for trade. Family units were nucleated, dispersed, and relatively fragile. When extended, they tended to be extended ritually and for instrumental purposes. Religion involved a combination of beliefs and rituals that were simultaneously responsive to the environment on which the Caboclo depended for subsistence and to the traditions of the Church. In many of its festive aspects, religion constituted a communal enterprise but this did not extend much beyond the boundaries of the neighborhood or vila.

The vila itself assumed the character of a relatively autonomous unit within a município, but beyond its frail boundaries authority was not generally recognized except as it was imposed in one form or another. Within the vila, or the cidade to which it was oriented, the trading post, the church, the primary school (if there was one), or the rubber field (if one was nearby), provided the loci for three or four power positions: specifically, the priest, the merchant or trader, the teacher, and the large landowner or his representative. These and similar positions represented the various layers of stratification within the fabric of Caboclo society.

Ultimately, Caboclo society seems to have derived its sense of public order from what might be called essentialist norms: i.e., rules that were presumably consistent with the longstanding tradition of formal legal codes in Brazil. Such rules were articulated and enforced by civil authorities with respect to contracts, the payment of debts, and the occupation and ownership of land. Conformity to these rules was further reinforced by the Brazilian version of Catholicism, a religious system that mixed rather easily with folk beliefs and practices but that also sought to interdict forms of behavior deemed immoral and, therefore, unacceptable. Combining the institutional dimensions of Caboclo society, one might generally describe the Caboclo culture as conservative, extremely deferential with respect to authority, and relatively adaptive in the context of developmental change.

The Urban Formation

Although he wrote mainly of the Northeast, Gilberto Freyre (1963) has richly described the urbanization process for Brazil. In *The Mansions and the Shanties,* Freyre emphasized that for more than three centuries the rural environment in Brazil remained much more important than the urban. This was certainly the case during the colonial period. Before the small cidades of the colonial period, there were the large land grants, the plantations, the masters, and the slaves. The masters were the nobility, or they were persons favored by the nobility, and they were completely rooted in the rural sector. Cidades originated as administrative centers or the loci of markets. Some developed in land grants given to religious communities and, until the Jesuits were expelled from Brazil in 1759, these remained under ecclesiastical control. Others developed in relationship to land privately owned and they were controlled mainly by the rural aristocracy.

As described by Freyre, the influence of rural life over the urban was accentuated in almost every aspect of the cultural life of these cidades.[9] Cultural norms were articulated by agrarian elites in respect to leisure, cuisine, regarding the relationship between individuals of different ages, sex, and classes, and concerning politics and commerce.[10] Except for Recife and Rio, the only two Brazilian cities that Freyre considers to have developed a significant pattern of cosmopolitan influence prior to the late nineteenth century, cidades remained largely the social constructs of elites whose economic interests and cultural traditions were essentially rural and parochial. This pattern of local control persisted until at least the end of the Old Republic (1930).[11] According to Flynn (1978: 13–16), the core of this system continues to exist and even today it exerts considerable influence in Brazilian political life.[12]

The history of urban development for the Amazon Region remains to be written.[13] Nevertheless, in terms of what has been reported and except for variations that may be attributed to the peculiarities of the region's environment and extractive economy, the pattern of urban development in the Amazon bears striking similarities to that described by Freyre for the Northeast. During the colonial period, the small cidades of the Valley, including Manaus and Belém, were formed by the same economic and political forces that forged the institutional dimensions of Caboclo culture. For the most part, these cidades—e.g., Santarém, Itacoatiara, Manacapuru, Tefé, Obidos, Humaitá, Porto Velho—were mission stations, or forts and centers of colonial administration, or ports of call where forest products could be exchanged for imports and warehoused for shipment. The establishment of Manaus, as described by Alexandre Rodrigues Ferreira in 1786, is a case in point:[14]

> The Fort is constructed in front of a small village of Indians and of some white residents. It is divided into two *bairros* along the northern

margin. In the first exist most of the inhabitants and it is divided into three streets... The Church is situated in the middle of the first street between the residences of the priest and of the *comandante*. The *brancos* (whites) own eight houses of which four are in the first street and four in the second. The better houses belong to the white residents... The Indians live in 36 houses of *palha* (straw) of which only a dozen are well preserved.

The commercial district was located near the Fort; the house of the Governor near the Church. As the cidade grew, this zonal pattern was generally maintained. The public market, always a gathering place where Indians and Caboclos came to sell their produce and forest products and buy clothes, food, fuel, and medicines, continued to be situated on the shore of the Rio Negro. The property adjacent to the market increased in value and became the location of public administration, commercial houses, the offices of lawyers, doctors, and the like. As Benchimol (1977: 73) reports, in this 'nerve center' the 'better elements' of the city met to converse and pass the time.

During the colonial period, residences and commercial outlets were located in the same streets. Subsequently, the places of business remained located in the center, close to the market and the offices of public administration. Wealth, concentrated in the hands of governmental and commercial elements, marked a division between the central and peripheral areas of the city. The most desirable homes were situated near the commercial center. Beyond this, on the periphery, were constructed the *'pensões de mulheres da vida'* (houses of prostitution) and the residences of the less well-to-do. As the city grew, the pattern of invasion followed this line of demarcation.

Also during the colonial period, the stratification system in Vila da Barra, as Manaus was then called, was simple and pluralistic. Not without considerable resistance, the Portuguese conquered and established control over the Indians. The social order to which this gave issue did not constitute a class structure based in the institutions of a common culture. The two populations differed categorically, by culture and by race, and the Indians were differentially incorporated by force of arms. However, this situation did not persist. The Portuguese population was deficient in women and, on April 4, 1758, a law was passed that both encouraged and legalized the marriage of whites with Indians. While Indians continued to occupy an inferior position in the community, through marriage, Christian baptism, and the ritual extension of kinship, a mestizo population emerged in the urban sector with a cultural profile somewhat different from that of the rural Caboclo. It was comprised not of horticulturalists and collectors but of artisans, clerks, peddlers, domestics and, in some cases, the children of merchants of considerable wealth.

By the time of Independence in 1822, the plural structure that came to exist during the colonial period in the larger urban settlements of the Amazon Valley was being transformed into a social class system. Within this system the Portuguese and their descendents retained superior status and power. However, as the population of *Manauaras* (i.e., persons born and raised in Manaus) grew, native sons, many of whom were of mestizo origin, established themselves in businesses of their own and assumed a position of intermediate status. Below them was what must have been the majority of the mestizo population —clerks, artisans, dock workers, domestics, and the like. And at the bottom, living on the periphery of the city, as many do today, were the rural Caboclos and Indians who continued as cultivators, extractors, woodcutters, and fishermen. Benchimol (1977: 80) reports that in 1836 this class system was seriously threatened by the *Guerra dos Cabanos* (War of the Cabanos), when out of a sense of oppression a group of Caboclos and Indians revolted against the provincial government in an attempt to expel the Portuguese and their descendents from Manaus.

Because of their favorable location, Belém and Manaus became key ports of trade, state capitals, and the largest and most important urban centers in the Amazon Valley. However, their population growth was in no sense explosive. In 1833, the thirty-three streets of Belém were reported as disappearing into the surrounding plantations and farms. Beyond these, accessible only by river, were bush settlements and administrative hamlets. By 1848, Belém's population is reported to have been only 15,000 (Wagley 1953: 46). When the Captaincy of St. Joseph of the Rio Negro was first established in 1757, and Vila da Barra (later Manaus) was implanted, the entire population of what is now the state of Amazonas is estimated to have been less than 20,000 (Bentes 1983: 21–22). It required more than a century for Manaus to accumulate a population of approximately 30,000.

From a demographic point of view, the rubber boom had an important impact on the Amazon Valley. Between 1872 and 1900, the population of the Northern Region (which includes Amapá, Acre, Amazonas, Pará, Rondônia, and Roraima) increased from 332,847 to 695,112—a relative increase of 108 percent.[15] By comparison, the relative increase of population in Amazonas, a major source of rubber extraction, was 334 percent (from 57,610 to 249,756). During the same period, the urban populations of Manaus and Belém increased, respectively, by only 71 and 56 percent. The total population of Belém, the major center of export and commercial activity in the Valley, grew from 61,997 to 96,560 inhabitants; that of Manaus from 29,334 to 50,300. Thus, relative to the urban growth of Belém and Manaus, the demographic impact of the rubber boom was disproportionately rural. Nevertheless, from a sociocultural point of view, the urban impact of the boom was rather extensive.

The primary source for the capital with which the aviadores (import-export firms) of the rubber trade were established in Manaus and Belém was foreign. It was held mainly in the hands of English investors and Portuguese merchants and speculators who acquired titles in Belém to large tracts of land in Amazonas and rushed to Manaus to establish their enterprises. These investors became a significant force in the political, economic, and social life of the city. The English, for example, undertook the construction of Manaus' port facilities, its electrical plant, and the trolley lines that no longer exist. They also introduced the use of steamboats for plying trade along the river system, cutting by more than three weeks the passage between Manaus and Belém. The Portuguese, on the other hand, created the major import-export establishments, the warehouses and, in some cases, the sawmills which furnished the lumber required by these developments. The Manauaras, particularly the native sons of the former elite, were relegated to a lesser status in the context of these extractive and commercial enterprises (Benchimol 1977: 81). For the most part, they moved into the professions, filled the politically sensitive upper ranks of public administration, or they operated the smaller businesses and retail enterprises that also became important to the commercial life of the city.

The social and cultural heterogeneity of Manaus was deepened further by the addition of still other immigrants. Syrians and Lebanese drifted into the city to become hucksters and peddlers in the more informal sector of the economy. More importantly, there was a wave of migrants from the drought-stricken state of Ceará to fill the ranks of the working class. Some Cearenses, however, came to Manaus as seringalistas (proprietors of rubber holdings) and they were well established in the aviamento system. Benchimol (1977: 81–82) reports that because of their wealth and their influence among the large number of migrants from Ceará, these seringalistas moved rapidly up the social and political pyramid in Manaus. They were so successful in manipulating elections in the places in which they lived that the Manauaras often referred to them as the *'Coronéis de Barranco.'* The more successful of these seringalistas from Ceará sent their sons to study in Europe and, following the boom, they became an established element among the local elite.

With all of these changes, the arts and professions flourished. The

Teatro Amazonas became famous for its ostentatious construction as well as for the artists who were brought from Europe to perform there. Social life began to revolve around private clubs (e.g., Ideal, Rio Negro, etc.), the most exclusive of which admitted only families of high income and status. The city acquired a cathedral (and a bishop), hospitals, and a school system that by 1910 included a university. It also acquired a Federal military battalion whose commandante enjoyed a status similar to that of the bishop and the Governor.

While the city provided opportunities for upward mobility, these opportunities were never as great as the influx of aspiring migrants. Moreover, significant status mobility enjoined forces and resources that were generally beyond local control. Nevertheless, the social class structure of Manaus deepened with new divisions—divisions between people of local origin and people from the outside, between Brazilians and foreign nationals (including Portuguese), between Manauaras of various strata and migrants from Ceará and Pará, between ethnic and racial groups, between 'urbanites' who lived and worked in the city and Caboclos who came to the city to trade or find better working conditions for themselves and their children, and between the employed and the unemployed. Even the religious life of the community was divided between the Prelacy of Manaus, the bishop who overseered the Prelacy, and the different missionary societies that established themselves in Manaus in order to missionize the interior; the latter were answerable primarily to their 'congregations' and not the Prelacy or its bishop.

In all these respects, the rubber boom brought to Manaus (and presumably Belém) a social and cultural milieu, a form of urban life, that differed substantially from the Caboclo formation that more directly expressed itself in the smaller cidades and hamlets of the region. Manaus was considerably more diversified and heterogeneous in the composition of its population, more deeply stratified in its social structure, and immeasurably more dynamic in its patterns of mobility. Still, while Belém and Manaus dominated the economic, political, and to some extent the cultural lives of Caboclo populations in the interior, these cities did not contain significant populations of urban origin. Both cities were largely artifacts of the extractive economy to which they were linked. While the wealth generated by this economy created for a time a splash of European culture in Manaus, except for a few foreigners, this was little more than an operatic production on the part of suddenly rich men to cover their rural origins and status identities by ludicrously displaying a highly polished veneer of cosmopolitan values and manners. The elite that dominated Manaus constructed a more elaborate, but still a modified version, of the cultural tradition described by

Freyre (1963) for the landed aristocracy of the Northeast and other parts of Brazil.

This urban formation persisted without much disruption in the Amazon Valley until very recent times. During the depression years that followed the rubber boom, while the local elites remained in place, struggling as best they could to maintain a way of life they could no longer afford, most of the Europeans left. At the same time, there was an influx of population from the interior. It was comprised mostly of Caboclos whose way of life had been so dependent on the trade in forest products that they could not subsist without it. Thus, in search of whatever employment they could obtain, they migrated to urban centers, first to the smaller cidades and then to Manaus and Belém. Because of this influx, between 1900 and 1940, the populations of Manaus and Belém more than doubled. The economy and urban development of these cities, however, stagnated as did the economy of the entire region. Until the 1960s, the Amazon Valley attracted the interests of relatively few entrepreneurs and politicians of national influence except for the military.[16]

The Zona Franca

As previously noted, the first serious steps taken to develop the Amazon Valley came in 1953 with the creation of the *Superintendency for the Economic Valorization of Amazônia (SPVEA)* by the government of President Getúlio Vargas.[17] By law, SPVEA was to receive three percent of the regional budget to finance its operations and begin a program of socio-economic planning. These funds never materialized but, in 1955, SPVEA submitted to the Brazilian Congress the *Plano de Valorização Econômica da Amazônia*. The plan was subsequently modified in 1966. During the interim, SPVEA embarked on an ambitious program of infrastructural development, the major monument to which is the Balém-Brasília highway, a road that plunged through 2,000 kilometers of virgin forest, linking Amazônia's major port to the then new federal capital in the center of Goiás. Although SPVEA sought to encourage private enterprise in the region, without sufficient Congressional support it had no funds with which to stimulate investment. Subsequently, however, SPVEA became a funnel for limited federal funds but their allocation was largely determined by local authorities in the region.

Following the military coup of 1964, the presidency of the republic was assumed by Marshall Humberto Castelo Branco. As many writers have noted (e.g., Davis 1977: 32–43), this change in government was

extremely important for Amazônia. Having been headquartered in
Belém for several years as the military Commander of the Amazon and
of the 8th Military Region, President Castelo Branco was familiar with
the problems of the area and with the problems confronting SPVEA. He
shared the military's long-standing vision of a fully developed and
nationally integrated Amazon Basin. He also considered the development of these frontier regions a political instrument. It provided the
means by which the migratory flow of excess population from the
Northeast to the favelas of Rio and São Paulo could be diverted to the
colonization of the interior and thereby remove from the industrial
South what was considered to be a major source of political instability.
Thus, for reasons of security as well as economic reasons, he viewed
the development of Amazônia as a matter of national urgency.

Soon after taking office, President Castelo Branco appointed General Mario de Barros Cavalcanti as head of SPVEA with instructions to
revitalize its developmental efforts and programs. Subsequently, based
on General Cavalcanti's recommendation that the Federal Government
completely reformulate its policies and programs in respect to the
region, President Branco launched *Operation Amazônia*. In and of itself,
Operation Amazônia was not much of a development program. Its projects were limited in scope and mainly designed to create by way of new
legislation the legal instruments deemed necessary to facilitate development efforts. However, *Operation Amazônia* did provide the basic orientation for future policy in the region.

Under *Operation Amazônia* SPVEA was replaced by a new agency, the *Superintendency for the Development of Amazônia* (SUDAM) and
the 'legal Amazon,' defined by Article 199 of the Constitution (see Map
1), became its area of responsibility for the coordination of federal
action for the economic valorization of the region. To accomplish its
objectives, SUDAM was given extensive powers and considerable independence of action. Its budget was to be comprised minimally of two
percent of the taxes collected by the Federal Government and three
percent of those collected by the States, Territories, and Municípios of
Amazônia. It could derive additional income from the interest on bank
deposits, from services rendered to companies in which it participated,
from gifts, subventions, or contributions made to it by other entities,
from the investment of its own capital, and from tax exemptions provided by other government agencies. It could contract loans from within
or outside the country. It also was empowered to proceed directly with
its own personnel and resources, or by contract with other entities,
public or private, national or foreign, utilizing as its financial agent the
Bank of Amazônia, S.A. (BASA).

As an additional benefit to the private sector, SUDAM was authorized to invest the proceeds from BASA securities in whatever research or private firms it considered important to the development of Amazônia. Further, to attract private capital (both foreign and domestic), by Law 5122 (September 28, 1966), firms sanctioned by SUDAM could qualify up to 100 percent exemption from their federal income tax (until 1982). They also were allowed tax credits up to 75 percent of the value of whatever BASA securities they might acquire. Finally, they could deduct 50 percent of their total tax bill when the resulting savings were invested in agriculture, livestock, industry, or services approved by SUDAM.

SUDAM's role in the promotion and execution of certain types of development action was lessened somewhat by the creation, or in some instances the reorganization, of more sectorial agencies as a result of subsequent planning by the Federal Government.[18] Nevertheless, SUDAM embodied the ideology of development articulated by *Operation Amazônia* and this ideology has generally persisted throughout the successive Governments that followed upon that of President Castello Branco, which terminated in 1967. Accordingly, future policy in the Amazon would be oriented toward 'development poles,' encouraging immigration, the establishment of stable and self-sustaining population groups, providing incentives to private capital, infrastructure development, and research with respect to natural resource potential. The overall content of the program called for the effective occupation of the region and its political and economic integration within the larger national society.

The economic content of the program encompassed agriculture, the extraction of minerals and forest products, and industrialization. In terms of agriculture, earlier programs gave emphasis to land distribution and colonization but, in the end, the strategy became one of promoting large-scale agroindustrial enterprises, particularly for the production of beef and beef by-products (Davis 1977: 21–46, 111–57; Ianni 1979: 219–29; Bunker 1985). In regard to minerals, with the assistance of a cooperative program between the Brazilian Department of Mineral Production, the Mineral Resources Research Company, the U.S. Geological Survey, Project Radam, the U.S. Agency for International Development, and more than 200 geologists and engineers, the mineral frontier of the entire region was mapped and opened for development by Brazilian and multinational firms.[19] Developments in the extractive sectors of the economy have generally conformed to an enclave-export model and, as Mahar (1979: 117) notes, the largest projects related to these developments tend to be located in eastern Amazônia (e.g., Carajás and Jari).[20]

With regard to urban industrialization, as Mahar (1979: 114–18) relates, since the era of SPVEA, the approach has vacillated somewhat between the import-substitution and the enclave-export models. The distinction seems rather meaningless. The import-substitution model was given emphasis prior to Operation Amazônia and it represented an unsuccessful attempt to reduce regional dependency upon the dynamic industrial centers of the South by promoting industries (e.g., food, beverages, clothing, chemicals, etc.) that would supply the demand for imports. The enclave-export model came into prominence with the creation of the Zona Franca de Manaus (ZFM). It proceeded from the assumption that by promoting industries that assemble imported components, not only will backward linkages with the regional economy emerge but, as the market for these finished products expands, it will provide the demand needed to stimulate industrialization with respect to imported components. With either approach, the ultimate commitment is to the promotion of import-substitution industrialization in key urban centers. The role of the public sector is primarily that of attracting capital to the region by providing fiscal incentives and the necessary infrastructural development.[21]

Whether it involved land-intensive projects in agriculture or capital-intensive projects in industry, the development ideology prescribed under *Operation Amazônia* conformed to a center-periphery model in terms of which private enterprise, domestic or foreign, was to assume a role equal to, if not more important than, that of government. Accordingly, the human and natural resources of the region were to become harnessed to a national economy for which the centers of decision were located primarily in the industrial South, particularly São Paulo, or outside the country.

With regard to urban industrialization, the most monumental achievement of *Operation Amazônia* was Decree Law 228 (February 18, 1967), which established the Zona Franca de Manaus (ZFM) and its supervisory organ, the *Superintendência da Zona Franca de Manaus* (SUFRAMA). The intent of this law was to create through fiscal incentives an industrial, commercial, and agricultural center in Manaus that would serve as the "development pole" for the western Amazon. As previously noted, firms locating within the ZFM were to be exempt from import and export duties and from the federal manufacturer's sales tax (*Imposto sobre Produtos Industrializados*). Goods exported from the ZFM to domestic markets were also exempted from the IPI and those exported with a foreign import content were subject to duties at a rate reduced in proportion to the value added in the ZFM. As an additional stimulus, SUFRAMA undertook and completed in 1973 the construction of an industrial park (*Distrito Industrial*), located five kilometers from the center of Manaus. Accessed by paved roads and served by all the necessary public utilities, the park includes hotel facilities and a permanent Industrial Exposition for the commercial and educational display of industrial products by firms located in the ZFM.

The choice of Manaus for this project was clearly more political than economic. The city is remotely located in the western Amazon where it is connected mainly by expensive air and fluvial transportation systems to the centers of finance and population that provide the most important capital and product markets in Brazil. This locational disadvantage entails high costs not only with respect to construction materials (e.g., cement, steel, etc.), capital equipment, unit components, and the export of finished products, but also in terms of the organizational burden required to coordinate and maintain these flows. This is particularly the case for industries that bear absolutely no relationship to the natural resources of the region. Moreover, these costs are not offset by the price of labor which is only marginally lower in the Amazon than it is in other regions where factor inputs and product markets may be combined. Nor are these locational costs offset by the cost of living in Manaus. Food, housing, fuel, medical care, indeed virtually everything that contributes to the overall cost of living, is generally higher in Manaus than for most other regions of the country.

Nevertheless, these locational disadvantages have not outweighed the value of the fiscal incentives provided by SUFRAMA and SUDAM (see above) for attracting industry to the ZFM.[22] That this is the case may be demonstrated by the success with which SUFRAMA implanted industries in the city during the first fifteen years of its existence, between 1967 and 1982. Table 1 summarizes data in this regard.

As Table 1 reveals, with the creation of the Zona Franca, Manaus entered a period of economic growth very different from the 'boom' it experienced when rubber dominated the regional economy. The new 'boom' is urban-based. It has been fiscally induced and it is almost completely unrelated to the extraction of forest products or to the processing of the region's natural resources. It does not engage anything like the exchange network that characterized the aviamento system. Rather, it involves a diversified complex of national and multinational firms (208 as of 1984), primarily engaged in the manufacture and sale of a wide range of industrial goods, including relatively sophisticated electronic consumer durables, motorcycles, and watches, mainly for national consumption and export.

Table 1 also reveals the development bias of SUFRAMA which has favored so-called capital-intensive industries that have no significant linkage to regional resources.[23] The industries that may be included in this

Table 1. Distribution of Industrial Firms Implanted in the Western Amazon as of December 1982 by Specification, Location, and Industrial Sector

Industrial Sector	Industrial District/Manaus			Elsewhere/Manaus			Interior/Amazonas		
	Firms N	Workers N	Fixed Investment (Cr$ 1,000.)	Firms N	Workers N	Fixed Investment (Cr$ 1,000.)	Firms N	Workers N	Fixed Investment (Cr$ 1,000.)
Electronics	27	19,162	18,319.6	8	1,380	2,017.5	-	-	-
Beverages	3	-	-	5	1,622	6,520.1	3	904	6,425.9
Metallurgics	3	213	2,223.3	11	830	10,946.5	-	-	-
Machinery	5	610	2,646.5	3	107	141.8	-	-	-
Transport. Material	4	3,103	19,382.0	7	1,461	2,643.4	-	-	-
Lumber	-	-	-	21	4,065	14,127.0	8	1,222	6,326.7
Paper, Cardboard	1	79	219.3	1	13	30.3	-	-	-
Leather, Hides	-	-	-	1	171	89.3	-	-	-
Chemicals	4	113	305.1	5	426	1,476.9	-	-	-
Perfumes, Soaps	-	-	-	3	403	2,024.4	-	-	-
Plastics	10	2,146	5,475.0	1	327	785.2	-	-	-
Clothing	3	361	315.6	1	21	17.0	-	-	-
Food Products	3	117	569.4	11	1,023	5,033.0	1	60	65.0
Graphics	1	69	118.3	3	70	188.6	-	-	-
Textiles	3	276	2,818.9	4	2,638	5,576.9	1	300	64.9
Non-metallic Minerals	2	387	620.8	3	149	9,562.6	-	-	-
Furniture	2	431	719.3	5	99	382.5	-	-	-
Rubber Products	-	-	-	-	-	-	2	110	284.2
Watches	11	1,523	3,760.8	1	660	5,325.5	-	-	-
Optics	2	128	257.4	5	786	1,425.2	-	-	-
Misc. (toys, etc.)	11	2,168	5,484.4	2	57	279.2	-	-	-
Total	92	30,896	63,235.7	101	16,298	68,603.2	15	2,596	13,166.6

Source: SUFRAMA (1983: 16). Fixed investment refers to infrastructural development by SUFRAMA.

category comprise no less than 90 (47 percent) of the 193 firms in Table 1 which have been located in Manaus. The production of these firms is concentrated in six industrial sectors: electronics, metallurgics, transportation equipment, plastics, watches, and optical equipment. These firms manufacture the most sophisticated products exported from the ZFM. Combined, they represent 55 percent of the total fixed infrastructural investment of SUFRAMA and they account for approximately 67 percent of the jobs that have been directly created as a result of the ZFM. Moreover, the companies that make up this group of industries are those that are most firmly based in the Center-South, principally São Paulo, and the largest of these are either divisions of or associated with multinationals (e.g., Philco, Sharp, Toshiba, Philips, and Honda).

By comparison, SUFRAMA has stimulated practically no industrial development in the interior of Amazonas. And in Manaus, firms that might conceivably have a resource base in the more traditional economy of the region, whether attracted to the ZFM as a result of fiscal incentives or locally reorganized with SUFRAMA's financial assistance, comprise only 25 percent of the 193 establishments reported in Table 1. Included in this group are enterprises having to do with lumber and the manufacture of wood products, clothing, food processing, textiles, and furniture. Combined, these enterprises contribute 22 percent to the number of newly employed workers and they represent only 19 percent of SUFRAMA's investment in ZFM projects. It should be noted also that some of these firms, FAMASA (*Fábrica de Artefatos de Madeira da Amazônia S/A*) for example, which is owned by *Sharp do Brasil,* have been organized by affiliates primarily for the manufacture of products used (e.g., television cabinets) in the assembly or shipment (boxes) of other industrial products. Notwithstanding these cases, the wood and food processing industries particularly have experienced considerable growth as a consequence of the ZFM but relatively little of their total production is exported outside the city and its environs.[24]

Significantly, except for very limited and specialized sectors of the economy (e.g., small-scale agriculture, jute, rubber tapping and the collection of a few other forest products), the aviamento system which once connected the Caboclo formation to urban developments in Manaus is barely in evidence. The system was seriously disrupted by the deep depression that followed upon the eclipse of the rubber industry. It has persisted mainly in relationship to small-scale production in the agricultural and extractive sectors but, in more recent years, these have also been disrupted by agro-industrial developments on the one hand and, on the other, by the demographic impact of industrial development in the ZFM. In addition, as noted above, the linkages established by most new industries in Manaus are forward and directed outside of the region both with respect to imported components and the export of finished products for sale in national and international markets. This directionality of imports and exports engages commercial relationships that are largely impersonal between affiliated firms, wholesale and retail establishments, with banks and other credit institutions, and between private enterprises and the various bureaucratic agencies that represent Federal and State governments. The texture of these relationships do not assume the character of patron-client linkages: rather, they are invariably bureaucratic, political, legalistic, and contractual.

The development, extension, and maintenance of these relationships, both within and outside of government, have given rise to new class. For the most part, this class is not of local origin. It is comprised mainly of bureaucrats, technocrats, and functionaries on assignment in Manaus. These are university-trained individuals who have been drawn into the vortex of the development industry as well as the newly developed industries. They come mainly from metropolitan centers like Brasília, São Paulo, Rio, Campinas, Belo Horizonte, Recife, Porto Alegre, or Belém, or abroad. To the extent that such individuals engage in patron-client-like relationships, they do so in a political arena formed by the bureaucracies in which they work. Except as the agencies of the state of Amazonas may be involved, the major centers of decision within these bureaucracies are not generally located in Manaus or the interior of the western Amazon.

The ideology of development in the western Amazon, as evidenced by Federal programs and the investment of public capital in the ZFM, is one that seeks to shift the dynamic center of the economy away from the extractive industries of the past. It has given priority to import-substitution industrialization by promoting the implantation of urban-based industries in the private sector for the production and export of a wide range of consumer durables to markets that are mainly located outside the region. This development ideology generally conforms to a center-periphery model in terms of which the overall economy of the region, and certainly the economic well-being of most of its population, is almost totally dependent upon national and multinational firms based in the Center-South and upon the fiscal bargains that these firms have struck with the State in the form of federal legislation.[25]

The Federal government's development projects in Manaus and the western Amazon have almost completely transformed the material and cultural foundations of the Caboclo and Urban formations previously described. This transformation is most immediately evident in terms of the spatial redistribution of population within the region and, more specifically, within those areas most directly affected by the Zona Franca—i.e., the state of Amazonas and its capital city, Manaus. By way of concluding this summary of historical material, it is instructive to briefly consider the demographic impact of these developments and their most immediate effect on the urban economy in Manaus.

Migration and Urban Growth

The overall pattern of population movement induced by development programs and projects is complex and has been extremely difficult for researchers to track. It involves both inter- and intra-regional movement from urban-to-urban places, from urban-to-rural places, and from rural-to-urban places. Apart from urban-based industrialization, these various movements have been stimulated by colonization projects, many of which have not been sustained, by urban growth in relationship to resource frontier projects (e.g., Araguaia Paraense), and by the insertion of large-scale agroindustrial projects. Clearly, the struggle for land and the proletarianization of rural work enjoined by many of these developments (Ianni 1978; Martins 1980; Bunker 1981; Fowerak-er 1981) have displaced rural populations to unsettled frontiers, but it also has contributed significantly to urban growth.

In a recent analysis, Mougeot and Aragón (1983: 9–26) write of the *despovoamento* (depopulation) of the Amazon region. Despovoamento does not refer to an absolute decline of the regional population; rather, as Mougeot and Aragón argue, it refers to the conjunction of four tendencies that have come to characterize movement within the region since 1960. The first is the increasing tendency of the population to aggregate in smaller portions of the total area. The second is the increasing tendency of the native-born population to emigrate from the region. The third is an increasingly accelerated rate of residential transitoriality within the region as people move from one location to another. And the fourth tendency is the increasing difficulty that the inhabitants of the region have in appropriating space in which to live or make a living.[26] Elsewhere, Mougeot (1984: 23–30) has noted that development programs that were aimed at promoting inter-regional migration and colonization have resulted in little net gain for the region. Between 1960 and 1970, only 2.3 points of the 40.3 percent increase in the regional population could be attributed to the influx of population from other regions. The net in-migration among municípios within the region was three times higher than the net gain from other areas of Brazil.

Whatever the redistributional effects that can be attributed to development programs, they have been primarily intra- rather than inter-regional and they are significantly associated with rural and urban population losses. A comparison of 1950–60 with 1960–70 municipal rates of change indicate that an increasing number of the area's 144 municípios were losing both their rural and urban populations relative to the natural rate of increase for the region as a whole. Mougeot (1984: 31–39) attributes these developments to, inter alia, unbridled changes in the region's agrarian production and land-tenure systems, the increasing concentration of land ownership in large agropastoral enterprises that provide relatively little employment other than on a short-term basis, to the abandonment or reorientation of rubber estates, and to the closing of frontier areas as a consequence of land conflicts.[27]

At the regional level, the internal redistribution of population has been most marked with respect to its urban concentration. While the total population of the area increased by 40 percent between 1960 and 1970, the growth in urban population was 67 percent. However, as Mougeot and Aragón (1983: 15–16) have noted, the rural-to-urban movement of population has not been uniform throughout the region. Between 1950 and 1980, the proportion of population residing in urban settlements of up to 5,000 inhabitants fell from 23.5 to 7.0 percent. During the final decade of the period, the urban network lost 20 cidades in this category. In the same interval, the proportion of population residing in cidades with populations in excess of 100,000 increased from 44.0 to 57.4 percent.

What, precisely, is the relationship between migration and the creation of the ZFM? It is difficult to give a precise answer to this question. The best currently available study of the migratory process in relationship to the ZFM is one made by Rosalvo Machado Bentes (1983) in 1979. With support from CODEAMA (*Comissão de Desenvolvimento do Estado Do Amazonas*) and its staff of researchers, Bentes conducted a survey of 2,000 households (a two percent sample of all households in Manaus), stratified by bairros. Of the heads of households interviewed, 76.6 percent were migrants. Of these migrants, 57 percent originated in the state of Amazonas.

In addition to the demographic data collected, Bentes also queried informants concerning their reasons for migrating and their occupations. Over 44 percent of the migrants indicated that they left their last place of residence for economic and financial reasons or for reasons of work (Bentes 1983: 82). Almost 21 percent left for reasons of family (they generally migrated with their parents). Seventeen percent migrated for a variety of personal reasons and almost nine percent migrated for reasons of education. As for selecting Manaus as a place to live, the frequency distribution of reasons given discloses a somewhat different order of priorities. Only 19 percent selected Manaus for economic reasons or reasons of work. Almost 21 percent came to Manaus for reasons of family and close to 12 percent came for personal reasons. Of the migrants queried by Bentes, only 1.3 percent indicated they selected Manaus because of the ZFM. When one takes into account the occupation of migrants (Bentes 1983: 96), the pattern is no less complicated. Only 27.9 percent of the migrants worked in agriculture or the extraction of forest products before coming to Manaus. A little over 11 percent arrived as students, 4.9 percent as comerciantes or vendors, 4.8 percent as functionaries, 4.1 percent as construction workers, and 3.4 percent as housewives. The number of migrants whose occupations was so varied as to fall below the one percent level comprised 29.7 percent of the entire sample.

On the basis of these data, Bentes (p. 92) concluded that the motives of migrants to leave their places of residence are generally tied to the material difficulties of overcoming the problems of isolation and underdevelopment in the interior of Amazonas and neighboring states. Thus, according to Bentes, migration to Manaus seems to be as critically related to factors of expulsion as it is to the economic impulses generated by the Zona Franca. Despite the quality of Bentes' research, this conclusion is questionable due to one deficiency in his report: he did not analyze the mass of data he collected so as to differentiate between those migrants who came to Manaus before the ZFM was established (a great many of whom came as young children with their parents or who came for personal reasons or reasons of education) and those who migrated to the city after 1967.[28] Fortunately, for purposes of the present study, Bentes made available the raw data which he collected in Raiz, the bairro in which the author focussed his collection of data relating to neighborhoods and working-class families.

Analyzing Bentes' data for this particular bairro, approximately 79 percent of its 3900 household heads are reported to be migrants. Of this group, 58 percent migrated to Manaus before 1967 and the remainder migrated after the ZFM was established. The motives for coming to Manaus differ rather significantly between these two groups. Among the migrants who moved to Manaus before the ZFM was established, 45 percent came for economic reasons and 33 percent came because their parents elected to migrate (Bentes did not collect data relating the migratory motives of parents). By way of contrast, 68 percent of the migrants arriving after the ZFM was established gave economic reasons for moving to Manaus and only four percent attributed the move to parents. Not to downplay the factors of expulsion that Bentes emphasizes, the data he collected in Raiz suggest that in the case of migrants arriving after 1967, the economic impulses of the ZFM may figure more significantly in their decision to move to Manaus than the factors of expulsion.

Concurrent with colonization projects and other development efforts instituted by the Federal government in Amazônia, there has been a significant shift of population from rural hamlets and small cidades like Itá to major urban centers. This movement has been most pronounced for the states of Pará and Amazonas and for centers of industrialization like Belém and Manaus. Between 1967 and 1980, with the creation of the ZFM, the despovoamento of Amazonas and the concentration of its population in Manaus has been particularly dramatic. Table 2 summarizes data relating to the population of the Northern Region, the State of Amazonas, and the Município of Manaus for the period 1872–1980.

Table 2. Population of Northern Region, Amazonas, and the Município of Manaus, 1872–1980

Year	Northern Region	Amazonas	Manaus	Manaus % of Amazonas	Manaus % of Northern Region
1872	332,847	57,610	29,334	50.9	8.8
1890	476,370	147,915	38,720	26.2	8.1
1900	695,112	249,756	50,300	20.1	7.2
1920	1,439,052	363,166	75,704	20.8	5.3
1940	1,462,420	438,008	106,399	24.3	7.3
1950	1,844,655	514,099	139,620	27.2	7.5
1960	2,561,782	708,459	173,703	24.5	6.8
1970	3,603,860	955,235	311,622	32.2	8.6
1980	5,890,000	1,430,314	634,756	44.4	10.8

Source: IBGE, Anuário Estatístico do Brasil, 1980, pp. 76 and 79.

From Table 2, it may be observed that between 1950 and 1970, before the creation of the Zona Franca, Manaus' proportion of the state and regional populations was declining. With the creation of the Zona Franca, this trend was reversed. In fact, between 1970 and 1980, while the population of the Northern Region showed a relative increase of 63 percent, and that of Amazonas (excluding Manaus) increased by only 23 percent, the population of Manaus itself more than doubled. Clearly, these figures suggest that the industrialization that followed upon the

ZFM not only siphoned population from the rural interior of Amazonas but it also attracted a fair number of migrants from other areas of the country. However, figures relating to population growth do not give sufficient focus to the profundity of the structural changes in the economy which the *Amazonenses* experienced during this period. Table 3 presents data relating to the distribution of the economically active population, by economic sector, in Amazonas and the município of Manaus for the period 1960-80.[29]

Table 3. Economically Active Population by Sector of Activity in Amazonas and in the Município of Manaus: 1960 and 1980

Sector of Activity (Col. Pct.)	Amazonas 1960	Manaus 1960	% in Manaus	Amazonas 1980	Manaus 1980	% in Manaus
Agriculture/ Extraction*	151,041 (70.1)	8,480 (21.7)	5.6	177,871 (40.0)	8,879 (4.1)	5.0
Public/ Adm.	3,235 (1.5)	1,946 (5.0)	60.2	14,741 (3.4)	12,005 (5.6)	81.4
Defense/ Security	2,042 (1.0)	974 (2.5)	47.7	8,399 (1.9)	6,845 (3.2)	81.5
Industry	10,874 (5.1)	5,221 (13.3)	48.0	91,999 (21.1)	77,485 (35.9)	84.2
Transport/ Communica.	8,205 (3.9)	4,442 (11.3)	54.1	17,019 (3.9)	13,665 (6.3)	80.3
Commerce	13,659 (6.4)	6.389 (16.3)	46.8	41,095 (9.4)	33,103 (15.3)	80.5
Services	14,939 (7.0)	7,211 (18.4)	48.3	50,030 (11.5)	40,266 (18.7)	80.5
Public Services	5,176 (2.4)	2,537 (6.5)	49.0	25,170 (5.8)	17,357 (8.1)	69.0
Other**	3,786 (1.8)	1,997 (5.0)	52.7	8,745 (2.0)	6,009 (2.8)	68.7

* Includes mining.
** Includes activities not well defined.

Table 3 reveals that between 1960 and 1980 the number of economically active persons in Amazonas increased by 104 percent as compared to 452 percent for the município of Manaus. Although growth occurred in all sectors of economic activity for both the state and the município, there was a substantial decline in the proportion of persons economically active in the agricultural and extractive sector. However, within the state, 81,000 workers were added to the industrial sector and no less than 89 percent of this growth occurred within the município of Manaus. In effect, as a consequence of the Zona Franca, by 1980 the economic center of gravity in Amazonas had moved significantly away from the interior—away from the economic activities associated with the Caboclo formation—to Manaus where 50 percent (as compared to 18 percent in 1960) of the state's economically active population found work.

In conjunction with this locational shift in employment opportunities, the urban labor market was structurally modified in several respect. For one thing, by 1980, industry had clearly become the leading sector of opportunity in terms of urban employment. Further, of the wage workers counted as economically active in this sector (approximately 64,000), informants at SUFRAMA estimated that at least 40 percent or more were employed by the industrial firms recently implanted in the Zona Franca. Thus, with the Zona Franca, growth in the city's traditional industries (e.g., construction, the processing of wood, food, fibers, and the like), became largely dependent upon the economic well-being of this new hegemonic industrial sector.

Another change in the structure of the urban labor market concerns the impact of these developments on the occupational position of economically active persons in the urban economy. Table 4 presents calculations to this effect.[30] From the data summarized in this table, we may note the following:

First, between 1960 and 1980 the number of individual employers (not firms or corporate enterprises) increased by approximately 929 percent (from 341 to 3,499). Despite this growth, the overall proportion of employers among the economically active population of the city remained relatively unchanged: 1.3 percent in 1960 as compared to 1.9 percent in 1980. This suggests perhaps that the ZFM has not altered the economic structure in such a way as to expand the proportionate representation of bourgeois elements within the local class system. Indeed, the social space available in the system to individuals with bourgeois aspirations appears to be no larger today than it was before the Zona Franca.

Second, the number of wage workers increased from 15,517 to 133,370, roughly 761 percent. Industrial employment provided for almost 51 percent of this increase in wage employment. Whatever, by 1980, more than 73 percent of all economically active persons in Manaus

Table 4. Distribution of Economically Active Population in Manaus by Position in Occupation and Sector of Economic Activity for 1960 and 1980

Sector of Activity (Row Pct.) (Col. Pct.)	Individual Employers		Position in Occupation Employees		Autonomous Workers		Other*		Total Manaus
	N	%	N	%	N	%	N	%	
Industry	74	(1.4) (21.7)	4,200	(80.4) (27.1)	589	(11.3) (6.8)	358	(6.9) (30.1)	5,221
Commerce	235	(3.7) (68.9)	2,400	(37.6) (15.5)	3,486	(54.5) (39.4)	268	(4.2) (24.5)	6,389
Transportation/ Communications	6	(0.1) (1.8)	3,837	(86.4) (24.7)	577	(13.0) (6.5)	22	(0.5) (2.0)	4,442
Public Services			2,237	(88.2) (14.4)	79	(3.1) (0.9)	221	(8.7) (20.2)	2,537
Commercial Services	26	(0.3) (7.6)	2,843	(39.4) (18.3)	4,119	(57.1) (46.5)	223	(3.1) (20.4)	7,211
Total 1960	341	(1.3)	15,517	(60.1)	8,850	(34.3)	1,092	(4.2)	25,800

Table 4. (Continued)

Sector of Activity (Row Pct.) (Col. Pct.)	Individual Employers		Employees		Autonomous Workers		Other*		Total Manaus
	N	%	N	%	N	%	N	%	
Industry	886	(1.1) (25.3)	64,096	(82.7) (48.1)	11,458	(14.8) (27.6)	1,046	(1.3) (29.6)	77,485
Commerce	1,472	(4.4) (42.1)	16,741	(50.6) (12.6)	14,428	(43.6) (34.8)	462	(1.4) (13.1)	33,103
Transportation/ Communications	258	(1.9) (7.4)	9,026	(66.1) (6.8)	4,155	(30.4) (10.0)	226	(1.7) (6.4)	13,665
Public Services	98	(0.6) (2.8)	16,274	(93.8) (12.2)	601	(3.5) (1.4)	384	(2.2) (10.9)	17,357
Commercial Services	785	(1.9) (22.4)	27,234	(67.6) (20.4)	10,835	(26.9) (26.1)	1,412	(3.5) (40.0)	40,266
Total 1980	3,499	(1.9)	133,370	(73.3)	41,477	(22.8)	3,530	(1.9)	181,876

Position in Occupation

* Includes mainly unrenumerated.

worked for wages and almost one out of every two of these workers was employed in the industrial sector and more than one out of every three economically active persons in Manaus was an industrial worker.

Third, the number of self-employed or autonomous workers also increased, from 8,850 to 41,477 (369 percent). However, while the proportion of wage workers among the economically active increased from 60 to 73 percent, that of self-employed workers declined from 34 to 23 percent.[31] This would lead one to suspect that the informal sector in Manaus is not necessarily comprised of workers who, because of their lack of skills, cannot find work and thus have been relegated to work in the informal sector as a consequence their marginalization by developments in the Zona Franca.

To summarize: the ideology prescribed by the Brazilian government under *Operation Amazônia* conforms to a center-periphery model. In terms of this model, private enterprise is to assume major responsibility for developing and integrating the human and natural resources of the region within the national economy. A showcase example of a project conforming to this model is the creation of the Zona Franca and the industrialization of Manaus. This particular project has had a significant impact on the extractive economy of Amazonas and the rural-urban distribution of its population. In effect, the industrialization of this old port city has drawn an increasing proportion of the population out of the rural hamlets and small cities of the interior, out of the mode of production traditionally associated with the subsistence activities and the exchange of forest products by Caboclos, and into various forms of urban employment.

Because of this industrialization project and the migratory flows it triggered, Manaus now contains almost half of the economically active population of Amazonas. Approximately two percent of this population is comprised of individuals (mainly in the commercial sectors) who employ non-kin to assist them in their enterprises. Less than 23 percent of this population is self-employed in the so-called informal sector. Most of the economically active population in Manaus, 73 percent, is comprised of workers who commoditize their labor in exchange for wages. Almost half of these wage workers are now employed in the industrial sector. A substantial majority of the remainder are individuals who perform clerical and other types of white collar work in the commercial and public sectors.

Rooted as they are in structures that are most responsive to external forces, especially forces influencing the corporate interests of capitalist firms and enterprises, how have these changes affected the social and cultural lives of various segments of this working-class population?

Have they, as modernization theorists might suggest, served to draw all but the most traditional elements of the population (i.e., recent migrants of rural origin) into the mainstream of the economy by providing employment opportunities that allow most working-class families to share substantially in the material and cultural benefits of capitalist development? Or, as other theorists might suggest, have these changes served to marginalize further the mass of the working-class population by labor processes that only expand and deepen the previously existing economic and social inequalities? Alternatively, we may ask: is it that in relationship to these changes different sectors of the economy enjoin somewhat different labor processes and these labor processes, in turn, have been selective for workers who differ because of their social and cultural origins?[32]

In the following chapter, based on case studies and related data, the labor process is examined in relationship to the organization of firms, enterprises, and economic sectors. In chapter 3, the analysis turns to the consideration of workers in relationship to employment in the new industrial, traditional industrial, white collar, and informal sectors of the economy.

The Labor Process: Firms, Enterprises, and Economic Sectors

The labor process concerns the way in which labor is recruited, appropriated, and valued in relationship to firms and enterprises. The centrality of this process for the present analysis is twofold. Whether they be employed for wages or self-employed, the labor process underscores the relationship of workers to their work. At the same time, it draws into the picture the relationship of work to the economic and social lives that workers and their families live in their respective neighborhoods and communities. In other words, the labor process enjoins on the one hand the type of work that individuals do in order to live and, on the other, the social lives they must live in order to perform that type of work.

As reported in the previous chapter, the new industrial sector (e.g., electronics, optics, watches, motorcycles, plastics, etc.) now forms the core of the economy in Manaus. The hegemony of this sector, however, does not order or define the labor processes that exist in other sectors. It remains the case in Manaus that labor is recruited, valued, and appropriated according to somewhat different norms and cultural practices in different sectors of the economy. The significance of this for workers employed in different sectors will be considered in the chapter to follow. In this chapter, case studies are employed by way of describing the labor processes thought to be more or less typical of firms and enterprises in the new industrial, traditional industrial, white collar, and informal sectors. The analysis begins with the organization of electronic enterprises in the hegemonic sector.

Hegemonic Industries

The electronics industry originated with the Zona Franca. Except for the more recent establishment of FAMASA, a wood-processing firm that specializes in the fabrication of cabinets and similar artifacts for the final assemblage of television and stereophonic speakers, this particular industry maintains relatively few backward linkages to the natural resources of Amazonas.[1] Practically all the components used in the assemblage of products produced by the industry—mainly radios, televisions, videotape units, video games, tape recorders, stereophonic units, and the like—are imported. In 1982, the electronics firms in Manaus imported 73.8 percent of their capital goods and 73.1 percent of their assemblage components and primary material from the industrial South; the remainder was imported from abroad.[2]

Similarly, except for what is distributed through the commercial sector to the very limited product market in the Amazon, electronics engages few forward linkages to the local economy. In 1982, the industry contributed 70.4 percent to the total sales of the state's industrial sector. Most of this production was exported to São Paulo, Rio de Janeiro, and Rio Grande do Sul for distribution in the national and international markets.[3] However, the forward linkages that do exist should not be underemphasized. Thousands of tourists arrive in Manaus each week from other regions of the country to purchase televisions, sound equipment, VCRs, and the like, at prices that are discounted by tax exemptions available only within the Zona Franca.[4] Indeed, Manaus' commercial district has become a virtual supermarket for the purchase of these consumer durables.

Dependent as it is on imported components and markets external to the region, Manaus presents the electronics industry with rather formidable locational disadvantages. Nevertheless, the industry conforms to the federal government's development ideology and between 1967 and 1982, SUFRAMA promoted the implantation of 35 firms in this sector. This represented only 18 percent of the total number of firms that SUFRAMA attracted to the ZFM.[5] Still, these 35 firms accounted for almost 44 percent of the 47,194 new jobs attributed to the industrial sector as a result of SUFRAMA's efforts (SUFRAMA 1983: p. 16). In 1983, SUFRAMA approved 53 additional industrial projects of which 25 were directly related to the electronics industry.

The penetration of the electronics industry by multinational firms is not always easy to discern. Of the 43 firms operative in this sector in 1983, no less than 22 could be clearly identified as affiliates of multinationals (e.g., Evadin, Motorádio, Philco, Philips, Toshiba, etc.).[6] Combined, these affiliates accounted for 65 percent of the 21,860 workers employed in the industry. Although Gradiente, a Brazilian-based firm, is the largest employer (4,091 workers), 65 percent of the nationally-based firms employ fewer than 150 workers. By way of contrast, 57 percent of the multinational affiliates employ more than 250 workers and six of them report payrolls in excess of 1,500 workers. Except for Gradiente, the electronics industry in Manaus is obviously dominated by affiliates of Japanese, European, and American-based multinationals. In addition, many of the smaller firms operating in the industry are directly linked to these multinationals or dependent upon them for the sale of coils, capacitators, switches, resistors, and the like.[7]

Two firms, identified here as Agá and Jota, were selected for intensive research.[8] Both are typical assemblage industries. Both produce essentially the same lines of finished products, including televisions (black and white as well as color), amplifiers and assorted stereo equiptment, tape recorders, radio-phonograph and radio-tape units, turntables, tape decks, radios with and without tape players, auto radios and tape players, and video cassette players. Both were established in Manaus in the early nineteen seventies. When established, both firms employed in excess of 1,500 workers.[9]

Agá belongs to a group of companies that are 100 percent owned by a foreign-based multinational. Within this group, Agá is separately incorporated as an affiliate. Its parent board of directors sits outside of Brazil. Within the Free Trade Zone, Agá is organized as a limited society (*sociedade limitada*). As such, shares in the firm are not traded in the Brazilian market. Officially, Agá claims to be an independent corporation whose administration sits in Manaus. In fact, however, the company's central office is in São Paulo, where the corporate headquarters for the parent company's multinational investments in Brazil are located. Major administrative decisions—decisions relating to such critical matters as contracts, marketing, production schedules, capital needs, the use of allocated import quotas in respect to components, and the like—are taken in São Paulo. Communications between higher level administrative officers in Manaus and São Paulo are virtually a daily routine. As often as not, the managing director of Agá is in transit between Manaus and São Paulo.

The corporate structure of Jota differs somewhat from that of Agá. Jota is organized in Brazil as an anonymous society (*sociedade anônima*). Shares in the firm are traded in the Brazilian market. Because the majority of these shares are purported to be owned by Brazilians, Jota claims to be a Brazilian firm and knowledgeable informants at Agá concur that Jota is predominantly owned by Brazilian interests. However, Jota's product line is solidly identified with a Japanese multinational and informants at the company were disinclined or not at liberty to discuss the precise nature of this affiliation. Jota's officials, like those at Agá, claimed that the company's central office is located in Manaus. However, like Agá,

Jota is one of a group of production units for which major decisions are taken in São Paulo.[10]

In Manaus, both firms have secured production sites in the new industrial park. The physical plants of both combine several production units housed principally in large, aluminum-constructed, air-conditioned buildings which do not create the impression of a long-term capital investment commitment.[11] These areas are fenced off from nearby plants and protected by security personnel. Admission to the plants by workers or visitors is by identity card or special passes. In order to move from one building to another, these credentials must be visibly displayed at all times.

At the time of research, Agá listed 987 workers on its payroll. Eleven (1.1 percent) of this number were classified as administrative officers and engineers in charge of production. Ninety-six (9.7 percent) were classified as office personnel. Thirty (3.0 percent) were classified as *técnicos* (low level technicians). The remaining 850 (86.1 percent) are mainly assembly line personnel who were classified as "qualified workers." Approximately 60 percent of the latter are female assembly workers, called *montadoras*.[12] In 1984, Jota's labor force was 55 percent larger than that of Agá (1,531 as compared to 987 workers). However, its stratification differed but slightly. At Jota, 10 (0.7 percent) of its workers were classified as administrative officers and engineers. Approximately 11.6 percent (178) were listed as office personnel. Seventy workers (4.6 percent) were classified as technicians (técnicos). Unlike Agá, Jota seems to differentiate between the latter and "qualified operators." "Qualified operators" are primarily inspectors who work under the supervision of middle-level technicians (high school graduates) and they comprised 2.2 percent (33) of the total labor force. Jota also considers assembly workers, the vast majority of whom are women, to be "unqualified operators." At the time of research, "unqualified operators" comprised 1,240 (81.0 percent) of Jota's total labor force.

The personnel directors of Agá and Jota were not able to provide data relating the percentage contribution of workers' salaries to the overall cost of production. However, at Agá, the director did emphasize that wages and salaries represented "a very small percentage of the total cost of production." A substantial majority of the assembly line workers are paid the minimum salary.[13] Technicians are generally paid between two and four times the minimum salary and most office workers receive two times the minimum salary or less. At one time, Agá provided a system of merit increases in addition to minimum salary adjustments. Because of the recession, this practice was terminated in 1981. In light of these data, excluding the salaries of managers and the cost of fringe benefits, Agá's monthly payroll in Manaus may be very crudely estimated at approximately U.S. $125,000–150,000. Interviews with workers as well as union officers indicate that the wage structure is relatively uniform throughout the industry. Thus, because of the size of its labor force, it may be assumed that Jota's monthly payroll is approximately 55 percent larger than that of Agá. However, there exist no data to suggest that wages and salaries at Jota contribute proportionately more to the overall cost of production than they do at Agá.

The organization of both firms combines divisional and departmental units in characteristic bureaucratic fashion. On the administrative side, general managers are delegated the responsibility of supervising the day-to-day direction of the plants by resident directors who travel frequently to São Paulo. Such personnel as the directors of industrial relations, chief accountants, and chief engineers assume functionally specified responsibilities. Each of their units have departmental or divisional subunits with their own administrative heads. These divisional units or subunits are further divided into functionally-specific departments or sections, each of which has its own supervisor or "chefe."

The higher levels of management at both firms are generally occupied by university-trained specialists appointed in São Paulo. These personnel are recruited in Brazil if possible. Although administrative vacancies and vacancies for advanced technicians (e.g., engineers) are announced in the local newspapers, both firms claim they have been unsuccessful in recruiting these higher level appointments from within the region. None of the top administrators at either firm originate in Manaus and both employ engineers who are not Brazilian and who have been recruited or transferred to Manaus from outside the country. At the time of research, no Manauaras or Amazonenses occupied positions above the level of technician or office staff at either firm.

With respect to recruitment of técnicos (low-level technicians), qualified and unqualified workers, and office personnel, both firms advertise vacancies within the plant and, when necessary, in the local papers. Agá claims to give preference to applicants of regional origin; Jota does not. Except for higher level appointments, for which education and previous experience are important, and apart from the applicant's regional origins, Agá claims that the only official criterion for employment is the applicant's aptitude for the work that will be assigned. Additionally, Jota gives considerable emphasis to the applicant's age, previous experience, level of education, and social origins.

At Jota, the director of industrial relations indicated that the company has a strong preference for hiring workers who were born or raised in the city, preferably under thirty years of age, and who have completed or hope to complete a secondary school education. Jota is disinclined to hire migrants from the interior of Amazonas. In explaining these preferences, it was stated that the company considers assembly workers a cost factor that must be periodically adjusted to product demand. Older workers with limited education, it was stated, create difficult personnel problems. Such workers often want to make a career of assembly work and they become agitated when laid off. Younger workers with some educational background, according to the personnel director, are not so negatively affected. They have fewer responsibilities and more opportunities for employment elsewhere.

Rural migrants, he emphasized, present other problems. "They are not used to urban life and they have no technological affinity. They are so fascinated with television that they stand about watching it rather than doing their work." "In addition", he noted, "workers from the interior are too independent. They are verbally violent. You give them a little attention and they think they can do and say what they please. You tell one of them to do this or that or he is going to get fired and he says: 'Fire me. I can still fish.' This mentality is continuous across generations: fathers from the interior want their children to think like people from the interior. They are a source of too many problems and we prefer not to employ them."

With reference to assembly workers, aptitude for the job primarily refers to the applicant's digital dexterity. Applicants are given standardized as well as non-standardized tests to measure their digital adroitness, knowledge of electrical circuitry, and their ability to read and follow instructions. Based on these tests, candidates are selected from the applicant pool for further screening by way of a personal interview with the director of industrial relations or the supervisor of the division to which the employee will be assigned. The interview is relatively brief and unstructured. Its purpose is to provide a quick assessment of the applicant's character and personality. All of this is more or less standard procedure at both firms.

The general perception of workers of the interview situation is that they are more likely to be successful if they do not ask questions, particularly questions relating to pay, benefits, rank, or the possibilities of promotion. Workers believe that docility rather than aggressiveness, and an attitude of deference rather than one of independence, are critical to securing a job, and many of them were able to cite cases in support of this belief. Successful applicants are given a brief orientation to familiarize them with the company, its rules and regulations, its production facilities, and its benefit structure. The new employee is then assigned to a department where the supervisor arranges whatever training may be needed for specific placement.

At Jota, but not at Agá, técnicos and qualified workers (mainly line inspectors, i.e., workers with previous experience in the industry) who are recruited outside the plant are given a probationary status. This means that despite their previous experience and training, and notwithstanding the fact that they may have been earning two or three times more than unqualified workers at their previous places of employment, they will receive the same salary as unqualified workers. Unless they are subsequently promoted from within the plant, these qualified workers remain at the same salary level as unqualified workers. In effect, the number of qualified workers is kept at a minimum. When their number becomes excessive, they are selectively dismissed and replaced by workers at beginning wage levels who are often equally experienced and qualified. This practice is disclaimed by the personnel managers of both firms. However, numerous informants, including labor leaders, claimed that this is a widespread policy in the electronics industry and that Jota is particularly notorious for using it.

The training process among these firms is not as complicated as it may first appear. Line inspectors require somewhat more training than assembly workers. However, line inspectors are few in number. Moreover, they are either recruited from what has become an excessive pool of such workers in Manaus or they are selected from among favored assembly workers or perhaps workers who have taken an electronics course in school or with SENAI (*Serviço Nacional de Aprendizagem Industrial*). Line inspectors test and sometimes repair faulty units. Assembly work, on the other hand, is divided among a series of simple repetitive tasks. Each worker is assigned a specific task. The task usually consists of inserting three or four color-identified transistors or relays in the designated holes of prefabricated circuit panels. Most soldering is done automatically by machine. The work is dexterous and may improve with practice, but it requires a minimum of training (perhaps fifteen minutes), little or no education, and no exercise of independent judgement. Regarding assembly work, the director at Jota stated: "I hate to see people work on the production line. It is stupid, dull, mechanical work, and it requires no intelligence."

It is claimed that gender is not a criterion of selection for assembly work. However, there is a disproportionate representation of women among assembly workers and it generally obtains throughout the electronics industry. The explanation given for this by administrators is that women are more dexterous and perform better on tests designed to measure dexterity. One informant added: "they are not as easily bored by dull, tedious work." Male workers suggest that the companies prefer women because they are more docile, less inclined to register dissatis-

faction in respect to wages and working conditions, and more sub-
servient in their demeanor in the presence of supervisors. In 1984 more
than half of the assembly workers at Agá and Jota were women.

Assemblage industries in the hegemonic sector are constantly hiring and dismissing workers. Because of the nature of the work involved
and the limited training required to perform it, the electronics firms
especially tend to view assembly workers as a production factor that
they can easily adjust to market assessments made in São Paulo. Even
while waiting a few weeks for the arrival of imported components or for
SUFRAMA to extend import quotas that have been exhausted, a particular firm may dismiss workers. Because of their number, montadoras
are particularly vulnerable to these adjustments. Also because of these
adjustments, it is frequently the case that an assembly worker will leave
the employ of one company to take a job with another because she or
he has a "friend" to whom she or he wants to be near. Consequently,
there exists in Manaus an experienced pool of assembly workers from
which the electronics firms can draw upon whenever necessary, and it
is common to encounter individuals who have been virtually cycled, or
who have cycled themselves, from one firm to another. Related to these
factors, data collected by union officials reveal that the level of employment for any particular firm in the electronics industry can vary on a
monthly basis by as much as one hundred or more workers.

With some variation, the work week at Agá and Jota is forty-five
hours extended over a five-day period. For assembly workers, the
tempo of work is mechanically controlled by the line to which they are
assigned and it varies according to what is being assembled. In all
cases, however, the speed at which components are moved is based
upon studies that are periodically made by industrial engineers. These
studies seek to maximize the assembly of finished products while mini-
mizing the number of faulty units at various points of inspection. Faulty
units are withdrawn and transported to a special section for repair. In
order to maximize production and minimize costs, assembly lines may
be slowed or speeded up; tasks may be modified and more workers
added; or inefficient workers may be removed.

The inspection process itself is rationalized as an empirical measure of the efficiency of particular workers and thus, it provides justification for the dismissal of workers who are not considered productive.
Although the inspection process is relatively focused on the task at
hand, it engages constraints that extend well beyond the physical operations involved. It particularly limits the sociability of workers. Despite
their physical proximity, when the line is in motion, assembly workers
must take care not to be socially distracted from their assigned tasks;

otherwise, they run the risk of making errors which can lose them their jobs. Accordingly, when the line is engaged, conversation among assembly line workers is physically confined to individuals working in close proximity to one another. Friendship groups or cliques form only when breaks are scheduled or in conjunction with formally organized events. In respect to the latter, both firms provide recreational facilities and a regular schedule of recreational activities.[14]

Accordingly, assembly line production entails a relatively strict system of industrial discipline. Inefficiency is grounds for dismissal. Tardiness, unexplained absences, or any behavior deemed disruptive of assembly line operations, are not tolerated. An unexplained absence automatically invokes a warning as well as a loss of pay; if repeated, it is considered grounds for dismissal. If a worker is fifteen minutes late, an hour's pay is lost. When more than fifteen minutes late, the worker is dismissed for the entire day. If tardy four times within the period of a month, the worker may be permanently dismissed. At Jota, except for administrative staff, all workers punch a clock and are paid accordingly. At Agá, only assembly workers are required to punch a clock.

In conjunction with these regulations, both firms maintain a file for each worker in its employ as well as a file for workers who have been dismissed. These files contain personnel data. They also contain data relating to tardiness, absenteeism, general conduct, and job performance. In terms of general conduct, such reports are unsystematic, subjective, and extremely variable in content. Positive evaluations are seldom recorded and no evaluation simply indicates that the worker's performance and conduct have been generally satisfactory.

Positive evaluations need not be recorded as there exists very little prospect for promotion at either of these firms or within most of the firms that comprise the new industrial sector. At Agá, on the production side of the industry and below the level of senior management, there exist only thirty positions (occupied by técnicos) to which 850 assembly workers might reasonably aspire. At Jota, the comparable number is 103 positions relative to 1,240 assembly workers. At Jota, it is reputed that these positions are sometimes vacated by layoffs. According to workers, this is not so often the case at Agá. Whatever, promotions are few and far between and when they do happen, they tend to be marginal in terms of both salary and status. Office workers are no exception to these circumstances. Indeed, Agá's director of industrial relations considers the lack of opportunities for advancement to be the firm's most negative feature and a major source of difficulty relative to the motivation of workers.

If the lack of opportunity for status mobility is thought to be a negative dimension of employment, the industry's benefit structure is touted to be the opposite. Agá and Jota proclaim to offer all categories of workers educational benefits by way of special training courses, nursery school care (*crèche*) for the children of working mothers, indemnification or FGTS (*Fundo de Garantia por Tempo de Serviço*), accident insurance, and health coverage at private clinics in addition to INPS (*Instituto Nacional De Previdência Social*). Both firms maintain a group life insurance program for workers who wish to participate. Both subsidize a hot lunch program. By contract with SUFRAMA, both partially subsidize the transportation of workers to and from their respective neighborhoods by private buses. Both provide recreational facilities, athletic fields and, in the case of Jota, a swimming pool. Both partially subsidize club activities, including an organized program of competitive sports. And finally, both firms offer workers the opportunity to purchase electronic units (televisions, radios, stereophonic equipment, etc.), by way of payroll deductions and at factory discounted prices. However, except to top-level managers, neither firm offers its employees a supplementary retirement program or housing assistance.

On the face of it, this package of benefits appears quite generous. Indeed, it is generous in the sense that it provides some services that are not generally available to workers in other industrial sectors. However, when viewed more closely, the benefit structure of the electronics industry is not entirely what it is proclaimed to be. For example, all registered employers are required by the federal government to pay an amount equal to eight percent of the employee's salary to an indemnification fund (FGTS) which remits the accumulated credits to workers in the event they are laid off through no fault of their own. By law, workers may borrow against this fund for such purposes as buying or constructing a house. To assist workers in negotiating loans backed by funds to which they are entitled, and then to proclaim this as a social service benefit (as in the case of Agá), is to proclaim a benefit that is more spurious than real.

The FGTS benefit, which is a tax imposed upon the employer, is clearly beneficial to workers. It should be noted, however, that the FGTS is also beneficial to employers. The fund is often used by employers to dismiss undesirable, inefficient, or surplus workers. Such workers can be discharged in a manner as to qualify them for indemnification payments. Sometimes these accumulated credits are sufficient for a worker to buy or build a house or to establish himself in the informal sector. This temporary windfall eases the loss of employment. In this manner, FGTS benefits tend to reinforce a calculus according to which labor is a factor input that can be readily adjusted to market assessments without engaging a more deeply constructed social concern for the worker's long-term interests or needs.

Similarly, for each registered worker, employers must contribute payments to INPS. This entitles workers to federally supervised retirement benefits and to health treatment, including the treatment of accident cases, at public clinics maintained by INAMPS (*Instituto Nacional de Assistência Médica da Previdência Social*). Why then, in addition to these payments, do the hegemonic industrial firms like Agá and Jota maintain contracts with private health clinics? The explanation provided by informants is that workers who absent themselves from the job find it too easy to qualify for wages they have not earned by obtaining medical excuses from government-operated clinics. Thus, by maintaining contracts with private clinics of their own selection, these industrial firms are assured that medical excuses will not be easily obtained and, at the same time, they appear to be providing a higher quality of care than that provided by public clinics.[15]

The concern for industrial discipline also extends to the design of other proclaimed benefits. The transportation of workers to and from their respective neighborhoods, for example, is a service designed by industry to facilitate industrial discipline. Although touted as a benefit, the transportation service operates according to schedules set by the industries that use it, thereby removing the vicissitudes of public transportation as an excuse for workers being late or sometimes absent. Moreover, while the cost of this service is borne primarily by the firms themselves, the workers who use the service are required to pay a nominal fee by way of regular payroll deductions. Similarly with the crèche. Maintained by SUFRAMA on behalf of the industries that subsidize it, this benefit is designed to facilitate the employment of women without compromising industrial discipline by allowing those with young children an excuse for tardiness or absenteeism.

In sum, beyond their conformity to federal requirements, many of the benefits provided by these firms are clearly designed to reduce production costs by facilitating the maintenance of a disciplined labor force. Even so, workers must share in the cost of some of these benefits. They contribute to the cost of transportation and hot meals. They obviously must pay for whatever they purchase at discounted prices. They also pay for whatever they consume whenever they use club and pool facilities or participate in social events. In these respects, the benefit structure of the hegemonic industries is not nearly as impressive as is generally proclaimed by SUFRAMA and by the companies involved.

The workers at Agá and Jota have a labor union (*Sindicato dos Trabalhadores Nas Indústrias Metalúrgicas, Mecânicas e de Materiais*

Elétricos de Manaus). Membership in the union is not compulsory. However, by law, employers are required to remit an amount equivalent to two percent of their total payroll to the union. This remittance is uniform throughout the industry and it is deducted from the salaries of individual workers independent of their membership status. As a consequence, registered members as well as non-members are required to support the union. Registered members pay dues in addition to the regular two percent deduction. The union maintains a union hall. In addition to administrative offices, meeting rooms, and some recreational space, the union hall houses a medical clinic, a dental clinic, and a dispensary for members who wish to use it.

Again by law, the electronics industry has to negotiate an agreement with the metallurgical union every August. Based on interviews with administrative personnel at Agá and Jota, with union officers, and with workers, this process of negotiation is largely ritualistic. The union always asks for wage adjustments slightly above the minimum set by the government and, after suitable resistence, the firms involved are generally prepared to make limited concessions for selected categories of workers. These limited concessions always seem to have been sufficient for the union to renew its contract. Strikes or work stoppages relating to contract negotiations were unheard of in Manaus.

At the time of research, it was extremely difficult for labor unions to legally engage in strike action in Brazil.[16] Labor laws required contract disputes between employers and unions to be arbitrated through a system of government controlled labor courts and these courts have been most friendly to capitalist interests. Arbitration procedures in the labor courts can be prolonged and, while in process, it is extremely risky for labor leaders to engage in organized work stoppages or strikes. Not only are such strikes illegal, but neither the unions nor the workers command the resources necessary to sustain these actions or to settle the disputes that provoked them. Ultimately, such disputes must be returned to the labor courts for settlement. Thus, strikes resulting from a breakdown of contract negotiations are relatively uncommon. When strikes do occur, they generally constitute a form of political action taken in support of a movement, a party, or, in some cases, a faction within the union itself.[17]

The most significant differences existing between the structure and organization of Agá and Jota, differences that might well be generalized to other firms in the hegemonic industrial sector, relate to their managerial styles and their philosophies of industrial relations. As expressed by its director of industrial relations, Agá seems to acknowledge that its wage and benefit structure are not what they should be in order for workers to "maintain an acceptable standard of living in Manaus," where the cost of living is considerably higher than it is in the industrial cities of the south.[18] Further, he noted that the electronics workers in Manaus form a labor force that is new and very different from what tends to exist in the region's traditional industries. For these reasons, he emphasized that Agá must discover ways to promote their development as industrial workers and this, he suggested, would require more consultation of workers by their supervisors.

Jota's director of industrial relations articulated a very different point of view. "Jota", he stated, "considers its wage structure adequate for what workers are asked to do and its benefit structure is the best in the industry." More significantly, he emphasized again that assembly workers are an "expendable factor" in the production process: "They cannot be viewed as permanent employees. We do not expect them to make careers of this work. They are hired when needed and let go when not. While here, they have better work conditions than they can obtain elsewhere in Manaus. If they are dissatisfied with these conditions, they are free to leave. They can be easily replaced and their replacements can be quickly trained."[19] "Indeed", he added, "the day will soon come when we will replace most of these workers with machines."

These differing views extend further. From the perspective of Agá's director of industrial relations, labor legislation regulating the organization of unions and CIPAs (*Comissões Internal de Prevenção de Acidentes*) has been of mutual benefit to employers and employees alike. From the perspective of Jota's director, the opposite is the case. In his view, the "unions in Brazil are useless, particularly at Jota." "The unions do what the government tells them to do anyway and Jota gives more and better benefits than the unions demand. They may protect workers' rights but that would not be necessary if the workers would learn their rights. The unions just drain money from the workers for nothing." As for CIPAs, he stated: "They are required by law but they are generally useless. The first person who worries about a fire in the plant is the manager and not the worker. The worker is motivated to be elected to a CIPA because he knows that, by law, CIPA representatives cannot be fired."[20]

The views expressed by these administrators are not independent of the policies and programs that prevail at their respective companies. At Agá, for example, several months of planning were recently devoted to the institution of a program designed to engage workers in discussions relating to company operations and decisions. The program involves the organization of workers' councils within departments and divisions. Supervisors and department heads are required to schedule weekly meetings with these councils in order to explore the views of workers with respect to conditions of work, job assignments, and departmental routines. As of the time of research, the program was new and experimental. Because of this, the director would not project the range of decisions that might be affected by these discussions. However, in the form that the program had been authorized by the São Paulo office, workers clearly would not be allowed to significantly influence decisions relating to administrative appointments, the organization of production, wages, or capital investments.

Agá's recruitment policies are also affected by its philosophy of industrial relations. One such policy has to do with the recruitment of older workers. Another concerns the recruitment of workers who originate in the interior of Amazonas and who have migrated to Manaus in search of employment. Unlike Jota, Agá claims not to discriminate against the employment of older workers and migrants from the interior in favor of younger applicants of urban origins. In regard to migrants, Agá claims to share the government's commitment to a program of regional development.

Another difference between the two firms concerns the employment of family members. Unlike Jota, Agá does not prohibit the employment of two or more members of the same family, providing they can be assigned to different departments or assembly lines. Agá's policy in this regard was explained as follows: "The salary we pay assembly workers is small. We know that it is small. If there are two or three workers in a household who can work here, the family can enjoy a higher standard of living. It is better for them and it is better for us. They can come to work together; they can eat here together; and they can go home together. We have not seen problems with this policy."

Agá and Jota are but two of the thirty-five or more firms that now comprise the electronics sector of Manaus' new industrial economy. This hegemonic complex of industries exhibits the characteristics of what Cardoso (1973) calls associated-dependent development. The enterprises that make up this complex are extensively dependent upon external sources of capital for their formation, organization, and direction. In this location, they are almost completely dependent for their production upon the importation of unit components. They are equally dependent upon external markets for the distribution and sale of their finished products. And, ultimately, their profitability is as dependent upon the fiscal incentives of the Zona Franca as it is upon production costs and the marketability of their products. Despite these dependencies, these enterprises have created in Manaus a considerable demand for labor. However, in the context of these dependencies, within the hegemonic industrial sector there exists no intrinsic relationship between profits and wages. In a de Janvryian (1985) sense, these industries are socially disarticulated: they tend to feed on cheap labor. That this is the case is clearly evident in respect to the previously described labor processes.

Like Agá and Jota, except for some variability in their philosophies of industrial relations and in managerial styles, most of the firms that make up this hegemonic sector do not differ significantly in the rationalized character of their bureaucratic organization or in the labor processes that this type of organization enjoins. These firms define and recruit labor with reference neither to persons or skills. Individuals are not recruited because they are known by some trusted employee, or belong to a household that is known to need income, or they are known by some respected teacher or clergyman. On the contrary, to the extent that some measure is taken of persons, it is generally taken with reference to attributes (e.g., gender, social origins, personality, and the like) that might insinuate themselves so as to somehow interrupt the efficiency of the production process. And the skills required by the mechanically structured production processes of these enterprises are so minimal that they assume the general character of labor power.

Thus, in terms of the labor processes characteristic of this new hegemonic industrial sector, workers as persons are of little or no social value to the firms that employ them. Moreover, whatever skills these workers may have acquired by virtue of experience or special education are also of little value. For the most part, all these firms require of workers is their general ability to expend energy in the performance of work. In Manaus, independent of whether or not not this labor energy happens to be excessive or scarce, its value as a commodity has no market determination. Given the fiscal incentives of the Zona Franca, for the most part, the commodity value of labor in the hegemonic industrial sector is politically tied to the minimum wage.

Peripheral Industries

The extractive economy that dominated the Amazon until the creation of the Zona Franca essentially combined subsistence activities with pre-industrial and industrial modes of production within a mercantilist form of capitalist organization. Although international markets ultimately determined the export value of forest products, at the regional and local levels, the exchange quotients of food and other products were fundamentally based on the system of debt relations that enjoined producers and brokers within the aviamento system. Extractors, whether of rubber, vegetable oils, *castanha* (cashew nuts), or animal skins, required simple tools and little else by way of capital inputs. Only at major centers of commerce was this extractive mode of production joined to industrial processes that provided opportunities for wage employment as such.[21]

While historical data are meager, it would appear that the wood-processing industry that existed throughout the region generally conformed to this mercantilist pattern of organization in its extractive dimensions. Benchimol (1977: 674–76), for example, makes brief reference to the "many decades" during which timber was felled by cutters who worked mainly in the *várzea* (floodplain), and who depended upon a system of credit not unlike the aviamento. Logs, extracted from the várzea, were generally floated to barges and delivered by river to holding ponds attached to sawmills located in the larger urban centers.[22] The whole process was directed by family firms that assumed the role of aviadores in terms of the linkages between themselves and woodcutters in the interior, and the role of industrial employers with respect to the sawmill workers in the *serrarias* (sawmills).

Although the wood-processing industry in Amazonas continues to be predominantly in the hands of family firms, and while its overall contribution to foreign trade remains small relative to other industries, on the extractive side, the organization of production has been extensively altered by technology as well as the construction of highways and secondary roads. New technology and secondary roads have opened large areas outside the floodplain of the várzea to the extraction of timber. With this penetration has come a proliferation of independently organized contractors who operate cutting enterprises with the use of power tools and heavy equipment, and who negotiate the sale of logs with bidders from among the *serradores* (sawmill operators). These developments have weakened or, in many cases, broken completely the control of extractive activities through the credit monopoly that urban-based serrarias previously exercised. Most sawmill operators no longer combine their industrial activities with the ownership of woodlots and the cutting of timber.

Throughout the period of the rubber boom, the wood-processing industry contributed practically nothing to the export economy of Manaus. To a considerable degree, this continues to be the case. In 1976, Manaus was listed as having 54 serrarias (Bruce 1976: 42).[23] This number represented almost 19 percent of the 287 serrarias listed for the entire Northern Region. While 45 percent of the total production of the Northern Region was destined for international markets, almost 80 percent of the total production in Manaus was for the local market. The explanation given for this market orientation by the owners is that transportation costs from Manaus are simply too excessive for them to be competitive with producers in the Lower Amazon. Thus, most of what the wood-processing industry in Manaus exports to national and international markets is comprised of laminated woods, pallets, and concrete forms produced by *fábricas de compensados.*

Fábricas de compensados, as distinguished from ordinary sawmills, are factories where logs are sawed and processed mainly for the fabrication of laminated woods and related products. [24] This industry is not large in comparison to other industrial sectors, but it does form a large component of the wood-processing industry. The technology is relatively new to Manaus. Most fábricas de compensados came into being with the incentive structure of the Free Trade Zone. In 1976, based on information compiled by Benchimol (1977: 794), only seven fábricas de compensados are listed for the entire Northern Region and four of these were located in Manaus. These four produced a total of 59,000 cubic meters of board valued at approximately U.S. $14.7 millions. Twenty-five percent of this production was of concrete forms. Of the total production, 40 percent was destined for export outside of Brazil. An additional 40 percent was destined for export to national markets and the remainder for sale in Manaus.

As of 1983, SUFRAMA (1983:16) had provided fiscal incentives with which 12 serrarias and 7 fábricas de compensados were newly established or modernized in Manaus. Related to these developments, between 1960 and 1980, the number of wood dealers and cutters in the State of Amazonas increased from 1,808 to 3,105. During the same period, employment in the wood-processing industry in Manaus grew proportionately. The 19 firms listed by SUFRAMA provided employment for 4,065 workers. Of these workers, 2,963 were employed by fábricas de compensados, the remainder (1,102) by sawmills. It should be noted that the largest of the compensados employs close to 1,000 workers. Moreover, up to 50 percent of the labor force in some compensados is comprised of women (de Castro et al., 1984). By way of contrast, almost all of the sawmills in Manaus employ well under 100 workers (averaging approximately 50) and relatively few of these sawmill workers are women. Three of the seven compensados in Manaus, all relatively new, are national or multinational affiliates.[25] Almost all of the sawmills are operated by locally owned, family managed firms. Thus, by way of contrast to the compensados, the sawmills are smaller firms and they enjoin a more traditionally organized industrial mode of production.

Two serrarias were selected for study in this peripheral or traditional industrial sector. Both are family owned enterprises. The first, *Serraria Amazonense,* was established in Manaus early in the century by a Portuguese immigrant, Augusto Fernandes, who became the founder of one of the city's influential business families. The second, *Serraria Paranaense,* was founded in the state of Paraná by Albert Schmidt, a former truck driver of German origin, and shifted its operations to Manaus because of the Zona Franca.[26]

The comparison of these two family firms, one old and indigenous to the city and the other relatively new and a product of the Free Trade Zone, is illuminating with reference to the heterogeneity of peripheral industries as it concerns some aspects of the labor process. Unlike the hegemonic industries that are externally dependent and that generally conform to a uniform pattern of bureaucratic organization in all that affects the labor process, these family owned firms are much more personal in their organization and management as well as in the way in which they recruit, appropriate, and value labor.

Serraria Amazonense continues where it was originally located in Bairro Educandos, a bairro not far from the center of Manaus. The mill is situated on an *igarapé* (a small bay or water inlet) that provides shipping access to the Rio Negro as well as sufficient water for a holding pond large enough to maintain a surplus supply of logs. Most of the workers employed by this mill live in nearby urban neighborhoods. None live at the mill. The mill itself is comprised of two factory sections, one containing the heavy equipment needed for the stripping and sawing of logs, the other a smaller section where lighter boards are planed and finished. A small building is located to the rear of the main office and used exclusively by cooks who prepare a midday hot meal for workers. The firm maintains its *depósito* (storage yard) on the site. Combined, the mill and the depósito occupy about 9,000 square meters. From this one depósito, Serraria Amazonense's entire production is stored, sold, and shipped to local contractors and buyers. Nothing of what is produced is exported to markets outside the immediate region and the firm claims to have no affiliates located elsewhere in Amazonas or Brazil.

Serraria Amazonense's management has always been a family affair. Two sons, Eduardo and Roberto, were raised in the business. Sometime after the death of the father, Roberto insisted on expanding the business to include production for export. According to informants, the company begin to incur credit commitments that were not offset by the profits realized in the export market. Subsequently, Eduardo elected to purchase the shares owned by Roberto and continue the the firm as originally established, producing lumber for the local market. In 1961, Serraria Amazonense was reincorporated as a limited society. Eduardo, who owns the majority of shares, became director and manager. Eduardo's mother participates in the company and holds minority shares.

According to Eduardo, Serraria Amazonense has expanded its overall production by more than 60 percent since the creation of the Zona Franca. This growth in production was achieved by the installation of some new equipment and the employment of additional workers. Capital for these developments was raised by the reinvestment of profits and federal grants from SUDAM and SUFRAMA. Today, excluding fábricas de compensados, Serraria Amazonense claims to be the second largest employer among the serrarias in Manaus. In terms of production, according to Eduardo, it probably ranks third among the city's sawmills. As organized, the firm does not possess timber grants. Rather, it negotiates the purchase of logs from a number of independent contractors, most of whom cut in the várzea.

Serraria Paranaense, like Serraria Amazonense, is also a family-owned enterprise. It is reputed to have struggled for many years to establish itself in the State of Paraná, where timber resources have been extensively depleted. It was founded by Albert Schmidt who, in response the the fiscal incentives of the Zona Franca, acquired timber contracts with loggers in the interior of Amazonas and elected to move his milling operations to Manaus. The move from Paraná to Manaus was carried out over a period of three years. The sawmill's principal depósito and main office is located in Bairro Educandos. More recently, a second depósito and a larger company office have been constructed in Bairro Cachoeirinha, not far from Bairro Educandos.

Serraria Paranaense's sawmill is located at Enseada do Marapatá. Enseada do Marapatá is situated in a heavily forested area attached to the Industrial Park, above the flood plain of Rio Negro and some eight kilometers distant from the company's depósito in Educandos. The particular site occupied by the mill is on a bluff above a holding pond that forms a small part of the bay. The site extends approximately 257,000 square meters and perhaps half of this land remains uncleared. Adjacent to the mill is a nicely constructed dwelling occupied by a retired worker who serves as a security guard. From this house, he and his wife also operate a snack bar where workers can buy soft drinks while on break, and beer in the evening. On the other side of the mill is located a large shed where lumber is temporarily stored out of the weather. Nearby is a third structure that houses the mill's machine shop. The mill office occupies a small building containing a single room where the manager, one clerk, and two overseers have desks.

Across the road from the office, perhaps 75 meters distant, is a series of five single unit dwellings—each with a kitchen, two bedrooms, and a living room—overlooking the bay and the forest beyond. This line of dwellings follows the curvature of the bay, away from the mill area. Where it turns to the north, there begins a second line of seven duplexes containing fourteen apartment units. These are fronted by a large field that serves as a recreational area. Nearby, another building provides a room for a school. A short walk through the forest leads to a clearing in which six additional dwellings have been constructed overlooking the bay. All of these homes are provided with electricity and potable water and all of them are occupied, rent free, by mill workers and their families.

The physical features of Serraria Paranaense are in striking contrast to those of Serraria Amazonense where nobody lives, and where piles of lumber are stored in locations that are seemingly free of sawdust and other debris, which is allowed to spill over into the igarapé. Very little lumber is stored at Serraria Paranaense. It is trucked to the depósitos in Manaus almost as soon as it is produced. The mill and the entire area surrounding it are kept clean at all times. At Serraria Amazonense, Saturday morning is a six-hour work period for the production of lumber. At Serraria Paranaense, it is a six-hour work period during which the entire crew is engaged in oiling machines and cleaning the area of debris, which is hauled to dumping sites in the forest.

The two depósitos owned by Serraria Paranaense are located in urban bairros and they assume a similar character. Each comprises an area of approximately 14,000 square meters. Each is fenced off from the adjacent neighborhoods. In both, the lumber is stored mainly under well-kept sheds, out of the weather. On Saturdays, work crews clean the yards and maintain the equipment. Both depósitos provide areas, away from the tumult of workday activities, where housing units have been constructed for employees. At Depósito Educandos, where the main office for Serraria Paranaense is situated, ten single unit dwellings of various size and appearance have been constructed. One of these is occupied by the family of Paul Schmidt, son of the company's proprietor. In recent years, Paul has assumed increasing responsibility for the day-to-day management of Serraria Paranaense and Depósito Educandos. However, Paul's father remains active in the firm. He maintains his office at Depósito Cachoeirinha and visits the sawmill at Marapatá several times each week.

As previously noted, Serraria Paranaense and its depósitos were established in 1970. Since that time, the firm claims that its production and sale of lumber has more than doubled. This growth, like that of Serraria Amazonense, was accomplished by the reinvestment of profits supplemented by grants from SUFRAMA. In terms of production, the firm is now considered to be one the largest serrarias in Manaus. Other than the operations already mentioned, the firm claims to have no affiliates elsewhere in Amazonas or Brazil. Like Serraria Amazonense, it negotiates the purchase of logs from independent contractors and does not possess timber grants of its own. Its entire production is distributed in local markets which, based on the assessment of its proprietors, are not very likely to improve over the next few years. As a consequence of this assessment, plans for the further development of Depósito Cachoeirinha, which was to become a wholesale-retail outlet for construction materials in addition to lumber, have been postponed.

Both these serrarias are directly managed by their respective proprietors. Neither firm has what might be called a personnel manager. At Amazonense, Eduardo Fernandes' office staff includes himself, a chief accountant, several secretaries and/or bookkeepers, a sales manager, and a yard manager who oversees the operation of the mill as well as the sale and delivery of lumber. The yard manager has two assistants working under him—one in the mill and the other in the yard. Including secretaries, bookkeepers, and field salesmen, the entire managerial and office staff is comprised of nineteen persons. All of these individuals are Amazonenses, and all but the chief accountant reached their present positions by promotion from within the firm. Only Eduardo and the chief accountant hold university degrees. At Serraria Paranaense, the office and managerial staff for the mill and two depósitos number twenty-one. However, except for a few secretaries and bookkeepers, the entire staff are Paranaenses (i.e., persons who were born in the state of Paraná) and only the chief accountant and the proprietor's son, Paul, hold university degrees.

In October 1984, Serraria Amazonense listed a total of 167 persons on its payroll, of whom 11 percent were classified as managers, technicians, salesmen, or office personnel. The salaries and commissions of this group, combined, contributed four percent to the firm's total cost of production. Of the 148 yard and mill workers, only eight were classified as "qualified operators" and these were individuals who operated various types of machinery and heavy equipment. The salaries of this group also contributed four percent to the cost of production. The remaining 140 yard and mill workers, most of whom received one minimum salary per month, contributed 14 percent to the cost of production. In other words, 22 percent of the total cost of production is attributed to the payment of salaries and commissions, the remainder to taxes, interest payments, utilities, the purchase of logs, maintenance, depreciation, and losses incurred in the processing of wood.[27]

By way of contrast, excluding proprietors, the regular payroll at

Serraria Paranaense included only eighty-five workers (approximately half the number employed at Serraria Amazonense). Of these, twenty-one are managerial and office staff, three are technicians, and sixty-one are "unqualified operators." The salaries and commissions of this group also contributes twenty-one percent to the total cost of production. However, most unqualified operators at Serraria Paranaense, in contrast to those at Serraria Amazonense, receive two minimum salaries per month in addition to their housing and utilities. Because of these salaries and benefits, Serraria Paranaense is reputed to have the best wage structure of the sawmills in Manaus.

There are few positions at either of these serrarias for which the recruitment of workers gives focus to previous experience, level of education, or technical training. Top supervisory positions are filled by members of the family independent of their educational qualification. In both serrarias the chief accountants or head bookkeepers have university degrees and they assume the role of office manager. Below these, the only positions for which a high school certificate is a matter of some consideration are those occupied by secretaries and bookkeepers. Yard and mill supervisors, for which four to eight years of education may be necessary, are filled by promotion from the ranks of experienced workers. Machine operators, for whom some technical formation is necessary, are similarly recruited. As far as anyone could recall, neither firm had ever announced or advertised a vacancy. The recruitment of office workers and yard and mill workers at Serraria Amazonense is by word-of-mouth and personal contact. Prospective applicants usually come to the yard or office manager on the recommendation of friends or relatives who work for the company. Indeed, 65 percent of the workers interviewed had one or more relatives employed by the firm. If prospective applicants are physically suitable and meet the yard manager's approval, they are given a brief interview with the proprietor and generally hired. Even though they are personally known or related to someone in the firm, as far as could be determined, all new hires are given probationary status.[28]

The recruitment procedures at Serraria Paranaense differ but slightly from those at Serraria Amazonense. Whereas the latter employed thirteen women outside the office, Serraria Paranaense does not employ women, except in secretarial positions. It is the stated policy of Serraria Paranaense to recruit almost all of its employees from the State of Paraná and to pay their moving expenses to Manaus. The only exceptions to this are office workers and three Amazonenses who were hired and placed at the mill. The explanation given for this recruitment policy was that "workers from Paraná are more productive, reliable, and considerably less troublesome than Amazonenses." The latter, it was claimed, are relatively productive in the interior "where they have experience" but, in Manaus, "... they absent themselves too frequently from work and for little or no cause they are inclined to move from one employer to another."

When Albert Schmidt moved his serraria from Paraná in 1970, he brought 52 workers and their families with him. In 1976, when the business was expanded, he went to Paraná and recruited an additional 26 workers. At the sawmill, only three workers are Amazonenses and these were recruited specifically to help sort and classify logs, a type of work for which they were particularly qualified by virtue of having been woodcutters in the interior. Vacancies at Serraria Paranaense are never announced locally. They are filled by sons or other relatives of workers employed by the company. Seventy percent of the workers interviewed at the firm have one or more relatives employed there. Recruits are trained on the job and if, by chance (only one case was cited), they do not fulfill the expectations of managers and overseers, they are discharged. "Discharged workers," it was stated, "can use their indemnification pay to return home or look for employment elsewhere in Manaus."

Both serrarias maintain a simple personnel file for each worker. However, there exists no system of worker evaluation apart from the observations of overseers, and these observations are recorded only if a worker is to be put on report or fired. Timeclocks exist neither at the sawmills nor the depósitos. Absenteeism or tardiness, depending upon the circumstances, may be cause for admonition, a salary deduction, or dismissal. These rules aside, it is evident to even the most casual observer that the labor force at Serraria Paranaense is considerably more disciplined, or self-disciplined, than workers at Serraria Amazonense. Compared to the latter, workers at Serraria Paranaense are seldom seen idle, and they are reputed by their overseers to almost never require disciplinary action for tardiness or absenteeism.

Whatever the evaluation of individual workers, the opportunities for promotion are practically nonexistent within these family owned enterprises. The positions available above the level of "unqualified worker" are very few in number and, except for reasons of health or death, they are rarely vacated before retirement. Workers of advanced age or with injuries are generally assigned lighter duties. All of the workers at Serraria Amazonense, and most at Serraria Paranaense, belong to the union (*Sindicato dos Trabalhadores de Madeira*). The producers in the wood-processing industry, the owners and their representatives, form their own association (*Federação Das Indústrias de Madeira*) and it, rather than the individual firms, negotiates contracts with the sindicato.

The proprietors at Serraria Paranaense maintain that federal labor regulations have been beneficial to the company as well as its employees; those at Serraria Amazonense maintain the opposite. Despite this difference in views, union membership, and indeed the union itself, is a matter of general indifference to the management at both firms. The office managers at both firms confessed that the union has virtually no influence on the determination of wages and its only other influence is by way of the CIPA committees that monitor safety regulations. Although neither company has ever experienced a strike or work stoppage, the wage structure at Serraria Paranaense is considerably higher than that of its competitors in the industry. It is also higher than the wages set by the union contract in force at the time of research.

Serraria Amazonense's benefit structure does not extend beyond its conformity to the requirements set forth in the federal labor code. This involves the firm's contribution to INPS, to FGTS, and the provision of accident insurance. A midday hot meal is provided. Except for the extension of credit for the purchase of lumber at discounted prices, no contribution is made to housing. Only the yard manager has regular use of a company vehicle. There is no supplementary retirement program. And the company makes no contribution to whatever social functions its employees may want to organize.

The benefit structure at Serraria Paranaense is considerably better. In addition to federal requirements, the company provides all its employees the opportunity to live in company housing at no cost to themselves. Electricity and water also are freely provided. The houses vary somewhat in size, but all are well constructed, screened, and maintained by the workers with the use of company tools and supplies. At the sawmill at Marapatá, the company maintains a classroom for the children of workers (the teacher, however, is paid by the state). Recreational areas are also provided along with some equipment. There exists no supplementary retirement program, but a small number of "deserving" workers are kept on as watchmen or janitors after reaching the age of retirement.[29] In addition to these benefits, Serraria Paranaense provides regular transportation to Manaus for its workers at the mill in order that they may do their weekly shopping. Transportation is also provided in case of medical emergency.

The normal workweek for mill and yard workers at both serrarias is 56 hours. It terminates at noon on Saturday. Needless to say, the work is primarily manual, arduous, and dirty. At the machines, the work can be quite dangerous. Except for machine operators, work tasks are variable. An individual may be assigned to assist a machine operator, transport or stack lumber, load trucks, remove debris, make repairs, or whatever else the overseers deem necessary. At neither serraria are workers encouraged to participate in decisions. It is clear, however, that at Serraria Paranaense, workers are expected to keep busy and exercise proper judgment without constant supervision. Overseers at Serraria Paranaense are not as occupied keeping workers busy or telling them what to do as they appear to be at Serraria Amazonense. If either serraria needs to increase production in order to meet contract obligations, it accomplishes this by extending the hours of individuals who volunteer to work in the evening at the normal rate of pay.

While neither serraria is bureaucratic in its organization, both are clearly authoritarian. Still, their managerial styles differ somewhat. Employees at Serraria Amazonense refer to Eduardo Fernandes as *patrão,* denoting his position of authority. This status identity does not entail a connotation of patronage or personal relationship. Indeed, outside the main office, workers almost never engage the proprietor of the company in personal conversation. In fact, unless a problem exists, they rarely see the patrão in the mill or the yard. Clearly, except for his closest associates—e.g., the yard manager—Eduardo Fernandes takes little personal interest in his employees or their problems.

At Serraria Paranaense, the opposite tends to be the case. Perhaps the reason for this is that Albert Schmidt has formed a labor force in Manaus whose regional origins and kinship extensions have imparted to it the quality of a small ethnic ghetto in an area that is very different and very distant from their native state of Paraná. When he or his son visit the mill or the depósitos, they do not pass without chatting with various workers. Much of it is small talk, but it affords workers the opportunity to speak to the patrão of their work, their families, their children, their friends in Paraná, or whatever else they deem to be of mutual interest. Similarly, the patrão and his son join the company's employees in a little celebration at Christmas. Sometimes they even join them in the celebration of a birthday. Workers can negotiate small loans with the company to help buy consumer durables or defray the cost of visiting a sick parent in Paraná. In all these respects, the authoritarian management of Serraria Paranaense is somewhat modified by relationships of more personal nature. And clearly, the workers at Serraria Paranaense consider this important; most indicated that they would return to Paraná before taking a job elsewhere in Manaus.

These sawmills are but two of a large and heterogeneous category of enterprises of the type that no longer dominate the industrial economy of Manaus. To the extent that we may generalize from these two cases, related data, and informant interviews, most of the firms of this category operate relatively small-scale enterprises engaged in the transformation or processing of wood, food, fiber, or other products originating in the region. Although mechanized in varying ways and to varying degrees, the production processes characteristic of these industries generally remain labor intensive. The work they provide is largely manual and while it requires some degree of physical fitness, it demands little skill and virtually no education. With the creation of the Zona Franca, this group of enterprises has become increasingly peripheral in the sense that it no longer forms the economy's industrial center of gravity. Some of the firms that make up this category are indigenous in the sense that they were founded by Manauaras long before the creation of the Zona Franca. Others have come to Manaus because of the Zona Franca. Whether indigenous or new, in response to urban growth and with assistance from SUFRAMA, many of these firms have substantially expanded their operations. Currently, they provide employment for perhaps one-third or more of the city's industrial workers.

Apart from these features, what most distinguishes these traditional industries from those of the new hegemonic sector is the fact that virtually all of them are locally capitalized, family-owned, and family-managed. Several factors affecting the labor process follow this local ownership and family control. For one thing, while the managerial structures of these firms tend to be highly infused with an authoritarian paternalism, they are not bureaucratized. Beyond this, they vary according to family tradition in their management and in the formality of the relationships that obtain between owners, managers, and workers. Independent of this variability, production processes are rarely engineered or rationalized, work is not carefully regulated, and workers are not closely supervised. In fact, except as machinery is involved, most workers and work tasks are interchangeable, and it is often the case that work tasks are assigned on the basis of ad hoc decisions that reflect a concern for the person of the worker (e.g., a concern for his or her age, friendship network, health, and the like).

Because the work in these industries is mostly manual, these firms do not recruit workers with reference to educational achievement, skills, technical formation, and the like. At the same time, because work in these industries is not mechanically structured and regulated, these firms are very much concerned with recruiting persons who will work without constant and close supervision. Accordingly, these traditional industries tend to define workers as persons and they recruit workers in terms of character reference. The types of persons who seek employment in these industries do not carry with them letters of reference. Thus, to be recruited, a prospective employee must be known by someone who is known by a proprietor. In effect, the prospective employee must be socially connected as a friend or a relative of someone in or close to the firm who can vouch for his/her character. This is not to suggest that the labor processes enjoined by these traditional industries do not accord the labor of workers commodity value: clearly, they do. However, workers are not exclusively defined in terms of the commodity value of their labor. They are also defined as the "friend" or "relative" of Angenaldo and Angenaldo has social value. As the proprietor or yard manager knows, Angenaldo has been for many years a steady, obedient, and loyal worker.

The Commercial and Public Sectors

Industrial development in Manaus has stimulated immense growth in the "white collar" sectors of employment. In the public administration and social service sectors, for example, the number of economically active workers increased from 4,183 in 1960 to 35,124 in 1980 (a relative increase of 716 percent). The growth in employment was even greater in the commercial and commercial service sectors, increasing from 5,243 to 43,975 (739 percent). These particular sectors of the economy are of interest in the present study because in terms of the labor process white collar work generally enjoins statuses to which upwardly mobile workers often aspire. Thus, for the purpose of comparative analysis, a sample of white collar workers and their respective households was included in the study.[30]

Except in the most general terms, it is difficult to contextualize the labor process in reference to white collar work in Manaus. In the private sector, the labor process involving white collar workers may attach to family-owned enterprises of varying types and scale as well as enterprises owned and operated by national or international firms (e.g. banks). In the public sector, the "firms" are formed by the federal, state, and local governments. The federal and state governments are certainly the largest and most significant employers of white collar workers, including accountants, bookkeepers, social workers, primary and secondary school teachers, librarians, paramedical personnel, secretaries, office clerks, messengers, communications workers, technicians, and the like. A small dictionary of acronyms would be required to detail the bewildering complex of even those federal and state agencies that have come into being in conjunction with what might be called the "development industry" in Manaus. Such a list, of course, would exclude not only their departmental divisions but also a very large number of pre-existing ministries, superintendencies, bureaus, divisions, and departments.

These ministries, superintendencies, or departmental divisions

disclose common structural features. They are bureaucratically organized and administered. Although personal connections may enhance
access to employment opportunities, mainly in terms of the dissemina-
tion of information regarding vacancies, recruitment is generally selective and based on examination, educational background, technical training, or experiential qualification. Generally, work discipline and
behavior are sharply defined by bureaucratic rules and regulations. For
the most part, these are unevenly administered by supervisors who are
described by workers to be "discriminatory," "strict," "friendly," "intoler-
ant," "just," or "unjust," "considerate," and the like. Personnel evaluations in these public bureaucracies are prescribed and presumably systematic. They occur annually or biannually and they must be personally
communicated to the worker by his or her supervisor. The system provides that such evaluations may be contested; generally, they are not.

Opportunities for promotion in the departments of the public sector are variable and by grade. In theory, promotions are based on an
assessment of merit, seniority, or the acquisition of additional training;
in fact, it often helps to have an influential connection relative to one's
"chefe." Whatever, promotions tend to be strategically staggered by
individual departments or units so as to ensure the support of higher
level administrators. Unless the unit is expanding, promotions are few
and infrequent. An office worker, for example, may be employed five-to-
seven years before being promoted to the rank of secretary. A secondary school teacher or a nurse's aid, regardless of merit or seniority,
may never be promoted. In the federal service, local decisions are submitted as recommendations to departmental superiors in Brasília. Within the state service, final decisions are taken in Manaus. In both cases, a
worker's promotion may ultimately depend upon the political status and
connections of his or her unit director vis-à-vis these loci of power. In
fact, the prosperity of entire units may depend as much on the political
connections of their supervisors as upon their functionality.

The salary structure in these organizations is tied to rank. Among
the informants interviewed, it ranged from two minimum salaries for a
nurse's aid or primary school teacher to ten minimum salaries for an
assistant personnel officer with a federal agricultural research organization operating under the Ministry of Agriculture in Brasília.

The benefit structures that obtain in these public service organizations are surprisingly uniform and prescribed by law as well as bureaucratic regulation. They include all of the usual benefits provided in the
hegemonic sector. In addition, they may or may not include some educational benefits for workers and/or their dependents. They usually
include group life insurance, for which workers must make a contribu-

tion. They may include preferential access to loans for the purposes of housing. More importantly, from the point of view of workers, the benefit structure of federal and state employment includes the opportunity of achieving the status of *estatutário*. Independent of their particular occupational assignment, workers who achieve this status, if they work for the state rather than the federal government, no longer qualify for FGTS (indemnification payments) because, except for unusual cause, they cannot be dismissed. They have, in effect, the security of permanent employment. It is because of this benefit that many university and secondary school students in Manaus aspire to government employment.

Virtually all of the workers in federal or state employment form what might be called "white collar" *sindicatos* or labor associations. It is primarily these organizations that provide white collar workers with whatever social and recreational facilities as may attach to their employment. A few of these organizations are quite active in this regard. One or two even sponsor consumer cooperatives for the purchase of food and medicines. Many, however, do not have facilities comparable to many of the industrial unions. As a consequence, they are not particularly active except when contract negotiations are underway or when officers are seeking re-election.

Despite these uniformities, from the point of view of informants, these organizations are highly variable in the social ambience of the workplace. Some are tightly structured and administered: others are not. Always, the decision-making process is hierarchical but some encourage worker participation by scheduling weekly or monthly staff meetings. Some are beset by internal politics, gossip, backbiting, and competition. Others are "friendly" and "informal." Whatever the case, workers are not frozen to mechanically structured work tasks which preclude anything other than casual encounters with work mates and directive encounters with supervisors and administrators. The labor process is such that workers have commodity value for their training, educational qualifications, and experience. However, they also have a personality quotient which may significantly enhance or diminish their status, and ultimately their commodity value, within the bureau.

The commercial sectors of the economy present quite a different picture. With the Zona Franca, an increasing number of retail, commercial service, and financial establishments in Manaus have come to be owned and operated by nationally organized firms. However, the majority of commercial establishments (e.g., hotels, clothing stores, auto parts agencies, retail outlets for furniture, watches, televisions, etc.) are locally owned, family-managed enterprises. This also tends to be the case with commercial service establishments (realty firms, printing firms, xerox services, etc.). With respect to the labor process, the differences between the nationally-based and locally-owned firms are extreme. Illustrative of these differences is the contrast between the organization of banks and family-owned retail establishments.

Typically, the banks in which a few workers were interviewed are externally directed, locally managed, and bureaucratically organized. The higher echelons of management are generally university trained personnel who have been transferred to Manaus from other regions. Below them, there may exist department heads who have been locally recruited on the basis of qualification or previous experience. Combined, this managerial staff may comprise between 10-to-20 percent of a payroll that may include 40-to-100 employees. The overall performance of these establishments is regularly and systematically reviewed by representatives from their corporate headquarters (usually located in São Paulo, Rio, or elsewhere) and particular branches or divisions are graded vis-à-vis one another in terms of their performance.

The majority of employees in these establishments are cashiers, secretaries, office workers, bookkeepers, accountants, and the like. Half or more are women. Recruitment to these positions is by examination. A high school education is a virtual prerequisite to passing this examination. Once recruited, employees are ranked according to grade. Employee evaluations are scheduled and systematic. Promotion is based not only on job performance but also on performance in training courses regularly provided for employees who may or may not elect to take them. In one bank included in the study, employees were required to successfully pass ten training courses in order to be promoted to a higher grade.

Salaries are structured by grade. Depending on grade, a cashier for example may receive one or two minimum salaries. A low-level supervisor may receive three or four, an accountant five or perhaps more. The benefit structure of these establishments do not generally exceed those that are prescribed by law. Workers may or may not belong to unions or professional associations. Relative to industrial workers, the workday for many white collar workers is not long. State functionaries and bank clerks, for example, sometimes work only five hours/day. All others tend to work forty hours/week. Still, work discipline is strict, employees are closely supervised, and deviation from prescribed regulations is only briefly tolerated before it results in dismissal. However, on the whole, jobs are relatively secure.

The labor process that obtains in many of the locally owned, family-managed, retail firms is considerably different from that of banks and other nationally organized enterprises. Whether they employ as few as five or as many as twenty workers, these enterprises are not bureaucratically organized. Most of the employees of these firms are sales clerks. The work that they do is neither specialized nor functionally structured. It requires some degree of interpersonal skill but not much training. The only specialized position may be that of a secretary. The proprietors themselves do most of the accounting and bookkeeping. Perhaps with the assistance of one or two senior clerks, the proprietors also do most of the supervising. Sometimes this is done from a strategically located cashier's cage. Or, it may be carried out from an office where the proprietor has a view of virtually everything happening in the sales department of the shop.

In any event, the labor process in these small commercial enterprises involves a great deal of personal communication between employers who are proprietors and their employees. From discursive observations, in the public context of this process and independent of the age and gender of the worker, most proprietors seem to appear as authoritarian figures of significant status and as such, they command deference. Employees, on the other hand, can be dealt with in public by their employers even to the point of embarrassment. Interviews suggest that the evaluation of personnel rarely involves the application of systematic measures. Rather, it consists of an accumulation of impressions arising out of the labor process. The overall character of these impressions is affected not only by work performance but also by the flow and intensity of business, the registration of customer complaints, the appearance and demeanor of the employee in situational encounters, and the personality of the proprietor. According to informants, in most cases the worker never knows how well he or she is performing his/her work. Ultimately, this makes little difference. Individuals are fired at will and the proprietor need not explain his decision. And, if retained, the only positions to which individuals might be promoted are those of cashier or head clerk and such promotions do not seem to involve a very substantial increase in earnings over the minimum wage that most workers are paid.

Recruitment by these firms is not systematic. Vacancies become known by word-of-mouth among the proprietors and employees of adjacent shops and they are related to friends and acquaintances or to strangers who happen to inquire. Unlike in the traditional industrial sector, except as the family of the proprietor is involved, networks of kin are not evident in these shops according to informants. If a vacancy happens to exist when an inquiry is made, an interview with the proprietor may follow. If the position is offered, the new employee may or may not be asked to fill out an application form or a worker registration card. It is not an uncommon practice among these firms to retain workers on probationary status, to pay them less than the prescribed minimum wage, and to withhold the employer's signature from their work card. In this way, the proprietor reduces his labor costs by circumventing federal labor regulations. These unregistered workers will not be entitled to health, indemnification, and retirement benefits. Workers know that this practice is illegal; they also know they will be dismissed as incompetent, if they complain, and this might make it difficult for them to find another job. Even when registered, almost all of these employees will receive but one minimum wage. In addition to this, a small sales commission may be paid a head clerk.

Accordingly, the conditions of work and the wage and benefit structures these small family-owned commercial establishments provide do not often measure up to those that obtain in government, in nationally-based commercial establishments, or in industry. When they do, they rarely exceed the wages and benefits prescribed by federal labor legislation. There exists little opportunity for promotion in these firms. The employment they provide is relatively insecure. Because of these conditions, many of the workers employed by these firms are individuals who are more or less continually looking for better jobs, particularly with nationally-based commercial enterprises. Others, because of their sales experience, may turn to self-employment in the informal sector.

Leaving aside the tremendous variability that characterizes the public and commercial sectors of the economy, the labor processes enjoined by white collar employment, whether in government or commerce, disclose some common features of considerable significance for understanding the social and cultural dimensions of working-class culture in Manaus. One such feature relates to recruitment. Recruitment by the establishments that form these sectors is generally selective for workers very different from those typically employed in the hegemonic and peripheral industries. Recruitment by these establishments is particularly selective for individuals of certified educational achievement, usually at the high school level or beyond (this is a general requirement even for most retail clerks). Often, it is also selective with reference to previous experience, gender, personality, and physical appearance.

As a consequence of the type of workers employed and the nature of the work they do, the workplace assumes a physical and social ambience very different from that of the factory or the sawmill. Physically, the workplace is lacking in the dirt and the noise associated with industrial machinery. The work is no less supervised, but work routines allow workers more independence and social interaction. Also, except in the family-owned establishments of the commercial sector, promotions are possible. The criteria for promotion may include seniority, but usually seniority will not give way to work performance, additional training, or certification by examination. Whatever the criteria, they are generally made known to everyone concerned and the evaluation of workers proceeds routinely, often engaging the worker under review in the evaluation process.

All of this underscores the fact that white collar work in these sectors is neither primarily mechanical nor manual; rather, it is thought to be "mental." Workers perform tasks that, in varying ways and degrees, require them to think, to use their minds, to exercise a trained intelligence. Although they perform these tasks in a multiplicity of contexts, even when working as bookkeepers or accountants, they are also required to interact personally and sensitively with others, including officials, supervisors, scientists, doctors, patients, students, clients, customers, and fellow workers. They are in effect, not operários, montadores, or mão de obra, but white collar workers and they are viewed as such by the firms that employ them.

The Informal Sector

Autonomous workers in Brazil are defined as self-employed individuals who, if they employ others, employ only members of their families or households. In 1960, self-employed workers in Manaus numbered 9,946 and they represented approximately 34 percent of the economically active population. Largely because of the employment opportunities created by new industrial development, by 1980, this proportion of self-employed workers declined to 21 percent. Despite the disproportionate shift to various forms of wage employment, however, the overall number of self-employed workers climbed from 9,946 to 42,086 (a relative increase of 323 percent). Most significantly affected by this increase were the industrial (particularly the construction trades), transportation, and commercial (especially retail trade) sectors.[31]

In Manaus, autonomous or self-employed workers often refer to themselves as having a "biscate" and they are known to others as *biscateiros* (*biscateiras*, if female). The work identity of biscateiros is not easy to delineate. In some contexts, the term has specific reference to an "odd-jobber." And indeed, many self-employed workers are individuals who command various skills and who contract their labor in the performance of a wide variety of odd-jobs, including domestic work. Such workers are not paid a wage for a repetitive and unending performance of a task; rather, they are paid for a job, a piece of work of defined character undertaken for a fixed price. Thus, a biscateiro may own a truck with which he contracts hauling jobs. He may own a car with which he operates a taxi service. Or, he may do jobs out of his home, repairing television sets, watches, automobiles, or sawing wood. Similarly, a biscateira may take in washing, do sewing, or dress hair in her home.

However, Manauaras also apply the term to individuals who engage in transactions that cannot be easily construed as a piece of work for a fixed price. A biscateiro may sell belts and other goods from a display board, watches from a small glass showcase, or perfumes from a tray or cardboard box. A biscateira may sell costume jewelry, small articles of clothing, maps, shoes, or leather goods from a stand that is dismantled and stored at the day's end. These individuals may move about the city or they may situate themselves each day at approximately the same location. On the other hand, a biscateiro may own a *balcão* (a counter or small shop) from which he sells dry goods, fruits and vegetables, or newspapers and magazines. A biscateira may cook food and sell it from her home or at a street stand. At some point, such enterprises may be sufficiently capitalized as to be relatively established in a fixed location—in front of a home, in a market area, or in the street. At this juncture, biscateiros tend to identify themselves not as biscateiros but as comerciantes. The comerciante is one who owns and operates an established small-scale business, often with the assistance of some members of his or her family. It is at this point that the organization of the enterprise begins to assume the character of a small firm and the distinction between the formal and informal sectors begins to blur.

Nevertheless, it is clear that with respect to the labor process these autonomous workers function primarily in the informal or small-scale sector of the economy. Regardless of the work they perform or the enterprises in which they are engaged, and independent of whether or not their engagement is officially registered, what most distinguishes these workers is their autonomy. They do not commoditize their labor but, instead, they commoditize some product or service of their labor. The distinction may not seem important. Culturally, however, it underscores the fact that biscateiros do not work for wages and, thus, they do not compete in a market for labor. More than this, these self-employed workers largely determine for themselves the kind of work they will do, where they will do it, when they will do it, and for how much they will do it. They do not have to take orders, submit to authority, or worry about relationships with chefes or patrões. Their workmates, if they have them, are of their own choosing. If they work the streets as hucksters and peddlers, they have considerable freedom of movement. By selecting their locations, they select their associates: i.e., the street people with whom they will visit and cooperate.

If autonomous workers pay wages at all, they pay them to members of their households. They do not assume the the binary status relationship of employer-employee in respect to these workers. Rather, they retain the familial status identities that normally obtain within their respective households. Thus, autonomous workers relate to their "employees" as husbands, wives, parents, siblings, and the like. The division of labor does not engage a sharp definition of functionally differentiated tasks. Most generally, it based on the authority of parental status, age, on values relating to gender, the consideration of personal interests, perhaps the acquisition of skills, or on the consideration of several of these factors. Whatever, work relationships do not engage the authority structure or market-oriented values that employers generally assume in relationship to the wage workers they employ.

The income of autonomous workers, as we shall see in the following chapter, is variable. On average, it is better than that of most industrial workers and better than that of most workers employed by locally owned firms in the commercial sector. Also, most autonomous workers have access to health benefits by self-registration or by registration as a "dependent" of a wage worker within the household. However, the benefit structure of autonomous work cannot be measured simply in these economic terms. Judging from informant interviews, at one time or another most autonomous workers have been employed for wages and less than thirteen percent of them would exchange their self-employment for wage employment, particularly in industry or the locally owned establishments of the commercial sector. Time and again, what emerges from in-depth interviews is the preference these workers have for their autonomy and for the work they are doing. In words summarizing their views: "I am my own patrão and the work I do is interesting."

All of this is not to suggest that the labor process in the informal sector is without the usual structural constraints. The markets in which these self-employed workers operate are ultimately dependent upon developments in the formal sector. These developments are beyond their control and often it is extremely difficult for them to know and assess these developments. Accordingly, income can be irregular and unpredictable. The availability of capital is generally a problem. Not infrequently, domestic needs exacerbate this problem. Also, where family labor is involved, work requirements are sometimes a source of strained relationships among members of the household, particularly when they run counter to individual interests and priorities. Problems also exist for those who work the streets. It is difficult for them to work when the weather is bad. At times, they are not well treated by customers. They are disliked by the merchants. At the instigation of the merchants, they are often harassed by the public authorities. And always, they have to protect their goods from thieves.

In sum, the labor process among autonomous workers is embedded in the interstices of the economy, in the spaces left open to individuals and households by firms because their markets are too small to conform to economies of scale. The conditions of work in these spaces are extremely variable. The work itself may be primarily manual, mechanical, or mental; in most cases, because the self-employed worker has to be in some sense a manager, the work has to be as mental as it is manual or mechanical. Moreover, relative to many types of wage employment, the work provided in these spaces is not economically unrewarding. For this reason, if for no other, these spaces provide an opportunity for individuals (and sometimes whole households) who prefer to manage their own affairs rather than allow them to be managed by others.

Firms, Enterprises, and Economic Sectors

In summarizing, it is instructive to consider the data presented here in more general terms. With regard to the labor process—i.e., how labor is recruited, appropriated or used, and valued—several sets of factors come into play and it seems that they can vary somewhat independently. One set of factors has to do with the character and organization of firms. It clearly makes a difference whether firms are bureaucratically organized and managed. Those that are, tend to define and recruit labor not with reference to persons but with reference to skills. Such firms seek to exclude from work activities whatever personal attributes of workers are thought to present a potential for destructuring the rational organization of work that these firms seek to maintain. Thus, by recruiting skills or simple labor power, these firms tend not only to depersonalize workers in the recruitment process by giving more or less exclusive focus to skills or to labor power as such, but they also depersonalize workers in their productive arrangements, in their mechanical systems of evaluation, and in their exclusion of merit considerations in the payment of wages. The opposite tends to be the case among non-bureaucratically organized firms.

As we have seen, in Manaus bureaucratically organized firms are generally, but not exclusively, those that were attracted to the city by SUFRAMA and the fiscal incentives of the Zona Franca. For the most part, these firms are externally capitalized. They are nationally- or multinationally-based. The enterprises in which they are engaged generally have no significant linkages with the traditional economy of the region. The non-bureaucratically organized enterprises tend to be locally capitalized, family-owned and managed, and more or less engaged in the production of goods and services that are not new to the urban and regional economies. Despite these differences, with respect to the labor process, the data presented here suggest that more is involved than the capitalization and managerial organization of firms. Also important is the type of enterprise in which the firm is engaged: more specifically, the type of work which the enterprise provides.

For example, Agá and Jota are assemblage industries in which most of the work is of a mechanical type that requires no experience, very little training, no mental adroitness, and no physical strength; it requires only digital dexterity. Digital dexterity is a skill or capability that is not commonly associated with the cultural perception of individuals as persons and, thus, it is an attribute that invites depersonalization. Accordingly, it is conceivable that an enterprise engaging a very different kind of work activity might call forth dimensions of the human personality that significantly obstruct the tendency by bureaucratic organizations, independent of their capitalization, to "depersonalize" the labor process. Indeed, this seems to be the case with the white collar workers employed by federal or state bureaucracies. It also seems to be the case with many white collar workers employed by nationally- and multinationally-based commercial enterprises. It follows that one cannot infer a particular type of labor process from the capitalization and bureaucratic organization of dependent capitalist enterprises. One must also consider the character of the enterprise itself and whether or not the work it provides engages skills and attributes that do not allow firms to easily depersonalize the worker while treating his or her labor as a commodity.

And what of economic sectors? From the data presented in this chapter several conclusions may be drawn. First, the most depersonalized type of labor process is found in association with the assemblage industries that, because of the Zona Franca, now form the hegemonic sector of the urban economy. In this sector, the commodity conception of labor is virtually complete and it extends from the assembly line to include even office personnel. On the other hand, the most personalized labor process encountered in this investigation tends to be associated with the traditional industries that have been made peripheral by developments in the Zona Franca.

Second, apart from their heterogeneity, virtually all of the firms in the commercial and service sectors, including departments associated with the state and federal governments, involve work activities for which the more personalized attributes—e.g., mental adroitness, previous experience, education, presentation of self, etc.—are acknowledged and in some sense valued.

Third, the labor processes that obtain in the hegemonic, traditional industrial, and white collar sectors stand in sharp contrast to that which exists in what we have called the informal sector. In the former sectors, no matter how workers may be differentially defined and valued by firms, both firms and workers conceptualize labor as a commodity and negotiate its exchange for wages in the market. Self-enterprising workers in the informal sector do not present themselves, nor do they present whatever skills they may command, in the market to be exchanged for wages. Thus, there appears to be a significant difference in the cultural psychology of wage and self-employed workers as a result of the fact that the latter are not directly dependent upon the decisions of firms for their economic and social well being.

In sum, the configuration of factors relating to firms, enterprises, and the labor process is such that, according to the sector of their employment, we should expect significant differences to exist in the social and cultural origins of workers, their mobility experiences, their objective and subjective status identities, their attitudes toward work, and the way in which they perceive their social lives to be related to the work they do. These are matters of consideration in the chapter to follow.

CHAPTER 3

Economic Sectors and the
Social Differentiation of Workers

Having outlined how the labor process is formed by the types of firms and enterprises that generally characterize key sectors of employment in the Zona Franca, we can now direct attention to how workers relate to these sectors of employment and the extent to which they are socially differentiated and stratified because of them. The chapter proceeds in five parts. First, I ascertain the extent to which these sectors of employment are in fact selective for workers who differ in their rural-urban origins, their gender, age, and level of educational achievement. I then show the extent to which the income inequalities that obtain among workers are related to the variables affecting their recruitment and their sector of employment. In the third section, I draw upon family histories to describe the intergenerational patterns of mobility that are generally associated with employment in different sectors of the new urban economy. In the fourth section, the reader's attention is directed to what workers in different sectors understand and think about their employers and the circumstances of their employment. Finally, using biographical data for purposes of illustration, I close the chapter with an analysis of how individuals in different sectors of the economy tend to conceptualize and structure their lives in relationship to their work.

The Social Selectivity of Economic Sectors

It may be recalled from chapter 1 that Manaus' working-class population is predominantly regional in origin. Its cultural heritage was largely formed by the linkages that existed between the extractive economy of the rural interior and the mercantile economy of the small urban

85

settlements for which Manaus served as the major center of trade. Because of its social class divisions, Manaus was somewhat more heterogeneous in its cultural formation than the settlements of the interior. However, the rural-urban distinction among working-class populations seems not to have involved cultural differences to which employers attached much value. Workers in Manaus were proletarianized by wage employment; those in the interior were semi-proletarianized by the necessity of collecting forest products and exchanging them for the credit they needed to buy necessities that they could not produce for themselves. Whether in the interior or the city, for the vast majority of workers the labor process mostly enjoined manual forms of work. The rewards for this work, as well as the social milieu in which it was performed, did not seem to allow for much social or occupational differentiation. This is no longer the case. Today, the firms and enterprises that characterize different sectors of the economy are selective for different types of workers. With reference to employment opportunities, workers are socially differentiated in terms of their rural-urban origins, their gender, age, and education.

Consider, first, the migratory origins of workers. In his study of the migratory process in relationship to the Zona Franca, Bentes (1983) reported that 76.6 percent of the 2,000 household heads interviewed in Manaus were migrants (defined as individuals born outside of Manaus) and 57 percent of this number originated in the small cidades and rural settlements of the interior. The migratory origins of the 88 household heads included in the present study does not differ significantly from that of Bentes' larger sample: 72 percent are headed by individuals born outside of Manaus, mainly in the interior of the region. However, when all of the economically active workers in these 88 households are counted (a total of 205), only 48 percent are migrants. Table 5 summarizes the distribution of these 205 workers by sector of employment and their migratory status.

From Table 5, it is obvious that there exists a considerable difference between migrants and non-migrants by sector of employment. Labor recruitment in the hegemonic industrial and white collar sectors of the economy appears to be very highly selective for non-migrants: i.e., for workers whose social and cultural origins are generally more urban than rural.[1] By way of contrast, recruitment in the traditional industrial sector is biased towards workers whose origins are mainly rural. Similarly, the self-employed workers included tend to be somewhat more rural than urban in their social and cultural origins. Moreover, those migrants who are employed in the hegemonic and white collar sectors are not generally an exception to the preference of

Table 5. Distribution of Workers by Sector of Employment and Migratory Status*

	Hegemonic Industrial		Traditional Industrial		White Collar		Self-employed		Total	
Migrants	N	(%)	N	(%)	N	(%)	N	(%)	N	(%)
Non-Migrants	34	69.4	8	17.8	40	69.0	25	47.2	107	52.2
Migrants	15	30.6	37	82.2	18	31.0	28	52.8	98	47.8
Total	49		45		58		53		205	

P < .001

*The significance of differences reported herein and all other tables is based on the X^2 test for k independent samples.

employers in these sectors for hiring workers of urban origin. Regarding this particular category of migrants, more than half of them came to Manaus with their parents at a very early age or, alternatively, they migrated from urban places.

Without burdening the reader with tabular data, it may be noted that the relationship between sector of employment and gender reaches an equivalent level of significance (P<.001). Thirty-one percent of the economically active males in these households were employed in the traditional industrial sector and 29 percent were self-employed. The remaining 40 percent were equally divided between the hegemonic industrial and white collar sectors. By comparison, 42 percent of the economically active women were engaged in white collar work; 30 percent were employed in the hegemonic industrial sector; 23 percent were self-employed; and only 5 percent were employed in the traditional industrial sector.

While *non-migrants* of both sexes are much more likely to find their way economically in the hegemonic industrial and white collar sectors, there does exist a significant difference in the sector of employment of male and female migrants. Female migrants are far more likely than male migrants to find employment in the white collar and hegemonic industrial sectors. At the same time, however, women born and raised in the interior are much less likely to find employment in these sectors than those who were born and raised in the city.

Age also is a significant factor (P<.01) in the social differentiation of workers by sector of employment. Almost 65 percent of the workers from these households who were engaged in the traditional industrial sector were over thirty years of age (in fact, 39 percent were over forty years of age). Self-employed workers revealed a similar age distribution. By way of contrast, approximately 76 percent of the workers employed in the hegemonic industrial sector, and 55 percent of those who were engaged in white collar work, were under thirty years of age. Regarding young workers (under thirty years of age) who were an exception to this pattern, interviews revealed that a substantial majority of them either followed their fathers into the informal and traditional industrial sectors or they left school to begin work at a very early age.

Clearly, what most differentiates workers in relationship to the labor processes that now obtain in different sectors of the economy in Manaus is their level of education. Moreover, this particular factor is itself related to the migratory status of workers, to whether or not they came to Manaus from a rural area in which educational opportunities were limited or unavailable, and to whether or not they arrived at an early or late age. Concerning the significance of this factor, consider first the data summarized in Table 6.

Table 6. Distribution of Workers by Sector of Employment and Level of Education

Level of Education

Sector of Employment	4 Years or Less		Completed Primary		Completed Secondary		
	N	(%)	N	(%)	N	(%)	Total
Hegemonic Industrial	3	5.8	19	26.4	27	33.3	49
Traditional Industrial	26	50.0	12	16.6	7	8.6	45
White Collar	1	1.9	19	26.4	38	46.9	58
Self-Employed	22	42.3	22	30.6	9	11.1	53
Total	52		72		81		205

$P < .001$

As the table reveals, 50 percent of the workers in these households who have completed no more than four years of education are employed in the traditional industrial sector. An additional 42 percent of these poorly schooled workers are self-employed in the informal sector. By way of contrast, almost 47 percent of the workers who have completed a secondary education are engaged in the white collar work. An additional 33 percent of this category are working in the new industrial firms of the hegemonic sector. Many of the workers employed in the hegemonic sector with a primary school education were attending secondary school at night. Those who were not tended to be employed as warehouse workers and the like. Workers employed in the white collar sector with only a primary school education generally fell into such low level occupational categories as office messenger, security guard, hospital attendant, store clerk, and the like. Still, with experience or special training, a few workers in this category did find their way into such occupations as nurse's aid, midwife, or typist.

In the context of Manaus and the Amazon region, educational opportunity is structured by a multiplicity of factors. Migratory origins is one. For example, among the non-migrant workers in these households, 52 percent had completed a secondary education. The comparable figure for migrant workers was only 25 percent. At the other end of the continuum, only 11 percent of the non-migrant workers, compared to 41 percent of those who were migrants, reported four years of education or less. Sixty percent of the migrants who have four years of education or less are employed in the traditional industrial sector and an additional 38 percent are self-employed.

Age at the point of migration is also a factor. Migrants who arrived in Manaus as children revealed a higher level of educational achievement than those who came as adults. Considering the general lack of educational opportunities in the interior, it was not too surprising to discover that among migrants no significant differences existed in the educational achievement of male and female workers. However, it was surprising to learn that among workers born and raised in Manaus, substantially more women (70 percent) than men (43 percent) had completed a secondary school education. In part, this would seem to explain the disproportionate representation of women in the white collar sector.[2]

It is unquestionably the case, therefore, that according to their rural-urban origins, their age, gender, and level of education, workers in Manaus are socially differentiated by the recruitment preferences that attach to the labor processes that now obtain in different sectors of the economy. The categorical differentiation or identification of persons in such status terms as these is not at all uncommon in industrial or even pre-industrial societies. However, whatever the terms that may be culturally appropriate, the social differentiation of persons is one thing; their stratification or differential economic empowerment is quite another.[3]

Status Inequalities

What, then, is the differential economic empowerment of workers according to these categorical status attributes and their sector of employment? If such workers have been differentially selected or recruited with reference to their urban-rural origins, their age, gender, and education, to what extent do these particular factors engage corresponding inequalities of income among workers who are employed in different sectors of the economy? Consider first the distribution of income by sector of employment (Table 7).

Table 7. Distribution of Workers by Number of Minimum Salaries and Sector of Employment

(Row Pct.)
(Col. Pct.)

Number of Minimum Salaries

Sector of Employment	One or Less N	(%)	Two–Three N	(%)	Four or More N	(%)	Total N	(%)
Hegemonic Industrial	28	(57.2) (25.9)	15	(30.6) (24.6)	6	(12.2) (16.7)	49	(100) (23.9)
Traditional Industrial	19	(42.2) (17.6)	21	(46.7) (34.4)	5	(11.1) (13.9)	45	(100) (21.9)
White Collar	33	(56.9) (30.6)	9	(15.5) (14.8)	16	(27.6) (44.4)	58	(100) (28.3)
Self-Employed	28	(52.8) (25.9)	16	(30.2) (26.2)	9	(17.0) (25.0)	53	(100) (25.9)
Total	108	(52.7)	61	(29.8)	36	(17.5)	205	(100)

$P < .05$

From Table 7 it may be observed that almost 53 percent of the economically active workers in the 88 households under study are pegged to one minimum salary/month or less.[4] For the most part, workers who earn this level of income are as likely to be self-employed as employed in the white collar or industrial sectors of the economy. However, it needs to be emphasized that the proportion of workers earning one minimum salary/month is higher among those employed in the hegemonic industrial sector than it is for any other group and it is lowest among those who are employed in the traditional industrial sector. It is also noteworthy that workers earning two or more minimum salaries/month are more likely to be found among those employed in the traditional industrial sector (57.8 percent) or among the self-employed (47.2 percent). Finally, it should be noted that while the majority of white collar (56.9 percent) and self-employed (52.8 percent) workers earn only one minimum salary/month, these two sectors of employment respectively account for 44.4 and 25.0 percent of the workers who report earning four or more minimum salaries/month.[5]

What these data seem to suggest is the following: first, the new hegemonic sector of the urban economy in Manaus has contributed less than the traditional industrial and informal sectors to improving the income status of individuals workers. Second, the status inequalities that obtain among workers in terms of their individual incomes are not large but to the extent that they exist at all, they are significantly related to the labor processes that obtain in different sectors of employment. Third, there is more space open for income improvement in the white collar sector, followed by the informal sector, than in either of the industrial sectors. However, it needs to be emphasized that among all four sectors of employment, the spaces open for income improvement are relatively small and they close quite rapidly as the worker reaches the level of six minimum salaries/month.[6] The question remains: how does this income distribution relate to the recruitment criteria according to which workers in these various sectors of employment tend to be categorically differentiated—i.e., their rural-urban origins, gender, age, and education?

Despite the fact that there exists a very significant relationship between the rural-urban origins of workers and the employment opportunities that are available in different sectors of the economy (Table 5), in terms of income or wages there exists no significant difference between workers whose social origins are rural rather than urban. This is the case not only for the entire sample of 205 workers, but also for workers who are self-employed or employed in the different industrial and white collar sectors. Thus, while workers whose social origins are more urban than rural may enjoy a competitive edge in gaining employment in certain industries or sectors of the economy, once employed, they do not command incomes or wages significantly higher than those workers whose origins happen to be rural.

The distribution of reported income assumes considerable significance in relationship to the gender of workers. As Table 8 reveals, 70.4 percent of the 71 females in this sample, compared to only 53.6 percent of the males, reported monthly incomes of one minimum salary or less. Approximately 79 percent of the workers who reported earning two-to-three minimum salaries, and 78 percent of those earning four minimum salaries or more, are males. Of the eight women in this sample who reported earning four or more minimum salaries, only two earned six and both of these were employed by the federal government.

Table 8. Distribution of Income by Gender

Number of Minimum Salaries

(Row Pct.) (Col. Pct.) Gender	One or Less		Two-Three		Four or More		Total	
	N	(%)	N	(%)	N	(%)	N	(%)
Male	58	(53.6) (53.7)	48	(36.8) (78.7)	28	(20.9) (77.8)	134	(100) (65.4)
Female	50	(70.4) (46.3)	13	(18.3) (21.3)	8	(11.3) (22.2)	71	(100) (34.6)
Total	108	(52.7)	61	(29.8)	36	(17.5)	205	(100)

P <.01

This general picture does not appear to change a great deal when income data for males and females are distributed by sector of employment. However, with reference to the labor processes that obtain in different sectors of employment, it needs to be recalled that firms in the hegemonic industrial sector place a high premium on the recruitment of female workers because of their presumed adaptability to assemblage work. Despite this preference, these industries assign female labor low commodity value in comparison to male labor. Without reporting tabular data, it may be noted that while 76 percent of the women interviewed in this type of work reported earning one minimum salary/month, 57 percent of the males engaged in this type of work reported earning two minimum salaries or more. In fact, 24 percent of the males reported earning four minimum salaries, a level of income that none of the women reported earning in this sector of employment.

It was found that age only commands significant (P<.01) income status as a function of the length of employment. In other words, in all sectors of employment, workers who report higher incomes are those who have accumulated the most seniority with particular firms or enterprises. Concerning age, it will be recalled that significant differences existed in the age of workers according to their sector of employment.

It also will be recalled that, typically, the recruitment preferences of firms, particularly in the hegemonic industrial sector, strongly favored the employment of workers under thirty years of age. Despite this preference, when the income level of workers is considered, no significant differences were found to exist among workers of different age categories by sector of employment. In other words, the preference for young workers, especially in the hegemonic industrial sector, does not bring to those who are recruited the reward of higher income, rather it gives them the promise of job *insecurity*. Because these firms periodically adjust their labor requirements to product market assessments, the overwhelming majority of young workers they employ will not accumulate the seniority needed to command the somewhat higher wages paid to the few workers who are their seniors. Those few who do accumulate this seniority are generally the ones who have been promoted and retained because, at their own expense, they have acquired some type of specialized technical training during the course of their employment.

It was previously shown (Table 6) that the recruitment and social differentiation of workers in the hegemonic, white collar, traditional, and informal sectors is significantly related to their level of educational achievement. Thus, it is appropriate to ask: what is the material value of education in the working class? Consider, first, the data relating the distribution of workers by level of income and educational achievement.

Table 9. Distribution of Workers by Level of Income and Educational Achievement

(Row Pct.)
(Col. Pct.)

Number of Minimum Salaries

	One or Less		Two–Three		Four or More		Total	
Level of Education	N	(%)	N	(%)	N	(%)	N	(%)
Four Years or Less	27	(51.9) (25.0)	20	(38.5) (32.8)	5	(9.6) (13.9)	52	(100) (25.4)
Completed Primary	49	(67.1) (45.4)	15	(20.6) (24.6)	9	(12.3) (25.0)	73	(100) (35.6)
Completed Secondary	32	(40.0) (29.6)	26	(32.5) (42.6)	22	(27.5) (61.1)	80	(100) (39.0)
Total	108	(52.7)	61	(29.8)	36	(17.6)	205	(100)

$P < .01$

As Table 9 reveals, there exists a significant relationship between level of educational achievement and income. Sixty-one percent of the workers reporting four minimum salaries/month or more have completed a secondary education. In this category of 22 workers, 8 have had some training at the University of Amazonas. At the other extreme, less than 30 percent of the workers reporting one minimum salary have completed a secondary education and this group represents two-fifths of the workers who have completed a secondary education. In fact, only 27.5 percent of the workers who have completed a secondary education earn more than three minimum salaries.

To what extent does this general relationship between income and education obtain in terms of different sectors of employment? The response to this question is not easily answered. It may be recalled from Table 6 that the recruitment processes in the hegemonic industrial and white collar sectors are particularly selective for workers who have completed a secondary education. However, when the data in Table 9 are distributed according to specific sectors of employment, the relationship between the level of income and education is only significant for the white collar sector. Among the workers in the white collar sector, while 81 percent of those without a secondary education reported earning one minimum salary, 57 percent of those with a secondary education reported earning two. However, it needs to be emphasized that the income level of 43 percent of the white collar workers with a secondary education is no higher than that of 85 percent of all workers without a secondary education. Gender preferences and income discrimination by gender seem to explain the low level of income among white collar workers with a secondary education. At least in terms of the sample under discussion, there were very few women with a secondary education who earned more than two minimum salaries in the commercial and service sectors and those that did were typically employed by Federal government.

These data suggest that, except perhaps for some white collar workers, educational achievement does not command significant value as measured by the payment of wages in relationship to the labor processes that obtain in various sectors of the economy. There is good reason for this. Independent of their sector of employment and of their level of educational achievement, the vast majority of workers in Manaus are chained by firms to the government's minimum wage structure. In theory, the minimum wage structure provides a floor below which firms are not to fix wages. In fact, this floor has become a ceiling above which, judging from our sample, the wages of more than half the workers employed in the hegemonic industrial and white collar sectors do not rise.

If, however, educational achievement up to the secondary level does not command significant value in terms of wages, it cannot be concluded that it commands no value at all. Clearly, without a secondary education (and certainly a university education) the worker will have virtually no opportunity for improving his/her income status. In addition, the mobility value of a secondary education differs rather significantly in relationship to the labor processes that exist in different sectors of employment and this, in turn, is generally reflected in the higher level of occupational status that most workers accord employment in the white collar sector. For example, among the 25 self-employed workers who reported earning two minimum salaries/month or more, 32 percent had completed a secondary school education. In the traditional industrial sector, only 23 percent of the 26 workers who reported this level of income had completed a secondary education. Of the 21 workers who earned this level of income in the hegemonic industrial sector, 62 percent had completed a secondary education. However, of the 25 workers in the white collar sector who reported earning two minimum salaries/month or more, no less than 84 percent had completed a secondary school education and within this group there existed several who were enrolled in courses at the University of Amazonas. Thus, within the hegemonic industrial sector, a secondary education offers some possibility of income improvement.[7] In the white collar sector, a secondary education has virtually become a prerequisite to income improvement.

Although the differences in reported monthly wages and incomes are not large among workers drawn from different sectors of employment, the differences are significant. Comparatively speaking, the traditional industrial and informal sectors have contributed to improving the income status of proportionately more workers than have the hegemonic industrial and white collar sectors. While the rural-urban origins of workers proved to be important with reference to their employment in different sectors of the economy, this factor did not reveal itself to be significant with reference to the income of workers in general or to the income of workers drawn from different sectors of employment. Gender proved to be generally critical with respect to wages and income and it also showed itself to be significant by sector of employment. The income status of workers differs significantly according to their age. However, this is a function of the length of employment and it is unrelated to the recruitment preferences that obtain in different sector of employment. Educational achievement, on the other hand, is generally related to the income inequalities existing among workers. While educational achievement does not make a significant difference in the income of workers within particular sectors of employment, it does emerge as a critical factor in respect to opportunities for promotion and income improvement, particularly within the white collar and hegemonic industrial sectors.

Intergenerational Patterns of Mobility

For many workers in Manaus, status mobility involves both horizontal and vertical movement. It may involve horizontal movement from self-employment in agriculture, sometimes combined with the extraction of forest products, to self-employment or wage employment in some urban location. The transition usually begins with the adult sons or daughters of *seringueiros* (rubber collectors) and subsistence producers in the interior. Because of floods, markets, size of family relative to the availability of land or forest products, or because of personal considerations such as family illness or the desire to provide their own children with an opportunity to attend school, these individuals are motivated to seek urban work. Usually, the parents of these migrants remain in the interior until they are forced by age or illness to join a son or a daughter in the city. It is generally the third generation that is born and raised in the city. And it is the third generation that has had little or no cultural experience with agricultural or manual labor in the interior.

Based on in-depth interview data relating to family histories, the households under study generally conform to the above pattern. However, there is substantial variation by sector of employment. For example, 65 percent of the workers employed in the white collar sector and 64 percent of those employed in the hegemonic industrial sector had grandparents who were engaged in agriculture or the extraction of forest products. Among the parents of these workers, only 16 percent were similarly engaged. By way of contrast, 89 percent of the self-employed workers and 88 percent of the workers employed in the traditional industrial sector had grandparents engaged in agriculture or extraction. No less than 46 percent of the parents of these traditional industrial workers continue to be employed in agriculture or extraction. For the self-employed workers, only 31 percent of their parents remained in the interior.

When the intergenerational mobility of informants is plotted with reference to their current sector of employment, a distinctive pattern emerges. For the most part, white collar workers and workers employed in the hegemonic industries are two generations or more removed from work experiences in the interior. The grandparents of approximately 35 percent of these workers quit the interior and the semi-proletarianized forms of work it provided for wage employment in Manaus or in one of the smaller urban settlements of the region. Many of the children of these early migrants obtained a primary school education and subsequently secured white collar employment in the public or commercial sectors. The grandchildren of these very early migrants have typically obtained a secondary school diploma and continue in white collar employment or, alternatively, they are employed in the hegemonic industrial sector.

When the parent(s) rather than the grandparents of contemporary workers are the ones who migrated from the interior, upon their arrival in Manaus they generally became occupied in the informal sector or they found employment in one of the traditional industries.[8] If the parent(s) arrived in Manaus at an age when their children were young enough to secure a secondary education, the latter tend to be employed in the new hegemonic industries. However, if they migrated when their children had already left school without a secondary education, then the children tend to have followed the occupations of their fathers, in which case they tend to be either self-employed or working in the traditional industries.

How do these horizontal patterns of mobility relate to vertical patterns. First, consider education. Eighty-one percent of the white collar workers and 88 percent of those employed in the hegemonic industrial sector, as compared to 49 and 34 percent of the traditional industrial and self-employed workers respectively, had completed a level of education higher than that of either of their parents. This is not surprising considering that the overwhelming majority of these white collar and hegemonic industrial workers are second and third generation urbanites and, thus, they have had more educational opportunities relative to their parents than workers in the traditional industrial and informal sectors. As previously noted, the majority of traditional industrial and self-employed workers are themselves migrants, typically from the rural interior of Amazonas or other states.

It is much more difficult to assess the occupational mobility of the workers interviewed relative to their parents. We do not have available for the population of this region some sort of scale according to which we can objectively compare the prestige or social worth of occupations. Moreover, interview data revealed important areas of value dissension regarding the prestige of work in different sectors of employment. For example, almost all informants seem to agree that any type of wage employment or self-employment in Manaus is preferable to agricultural or extractive work in the interior. Similarly, most considered wage employment in the hegemonic industrial sector more preferable than employment in the traditional industrial sector. Some workers in the traditional industrial sector, however, would not agree with this assessment. Needless to say, virtually all informants agreed that white collar work is more desirable than industrial work, particularly if it involved government employment. And, independent of their sector of employment, the majority of wage workers considered self-employment in the informal sector demeaning and lacking in prestige. However, almost all of the self-employed workers interviewed considered self-employment eminently more desirable than industrial employment. Allowing for these disagreements, one might consider upwardly mobile a move from agriculture to wage employment or self-employment in Manaus; a move from work in a traditional industry to work in the new industrial sector; a move from wage employment in the traditional industrial sector to self-employment; and a move from any of these to some type of white collar work.

On the basis of this admittedly crude scale of evaluation, it was determined that approximately 81 percent of all the workers interviewed had experienced some degree of mobility relative to the work of their fathers, in the case of males, or their mothers, in the case of females. However, rather significant differences again existed among workers according to their sector of employment. Because of the work of their parents, 83 percent of the workers in the hegemonic industrial sector have experienced intergenerational mobility. By comparison, because 39 percent of their parents were already engaged in white collar work, only 61 percent of the white collar workers interviewed had experienced intergenerational mobility. Similarly, because 31 percent of their parents worked in agriculture, 69 percent of the self-employed workers experienced intergenerational mobility. And, since 48 percent of the workers employed in the traditional industrial sector are doing the same work as their fathers, only 52 percent of this category had experienced intergenerational mobility in terms of their work.

The question remains whether intergenerational mobility assumes significant economic dimensions. To determine this, we compared the monthly income reported (in minimum salaries) by informants to that currently earned by one or both of their parents, if the latter were still working, or what they believed their parents to be earning at the point of their retirement or death.[9] In all, data in this regard were obtained from 182 workers. Of these, as far as economic empowerment is concerned, almost 59 percent of the workers interviewed revealed themselves to be immobile or downwardly mobile relative to one or both of their parents. More significant than this, however, are the differences that emerge among these workers with reference to their sector of employment. The largest proportion of workers who judged themselves to be economically immobile or downwardly mobile were employed in the hegemonic industrial sector, that sector of the economy which is most specifically and most directly the product of SUFRAMA's development project. Whatever their educational achievements and their sense of occupational mobility, more than 72 percent of the workers in these so-called high tech assemblage industries, as compared to less than 55 percent of the workers in other sectors, judged their monthly incomes to be no better than that of one or both of their parents.

In view of these considerations, how do these workers view their employment? More specifically, if the social differentiation of workers with respect to employment in different sectors of the economy does not enjoin a significant degree of stratification in terms of economic empowerment, what then are the status implications of their social differentiation? Do these workers, according to their rural-urban origins, gender, age, and education, view their work, their employers, the benefits of their employment, and one another differently? Is there any relationship between their social differentiation in the labor market and the way in which they view their life circumstances?

As Workers View Their Employment

Based on in-depth interview data, it is more than apparent that the attitudes workers hold with respect to the stability or permanency of their current employment are affected by a multiplicity of factors relating to the work they do, the firms for which they work and, in general, the labor market that now obtains in the Zona Franca. On a day-to-day basis, these workers collect and process a great deal of information and misinformation about their employers as well as other employers from supervisors, workmates, neighborhood friends, relatives and, to a lesser extent, the media. The complexity and the magnitude of this information is such that it is difficult to sort out precisely how it is factored by individual workers in relationship to their economic empowerment and the prestige they generally assign to work in different sectors of the economy. Nevertheless, in an effort to discern patterns in this regard, interview schedules were structured so as to elicit information regarding the way in which workers perceived their work, their employers, and the conditions of their employment, including factors relating to the possibilities of their promotion, incentive structures, the role and significance of labor unions, and the like.

It is instructive to consider, first, how these workers view their work and what they know or do not know about their employers.

When asked what they liked most about their current work, almost 78 percent of the workers of rural origin specified the work itself or the conditions of their employment. Less than six percent indicated that they liked most the people that they worked with. By way of contrast, almost 38 percent of the workers of urban origin indicated that what they liked most about their work was their workmates. Generally, workers over the age of thirty are those who most liked the work they were doing; workers under the age of thirty liked most the conditions of their employment or the people they worked with. These attitudes do not vary much by gender but they do vary significantly by sector of employment. Workers in the hegemonic industries most appreciated the work they were doing (63 percent) or the people they worked with (44 percent). They (22 percent) disliked most their wages and the benefits they received. White collar workers liked most the work they were doing (60 percent) and if they disliked anything, they disliked the conditions of their employment (20 percent). However, it is the white collar workers employed in the commercial sector, clerks and the like, who revealed themselves to be most dissatisfied with the conditions of their employment. Self-employed workers most appreciated (60 percent) the conditions of their work. When they complained of the conditions of their work (only 15 percent), they complained most about the public they serviced. Almost none of these workers expressed much satisfaction with their incomes and, except for workers in the traditional industrial sector, very few expressed any special attachment to the firms that employed them.

What do these workers know about the firms that employed them?[10] Most of the firms operating in the hegemonic sector claim to provide programs designed to inform new workers as to the organization of the firm, the conditions of their employment, the criteria of their evaluation, and the like. As often as not this information is distributed in a pamphlet, in which case the less educated workers do not read it, or the transmission of information is left to a supervisor, in which case the information transmitted tends to give focus to the work assignment itself and not to the firm, its organization, or its benefit structure.

Based on a content analysis of tape-recorded responses to open-ended questions, approximately 46 percent of the workers interviewed are generally well-informed about the structure and organization of the firms that employed them. This means, in effect, that they could describe the divisional organization of the enterprise as it existed in Manaus. They had a fairly accurate idea as to whether or not the enterprise is locally owned, nationally based, or organized as a subsidiary of a multinational. They could name the three or four key corporate officers at the local level. In regard to this kind of information, 54 percent of the workers were poorly informed or completely uninformed.

In terms of sector of employment, workers in the hegemonic industrial sector comprised approximately 56 percent of the most poorly informed group. Workers in the traditional industries were better informed but not because programs existed for this purpose. Rather, they were better informed because they were employed by smaller, locally-owned enterprises that had recruited them through relatives and friends who were employed by these firms. In addition to this variance, almost 70 percent of the well-informed workers were counted among those who had completed a secondary school education and 46 percent were employed in the white collar sector, mainly by the state or federal governments or by banks.

In light of these considerations, what has been the employment experience of these workers? First, it may be noted that during the course of their work careers, almost 71 percent of the workers included in the sample have changed jobs two or more times while living in Manaus. In fact, 27 percent reported having worked for three or more employers prior to their present employment. This mobility in and of itself bears no significant relationship to the rural-urban origins of the workers involved, to their age, gender, education, or to their current sector of employment. However, it is evident that there exist among various groups of workers differences in attitude with respect to their current employment and these differences are significantly related to the rural-urban origins of the workers involved, to their age, their gender, education, and to their sector of employment.

More specifically, almost 71 percent of the workers of rural origin considered their current employment to be permanent as compared to only 40 percent of the workers of urban origin. Sixty-seven percent of the workers over the age of thirty considered their current employment permanent as compared to 57 percent of those under the age of thirty. Sixty-three percent of the male workers considered their current job permanent; 62 percent of the female workers did not. Also, 63 percent of the workers with less than eight years of education considered their current employment to be permanent; 51 percent of those with more than eight years of education did not. And, with respect to sector of current employment, only 32 percent of the workers in the hegemonic industrial sector considered their current employment to be permanent. By way of contrast, 75 percent of the workers in the traditional industrial sector, 65 percent of those working in the white collar sector, and 63 percent of the self-employed workers in the informal sector, considered their current employment to be permanent.

In other words, workers of rural origin, older workers, males, workers with little or no education, in short, self-employed workers or workers who are employed for wages *outside* the hegemonic industrial sector, tend to consider their current employment to be nearly permanent. Further, interview data suggest that this predisposition to view their employment as nearly permanent engages a wide variety of attitudes and some of these are clearly grounded both in the recruitment variables under consideration and in the worker's sector of current employment. For example, workers of urban origin (58 percent) see more opportunities for advancement in their current work than do workers of rural origin (42 percent). Whereas 61 percent of the males see some opportunity for advancement in their current work, 67 percent of the females do not. Needless to say, the majority of the latter are women employed in the assemblage industries or as clerks, typists, telephone operators, and the like, in the white collar sector. As to sector of employment, despite the infrequent promotions in the hegemonic industries, 66 percent of these workers (almost all of them males) believe that they can advance or be promoted within the firms that employ them. By way of contrast, this view is held by only 50 percent of the white collar workers (mostly those employed in the public services) and only 30 percent of the workers in the traditional industries.

How do these workers view the *sindicatos* or labor unions in relationship to their work, the conditions of their employment, and their opportunity for advancement? First, it needs to be noted that only 56 percent of the workers interviewed belonged to a labor union (i.e., they reported themselves to be a *registered* member of a sindicato) and this varies significantly by sector of employment. Although there exist several associations of self-employed workers (e.g., street vendors, taxi drivers, news stand proprietors, etc.), very few (20 percent) reported belonging to one of these associations. Similarly, only 35 percent of the white collar workers (mainly bank clerks, teachers, medical workers, and the like) belonged to a union or a professional association. Ninety-five percent of the traditional industrial workers interviewed belonged to a union as compared to 63 percent of the workers in the hegemonic industrial sector.

Among all of these workers, union membership appeared to assume more the character of a ritual obligation than an expression of an organized political stance in relationship to their employers. For example, approximately 45 percent of the workers interviewed indicated that they did not know what, if anything, the unions had contributed by way of improving their conditions of work, their job security, income, or fringe benefits. Besides these, a substantial number of the workers interviewed claimed that they had derived no value whatsoever from the sindicatos. Specifically, 36 percent emphasized that working conditions had not improved because of the union; 37 percent maintained that salaries had not improved because of the union; and 46 percent felt that unions contributed absolutely nothing to job security. These data do not vary significantly with reference to the social origins, age, gender, and education of workers. They do vary somewhat with reference to their sector of employment. In general, workers in the traditional industries, most of whom belonged to a union, expressed more knowledge of unions than workers in the hegemonic industrial and white collar sectors. However, these traditional industrial workers also expressed less confidence in unions than did workers in other sectors.

If the majority of these workers were negative or uninformed as to what the unions contributed to the labor process and their economic well-being, they also expressed a very vague understanding of how their work was evaluated and what criteria their employers used for purposes of evaluation and promotion. For example, independent of their social origins, age, gender, and education, but not independent of their sector of current employment, less than 22 percent believed that in the case of promotional reviews, their employers would give considerable weight to the previous experience, technical formation, and professionalism of workers. The minority of workers who thought these factors to be important were located mainly in the hegemonic industries and the white collar sectors. A somewhat larger percentage of workers (33 percent) considered personal relationships with supervisors to be more critical to their promotion than previous experience, technical training, or professional demeanor. Workers who underscored personal relationships are among those who are more urban than rural in their social origins. They also tend to be under thirty years of age and employed in the hegemonic industrial and white collar sectors.

Related to the question of worker evaluation, it is interesting to note the extent to which workers considered relevant to their employment and promotion the very criteria we have shown to affect their recruitment and social differentiation within the labor market that now exists in Manaus. To begin: most workers (89 percent) did not consider their social origins to be a factor in their recruitment or evaluation and the few who did were employed mainly in the traditional industrial sector. Although most workers (65 percent) did not consider gender important, those who did are typically male, significantly more rural than urban in their social origins, over thirty years of age, and employed in the hegemonic industrial sector. Only 18 percent (a total of 38) of the workers interviewed considered education to be a very important factor in their recruitment and in their prospects for advancement. Of this number, half were employed in the white collar sector and half in the hegemonic industrial sector. The majority (68 percent) within both these groups had completed a secondary school education.

In sum, the recruitment criteria that in fact affect the opportunities of these workers in the labor market in Manaus are not considered by the workers themselves to be very important to their employment or promotion. And yet, it is clear that to varying degrees these factors are significantly related to the way in which these workers view their work, the conditions of their employment, and the opportunities they think exist for advancement within the firms that employ them. Further, it needs to be emphasized that these criteria and the perceptions they seem to structure are not without some objective basis in the occupational careers of these workers. Consider, for example, promotions and then the frequency with which these workers have changed employers.

Only 36 percent of these 205 workers interviewed had ever experienced some improvement in their job classification by way of promotion during the course of their work careers. The mobility of this select group tends to be centered in the white collar and hegemonic industrial sectors but not significantly so. It tends to be related to age and education but, again, the relationships do not reach statistical significance. What emerges as significant is the fact that 81 percent of the 74 workers whose job classification has improved since entering the labor market are males. Of the 71 females included in the study, only 27 percent have improved their job classification since entering the labor market.

This lack of mobility is undoubtedly related to the frequency with which many workers change employers in Manaus. However, in this regard, other factors are perhaps more significant. For example, almost 72 percent of the workers of rural origin in this sample have held their current jobs for more than three years as compared to only 31 percent of the workers of urban origins. Among workers under the age of thirty, 77 percent have held their current jobs less than three years as compared to only 30 percent who are over the age of thirty. Fifty-five percent of the males in the sample have held their current jobs four years or longer as compared to only 30 percent of the females. And regarding sector of employment, almost 70 percent of the workers in the hegemonic sector, where the turnover among females is even higher than it is among males, have held their current jobs three years or less. By way of contrast, 75 percent of the workers in the traditional industrial sector and 60 percent of those in the white collar sector have been at their current place of employment four years or longer.

The occupational career pattern of self-employed workers is somewhat different from that of other groups. As has been established, the income potential of self-employment in the informal sector is considered by workers in this sector to be better than wage employment in the industrial sectors. It is considered better particularly by those individuals who have less than eight years of education and who cannot hope to be promoted or improve their circumstances by movement into white collar employment. Many of these individuals view the informal sector as a locus of opportunity and an avenue of vertical mobility. Generally, the shift into the informal sector occurs at a point in their work careers when they have accumulated sufficient capital, either by way of wages or indemnification (Fundo de Garantia por Tempo de Serviço) payments, to become "independent" by establishing small scale enterprises in the informal sector.[11]

However, the perception of the informal sector as an avenue of mobility is one thing; earning a livelihood in the informal sector is quite another. In the commercial district street vendors are everywhere and their number as well as that of taxis is legion. And in the neighborhoods it sometimes seems that there are more small dress shops, bars, food stands, television and watch repairmen, than business to sustain them. Related to these small-scale enterprises, interview data reveal that there exists a great deal of variation in managerial skills. Thus, the death rate of these enterprises tends to be high and there appears to exist a great deal of movement into and out of the informal sector. In general, this movement is not the result of unemployment or the inability of the formal sector to provide sufficient opportunities for employment, rather it is due to the fact that the informal sector itself is highly competitive.

As a consequence of these circumstances, while 63 percent of the self-employed workers interviewed considered their self-employment to be permanent, only 36 percent had in fact been self-employed four years or longer. Moreover, most of the workers in this particular sample who did not consider their self-employment to be permanent are women, domestics and street vendors whose income in the informal sector was generally one minimum salary/month or less. We interviewed very few self-employed workers of this type and they were the ones who were prepared to leave the informal sector if they could obtain wage employment, particularly in the hegemonic industries. The overwhelming majority of self-employed workers emphatically expressed a strong preference for self-employment over wage employment.

Living Work and Economic Sectors

The relationship between social life and work is conceptualized here as *living work*.[12] The concept is intended to give focus to the fact that the social structures that affect the way individuals must work in order to live are simultaneously structures that generally affect the way in which individuals must live in order to work. There exists, in other words, a connection between the work that individuals perform for a living and the life they live in their respective families, neighborhoods, bairros, and in the larger society. By concluding the present chapter with biographical material which discloses how individuals in different sectors of the economy tend to conceptualize and describe their work with reference to the lives they live, or would like to live, we initiate here the analysis that is the focus of the chapters to follow; i.e., the analysis of the relationship between social life and work in the Zona Franca. The biographical sketches begins with a few cases drawn from among white collar workers.

As we have seen, white collar work tends to favor the employment of women. In 1980, approximately half of the wage workers in Manaus were employed in the white collar sector. Among women who were gainfully employed, no less than 65 percent worked in this sector. Still, it should not be overlooked that women contributed only 45 percent to the total employment in this sector. Francisco Brandão is a case of a male employed in this sector by a research unit of the Federal government.

Francisco Brandão was born in the interior. When he came to Manaus with his parents as a young man, he spent two years in a seminary. Later, while holding an internship at the Escola Ténica Federal in Manaus, he worked as a janitor in a church. After completing his internship, with "the help of friends and connections," he secured a job with an agricultural research firm supported by the Federal Government, an enterprise of a type that forms part of what I have called the "development industry" in Manaus. Francisco is now thirty-eight years of age, married, and has two young children. He has held his current job for nine years. He considers himself relatively well paid (five minimum salaries/month). He owns a modest home in Raiz, approximately thirty kilometers from where he works. In his work, he frequently has to travel to field sites that are even more distant. As a result of these circumstances, Francisco is away from home a great deal of the time. However, he emphasized: "I do not consider this a problem. Thanks to my work, I am living a good life."

When asked to describe this "good life," Francisco's comments gave focus not to his economic circumstances, his family, or his neighborhood, but to his work. He stated: "(My firm) provides excellent working conditions. It employs a great many scientists, some from Germany and France. (The firm) has nine different laboratories. When I supervise the application of poisons in field tests, I am given clothes, boots, masks, everything. There is not much promotion within the company and this makes for a lot of internal politics which I do not like. I prefer to be in the field, away from the internal politics and the people who observe us. But this is not a serious problem for me. The scientists there are of very high status and I work with them. I myself supervise the field studies which they organize. I supervise a small crew of *mão de obra* (unskilled laborers) whose positions are not so high as my own."

None of the scientists or field workers with this agricultural research unit are related to Francisco. He counts none of them among his close friends. Except at work, he has no association with them. "My close friends," he stated, "are only my wife, my father, my brother, my sister-in-law, and my mother-in-law. Because I have so little time, I try to be with them whenever I can be home. Sometimes, never more than once a month, my wife and I do a little something with my neighbor across the street. We take a little food with one another, perhaps a beer, or go to the cinema."

Like everyone else, Francisco must work in order to live. However, Francisco also lives mostly for his work. It consumes a great deal of his time but then, because he works with important and interesting people, with scientists, his work provides him with a good life. In effect, apart from his income, Francisco derives a sense of status from his employment. He does not consider himself to be an ordinary mão de obra. Because of his work he is a person; that is, he has social and not simply commodity value. Although Francisco does not consider his social and family life fragmented by his employment, he confesses to having limited time for his family and almost no time at all for his neighbors. Francisco works to live and he lives modestly well. However, because of the conditions of his employment, Francisco also lives to work.

Like Francisco Brandão, Linda Figueiredo also derives her status identity and sense of personal worth from her work. Linda has been a midwife at the state maternity hospital for twenty years. Besides this, she works at a private hospital. And, in her off hours, she earns additional income delivering babies for women who do not go to the maternity hospital. From this work, she reports a total income of approximately five minimum salaries. While important, it seems that this income is not entirely critical to her support.[13] Her work, however, is important because she derives from it not only her sense of self-worth but also her sense of independence.

Regarding her social situation, Linda stated: "The conditions at the hospital are not ideal. I work there only three days each week but the hours are long—12 hours per day. There are no incentives, no pay for extra hours. We are lacking in everything—bed space, supplies, facilities, medical assistance—everything. My daughter works in the hospital and most of my friends are there. Also, what I do is important. I help the mothers. Here in Manaus we have to continually struggle for better conditions in the health field. I am part of this struggle. We have an association and I am a member of the directorate. We organize parties, which I enjoy, but mostly we struggle for better days in the health field." In effect, more than she works to live, Linda lives for her work and her work almost completely structures her social life both at home and in the community. Because of her "speciality" she claims to be well known in the neighborhood but, she emphasizes, "I do not live much in the neighborhood. I see my neighbors only when passing in the street."

The case of Selma D'Almeida is a bit different from that of Linda. Selma thinks of herself as an accountant. She works for a private tourist agency subsidized in part by the government. Selma was born and raised in Manaus. Her first employment, at age seventeen, was selling clothes in a store. She worked there for two years and was laid off. She then worked for two years as a clerk in a music shop. She left the music shop when she became pregnant. Four years later, after she completed her secondary education with a course in accounting, her brother-in-law found her present position for her. When interviewed, she had been with the firm for six years and reported earning four minimum salaries.

Despite her occupational self-identity, Selma is not really an accountant. She works as a bookkeeper under the assistant to the chief accountant. Before moving to this particular position, she kept records in "storage and equipment." She related, "I like the accountant office better because there I work in what I have studied. Also, we have monthly meetings in the department and you can talk with the chief of your section. The workday is short in this department—only six hours." She continued, "We have an association. It sponsors a monthly social but I have never participated. Except for my brother-in-law, who also works there, most of our (her and her husband's) close friends belong to a group of couples that form the Christian Family Movement in another neighborhood."

Selma lives in Raiz, a bairro less than eight kilometers from her place of work. She is married to an insurance agent who averages seven minimum salaries, virtually a middle-class income in Manaus. In view of her husband's income, Selma was asked why she worked. She responded: "With the money I earn we can afford more of the things we want. I can give more help to my children's education. Besides, my work is not far, the hours are not long, and the job does not detract very much from my children, my husband, and my friends in the family movement." Thus, unlike Francisco and Linda, Selma's sense of worth in relationship to her work is more a function of the additional income it provides than the conditions of her employment or her occupational status. She does not completely discount the latter because she took care to inflate it by claiming to be an accountant. However, this seemed not be as important to her as what she could do with the income she derived from her work and the fact that she could earn this income working short hours and, thus, without disrupting her life with family and friends.

For purposes of contrast, Marlice Loureiro's is a case drawn from the lowest end of the occupational scale in the white collar sector. Marlice was born in Manaus, is twenty-one years of age, and has finished high school. While in high school, she had an internship as a receptionist for a travel agency but she was never paid for this work. Her first and only gainful employment has been clerking in a clothing store, located in the commercial district. The store is locally owned and family operated. In addition to Marlice, the proprietor employs seven clerks who are not members of his family. After more than a year at the store, Marlice has yet to receive a worker's registration card from her employer. Thus, she is not registered with INPS and, with commissions, she reports earning on average one minimum salary/month.

Marlice describes her work as follows: "We work five full days and Saturday mornings—fifty hours or more each week. Conditions are very good. The store is hot but they have some fans. The restrooms are clean. If you report five or ten minutes late in the morning, which sometimes happens because of the bus service, they do not let you begin work until the afternoon. I think I have friends there but they are not close. Most of my real friends are in the neighborhood. I like the work I am doing but my relatives make fun of it. They do not think it is important or interesting. I prefer to be a secretary but my hours do not make it easy for me to look for another position. Because of the long hours, I am tired when I come home. I have a little time with my family and less for my friends. I belong to a youth group but it is not often that I can participate. When I am home, I have to help my mother."

In general, white collar workers did not view their work simply as something they had to do in order to earn a living for themselves or their families. As much as they worked in order to live, most also lived in order to work. That is to say, their work enjoined an occupational status identity which in some sense corresponded to some set of mobility aspirations that they expressed for themselves or for their children. Accordingly, they did not mind organizing their family and social lives around their work. This, of course, was not so much the case with Marlice who, like so many workers in this sector, was employed as a store clerk, at the bottom of the scale. The case of Marlice illustrates that there are types of work in the white collar sector that do not enjoin the esteem of friends or relatives. Thus, some types of work in the white collar sector can be as alienating as work in other sectors. Alienating or not, what emerges from the comments of these and other white collar workers is the cultural view, not necessarily new in Manaus but certainly underscored by developments in the Zona Franca, that occupational identity and income are the measure of one's social worth as well as the basis for the esteem in which one is held by family and friends. Related to this, of course, is the view that employment in the white collar sector should enhance one's income potential and social esteem and, if it does not, then something must be wrong with the individual.

Given the relative uniformity of working conditions in the firms that comprise the hegemonic industrial sector, two examples may suffice to illustrate the type of alienation that most interviewees expressed.[14] The first concerns Evandro Oliveira. Evandro is twenty-four years of age, single, and lives with his parents and four siblings in Raiz. Since finishing high school in 1980, he has been employed as an assembly worker at Jota. Evandro related: "I entered Jota as an assembler. I was promoted to inspector but I still earn only one minimum salary. If I want to keep my job, I cannot complain about this. Too many people work there and if you complain, or when your salary improves, they replace you. They prefer to hire women because they can be more easily manipulated and there are many women who look there for work."

When asked how his work affected his life with family and friends, Evandro stated: "I think my work is important. On the line, I check each television unit and decide whether or not it is proper. You must understand, this is only relative. None of the work there is really important. Because I finished high school, I find it difficult to adapt myself there. Many people there are ignorant and stupid. Sometimes it is even difficult to talk with them. The company pushes them all the time and they never complain. Even those who study after hours do not complain when the company makes them work so late that they have to miss school. How long can this last? My parents see my work as a necessity, but I do not like to work in the District."

When asked why he did not like to work in the District, he continued: "One cannot have a future working in the District. Jobs are not safe. There are few promotions and you cannot get one unless you kiss everybody's ass. The District is isolated. The workday is only nine hours but you must spend two or three more hours on a bus. Some women signed a petition to have one of the bus drivers fired because of his behavior. He was fired and now everyone of those women is laid off. If you work in the District you have no time for anything else. My friends in the neighborhood joke about me working there. They cannot take what I do seriously. It has no future and without a future, how can one be dignified? We can forget the District. The majority who work there want to forget it on weekends. They don't even want to return there on weekends to use the pool or the club facilities. They only want to stay home, perhaps watch television, and rest. I took a course in computers and I have friends who are helping me find something better. People who work in the District have no life of their own."

In somewhat different words, Aldemira Barbosa projects a similar sense of alienation. Aldemira is thirty-one years of age, single, without children, and lives in Raiz with her widowed mother, two brothers, and her sister's children. She has completed eight years of education. In the fifteen years that she has been gainfully employed, she has worked for nine different firms, three of which are in the hegemonic industrial sector. She quit her job at one of these firms because they wanted to transfer her to the second shift (from 2 to 11 P.M..) and, she said, "working these hours, I could find absolutely no enjoyment in life." She was laid off at the second of these firms because "my supervisor was a pain in the ass and I made a complaint." At the time of interview, Aldemira had been working as a "helper" for six months at Jota. She earned slightly more than one minimum salary. She described her work as follows:

"My job is not very important. I have a little office on the assembly line from which I deliver gloves and other things that the workers need. If a girl needs relief, I replace her on the line. The work is not interesting and the hours are long. As you know, the factory is only a few kilometers from here but I have to leave home at four in the morning. Sometimes I miss the bus in the afternoon and I don't return until after four or five. I think Jota is one of the better companies in the District but most of us become tired of the work we do there. Sometimes you are laid off and don't know why. I think all the companies in the District have more value for people outside the region. They think people from here are stupid and lazy. Well, I am from the Amazon. I do not think I am stupid and I know that I am not lazy. However, the workers on the assembly line do not get much praise and they have no voice. If someone needs medical assistance, they say it is a lie. People are humiliated by supervisors and managers. Only once has my supervisor praised my work."

Asked how her work affected her social and family life, Aldemira responded: "What I do is not important, it is only important for my family that I work. It is difficult to make friends at the plant. There is too much bickering and competition for the chief's attention. My friends are in the neighborhood but all of them work. Some are married and (laughing) they have other problems. I also have a problem with my mother. She is old and needs my help. I have to get up very early to go to work. It's difficult if I watch a late television program. When I come home, I don't have much motivation to visit. If I could, I would go to a party every day, but I have only the weekend to do this. Sunday for me is dead. No one does anything interesting on Sunday. Sometimes I go to a movie or a discothèque on Friday or Saturday night. I have a close friend in the back who likes to do this."

Although most of the workers in the hegemonic sector considered their work to afford them more status than self-employment or work in the traditional industrial sector, only those classified as técnicos seem to derive an encompassing sense of social worth from their work. Técnicos either viewed their work as an opportunity to acquire skills for which they believed there existed unlimited demand in the Brazilian economy or, alternatively, they were convinced that there existed in their respective firms the opportunity for a lifelong career. Accordingly, after hours, they engaged in whatever technical training program these firms or SENAI offered that might be relevant to their advancement. In addition, in order to become better known, they oriented their social lives as much as possible around whatever club activities their firms promoted. Técnicos, however, form a very small percentage of the workers in these industries. The situation of Evandro and Aldemira is more characteristic of the majority.

Evandro, like most of those interviewed who had completed a high school education, defines his status and describes his social worth with reference to his educational achievements. He considers his status to be diminished by his work in the District. Because part of his income is needed by his family, his work does not negatively affect his relationships at home. However, in his view, it does diminish his standing among friends. As much as he tries to keep apart the work he does and the life he wants to live, his work intrudes. It limits his time and constrains his relationships with friends. It also precludes him from doing the things he would like to do: work with computers and take lessons in art. Evandro would prefer that the separate lives he lives be joined and, thus, his friends are helping him to find work that would make this possible.

Aldemira does not have Evandro's level of education and she does not particularly aspire to a career in the white collar world. Nevertheless, like Evandro, she derives no self-esteem from her work. In fact, she considers her work to be of little social value to herself or her supervisors and it is not an occasion for forming friendships. Rather, her place of employment is a place of frustration and humiliation. It is a world that saps too much of her time and too much of her energy. Still, it is a world in which she must participate in order to eat and to help feed her family. It exists quite separate from the social world she seeks to occupy, on weekends, when she is rested and free of its constraints.

Still, as previously noted, these assemblage industries have been widely propagandized for the technological sophistication of the work they provide, the benefit structures they offer, and the attractiveness of their production facilities— clean, safe, air-conditioned, etc. This propaganda gives special focus to the values and mobility aspirations that must be cultivated in order to enhance the developmental processes that have been instituted in the Zona Franca. Thus, despite their complaints or their sense of alienation, it is not surprising that many of the workers interviewed in the hegemonic industrial sector considered their employment in this sector be more desirable and commanding of higher status than self-employment or employment in the traditional industries. As a group, they considered work in the traditional industries to be dirty, difficult, and demanding of little or no technological sophistication. As for work in the informal sector, they considered it to be mainly for individuals who simply could not find or hold any type of wage employment.

Some, a few young males, thought they could make a career of their work in these industries. Most understood that this was not the case. However, many of the latter considered that their employment provided an opportunity for the acquisition of technological skills for which they believed there existed unbounded opportunities in the Brazilian economy. Some of those who aspired to become technicians or even engineers combined their work with night school or enrolled in special courses. For this minority of young men, work in the hegemonic industrial sector assumed the character of an educational investment. Their female counterparts, most of whom were unmarried, included those who needed employment in order to cover living expenses while finishing school. Once finished with school, if at all possible, they would not continue working on the assembly lines.

Except for those few who aspired to become technicians or engineers, the overwhelming majority of these workers expressed a higher degree of frustration and dissatisfaction with their work than any other group. Clearly, most of them worked in the hegemonic industries because jobs were available and they could not find work in the white collar sectors. Most of them worked in order to live. Very few of them lived for the work they were doing. Nevertheless, the work they were doing significantly structured the way in which almost all of them had to live.

For example, the workday for these workers is rigidly organized. It often begins at 5 A.M. or earlier, depending upon shift or division assignment, travel distance, and how long it takes individuals to prepare for the buses that will carry them to the factories. At this early hour, some workers elect to save a little money and breakfast at home; others will breakfast at the factory. Whatever the case, in order to avoid penalties for tardiness, all must be ready when the buses arrive. An individual's bus may carry some of his neighbors but, from observation, it seems that the ride to the factory is not much of a social occasion. More often than not, it is an occasion for a brief nap. At the factory, workers punch clocks and disperse to their particular divisions, work sections, and stations. From this point on, their work routines are invariable, tightly regulated, and sharply supervised. Throughout the day, their time is budgeted according to their work. There exists little latitude for deviation, individual expression, or independent movement. Even the midday meal and rest periods are scheduled in shifts by work sections and divisions.

Within these units or groups, workmates are seldom from the same neighborhood. Even when they are, they are not likely to be counted among close friends. In fact, office personnel indicated in interviews that there often exists a great deal of bickering and pent-up hostility on the assembly lines. Whether this is true or not, only 9 of the 48 hegemonic industrial workers interviewed (less than 19 percent) counted a workmate among his or her five closest friends. Moreover, if workmates do become friends, they seldom see one another except at work or unless they happen to live in the same neighborhood. At the same time, workmates are almost never relatives. Less than 20 percent of these workers have relatives employed by the same firm and workers who are known to be relatives are never assigned to the same division or work section.

Depending upon travel distance and work assignment, most of these workers will not return home until after 6 P.M. Some, mainly those attending school, will not return home until 9 or 10 P.M. in the evening. They will snack alone, perhaps watch a television program, briefly study an assignment, and retire. Those who arrive home at 6 P.M. or thereabouts, particularly the males, may visit with friends in the street or at the neighborhood bar before dining with whomever happens to be home. They will then watch a few television programs and retire. The women, particularly if married, will be confronted by household chores, the preparation of meals, and perhaps the care of children. Most of these women will not have much of an opportunity to visit with neighbors or watch a television program before retiring. For males and females alike, this routine is a very alienating process. Their social time and their family time are largely dictated by the organization of industrial time. They look forward to the weekend when they can live without working and, thereby, briefly organize their lives in terms of personal or family interests. Thus, these workers tend to work in one cultural world and live in another, to the extent that time and resources allow.

Compared to the hegemonic industrial sector, social life and work are not so sharply separated in the traditional industrial sector. Certainly this is the case for sawmill workers. Partly this is a matter of scale. These locally-owned, family-managed enterprises are smaller, less bureaucratically organized, and their work routines are not so technologically structured. As a consequence, there exists more opportunity for workers to engage in social relationships that are not task oriented. Such relationships are also amplified by the relative stability of the labor force and by patterns of recruitment that involve the hiring of friends and relatives.[15] These relationships are further amplified by the fact that urban neighborhoods, and in some cases entire bairros (e.g., Compensa, Educandos, Colonia, Santa Luzia, Morro da Liberdade) have formed around some of these industries.[16] Accordingly, a great many workers in this particular industry work with close friends and relatives. Their workplaces are frequently located close to the neighborhoods in which they live. The social worlds in which they live and work tend to converge. To a considerable degree, these workers construct their social lives in terms of their jobs and their jobs in terms of their social lives. The case of Luiz Alvez illustrates the extent to which this is possible in the employ of Serraria Paranaense.

Luiz is thirty-five years of age and has completed only three years of school. He came to Manaus with the serraria in 1972. He, his wife, and three children live in a house provided by the company. Regarding his work, Luiz related: "I learned my work from my father when I had less than sixteen years. My father is now retired but he still works as a security guard for Senhor Schmidt. My father has always encouraged me to grow in my work. I now operate a special saw in the mill and earn five minimum salaries." When asked if he had ever considered doing something else, Luiz stated: "I would not want to choose another patrão. I like my work. It is my life. I like my life with the serraria. My father works here and lives across the way. My sister's husband works here. My wife's father is a security guard here and her brother also works with me. I have another brother in Paraná who is now making plans to come here to work. Most of us here are from Paraná. Senhor Schmidt brought us here with the serraria. He is a very good patrão. I would prefer to live in Paraná because the food is better there. Sometimes I think I would like to live closer to Manaus, but all my friends live here. We work together and after work we sometimes have a little drink together. We go to the city together to shop. On weekends we visit, play dominoes, or have a game of soccer. We are a family here at the serraria and I would not want to choose to work for a different patrão."

At Serraria Amazonense, the convergence of social life and work is not as intimate as it is at Enseada do Marapatá and some of the workers who were interviewed expressed a feeling of alienation no different from that of Aldemira Barbosa and Evandro Oliveira. Still, despite the more urban setting of Educandos, the convergence of social life and work remains very much in evidence at Serraria Amazonense. Ariovaldo Lopes, for example, is sixty-one years of age. He was born in the interior and came to Manaus in 1954. Except for a brief course in mechanics at SENAI , he never attended school. Speaking of his situation, Ariovaldo related: "I now have so many relatives in Manaus that I cannot count them. They are all over the city. When I first came to the city, my brother and I went to work at another sawmill. We didn't like the patrão and stayed there only four years. We then worked as *bagulheiros* (ambulatory comerciantes), selling fruit and meat. We sold this business and then came to work at Serraria Amazonense. I have been here twenty-two years. I am now chief mechanic in the mill. The pay is not so good—only 2.5 salaries, but the patrão always helps me if I need urgent money. I work with two of my brothers here. My son also works here. We all live on the same street. Most of my friends work here. Many of us live in the same neighborhood. The patrão prefers workers who live nearby. If they are not kin, most of the workers here are either friends or neighbors. I will retire in three years but if the patrão will give me permission, I will continue to work. The money, of course, is always needed and the work is difficult, but I prefer to spend my days here with my friends. The patrão sometimes allows this. He finds lighter things for the older men to do if they want to continue work."

With regard to sawmill workers, it is not so much the case that they derive their status or sense of self esteem in terms of their work. Of course, some do. Many of them made the point by proudly asserting: "I like to work with wood" or "I have a good knowledge of wood." More important with regard to their lack of alienation is the extent to which their social lives, the time they spend with with friends and relatives, is very much a part of the time they must spend working and earning a living. The long hours that they spend at work, usually fifty-five hours each week, do not remove them from the associations that they enjoy; in fact, the one tends to be an extension of the other.

In short, many of the workers employed in these traditional industries are not only friends and relatives who have often worked with one another for a long period of time but, often, they are neighbors, people who live near one another as well as near their place of employment. As a consequence, the cultural worlds in which these individuals live and work tend to converge. These workers construct their lives in terms of their jobs and their jobs in terms of their lives. They work in order to live. However, they also tend to live with friends and relatives at work and to live their work with friends and relatives at home or in the neighborhood bars. And 75 percent of these workers consider their current employment to be permanent, which is to say that they expect to continue living their work as they have been living it.

Living work for self-employed workers in the informal sector is so diffusely structured that it is very difficult to draw simple comparisons to that of workers in other sectors. To begin with, it needs to be emphasized that self-employment in the informal sector in Manaus appears to be more an exercise of choice than the result of structural unemployment in the formal sector. Of the 53 self-employed workers interviewed, less than half had ever looked for wage employment. Of the 23 who had worked at some time for wages (mainly in the traditional industries), only 2 had moved into the informal sector as a result of having lost their jobs. Moreover, this exercise of choice is not entirely unaffected by the social origins of these workers.

For example, at least in terms of this sample, persons engaged in the informal sector come predominantly (64 percent) from households whose declared heads are also engaged in the informal sector. Fifty-seven percent of the economically active workers in these households are also engaged in the informal sector. By way of comparison, 86 percent of the workers employed for wages come from households whose declared heads are also employed for wages. Most of the parents of self-employed workers whose origins are rural were self-employed in agriculture, fishing, as *regateiros* (hucksters who sell goods along the river), or as independent artisans. Those whose parents were born in Manaus were also mainly hucksters, independent artisans, or comerciantes. Whatever the enterprise of their parents, a sense of tradition with respect to self-employment seems to have been formed in these households and despite the expansion of wage employment in the Zona Franca, this sense of tradition has in some measure persisted. What is it that keeps this tradition alive?

Interview data suggest that this exercise of choice is most influenced by three factors. The first involves economic considerations. The second has to do with mobility aspirations. And the third is related to time and the organization of work. Concerning the first, most of these workers considered self-employment in the informal sector to be more secure and more economically rewarding than whatever wage employment they might be able to obtain. As James Migueis stated: "If I work for myself, I always have money in my pocket. I can budget my expenditures so as not to be caught short. No one makes deductions from what I earn. If I want to earn more, I work more. If I work in the Industrial District, no matter how hard I work, I can earn only what they want to give me. And even then, they can say: 'James go home. We no longer need you.' What I do is a better way to make a living. Don't you agree?"

As to mobility aspirations, the majority of these workers considered their self-employment to provide them with more possibilities for economic and social advancement than the wage work for which they were most qualified. Francisco Chaves, for example, has a primary school education and is fifty-seven years of age. He came to Manaus as a heavy equipment mechanic with a construction company in 1971. Three years later, he purchased a lift truck with which to go into business for himself. Francisco stated: "In this country, even if you have a skill, you cannot improve by working for someone else. The unions are corrupt and the patrões will never reward your initiative. If you want to improve, you have to work for yourself. Unless you are a politician and can steal from the people, there is no other way."

Similarly, Edineia Lisboa, twenty-four years of age and with a primary school education, sells costume jewelry in the commercial district. When she first came to Manaus from Belém, in 1980, she worked for two years as a cashier in a supermarket. She stated: "Unless you have a lot of education, you cannot advance. You get only low paying jobs. My dream is to own a boutique, a small shop of my own. One day I decided to borrow money from my brother and bought some jewelry to sell in the streets. Sometimes I gross Cr$600,000 or more in a month. My profit is 35–40 percent. I now have an account at the bank. When I save enough, I am going to rent a boutique in the plaza. If I can do this, I can grow."

Apart from these considerations, what self-employed workers find most attractive about their work is the independence it affords them. Time and again, they emphasized that their work provided them a great deal of freedom. They could take measure of their own needs, interests, and social predispositions and structure their time and their lives accordingly. In the words of Lecino Rodrigues, a street vendor: "I would never take a job in the Industrial District. In the kind of work I do, I do not have to follow a schedule or punch clocks. I do not have to take orders. I do not have a boss telling me to do this or that. If I do not want to work in this location, I can go to another. When I want to work close to my friends, I can do so. If the weather is bad and I want to stay home, I will not be dismissed. *Minha vida é minha* (My life is my own)."

In conjunction with this independence, many of these informants also emphasized that they found their work socially engaging. Luiz Magalhães, also a vendor, described his work as follows: "What I like most about my work is dealing with people and making friendships. I am not isolated. The city attracts a lot of people from Rio, São Paulo, from other countries. It is a challenge to know these people, to talk with them, to know what they want, and to hear them tell of other places. I also have many friends in the streets. I look forward to being with them. I dislike it when the weather is bad. When I cannot work, I cannot be with my friends. Some days business is not so good, but I can see my friends and talk with them. I once worked in a store. I had no time for my friends and the boss would not allow us to *bater papo* (to chat idly) with friends or customers. My life then was more disorganized."

Among many of the self-employed who are commercially engaged, particularly as street vendors, friendship networks soften the rough edges of competition. For example, competitors who are friends help one another to become established. They teach their friends among newcomers "the tricks of the trade." In the words of Lecino Rodrigues: "If I want to leave, run an errand, or visit someone, my friends will look after my goods. They will even try to sell them for me." Lecino continued: "Competitors who are friends help one another. We share information. We watch for thieves in the streets and protect one another's goods. All of us want to make a living but unlike the comerciantes (merchants), we do not want to drive our friends from the streets, out of the neighborhood, or out of business."

Within this sector of employment, there do exist levels of stratification. Some of the self-employed workers interviewed spoke of themselves as biscateiros. Others thought of themselves as comerciantes. The cognitive frames for these terms are sometimes ambiguous but, in general, biscateiros think of comerciantes as merchants or proprietors of stalls or small shops at fixed locations downtown or in the neighborhoods. These enterprises can vary considerably in size but whatever their business, most begin to assume the characteristics of family firms. As such, they require a more substantial investment of capital than the smaller, more mobile, enterprises operated by biscateiros. These somewhat larger enterprises have a greater capacity to absorb family labor.

In addition, such enterprises usually entail the regular payment of over-head costs in the form of licenses, rents, utility bills, repairs, and the maintenance of larger inventories. Their proprietors also tend to make more frequent use of formal credit institutions and they reveal incomes substantially higher than that of most of biscateiros who were inter-viewed.[17] In the words of one informant: "Comerciantes are more impor-tant in business. They are more respected by the public and they are not always being harassed by the authorities." If they did not already think of themselves as comerciantes, almost all of the biscateiros inter-viewed aspired to establish "shops" and become "comerciantes."

In all these respects, living work in the informal sector was found to be less alienating than many types of wage employment. Neverthe-less, there did exist among some of these self-employed workers a painful acknowledgement that their own sense of status was not matched by that which others accorded them. Luiz Magalhães, for example, stat-ed: "Seriously, my father does not like me to do this work. Like many of my friends in the neighborhood, he thinks that selling in the streets is humiliating, that those of us who do it are a problem for the authorities. My father and some of my friends do not understand my work. Many people who see us do this work think we are humiliated, that we are here because we are starving, that we cannot do anything else to feed our-selves. They are wrong. Commerce is my specialization. It is a good pro-fession." In effect, Luiz felt that he does not derive much social recogni-tion from his self-employment as a street vendor. Nevertheless, he works among friends and they do not depreciate the self-esteem he derives from his work.

Lecino Rodrigues, who sells newspapers and magazines close to his neighborhood in Raiz, voiced much the same concern. "I like what I do because I make a good living and I can be with my friends. Still, I may have to find something better. My father- and mother-in-law do not think the work of a biscate is important. My mother also says this. She thinks that people who sell in the streets have no future. They are not registered and have no benefits. My mother always bothers me about this. She wants me to return to my job in the Industrial District. People who think work in the District is important have not worked there. They do not understand the work of people in the District. They have never felt the isolation of the District. In the District a worker is nobody. My wife agrees with me. She sometimes works with me here and she knows all the friends I have made in the neighborhood."

Guilherme Mindello, who left his job in the District to repair tele-vision units at home, phrased much the same problem of status when he stated: "The conditions of my work are good but my parents are very unhappy with it. They do not see it as a job. I have no patrão. My income is irregular because sometimes I have to wait for people to pay. Some of my friends think like my parents. They tell me that in order to be important you must have regular work and a very good patrão. I do not agree with this. I have my own tools and I fix radios, televisions, stereos, all kinds of electrical things. My clients are friends and neighbors—good people that I know. Sometimes I have to wait a little to be paid but I know these people and they will pay me because they are my friends and I do good work for them."

Workers in Manaus have been shown to be socially differentiated and, in varying degrees, socially stratified by the recruitment procedures associated with the labor processes that now obtain in different sectors of the economy. The criteria according to which workers are most differentiated include their rural-urban origins, age, gender, and level of education. Workers in the hegemonic industrial and white collar sectors have experienced considerable upward mobility with reference to the educational and occupational status of their fathers. However, relative to their fathers, most workers in all sectors of employment have not experienced much improvement in their economic status as measured by wages and incomes. Those workers who have improved their economic status relative to that of their fathers, for the most part, are located in the traditional industrial and informal sectors of the economy.

Although the difference in income status is not large among workers drawn from different sectors of employment, it is significant. On average, the incomes of workers in the traditional industrial and informal sectors are higher than that of most workers in the hegemonic industrial sector. They are also higher than the incomes reported by most white collar workers employed in family-owned enterprises of the commercial sector. However, in addition to the sector of employment, the gender of workers is also significantly related to the level of income. Across all four sectors of employment, women generally report lower incomes than their male counterparts. While educational achievement does not make an important difference in the income status of workers by sector of employment, it is a critical factor with reference to promotion and occupational mobility, particularly within the white collar and hegemonic industrial sectors.

On the whole, the recruitment criteria that in fact affect the employment opportunities of workers in the Zona Franca are not considered by the workers themselves to be very important in determining who their employers hire and promote. Despite these beliefs, it has been shown that these criteria do tend to structure the perceptions workers have of their work, the conditions of their employment, and the opportunities they think they have for advancement. Moreover, with regard to these perceptions, the differences that exist among workers are well grounded in their employment histories.

The relationship between social life and work for these workers tends to vary according to the biographies of individuals, the location of their work, and the sector of their employment. With reference to the latter, there exist certain similarities in the structural constraints imposed on the social life of workers in the white collar and hegemonic sectors. In both, individuals tend to live in one social world and work in quite another. To the degree that their work schedules remove them from their families and friends, their social lives tend to be somewhat fragmented. For the most part, they do not work with friends or close to home. Their days are consumed by the circumstances of their employment. Except perhaps for Friday evenings and Saturdays, they are not free to engage in "social distractions." Here, the similarity between the white collar and hegemonic sectors end as far as living work is concerned.

Many workers, but certainly not the majority, in the white collar sector are as preoccupied by their work as they are occupied. They find their work interesting and they claim to enjoy it. It affords some of them an opportunity to associate with "important people." Somewhat independent of their income, they derive a considerable sense of status from what they do for a living. Thus, they work not only to live but they also live for their work and this tends to orient their use of time. Like Francisco Brandão, they do not begrudge the fact that they have little time to relax with family, friends, and neighbors. Still, one must not forget the alienation of Marlice Loureiro. She derives little social worth from clerking in a clothing store and this type of worker is perhaps more typical of the white collar sector in Manaus than is Francisco Brandão.

Most of the workers interviewed in the hegemonic sector did not consider themselves to be socially compensated for the time they spend at work, apart from family and friends. On the contrary, they often complained bitterly that their work was dull and uninteresting and that their workdays were long and tiresome. Still, they preferred work in the Industrial District to work in the traditional and informal sectors. However, with all its insecurities and the bureaucratic indifference of supervisors, work in the Industrial District provided these workers with but a limited sense of social value. As in the case of Evandro, many of these workers felt that their work in the Industrial District diminished their educational accomplishment and their sense of self-worth and, in addition, gave them little social distinction in the community.

Although work in the traditional industrial and informal sectors is not highly regarded by employers or workers in other sectors, those who work in these sectors found their work to be less alienating. Partly this is related to the character of their aspirations. In general, sawmill workers did not aspire to do anything different and self-employed workers felt that there existed almost no limit to what they could accomplish by virtue of their own initiative. Mostly, however, the lack of alienation among these two groups of workers seemed related to the fact that the social worlds in which they lived tended to be co-extensive with those in which they made a living. This was especially the case with sawmill workers who reported a familiar and satisfactory relationship with a patrão, and who also enjoyed on-the-job relationships with friends, neighbors, and relatives. As for self-employed workers, despite their relatively low incomes and the low status they were sometimes accorded by others, they exercised more control of their labor time, and thus had more time to engage in what they considered to be meaningful social relationships, than most workers in the white collar and hegemonic sectors.

What emerges from these brief biographies is a general sense of how different workers viewed their social lives to be affected by the circumstances of their gainful employment. However, this is not the whole picture. The impact of developments in the Zona Franca does not begin and end with the firms and enterprises that have been implanted or expanded in various sectors of the economy. Nor does it begin and end with how individual workers consider their particular social lives to be affected by the labor processes that obtain in these different sectors of the economy. Also involved are households, families, neighborhoods, and the city itself. It remains to be considered how these aggregates have been affected by these developments. In the chapter to follow, I consider how household economies are shaped in relationship to various internal and external factors, including among the latter the sector of employment of their economically active members.

CHAPTER 4

The Economy of Households

Roberto DaMatta (1985) has suggested that *a casa e a rua* form the social spaces or universes that encapsulate the lives of most Brazilians. For DaMatta, the universe of the streets is a sphere of social action external to and symbolically differentiated from family and household. Among its various social spaces, the universe of the streets includes the domain of work. However externalized it may be, the domain of work is not unrelated to the internal domain of the household. Independent of whether or not they live to work or simply work to live, and apart from where they work, it is the case that most of the workers included in this study do not live apart from family and household. Indeed, in most instances, productive work and wage incomes not only determine household consumption but they also significantly affect relationships within the family. What is the income status and character of consumption within these working-class households and how do these relate to the organization of families?[1]

In addressing this question, the chapter begins with an assessment of some demographic features that distinguish the households under consideration. It then proceeds to the analysis of factors affecting household income and consumption patterns. The relationship of these to the social organization of families is the subject of the chapter to follow.

Household Composition and Income

It will be recalled that the households included in the present study are those of the 88 industrial and non-industrial workers that were selected with reference to particular firms and various sectors of employment.[2] Combined, these 88 households contained a total of 549 persons of whom 205 were economically active at the time of research.

Fifteen percent of these households contained up to three persons; 48 percent contained between four and six persons; and the remainder contained in excess of six persons.[3] Seventy percent of these 88 households are multiple income units. And, as Table 10 reveals, there is a significant relationship between the size of these households and the number of economically active persons included within them. Almost 49 percent percent (20 of 41) of the households with five or fewer members have only one breadwinner compared to 13 percent of the larger households. Only 12 percent of these smaller households contained three or more economically active persons. At the other extreme, almost 60 percent of the larger households contained three or more economically active persons and less than 13 percent contained only one. What accounts for the size of these households?

Table 10. Distribution of Economically Active by Household Composition

| (Row Pct.) (Col. Pct.) Economically Active Persons | Household Composition[4] | | | | | |
| | Five Persons or Less | | Six Persons or More | | Total | |
	N	%	N	%	N	%
1	20	(76.9) (48.8)	6	(23.1) (12.8)	26	(100) (29.5)
2	16	(55.2) (39.0)	13	(44.8) (27.6)	29	(100) (32.0)
3–More	5	(15.2) (12.2)	28	(84.8) (59.6)	33	(100) (37.5)
Total	41	(46.6)	47	(53.4)	88	(100)

P < .001

The composition of these households bears no relationship to the sector of employment of their economically active members, to the sector of employment of their household heads, or to whether or not the heads of these households happen to be migrants. Relative to their size, one factor of significance emerges: the age of their respective heads. The older the head of a household, the larger his family is likely to be.[5] Among the 41 households headed by individuals between 20–39 years of age, 61.5 percent were occupied by five or less persons. Conversely, among households headed by individuals 40 years of age or older, 65.3 percent contained six or more persons. As might be expected, the relationship between the size of these households and the age of their respective heads generally corresponds to the position in the domestic cycle at which households are encountered. However, the data suggest that the domestic cycle among these working-class households is extremely variable in terms of the relationships it enjoins.

More specifically, following marriage or the establishment of a consensual union, it is not uncommon for the couple to live a short time with parents or a close relative. This had been the case for almost half (47 percent) of the household heads interviewed. The choice of residence, whether with the parents of the wife, those of the husband, or with an uncle or an aunt, does not engage a culturally prescribed rule. The decision generally involves personal relationships and it is taken mainly for practical reasons. Among other considerations are the predispositions of the individuals involved, their economic status, the location of their residence relative to their work, and the availability of space. In other words, the decision is largely a matter of convenience and acceptability to all concerned. However, the preference for most couples is to secure a house of their own. Thus, as soon as it becomes economically feasible, most couples will move away from the household of their parents or other relatives.[6] Subsequently and not infrequently, if parents should become separated, widowed, retired, or infirm, a married son or daughter will return to the parental home and bring with them whatever dependent children they may have. Alternatively, one or both parents, particularly if infirm, will take up residence with one of their married children.

Because of this variability, the size of households tends not to be related to the domestic organization of family units. Sixty percent of households included in the study were formed by nuclear families; the remainder contained extended or composite families.[7] Households containing nuclear families are as likely to be as large as those with composite or extended families. Despite this lack of association between the composition of households and the organization of family units, there does exist a significant relationship between the constitution of families (nuclear or extended) and whether or not households form single or multiple income units. For example, while 38 percent of the 53 nuclear families in the sample formed single income units, this was the case for only 17 percent of the 35 extended families. However, if only multiple income households are considered, there exists no significant difference between nuclear and extended families with respect to the number of economically active members that they contain.

What these data suggest is that from the point of view of household economy, more important than the domestic organization of family units is their size and their position in the domestic cycle (i.e., their age and sex composition). The size of the household and the position of its family in the domestic cycle is very much related to the age of its head but it has very little to do with the head's occupation or sector of employment. Although the cultural preference is for households that contain nuclear families, if they are free and can find any kind of work, it is necessary that both the spouses who help form these households be gainfully employed. This is also the case for those adult children who continue to live with their parents.

As these households age and grow, under particular circumstances and for varying lengths of time, they may form extended or composite families. This form of domestic organization does not constitute a multiple income strategy. Such a strategy is already ingrained in the nuclear family of which the composite family is but a temporary extension. The economic unit is the household. Whether the household forms a multiple or a single income unit is largely a function of the domestic cycle and conditions affecting the labor and housing markets. This being the case, how do single and multiple income households differ in their economic and social characteristics? Consider, first, the economic characteristics of these households.

Single and Multiple Income Households

The economy of households may be treated in terms of income, housing, and patterns of consumption. To begin, it needs to be emphasized that the constitution of household income will not admit of simple analysis. Consider, first, total income. As previously noted (Table 10), there is a significant relationship between the size or composition of households and the type of income unit they form. More often than smaller households, larger households form multiple income units. And, as revealed in Table 11, there is a considerable difference in the total income of single and multiple income units.[8]

Although there exists a relationship between the size of households and the number of workers they contain, and between total income and whether or not households form multiple or single income units, it does not follow from that there exists a relationship between the size of households and total income. Indeed, when households are distributed by size and total income, there exists no significant difference between those having five or fewer persons and those occupied by

Table 11. Distribution of Single and Multiple Income Households by Total Income (Minimum Salaries/Month)

| (Row Pct.)
(Col. Pct.)
Total Income
(Min. Sal./Month) | Households | | | | | |
| | Single Income
Units | | Multiple Income
Units | | | |
	N	%	N	%	Total	%
3 or Less	14	(48.3) (53.8)	15	(51.7) (24.2)	29	(100) (33.0)
4–5	7	(30.4) (26.9)	16	(69.6) (25.8)	23	(100) (26.1)
6–More	5	(13.9) (19.2)	31	(86.1) (50.0)	36	(100) (40.9)
Total	26	(29.5)	62	(70.5)	88	(100)

P < .02

six members or more. There is good reason for this. Apart from the reproductive behavior of individual members, the formation of large households is primarily related to the domestic cycle of family units and to the availability of housing. The total income of households, however, is most significantly affected by the sector of employment of their economically active members. Data in this regard are summarized in Table 12.

As Table 12 reveals, the majority of white collar and hegemonic industrial workers included in the study are located in the higher income households. By way of contrast, self-employed and traditional industrial workers are located in the lower income households. Thus, the income structure of these households is more determined by the sector of employment of their economically active members than by their size or composition. Nevertheless, the size or composition of these households is very much related to whether or not they form multiple income units. Indeed, almost 67 percent of the households forming such units contain six or more persons. From this it follows that multiple income households, relative to single income units, have more people to support. Accordingly, as economists (e.g., Folbre 1986) argue, the per capita income of these households may more accurately reflect their economic circumstances than total income. Taking, again, the median family size (5.27 persons/household) as a breaking point, Table 13 presents the distribution of per capita household income by household composition.

Table 12. Distribution of Economically Active by Sector of Employment and Monthly Income of their Respective Households

(Row Pct.) (Col. Pct.) Sector of Employment of Active Workers	Monthly Household Income					
	Five Min. Salaries or Less N	 %	Six Min. Salaries or More N	 %	 Total	 %
Hegemonic	23	(46.9) (22.8)	26	(53.1) (25.0)	49	(100) (23.9)
Traditional	29	(64.4) (28.7)	16	(35.6) (15.4)	45	(100) (22.0)
White Collar	15	(25.9) (14.8)	43	(74.1) (41.3)	58	(100) (28.3)
Self-Employed	34	(64.2) (33.7)	19	(35.8) (18.3)	53	(100) (25.8)
Total	101	(49.3)	32	(50.7)	205	(100)

$P < .001$

Table 13. Distribution of Per Capita Household Income (Minimum Salaries) by Household Composition

(Row Pct.) (Col. Pct.) Per Capita Income	Household Composition					
	Five Persons or Less N	 %	Six Persons or More N	 %	 Total	 %
.01–1.00	22	(37.3) (53.7)	37	(62.7) (78.7)	59	(100) (67.0)
1.01–Above	19	(65.5) (46.3)	10	(34.5) (21.3)	29	(100) (33.0)
Total	41	(46.6)	47	(53.4)	88	(100)

$P < .02$

As Table 13 shows, there is a marked difference in the per capita household income of large and small households. Although the larger households generally contain more economically active workers, only 21 percent of these have a per capita income in excess of one minimum salary. Conversely, almost 66 percent of the households reporting a per capita income in excess of one minimum salary contain five or fewer members. While interesting, this finding is not particularly surprising. What is surprising is the fact that per capita household income appears not to be much affected by whether or not the household contains one or more than one economically active workers. For example, when one distributes single and multiple income households by their per capita income, no significant difference exists between them. Sixty-five percent of the multiple income households, as compared to 73 percent of those having a single breadwinner, report per capita incomes of one minimum salary or less per month.

What these data suggest is that in general large households have more income to spend than small households. However, on a per capita basis, the opposite is the case. Moreover, in the economic context affecting these working-class families, it appears that the difference in per capita income between small and large households cannot be easily reduced by the addition of economically active workers. For example, if one compares the per capita income of multiple income households containing five or fewer persons with those containing six or more (Table 14), the income difference between these households is significant. Almost 76 percent of the 41 multiple income households having six or more persons have a per capita income of one minimum salary or less. Fifty-seven percent of the smaller households report a per capita income of more than one minimum salary.

Table 14. Distribution of Per Capita Income of Multiple Income Households by Size of Household

Size of Household

Per Capita Income	Five Persons or Less		Six Persons or More			
	N	%	N	%	Total	%
.01–1.00	9	42.9	31	75.6	40	64.5
1.01–Above	12	57.1	10	24.4	22	35.5
Total	21	100	41	100	62	100

P < .01

However, if one controls for the size of household, comparing for example the per capita incomes of households having five or less members by whether or not they contain one or more than one worker, there is no significant difference between them. Similarly, no significant difference exists between the per capita incomes of larger households containing two workers and those containing more than two. In other words, the per capita income of these households is more significantly affected by their size or composition than by the number of economically active persons that they contain. The opposite is the case with total income.

We have seen that the total income of households is very much related to the sector of employment of their economically active members (cf. Table 12). Without relating tabular data, this is not the case with per capita income. Again, the total income of these households is primarily a function of their employment structure and this is affected by the sector of employment of their economically active members. The per capita income of these households, on the other hand, is more affected by their composition or size. A multiple income strategy allows these households to increase their total income. The amount that they can increase their total income depends, at least in part, upon the sector in which their economically active members are employed. However, because employers in Manaus seek to maintain wages at the minimum prescribed by the government, the addition of a worker within a household generally remits but the addition of one minimum salary. This is not sufficient to alter the overall economic status of households as measured by per capita income unless the household is relatively free of economically dependent members. This would seem to suggest that in the context of Manaus, a multiple income strategy is primarily one of survival and not one of economic mobility.

In order to improve their economic status, it is necessary for working-class households in Manaus to maximize income earnings while giving expression to those global consumption values upon which the hegemonic industries depend for their profitability and growth. To accomplish this, not only must husbands and wives work but, unless engaged in the better paying occupations of the white collar sector, they must also postpone or avoid establishing households that contain economically dependent parents and/or children. In other words, the economy fosters values that are supportive of the nucleation of households, instrumental relationships within households, and the weakening or dissolution of extended family networks. Before describing how the economy of households has affected domestic relations within them, it is instructive to consider the extent to which these households have internalized the consumption values of the industrial culture that now exists in Manaus.

Food Consumption

Perhaps one of the most significant changes resulting from SUFRAMA's efforts to engineer an industrial pole in Manaus has been the extent to which it has also engineered a consumption economy. Because of the Zona Franca and its assemblage industries, the city has become a veritable supermarket for the sale of high ticket consumer durables (e.g., television sets, stereophonic units, tape recorders, air conditioners, motorcycles, etc.), not to mention a seemingly endless variety of less expensive items (e.g., watches, toys, pocket radios, cameras, and the like). As evidence of this, on a monthly basis thousands of Brazilian tourists flock to the city by plane and by boat to make purchases at Free Port prices. Before the 1980–84 recession, the magnitude of this traffic was such that there existed more than 7,704 commercial establishments in the city which, when combined, reported monthly sales averaging approximately U.S. $32 millions.[9]

Needless to say, these developments have stimulated consumer wants among all categories of workers. However, more than for income, the analysis of consumption patterns poses both conceptual and methodological problems. For example, in presenting his theory of disarticulated development, Alain de Janvry (1985) discusses export-led, luxury-led, and wage goods-led growth patterns. In doing so, he is careful to note that the definition of luxury versus wage goods is relative; the same commodity can be a wage good in one country or cultural context and a luxury good in another. One might argue, for example, that for a low income household in Manaus a television unit is a luxury good and not a wage good. Objectively, such may be the case. Culturally, the opposite would seem to be the case. Indeed, independent of income or social circumstances, most of our informants in Manaus would consider themselves extremely deprived without a television unit and to suggest otherwise is nothing less than imposing an unacceptable cultural value.

To sidestep this type of issue, it was decided simply to allow the purchases made by households to express the cultural values to which their members subscribed. This, of course, posed a methodological problem. Time and finances did not allow for the collection of systematic data regarding household budgets and expenditures. Under the circumstances, an inventory was made of a number of items that would presumably give some cultural expression to the relationship between consumption values and economic circumstances.

Since health is fundamentally a matter of nutrition, consider first the consumption of food. Data were collected in respect to 55 food items. Concerning these items, it was considered important to sort out those that are more or less standard in the regional diet—e.g., rice, beans, manioc flour, milk, coffee, eggs, pasta, dried beef, chicken, sardines, fish, peppers, onions, garlic, bananas, mamão, limes, and the like, and those that might conceivably reflect the more variable tastes of households relative to their economic circumstances—e.g., cheese, potatoes, cabbage, lettuce, cucumbers, tomatoes, oranges, coco, palmito, pineapple, melon, various fruit juices, soft drinks, and beer. Time did not allow for the measure of caloric values or the quantities consumed. Thus, it was determined only whether or not particular foods were consumed on a daily, weekly, or monthly basis, or almost never.

In order to contextualize in more general terms the consumption of food items, based on various comparisons from the IPCM (Indice de Preços ao Consumidor de Manaus) drawn by CODEAMA in 1984, it is noteworthy that the price for various staple foods in the Brazilian diet were generally from 50 to 100 percent higher in Manaus than in São Paulo, where wages are considerably higher than those paid in Manaus. More specifically, the typical monthly expenditures of families earning up to 5.25 minimum salaries in Manaus were reported in October of 1984 (see Table 15).[10]

As Table 15 suggests, households in this category spend more than half their income on food and they spend a substantial proportion of the rest on other necessities. On the basis of these data, *A Noticia* maintained that in October of 1984 a family of four earning one minimum salary simply could not sustain an adequate diet without finding ways to generate additional income.

Clearly, the households included in the present study do not in any sense represent the poorest households in Manaus. Although 59 percent of these households reported earning five minimum salaries or less/month, only one revealed an income of but one minimum salary. This particular household was formed by a young couple with a newborn child living in one room without sanitary facilities or running water. The room contained one table, two boxes serving as chairs, one box which housed a few dishes, an electric cooking plate, an old refrigerator, and two hammocks. It also contained an inherited black and white television unit. The family was very poorly clothed and virtually its entire income was regularly consumed by rent, food expenditures, and electricity.

As far as the households under study are concerned, no significant differences were found in the types of food consumed or in the frequency of their consumption which related to per capita or total household income, to the sector of employment or migratory status of household heads, to the sector of employment of economically active

**Table 15. Typical Monthly Expenditures of Households
Earning up to 5.25 Minimum Salaries: October 1984**

	Commodity	Percent of Income Expended	Total
Food:	Fresh Meat	15.1	
	Fresh Fish	6.7	
	Bread	6.2	
	Vegetables	4.5	
	Cooking Oil	3.4	
	Flour	3.4	
	Milk	3.3	
	Beans	2.9	
	Fresh Fruit	2.8	
	Rice	2.3	
	Powdered Coffee	1.8	
	Sugar	1.7	54.1
Other:	Cooking Appliances and Utensils	5.2	
	Furnishings	3.2	
	Tobacco	2.7	
	Cooking Fuel	2.3	
	Cleaning Materials	2.	15.6
Personal Services:		1.4	1.4
Public Utilities:	Transportation	3.8	
	Electricity	3.4	7.2
Discretionary Income:		21.7	21.7
Total		100	100

members, or to their composition. Depending somewhat upon work schedules, school attendance, and the like, individuals in these families take three and sometimes four meals a day. Typically, those employed in the industrial sectors take one hot meal at work. Sawmill workers at Serraria Paranaense were an exception because most of these workers lived so close to their place of employment that they were able to take their midday meal at home. Some workers in the white collar sector were provided cafeteria services. Others patronized luncheonettes for their midday meal and, notwithstanding regional differences, this is when the principal meal of the day is taken.

Within households, food consumption patterns are quite similar and interview data suggests that they tend to be relatively standardized. Except for breakfast, which tends to be light, almost all of the households studied served bread, rice, and beans as part of the principal daily meal. On a weekly basis or more frequently, most substituted pasta or potatoes for rice and beans. Almost always these staples are accompanied by a serving of either fish, beef, or chicken. In fact, 77 percent of the households reported serving fish, chicken, and beef no less than two-to-four times each week. In general, fish is eaten more frequently than beef and although somewhat more expensive, beef is eaten more frequently than chicken. Chicken is often reserved for a Sunday meal. Pork, which is very expensive in Manaus, tends to be consumed primarily on such festive occasions as Christmas. Meat and fish, in effect, are considered a necessary part of every major meal and, on the whole, the diet of these households contained what might be considered an excessive amount of animal fats and protein.

The pattern is similarly standardized with respect to dairy products. Milk is taken by almost everyone with their morning coffee. Still, more than 77 percent of these households consumed milk separately and on a daily basis. Eggs are used for cooking and sometimes served boiled with breakfast. Whatever, 55 percent of these households used eggs on a daily basis and most of the remainder used them several times each week. Cheese, however, is a relatively expensive item in Manaus and even for the higher income households it was served only on a weekly basis. Still, this difference does not reach statistical significance within the sample.

The majority of households (68 percent) served various fruit juices, usually prepared from fresh fruits but sometimes in concentrate, or fresh fruits on a daily or weekly basis. Bananas are eaten almost on a daily basis except by those individuals who did not like them. Similarly with mamão. All but a few households purchased and used oranges once or twice each week. Watermelon and pineapple, when in season, are available but somewhat more expensive than other fruits and thus, independent of household income, they are less frequently consumed. Limes are used with virtually every meal for which fish is prepared.

A wide variety of vegetables are available in Manaus, including sweet potatoes, squash, couve, lettuce, cabbage, maxixe, peppers, onions, beets, and cucumbers. Because of tastes or expense, but again independent of household income, beets, cucumbers, and lettuce were less frequently purchased. However, almost all of these vegetables were consumed by more than two-thirds of the household sampled on a daily, weekly, or monthly basis.

Sweets, usually cakes, biscuits, or tapioca, are generally made within the home. These were served with at least one weekly meal in 73 percent of the households studied. Only 20 (26 percent) of the households served sweets more than once each week. Thirty-seven percent of the households reported that they almost never served sweets because "we don't like them" or "we prefer fruits."

Apart from coffee, milk, and fruit juices, beverages include primarily hot chocolate, soft drinks, beer, and cachaça (Brazilian rum).[11] Most households (71 percent) seldom or never made hot chocolate. Two-thirds of the households consumed soft drinks at least weekly or more often. In fact, soft drinks were frequently offered the author during interview sessions. In some cases these were available in the house; in most cases someone was sent to purchase a large bottle, usually of orange. Thirty-five percent of the households reported the consumption of beer almost on a daily basis and 59 percent reported its consumption at least on a weekly basis. Relatively few households reported the regular consumption of cachaça.

Based on observation, interview data appear to be quite inaccurate with respect to the consumption of alcoholic beverages. Industrial workers and workers in the informal sector in these households, especially males but also some females, frequently drink one or two beers at the conclusion of the workday. It may be taken at home or at a neighborhood bar. Alcoholic beverages, including cachaça, are consumed in large quantities on weekends, particularly Friday nights and Saturdays. Several of the young female industrial workers interviewed patronized a bar or nightclub at least once or twice a month. Weekend drinking bouts, involving the consumption of large amounts of beer and cachaça, were such a common occurrence among workers in the wood-processing industry that at times it made interviewing somewhat difficult. White collar workers, certainly the higher paid white collar workers, are not an exception in this regard. On weekends, somewhat independent of their occupational status or sector of employment, music, conversation, cards or dominoes, accompanied by a more or less continuous flow of drinks, were observed to constitute a major form of social diversion for a great many workers in the neighborhoods under study. The cost of such diversions could not be calculated but it is not an insubstantial part of a great many household expenditures and it was frequently referred as a source of family problems by women, social workers, priests, and ministers.

In sum, independent of household composition, employment structure, and family income, the consumption of food items on a daily and weekly basis discloses a diet which is more or less standard and relatively balanced in terms of nutrients. Clearly, whatever the values these households have internalized as a consequence of the consumption-oriented economy which SUFRAMA has created, these values appear not to have displaced the provisioning of families with an adequate diet. However, some change has occurred in the regional diet. Garlic, onions, tomatoes, oranges, potatoes, green peppers, eggplant, okra, for example, are not indigenous cultigens and they are difficult to grow in the Amazon. The demand for these foods, it seems, came with upper- and middle-class migrants from the south who were attracted or transferred to Manaus by the creation of the Zona Franca.

Another change relates to the cost of food. Development programs and policies in the region, and particularly the industrialization of Manaus, have substantially disrupted the local production of foodstuffs. As a consequence, Manaus has become increasingly dependent on high cost food imports from other regions of the country. If CODEAMA's cost of living surveys are correct and the purchase of food now absorbs more than 50 percent of the income of families earning up to 5.25 minimum salaries, it follows that the discretionary income available in these households will vary significantly in terms of their per capita earnings. It follows also that the expenditure of this discretionary income for consumer durables should simultaneously provide an indication of the consumption values that these households have internalized and the extent to which they are economically marginalized from the realization of these values.

Consumer Durables

Data for consumer durables were collected with reference to the following: proprietorship of house or apartment, construction style (brick or wood), number of rooms, and type of sanitary facilities. Other durables inventoried included such items as water filters, radios, electric fans, washing machines, stereophonic equipment, television units, sewing machines, telephones, automobiles, beds, hammocks, tables, stuffed furniture, and the like. The mode of acquisition of these items was not determined; their quality could not be objectively assessed; and their price value, involving faulty recall or completely subjective evaluations, could not be fixed.

Sixty-three (72 percent) of the 88 houses included in the study are privately owned by one or another member of the families that occupied them. Eleven families occupied houses that were provided, rent free, by the employer.[12] Fourteen houses were rented. Of the proprietors, only five acquired their house by inheritance. Thirty-one (49 percent) acquired their house with the assistance of SHAM (Sociedade de Habitação do Estado do Amazonas) and BNH (Banco Nacional da Habitação). The remaining 27 families (43 percent) acquired their houses either by private purchase or construction.

Owning a house was a value of considerable importance for most of the families included in the study. However, housing is a basic necessity; the proprietorship of a house is not. If proprietorship in and of itself expresses a consumption value, this is not particularly evident in relationship to income variables. At least in this sample, proprietorship is not significantly related to any of the income factors for which data were collected. Proprietors and renters, for example, do not differ in terms of their sector of employment. And, independent of whether they belong to multiple or single income households, total and per capita income differences between proprietors and renters do not reach even a minimal level of statistical significance.[13]

As far as proprietorship is concerned, two factors of importance emerge: household composition and length of residence in Manaus. Almost 62 percent of the households containing six or more persons are privately owned by one or another member of the occupant family; 68 percent of the houses rented or provided by employers contain families of five persons or less. Regarding length of residence, almost 62 percent of the proprietors included in the sample were born or lived most of their lives in Manaus. Sixty-eight percent of the non-proprietors are migrants who have lived in Manaus a relatively short time.

Length of residence is also related to the manner in which proprietors have acquired their houses. Most of the houses in the sample that were privately constructed or purchased are located in or very close to favelas, usually poorly drained lands in which individuals squat and build, buy, or rent a house at a very low cost. Families who have gained access to the more desirable public housing are those who have generally resided in the city long enough to have acquired a knowledge of the agencies involved and to have had applications processed through the qualification procedures of these agencies. Generally, it is the recent migrant from the interior whose knowledge and lack of urban experience necessitates renting, perhaps buying, or constructing a house in a favela.

If the proprietorship or rental of a house in and of itself is not particularly expressive of consumption values that enjoin the use of discretionary income, this is not the case with respect to the quality of house owned or rented. Independent of household composition, and independent of whether or not the household contains one or more than one economically active worker, the quality of housing is very much affected by family income and this, in turn, is significantly related to the sector of employment of family heads. Moreover, the quality of housing occupied by all workers included in the sample differs significantly by their sector of employment.

One dimension of quality concerns construction. Fifty-two (59 percent) of the 88 families in the sample occupied houses constructed of brick rather than wood. These houses are not only more costly to build or to rent, but generally they are better constructed, more permanent, less affected by termites, and require less frequent maintenance. Exactly half of these more costly houses were occupied by families reporting six or more minimum salaries. Nineteen (36.5 percent) were occupied by families reporting 4–5 minimum incomes. Only seven were occupied by families having three minimum salaries or less. By comparison, 22 of the 36 (61 percent) wooden structures were occupied by families reporting three minimum salaries or less and only 10 (28 percent) were occupied by families reporting six salaries or more.[14]

The construction quality of houses owned or rented is also significantly related to the sector of employment of household heads. Sixty-six percent of the household heads who were employed in the hegemonic industries, 58 percent of those employed in traditional industries, 39 percent of those employed in the informal sector, and only 7 percent of the heads employed in the white collar sector, lived in wooden structures. All eight of the retired heads included in the sample lived in brick-constructed houses. Apart from the sector of employment of household heads, as is shown below in Table 16, there is a significant difference in the construction value of houses by the sector of employment of all workers included in the study.

Other dimensions of quality involve space, specifically the number of rooms available, and the availability of sanitary facilities within or outside the house.[15] Houses containing four rooms or less are significantly related (P < .001) to the level of family income. Almost 76 percent of families reporting an income of three minimum salaries or less, compared to 39 percent of those reporting four-to-five minimum salaries, occupied houses that provided four or fewer rooms, including the kitchen. On the other hand, 81 percent of the families reporting six or more minimum salaries occupied houses that generally provided five-to-seven rooms. None of the working-class houses visited contained more than seven rooms. Significantly, the spaciousness of the house is unrelated to size or composition of the family. Many informants who lived in small houses expressed the desire to one day accumulate sufficient funds with which they could purchase or rent a larger and better constructed house.

Table 16. Construction Value of Houses Occupied by Workers and their Sector of Employment

(Row Pct.) (Col. Pct.) Sector of Employment of Econ. Active	Style of House					
	Brick		Wooden			
	N	%	N	%	Total	%
Hegemonic	26	(53.1) (20.6)	23	(49.6) (29.1)	49	(100) (23.9)
Traditional	19	(42.2) (15.1)	26	(57.8) (32.9)	45	(100) (22.0)
White Collar	48	(82.8) (38.1)	10	(17.2) (12.7)	58	(100) (28.3)
Self-Employed	33	(62.3) (26.2)	20	(37.7) (25.3)	53	(100) (25.8)
Total	126	(61.5)	79	(38.5)	205	(100)

$P < .001$ (If workers at Serraria Paranense are excluded, $P < .01$).

The availability of internal sanitary facilities—specifically toilet and bath or shower—is also significantly related to family income and sector of employment. Fifty-nine (67 percent) of the 88 homes included in the study had internal sanitary facilities. This is significantly related ($P < .02$) to the sector of employment of household heads and to the sector of employment of workers in general ($P < .001$). It is noteworthy that only seven percent of the 58 white collar workers were without such facilities. By way of contrast, 32 percent of workers in the informal sector, 37 percent of those in the hegemonic sector, and 47 percent of those in the traditional industrial sector, lived in houses that lacked internal sanitary facilities.

In light of these data, it is apparent that the larger and better quality working-class homes are occupied by families reporting higher levels of income. If one gives focus, for example, to the 29 families that reported household incomes of less than three minimum salaries, 72 percent of these families occupied wooden structures divided into four or less rooms. Most of these houses contained one or two bedrooms and the cooking and eating areas were undivided from what might be called *a sala de estar* (sitting-room). Although all of these families had electricity and running water, 66 percent were without bathroom facilities except as provided by an outhouse, or by the addition of a small privy extending over a drainage ditch which did not always contain a sufficient water flow to remove fecal contaminants from the vicinity of the house.[16]

Household furnishings are also expressive of consumption values and the level of discretionary income available after expenditures for food and basic housing. Regarding household furnishings, however, one must differentiate between those that are more or less necessary (e.g., stove, refrigerator, beds, hammocks, tables, chairs) and those that are not (e.g., radios, television and stereophonic units, telephones, electric fans, air conditioners, and the like). In general, the former category of furnishings, at least in a quantitative sense (it was not possible to assess quality except in highly subjective terms), are unrelated to the income and employment factors that otherwise differentiate these households. Many of these more necessary furnishings, however, did vary significantly in relationship to the size or composition of the family.

Refrigerators are absolutely necessary for the preservation of food in Manaus.[17] We encountered only one household that was without a refrigerator. This particular house, a very poor one occupied by an electronics worker, his mistress, and two children, and reporting a household income of slightly less than two minimum salaries, was constructed in a favela adjacent to the house owned and occupied by the informant's widowed mother. In this instance, food was stored in the mother's refrigerator. Similarly, a stove is necessary for the preparation of food and most working-class households in Manaus use a gas stove for this purpose. We encountered only two households that were without gas stoves. Again, these were very low income households and both employed a two-burner electric plate as a substitute for a gas stove.

Hammocks are indigenous to the Amazon region. The acculturation of the Caboclo to the urban way of life might be expressed through a series of objective signals. One of these is the replacement of hammocks by the use of beds. Although hammocks are widely used for sleeping purposes, particularly by children, beds are preferred. We encountered only one household without at least one bed (56 percent had three or more) and only four households were without a hammock (95 percent had two or more). The number of hammocks and beds with which households are furnished is significantly (P < .01) related to the composition or size of the family.

A similar pattern obtains with respect to such furnishings as eating tables, plain chairs, stuffed furniture, and the like. Independent of household income, these furnishings vary in quantity in relationship to family size. Only one household lacked a table on which the family could eat (that of the electronics worker who used his mother's refrigerator) and all but two households contained stuffed furniture. In fact, 83 percent of the households inventoried contained no less than four pieces of stuffed furniture.

More indicative of the extent to which these working-class households seek to penetrate the consumer economy is the expenditure of discretionary income for consumer durables that can be construed as "necessities" only with reference to the consumer values that the industrialization of Manaus has promoted in the media, on the streets, and at many places of work. The best examples of such items are television units, stereophonic equipment, tape recorders, telephones, radios, digital watches, water filters, bicycles, and automobiles. In every case, the purchase of such items is unrelated to the size or composition of households or to whether or not they form multiple or single income units. It is related, however, to the sector of employment of heads of households and to that of all economically active persons within households. Obviously, it is also related to household income, much more significantly to total household income than to per capita income, thus reflecting the relative independence of such purchases from the effects of household size or composition. For illustrative purposes, consider television units, stereophonic equipment, telephones, and automobiles.

Eighty-five (97 percent) of the 88 households inventoried contained a television unit (15 households actually contained more than one unit).[18] Even the one household we encountered without a refrigerator, a household in which four wooden boxes served as chairs around a makeshift table, contained a television (it also contained a stereophonic unit). Thus, a television in and of itself no longer represents the purchase of a luxury item for Manauaras. Most informants considered a television to be a household necessity. The purchase of a color television, however, is generally thought to be a luxury expenditure. Tables 17 and 18, respectively, present the distribution of black and white and color television units by household income and by the sector of employment of economically active household members.

As Table 17 reveals, these households begin to penetrate the consumption economy with respect to the purchase of television units at a level in excess of three minimum salaries. Regarding the purchase of color television units, the difference between households reporting 4–5 minimum salaries and those reporting 6 or more is not really significant. However, in light of the cost of food and the consumption of related necessities, the discretionary income of these mid-level working-class households is considerably lower than that of higher income households. How is it then that almost 73 percent of these mid-level households have purchased a color television?

In part, the answer may be found in Table 18 which shows that 67 percent of the hegemonic workers (compared to only 41 percent of traditional industrial workers and to 58 percent of self-employed workers)

Table 17. Distribution of Black and White and Color Television Units by Household Income[19]

(Row Pct.) (Col. Pct.) Television Units	Household Income (Minimum Salaries)							
	3 or Less		4–5		6 or More			
	N	%	N	%	N	%	Total	%
Black/White	17	(50.0) (63.0)	6	(17.6) (27.3)	11	(32.4) (30.6)	34	(100) (40.0)
Color	10	(19.6) (37.0)	16	(31.4) (72.7)	25	(49.0) (69.4)	51	(100) (60.0)
Total	27	(31.8)	22	(25.9)	36	(42.3)	85	(100)

P < .02

Table 18. Distribution of Black and White and Color Television Units by Sector of Employment of Economically Active

(Row Pct.) (Col. Pct.) Sector of Employment of Econ. Active	Television Units					
	Black/White		Color			
	N	%	N	%	Total	%
Hegemonic	16	(32.7) (20.5)	33	(67.3) (27.3)	49	(100) (24.6)
Traditional	26	(59.1) (33.3)	18	(40.9) (14.9)	44	(100) (22.1)
White Collar	16	(27.6) (20.5)	42	(72.4) (34.7)	58	(100) (29.2)
Self-Employed	20	(41.7) (25.6)	28	(58.3) (23.1)	48	(100) (24.1)
Total	78	(39.2)	121	(60.8)	199	(100)

P < .01

live in homes that have color televisions. It is not that the incomes of these workers is significantly higher but rather that many of these workers are employed in the electronics industry. Because of their employment, they are able to purchase this high-ticket item at factory discount and deduct the payments, without interest charges, from their monthly pay envelopes. It is noteworthy in this regard that 61 percent of the households containing at least one worker in the hegemonic sector also contain color televisions. Whatever the particular circumstances, as households achieve a level of income in excess of three minimum salaries, or as one or another of their members become employed in the white collar or hegemonic sectors, they are increasingly drawn into the consumption economy. That this is the case is particularly evident with respect to the purchase of stereophonic sound equipment. Table 19 presents the distribution of households containing such equipment by household income.

Table 19. Distribution of Stereophonic Sound Equipment by Household Income

(Row Pct.) *(Col. Pct.)* Household Contains	*Household Income (Minimum Salaries)*						
	3 or Less		*4–5*		*6 or More*		
	N	*%*	*N*	*%*	*N*	*%*	*Total*	*%*
Stereophonic Unit	9	(20.0) (31.0)	7	(15.6) (30.4)	29	(64.4) (80.6)	45	(100) (51.1)
No Stereophonic Unit	20	(46.5) (69.0)	16	(37.2) (69.6)	7	(16.3) (19.4)	43	(100) (48.9)
Total	29	(33.0)	23	(26.1)	36	(40.9)	88	(100)

P < .001

Of the 88 households inventoried, no less than 51 percent contained stereophonic equipment of an up-to-date vintage (Toshiba, Sharp, Gradiente, Philco, Phillips, etc.). Nine of these households may be included among the poorest 29 working-class households studied. However, more than color television, the purchase of such equipment expresses acquiescence to consumption values because even when purchased at factory discount prices, this equipment entails a considerable investment of household income. Moreover, if anything other than the radio amplifier is used, it entails a further investment of funds for the purchase of high fidelity records and/or tapes. It was observed that most working-class homes containing such units possessed very few, if any, records or tapes.[20]

Perhaps more than color television, the possession of stereophonic units appears to represent something of a status expenditure. That this is the case is suggested by the fact that while almost 73 percent of the households reporting an income of 4–5 minimum salaries owned a color television unit, only 30 percent of these households owned stereophonic equipment. By way of contrast, among the households reporting six minimum salaries or more, the number owning sound equipment (80.6 percent) is larger than the number owning color television units (69.4 percent). Also related to the status value of possessing stereophonic units is the importance of *bailes* or dances as a necessary part of almost all house parties. Whatever the occasion for giving a party, if a household does not possess sound equipment with which to play music, it will try to borrow it from neighbors or relatives.

As in the case of color televisions, the purchase of stereo units is significantly (P < .001) related to the sector of employment of the economically active members of these households. Seventy-two percent of white collar workers, 53 percent of those in the hegemonic sector, 45 percent of the self-employed workers, and 20 percent of traditional industrial workers, respectively, live in households containing these units. It is also noteworthy that 61 percent of the households containing stereophonic equipment also contain at least one worker in the hegemonic sector. Clearly, the purchase of such equipment is facilitated by a family employment connection, even if temporary, with one or another of the electronics firms.

Private telephone service, if considered a necessity in industrial societies, is a luxury for most people in Manaus. Public telephones are readily available in almost every urban neighborhood. Private telephones are cheaper than color televisions and stereo equipment. However, except for firms and individuals (businessmen, professionals, etc.) who in some sense are privileged, private telephone service is difficult to obtain. It generally involves a waiting list through which an application may be shuffled a year or even longer. As a consequence, there exists an illegal parallel market for the sale and distribution of telephone lines and a line purchased in this market can be quite expensive for a working-class household. Moreover, once available, a telephone line requires a regular monthly expenditure for a service that may be infrequently used and that, when needed, can be obtained at a nearby street corner. Table 20 presents the distribution of telephones by level of household income.

It is evident from Table 20 that the number of households containing a telephone increases significantly at or above the level of six minimum salaries. Without presenting tabular data, it may be noted that the distribution of telephones bears approximately the same significant relationship to sector of employment as the distribution of color television and stereophonic units, the only difference being that a somewhat higher percentage of households headed by self-employed workers contain telephones than households headed by industrial workers in the hegemonic and traditional sectors. Slightly more than 43 percent of the households containing a telephone are headed by a worker in the white collar sector.

Table 20. Distribution of Telephones by Household Income

Household Income (Minimum Salaries)

(Row Pct.) (Col. Pct.) House Contains	3 or Less		4-5		6 or More		Total	%
	N	%	N	%	N	%		
Phone (s)	4	(14.8) (13.8)	4	(14.8) (17.4)	19	(70.4) (52.8)	27	(100) (30.7)
No Phone	25	(41.0) (86.2)	19	(71.0) (82.6)	17	(27.9) (47.2)	61	(100) (69.3)
Total	29	(33.0)	23	(26.1)	36	(40.9)	88	(100)

$P < .001$

Most other consumer durables reflect the same pattern of consumption in relationship to household income and sector of employment. For example, only 28 percent of the households reporting three minimum salaries or less have one or more water filters, as compared to 65 percent of the households reporting two-to-four minimum salaries and 75 percent of those reporting six minimum salaries or more. Similarly with electric fans, radios, air conditioners, and bicycles. The number of these items possessed is significantly related to income factors, specifically level of family income and sector of employment.[21]

Sewing machines, either electric or mechanical, are a partial exception to this pattern. Sixty (68 percent) of the households had a sewing machine and the distribution of this item in relationship to such factors as household income, composition, and sector of employment was not statistically significant. Although almost half of the households without a sewing machine reported three minimum salaries or less, five of the eleven households containing electric units fell into this low income category. In all five cases the machines were used not only to make clothes for the family but also to take in sewing as a means of earning additional income for the household.

Perhaps the most expensive consumer durable to buy, operate, and maintain in Manaus is an automobile. Without reporting tabular data, 22 (25 percent) of the households studied possessed an automobile. Fourteen of these vehicles were owned by individuals in households reporting an income in excess of six minimum salaries. Only three households reporting a monthly income of three minimum salaries or less possessed an automobile. Thus, there is a significant relationship (P< .05) between household income and the possession of an automobile. However, no relationship exists between the possession of an automobile and the sector of one's employment. Among households inventoried, automobiles were possessed by nine white collar workers, seven in the electronics industry, three in the wood-processing industry (one of whom was a crew boss), and three self-employed workers. Six of the eight automobiles owned by individuals in the lower income categories were used by their owners, or some other member of the household, to operate a taxi service on a part- or full-time basis. Apart from these cases, automobiles did not provide a source of income; they were used exclusively for convenience and pleasure. The possession of an automobile, particularly by young males, has assumed the character of a highly valued status symbol in Manaus.[22] The most emphatic expression of this involved an electronics worker who had been dating a young man in the neighborhood for almost four years. She indicated that they planned to marry but the event had been postponed because her *novio* (fiancé) wanted first to buy an automobile and finish with the loan he incurred for its purchase.

To summarize, the cultural preference in Manaus appears to be for independent households occupied by nuclear families of up to six members. In 1980, excluding domiciles occupied by single persons or lodgers, approximately 61 percent of all households in Manaus conformed to this norm. The distribution of working-class households included in the present study also generally conforms to this norm.

Seventy percent of these working-class households form multiple income units, two-thirds of which contain no less than six members. Forty-five percent of the larger multiple income households contain three or more economically active workers. Clearly, the larger the household, the more likely it is to form a multiple income unit. And, as the data reveal, the percentage of single income units falling into the lowest household income category (i.e., households reporting three minimum salaries/month or less) is substantially larger than the percentage of multiple income units.

Notwithstanding the relationship of these factors, when households are distributed by size and total income, no significant difference exists between those having five or fewer members and those containing six or more. The reason for this is clear. Although total income is very much affected by a multiple income strategy, the income structure of households is more significantly determined by the sector of employment of their economically active members than by the number of members who are economically active.

However, when households are distributed by size and per capita income, independent of the number of economically active persons they contain, the number of smaller households falling into the higher per capita income category (i.e., in excess of one minimum salary) is almost twice the number of larger households. Given the minimum wage structure that prevails within the Zona Franca, the per capita income of households cannot be substantially altered by the addition of economically active persons. Most generally, an additional worker will add but one minimum wage or less to the household's total income. Assuming this added income brings with it no additional dependents, it will serve only to move the per capita household income closer to the minimum wage level by reducing the already existing number of dependents. If capital with which to form a successful small scale enterprise is lacking, it seems that the ultimate strategy for improving per capita income is that of a couple remaining childless, and free of dependent parents or other relatives, while pursuing careers in the higher echelons of the white collar sector. In short, the per capita income of households is almost completely a function of household composition and it is neither affected by the number nor the sector of employment of economically active household members. The opposite is the case with total income.

The significance of the sector of employment for the income structure of households is underscored by the fact that no less than 74 percent of the white collar workers encountered in this study were located in 24 upper income working-class households (i.e., households reporting six minimum salaries/month or more).[23] It is perhaps the case that the white collar sector has always been the major avenue of economic mobility in Manaus. However, with the creation of the Zona Franca, this avenue of mobility has widened considerably and, judging from the income data reported here, the economic empowerment gap between households whose members are predominantly employed in this and other sectors has also widened. While 56 percent of the hegemonic industrial workers were located among the higher income working-class households, this was the case for only 36 percent of the traditional industrial and self-employed workers, respectively.

The income status of households, at least above the level of one minimum salary, appears not to enjoin any significant differences with respect to diet and food consumption. Independent of household composition, income, or sector of employment, the pattern of food consumption across these households is relatively uniform and it generally conforms to a mixture of the standard Brazilian and regional diet. Without taking quantitative measures, the daily diet in almost all of these households seemed to be quite adequate and it is relatively well balanced in terms of protein, carbohydrates, and fats. Given the cost of food in Manaus, however, low income households are left with very limited discretionary funds with which to make other purchases.

That this is the case is evident not only in relationship to the quality of housing but also with reference to the purchase of high-ticket consumer durables, including color television units, stereophonic equipment, private telephone service, automobiles, and even less costly durables such as electric fans, radios, digital watches, water filters, and the like. With respect to the purchase of every one of these items, no significant relationship obtained between household composition or whether or not households formed multiple income units. However, their purchase did vary significantly with the level of total household income, the sector of employment of household heads, and the sector of employment of other economically active household members.

In light of these data, it would appear that households reporting less than three minimum salaries, and to a lesser degree those reporting up to five, have derived very little material benefit from the creation of the Zona Franca and the industrialization of Manaus.[24] Overwhelmingly, the members of these lower income households are employed in the traditional industrial and informal sectors of the economy. At first glance, this is somewhat paradoxical because as was noted in the previous chapter, on average, workers in these sectors do as well economically as most lower echelon white collar workers and workers engaged in the hegemonic industries. However, the incomes earned by most workers in these sectors are not sufficiently above the minimum wage to equalize the differential impact on multiple income units of such factors as the number and sector of employment of all economically active members. To illustrate the point, compared to other groups, a substantially larger percentage of the white collar workers interviewed reported earnings in excess of three minimum salaries. At the same time, approximately one-third (20 of 58) of all the white collar workers interviewed were encountered in eight multiple income households reporting total incomes in excess of six minimum salaries.

On the whole, the economically active members of low income households have all that they can do to feed, clothe, and house themselves and their families. Most of the families falling into this category were found living without sanitary facilities in poorly constructed and poorly furnished homes. Except for a wrist watch, a black and white television (often second-hand), and perhaps a radio, these families are excluded or marginalized by virtue of their incomes from the consumption economy that has developed around them. A multiple income strategy may help these families get by with a little less uncertainty and deprivation, but it does not substantially improve their overall standard of living.

In view of the relationship existing between the economy of households and the work enjoined by the labor processes that obtain in different sectors of the new urban economy, the question remains: how does all of this affect the organization of domestic groups and relationships within the family? This is the focus of the following chapter.

CHAPTER 5

Domestic Organization and Household Economy

When theoretically focussed, household studies have the potential of bridging the gap between the productive and reproductive lives of individuals, between the macroeconomic institutions and processes that envelop their work, and the microsocial institutions and processes that engage their living.[1] However, as Marianne Schmink (1984) relates in her very perceptive review of Latin American research, studies of the way in which the household is inserted into the productive structure of society at different income levels confront a plethora of conceptual and methodological problems. The household or domestic unit, as Schmink (p. 93) notes, refers to a resident group of persons who share most aspects of consumption, drawing on and allocating a common pool of resources (including labor) to provide for their material reproduction. Such units are analytically distinct from and may not exactly correspond to the sets of social relations that constitute families. Whereas the organization of households may be responsive to economic forces, the organization of families, their authority structures, and their division of labor, may be responsive to cultural and ideological forces that are not strictly economic. Schmink also underscores the tendency of analysts to reify households by imputing a consensus of decision-making strategies to them, or by assuming that their members share a common economic relationship to society and, thus, a common class position.

The conceptual differentiation of household or domestic units from "families" is commonplace in anthropology. It is also commonplace that family relationships are extended beyond the household or domestic unit. Schmink is quite correct in asserting that the organization of families may be responsive to cultural and ideological forces that are not strictly economic. However, as in the case of the parentela within the context of the Caboclo Formation (cf. chapter 1), economic circumstances may significantly diminish the responsiveness of families to the

153

cultural and ideological forces they articulate. In the analysis to follow, I assume that the members within the households under study are positioned within the working class. It does not follow from this assumption that they occupy a common class position. Indeed, it is one of the hypotheses of this study that the social differentiation of workers with reference to the labor processes that obtain in different sectors of employment enjoins a process of social stratification. It remains to be determined if this process of stratification has in some ways affected the organization of households, the types of families they house, and relationships within these families.[2] The chapter begins with a consideration of family type. It then gives focus to the economic division of labor within households and the status identities that the division of labor enjoins. The chapter concludes with an analysis of how these status identities seem to affect the domain of domestic relations in single and multiple income households.

Households and Family Units

It is difficult, if not impossible, to know precisely the structural impact on the family of urban-industrial development in Manaus. Since it was only in 1980 that IBGE tabulated data with respect to family type, it is not possible to assess demographic trends. Further, a search of secondary sources failed to discover a single contemporary or historical study on which a comparative analysis of family structure and household organization in Manaus could be based. The only approximation we seem to have of historical data is that provided in such ethnographic studies (e.g., Wagley 1953: 145–86), wherein the family structure among Caboclos is described in some detail.

As previously noted, among the Caboclos interviewed by Wagley in the little town of Itá, less than 25 percent claimed both civil and religious rites at marriage; 42 percent were married only in Church; 25 percent admitted to consensual unions; and the remainder reported a civil union.[3] Although people of all "social classes" in Itá shared the traditional ideal of a large, patriarchally united, extended family, this did not seem to significantly affect the composition of households; most homes contained but a nuclear family—i.e., a man, a wife, and their children. The man, according to Wagley, was considered the absolute head of the household but, because of his work as a collector, women in fact assumed a significant position of influence within the home. Moreover, since it was not uncommon for men to "walk out" of whatever marriage arrangements that existed, women often became heads of households.

Despite cultural values and norms, households typically housed a nuclear family in respect to which the *dona da casa,* if not completely independent, appears to have had considerable authority or influence. If such a family was embedded in a parentela, it appears from Wagley's account that this form of extended family was not particularly functional for the lower class households that comprised the vast majority of Itá's population.

According to Rosen (1982: 41–74), the Brazilian parentela or extended family system has been gaining strength in the urban-industrial context. In presenting his case, Rosen notes that to stay intact, the parentela needs a centripetal force sufficiently powerful to induce solidarity. Although affection and a sense of family loyalty are important, he argues that unless some form of mutual assistance exists the parentela eventually disintegrates. In pursuing this point, if I interpret him correctly, he suggests that urbanization has created a need for mutual assistance. Industrialization, presumably because of the employment it creates, has made accessible to lower strata households the resources with which they can, perhaps for the first time, provide mutual assistance. Ultimately, Rosen hypothesizes and seeks to demonstrate that the persistence or reconstitution of the parentela is most significantly associated with upwardly mobile lower strata families, particularly families that reveal a strong achievement orientation.[4] To what extent is this the case in Manaus?

First, a conceptual problem: what exactly is this modified extended family or parentela of which Rosen writes and how are we to recognize it empirically?[5] Briefly, it consists of a bilaterally extended network of kinsmen. The network can vary extensively in size, composition, complexity, and organization. Traditionally, particularly in upper-class families, it sometimes included hundreds of relatives and its organization was fiercely hierarchical and patriarchal. Its more contemporary modification, as described by Rosen (1982: 47–51), tends to be smaller, more limited in its genealogical memory, more loosely structured, less hierarchical or patriarchal, and considerably more voluntary in the determination of its social boundaries.

Conceptually, both in its traditional and more contemporary forms, it is important to emphasize again that the parentela is a kinship network and not a residential unit. Thus, without extensive kinship analysis, the precise boundaries of a parentela cannot be determined.[6] Traditionally, however, the core of this kinship network was formed by a residential unit which included the patriarch's family, perhaps one or more of his married children and, in some instances, other relatives. Such a residential unit approximates the definition of the "extended family" that has been adopted by IBGE in tabulating households by family type. A household is counted as containing an extended family if, in addition to a nuclear family, the household also contains another relative.[7] For purposes of the present analysis, the presence of such a unit may be taken as an indication that some aspect of the parentela is in some sense functional with reference to a particular household.[8] Accordingly, Table 21 presents the percentage distribution of family types as reported in 1980 for Brazil, Amazonas, Manaus, and for the sample of households under study.

Table 21. Percentage Distribution of Family Types (1980)

Type of Family

		Nuclear	*Extended*	*Composite*[9]
Brazil				
	Urban	71.6	23.8	4.6
	Rural	76.3	20.1	3.5
Amazonas				
	Urban	60.6	31.6	7.8
	Rural	73.4	23.7	2.9
Manaus (IBGE)		60.7	31.1	8.2
Author's Sample		60.2	39.8	—

Based on this somewhat unsatisfactory demographic measure, and considering such ethnographic data as provided by Wagley and others, it seems that Rosen's contention that the parentela is perhaps becoming more functional, and thus acquiring more strength, in urban areas than it probably enjoyed among the vast majority of rural populations is not without some merit. This is certainly the case in Amazonas where almost 32 percent of urban households, compared to 24 percent of those classified as rural, contains some fragment of the parentela. Among the households under consideration, the number of such families reaches almost 40 percent.[10]

However, leaving aside the possibility that the parentela is in some sense reinvigorated by urban-industrial forces, Rosen's thesis engages considerations of a more complex nature. Specifically, the logic of the thesis suggests that in the urban-industrial context the persistence or reconstitution of the parentela in modified form is, in effect, a consciously constructed resource strategy designed to improve the income status of families and thereby amplify the mobility aspirations of their respective members. If this is correct, the persistence or reconstitution of the parentela assumes the character of an independent variable in relationship to the income status of families and the mobility experiences of their individual members. Assuming the strategy works, that it is functional, extended families should disclose a higher level of income than nuclear families and the latter should reveal a lower level of status achievement than the former.

Alternative hypotheses are also possible. One might hypothesize, for example, that in the urban-industrial context the modified extended family represents a resource strategy designed more to secure the survivability of family units than to amplify the mobility aspirations of their members. It follows from this that the parentela assumes the character of a dependent variable and the constitution of such groups should be more evident with respect to those households falling into the lower income strata.

A third possibility is that the modified extended family is simply a temporary artifact of the domestic cycle and various problems associated with the conditions of urban life, or that it is the product of circumstances peculiar to one or another member of a particular household. Housing in Manaus, for example, is a difficult problem. A fragment of the parentela might come into being upon the marriage of a son or a daughter, or the migration of a relative, and exist only for whatever time they need to locate housing of their own. Which are the more tenable of these propositions with respect to the families investigated in Manaus?

In dealing with this question, it is instructive to remove from consideration variables of no significance. The reader may recall from chapter 4 that nuclear families are as likely to be as large in their household composition as extended families. Without bothering the reader with additional tables, it may also be noted that these types of families do not differ significantly with reference to the age, migratory status, level of education, income, or sector of employment of their respective heads. All of this is to suggest that the types of family units found in these households can neither be explained by their demographic composition nor by the social, economic, or occupational status of family heads.

Concerning the question as to whether or not the formation of extended families within households is in some sense a strategy designed to enhance their income or to give vent to mobility aspirations, it may also be recalled from chapter 4 that the relationship between family type and the constitution of multiple income units does reach a low level of significance ($P < .05$). Almost 77 percent of the single income households, compared to 53 percent of the multiple income households, contain nuclear families. Or, to put the matter differently, 83 percent of the households that contained some form of extended family unit constitute multiple income households. However, many multiple income households contain nuclear family units and, conversely, some extended family units are single income households.

Despite the relationship between extended family units and multiple income households, the difference in household income by family type does not even begin to approach an acceptable level of significance. While 51 percent of the extended family households, compared to 22 percent of the nuclear family households, report an income of six minimum salaries or more, exactly half of the 36 families achieving this higher level of income are nuclear. It is also the case that no significant difference exists between nuclear and extended families with respect to per capita household income.

Perhaps the reason that the income level of extended and nuclear family households differ but marginally is due to the fact that if only multiple income households are considered, those that are formed by nuclear and extended family types do not differ significantly with respect to the number of economically active workers living within the household. If the formation of extended families is a strategy designed to increase household income and thereby enhance the economic status of the family, as far as income data are concerned, the strategy does not appear to work within the urban-industrial context of the Free Trade Zone in Manaus.

Is it possible that this modified form of the extended family is fundamentally a survival strategy, that it is primarily associated with the effort of local income households to cope with harsh economic circumstances by forming multiple income units? Accordingly, one should expect to find families of this type disproportionately represented among households reporting three minimum salaries or less. However, this is not the case. Within the lower income stratum, no significant difference exists in the distribution of multiple and single income households by family type. Similarly, if one considers multiple and single income households with a per capita income of up to 1.0 minimum salary, there is no significant difference in the proportion of households containing nuclear and extended families. Among the multiple income households of the lower income stratum, respectively, 53 and 47 percent are occupied by nuclear and extended families.

Thus, as far as these particular households are concerned, the apparent reinvigoration of the parentela cannot be explained as a cultural artifact of resource strategies designed to secure or enhance household income or to facilitate economic mobility. If, in some subjective sense, the members of these households "think" in these terms, and we have no evidence that many of them do, then their calculations are misguided. As we have seen in the previous chapter, the most upwardly mobile households are multiple income units of small size, generally formed by husbands and wives employed in the white collar sector. For the most part, these are nuclear families. Nevertheless, in terms of demographic data, the parentela seems to have been reinvigorated in the urban context of Manaus. How is this to be explained?

Several factors appear to be involved. Perhaps they can best be illuminated by reference to case studies that illustrate the variety of circumstances resulting in the formation of these family units. Consider, first, the case of Inácio. Inácio was born in Belém but never knew the mother who discarded him in a trash bag at the time of his birth. He was brought to Manaus as a baby and raised by the person who found him and is now fifty-six years old. With only four years of education, he works as a messenger in the office of the Secretary of Education. Before taking this job, he owned and operated a fishing boat. When he fished for a living, he worked with his brother-in-law, the husband of his wife's sister. As Inácio and his brother-in-law were away from Manaus much of the time, his wife and three children lived in his brother-in-law's home. In 1968, when his fourth child was born, Inácio quit fishing and took his present job. He sold his boat and used the money to purchase the brickmade home in which he now lives.

In 1984, Inácio headed a household consisting of his wife, four daughters, three sons, a son-in-law, and one grandchild. Inácio, his wife, one son, and two daughters, including the one who is married, are employed; the remaining children are enrolled in school. The household became extended upon the marriage of his daughter. At the time of her marriage she was looking for work and her husband was enrolled in school. At the time of research, the daughter's husband had finished school and was looking for work. He also was looking for a house which he and his wife could rent or buy. Inácio's oldest son, Ulisses, was engaged and also looking for a house of his own. When asked why he didn't marry and live with his parents while searching for a house, he complained that the house was already too crowded and afforded too little privacy.

Because of the rapid urban growth that followed upon the industrialization of the Free Trade Zone, housing has become a serious problem in Manaus. It is particularly a problem for young couples who may be lacking a job, sufficient resources with which to rent or buy a home, or lacking in the knowledge or urban connections necessary to purchase a home. Whatever the case, it may be noted that when first mar-

ried, almost 48 percent of the heads of households interviewed lived for
a short time in one or the other of their parental homes while searching
for housing of their own. Housing in Manaus is particularly a problem
for individuals migrating to the city. José's household illustrates the
point.

José is an electronics worker, an inspector earning three minimum salaries. He was born in Manaus, completed high school, and is
twenty-nine years old. He has eight brothers and three sisters. Two of
the brothers and two sisters are students and live with José's parents in
a neighboring bairro. The rest are married and have homes of their
own in different parts of Manaus. José rents a poorly constructed and
poorly furnished house on the edge of a favela. He is not married but he
is head of an extended family household consisting of Maria, the
woman with whom he forms a consensual union, and two young daughters. The family unit is extended by the addition of Maria's sister, Antônia. Maria's sister works and she contributes whatever she wishes to
the support of the household. However, Maria's parents live in the
neighborhood. When asked why Antônia lives in José's house rather
than at home with her parents, it was learned that Maria's parents had
only recently moved to the neighborhood from Itacoatiara, a city almost
200 kilometers from Manaus. Antônia, a young girl of twenty years, had
migrated to Manaus in advance of her parents because José found her a
job in the factory where he works. Now that her parents were here, she
planned to move in with them as soon as they became settled in their
new home.

A somewhat similar set of circumstances explains the situation
with respect to Francisco's household. Francisco, thirty-six years of
age, worked in agriculture in the interior. He came to Manaus with his
wife and young child in 1978 in order to "live a better life." He now
unloads trucks for a transportation company. Franscisco owns a three-
bedroom house in Educandos, not far from where he works. Living in
the house are his wife, his daughter, his sister, Maria, and her husband,
Raimundo. The household is thereby extended with the addition of
Maria and her husband.

When Raimundo, Maria's husband, first migrated from the interi-
or, he came alone and he rented a room in Educandos. Almost immediately he found employment with Serraria Amzonense. After a few
months of work at the sawmill, he gave up his rented room, quit his job,
and returned to the interior to work. While there, he married Francisco's sister, Maria. Together, they decided that life would be better for
them in Manaus. When they returned to the city, Raimundo was again
employed by the sawmill. However, they could not find a place to rent

and they were forced to take up residence with Maria's brother, Franscisco. The arrangement is temporary. According to Raimundo: "I am now buying a house in two payments, one part from savings and the other part my father is giving me. We will move to the house as soon as I receive my father's money and make the second payment. We are anxious for this to happen because we will have a small garden at the house I am buying. Also, Francisco's house is very crowded for us."

Mônica is also a migrant from the interior but her situation is different from that of Raimundo. Mônica lives with her sister and brother-in-law, João Luiz. João, thirty-one years old, is a migrant from Pará. He works as a pharmacist for INPS and was transferred to Manaus where he met and married his wife, Maria. Maria is also a migrant to Manaus. Her family still lives in the interior of Amazonas. She is employed in the electronics industry. Together, with their two young children, João Luiz and Maria occupy a small rented apartment. The household is extended by the addition of Mônica. Mônica is seventeen years of age. She came to Manaus to live with her sister in order that she could attend secondary school. Mônica does not work but she takes care of the children while her sister works. When she completes her education, Mônica plans to return to her village in the interior and hopes to find employment as a secretary or primary school teacher.

Migration and the problem of housing are not the only circumstances resulting in the formation of some type of extended family household. Consider, for example, the case of Manoel, a twenty-five year old technician employed in the electronics industry. After losing his job in Parintins, Manoel's father found employment as a construction worker with the city and moved to Manaus in 1960. He brought with him his wife and seven children, five girls and two boys. They did not find it necessary to live with relatives when they arrived in Manaus. Before leaving the interior, Manoel's father came to the city and rented a very poor house in a favela near Compensa. Subsequently, he acquired a house in São Jorge by gambling with its proprietor. In 1968, he sold this house and with the money he purchased a larger home in Costa e Silva, a public housing scheme. As each of the children married, they rented or purchased a house of their own. All but two live in Manaus and only Manoel continued to live in the parental neighborhood.

Before he married, Manoel rented a house which he subsequently bought in Costa e Silva. Soon after his marriage, however, Manoel's father died, leaving his sixty-two year old mother living alone in the parental house. A year later, because his mother did not want to live alone, Manoel rented out his own house and moved his family to his mother's home. The household now constitutes an extended family. It consists of Manoel, his widowed mother, his wife, and three young children. The mother draws a pension but only Manoel works. The arrangement has allowed Manoel's wife to return to school in order to complete a secondary education.

Domestic problems of one type or another may also result in the formation of an extended family household. Senhora Antônia Barbosa's household is a case in point. Senhora Antônia is sixty-two years of age and a retired primary school teacher. Her husband, a rubber collector, disappeared many years ago. After his disappearance in 1954, she moved to Manaus with her two sons and two daughters "in order that they might go to school." She now heads an extended family household. It consists of one son, the youngest of the two daughters, and four grandchildren. All four of the grandchildren belong to the oldest daughter, three by one *amasio* or consensual union and one by another. The oldest daughter moved to Porto Velho with her latest amásio and left the children with the grandmother in order that they also might attend school in Manaus. From time to time, the daughter sends a little money to help her mother support the children.

Domestic problems of a somewhat different nature were involved in Valdomiro's household becoming extended. Valdormiro, forty-eight years of age, came to Manaus from Parintins with his family in 1972. He operated a biscate, sawing wood, with his brother. He lived only a few days at his brother's home and then rented the house that he still occupies. The family grew to include eleven children. All of them married and left the parental home. In 1983, however, Valdormiro's daughter, Valda Maria, "threw" her husband out because "he drank too much." A few months later, she sold the home that she and her husband had owned and returned to the home of her parents. When asked why she had given up her own home to live with her parents, she responded: "I don't like my father very much. He is like my husband. When he works, he spends all his money drinking. He makes life very difficult for my mother. I came here to make life easier for her. I work and support my mother and my children. In Manaus the man is always the head of the household, but I am more the head of the household than my father."

Or, as in the case of Lima Braga, an extended family unit may grow out of the simple desire to keep members of the family close to one another. Lima Braga is sixty-three years of age and works as a security guard in the industrial district. Before this, he worked as a day laborer in Manaus and before that, as a rubber collector with his father in the interior. His mother was born in Manaus and has many relatives living in the city. When Lima's father died, his mother returned to Manaus to live. In 1957, leaving his own family in the interior, Lima came to

Manaus to look for work. He lived with his mother and built a house next to her's on land that she had acquired by selling fruit in the market. In 1958, he returned to the interior to work and to be with his family. Two years later, in 1960, he moved his family to Manaus and occupied the house that he had built on his mother's land. Subsequently, Lima's oldest son married and also built a house on his grandmother's land. In effect, the entire family forms a modified parentela which occupies three modestly constructed wooden structures on a very small piece of land that is owned by the matron of the family, Lima Braga's mother.

In 1984, the household that Lima Braga headed included his wife, his four youngest sons, and three daughters. This unit itself was extended by the addition of a seven-year old grandchild, borne to an unwed daughter. It was also extended by the addition of the wife of his youngest son, Clovis. Six members of this particular household were economically active and, combined, they reported earning eight minimum salaries (a per capita family income of .74 minimum salaries). Each contributes half of their monthly income to the support of the household. When asked to explain this family arrangement, Lima Braga responded: "My mother had this small piece of land available on which we could build. My own home has plenty of room—three bedrooms, a sitting room, a kitchen, and an outside bathroom. And there is much harmony in the family. It is a happy environment. It is *muito sorte* (much luck) for us to live close to one another in this very large city."

These cases are more or less typical of the thirty-five extended family units that turned up in the sample. It is apparent from these cases that the formation of family units of this type is not without some economic benefits. However, in most cases, economic considerations are not the critical factor in their formation. Moreover, whatever the economic benefits that derive from the formation of these extended family households, the benefits do not generally accrue to all members of the household.

Upon his marriage, for example, Raimundo purchased a house and has since rented it out in order to return to live with his widowed mother. Raimundo derives a rent from this arrangement. Also, because of this arrangement, his wife can attend school without paying for the care of her children. Raimundo's mother, a widow with few expenses, her own home and a pension, does not need her son and his family to live with her in order to obtain whatever additional help she needed. Thus, she derives no economic benefit from this arrangement. Her only benefit is social or social psychological; she prefers not to live alone. Her son and his wife, however, do benefit economically from the arrangement.

Inácio's daughter married young, before her husband completed school. It has been economically beneficial and convenient for them and their child to live with her parents while her husband completes school. Her parents and her brothers and sisters derive little economic benefit from the arrangement. However, Inácio and his wife are pleased to have the company of their daughter and grandchild. Inácio's oldest son, Ulisses, is not so pleased. He contributes substantially to the household economy and he considers the house so crowded that he prefers to spend as little time there as possible.

José found a job for his sister-in-law. A recent migrant from the interior, she will live with José only until her parents are settled in Manaus. Although the sister-in-law contributes very little of her earnings to the household, the arrangement is temporary and it pleases José's wife to help her sister. On the other hand, João's situation is different. His sister-in-law is also a migrant from the interior. She lives with João and baby sits for his wife in exchange for the opportunity of attending secondary school in Manaus. According to João's wife, "I have to work because I want to help pay for my sister's education." The extended family arrangement, it seems, was not struck primarily for reasons of economy. João's wife works, so she claims, only to help her sister go to school.

Lima Braga and his sons have built two modest houses on a small piece of land owned by his mother. Coming to Manaus from the interior, the family considers itself lucky to be able to live close to one another in the city. Relative to the opportunity of remaining together, they do not consider important whatever economic benefits they have derived from building houses on their mother's land. As Lima Braga noted, when he came to Manaus in 1960 it was then not too difficult to find land on which to build a small house.

Clearly, in most cases these extended family households have not been engineered out of dire economic necessity or to enhance the economic status of the family. In many instances, they represent a response to problems emerging out of the urban context, problems related to migration, housing, the search for employment, or the desire for education. In some cases, they represent a response to problems peculiar to particular families—marital problems, an unwed daughter with child, problems associated with drunken husbands or fathers, or the loneliness of a widowed parent. Or, as in the case of Lima Braga, an extended household may be formed simply because members of the family want to live as close to one another as possible in a complex urban society where most of one's neighbors remain strangers.

Although the circumstances leading to the formation of these extended family households are extremely variable, their structure is not. In general, the kinship boundaries of these units are very narrowly drawn. They center primarily on the nuclear family, on the relationship between parents, their children and grandchildren, and between siblings. Beyond this, the boundaries tend to include only those persons who are married to or living with a son, a daughter, or a sibling. We rarely encountered a more distant consanguineal or affine, a cousin for example, in these households. And we rarely encountered mention of more distant relatives in terms suggesting that relationships with them were close or intimate. In most cases, the members of these households knew or had heard tell of more distant kin, but generally they seldom or never saw them and thus they did not know them well; they could not say if they were married, where they lived, or what they did for work.

Accordingly, the formation of these modified extended households seems not to involve a desire to constitute or maintain an extended family in the fashion of the much described parentela of Brazilian tradition. Rather, they were formed out of a sense of obligation rooted in the mutual affection that members of the nuclear family had for one another. Thus, there sometimes emerges a desire on the part of some to remain close and a willingness on the part of others to render one another whatever kind of assistance can be offered in the event that assistance is needed. Apart from this sense of loyalty and obligation to one's immediate family, the parentela does not appear to be particularly functional. And even if we consider these extended family households a modified form of the parentela, at least as far as this sample is concerned, the parentela appears not to be strategic with respect to the survivability or the economic mobility of the families in question. More critical for the economic status of households than family type is whether or not they form multiple income units. Moreover, the economic division of labor within these multiple income units has a significant impact on the status relationships among various members of the household.

Status Identities and the Economic Division of Labor

By the economic division of labor within households we are referring specifically to the conjunction of family statuses and gainful employment and not to the assumption of domestic tasks by different members of the family unit, nor to the differential contribution that individual members elect or are required to make to the household budget. At issue here is the question of who works, the kind of work they do, and how this sustains or alters status identities within the household, particularly those identities involving the authority structure that most of our informants considered to be traditional in the Brazilian family.

What is the family authority structure that most of our informants considered to be traditional? Briefly, informants emphasized that ideally the head of the household should be a male in the parental generation. In addition, the head should be the major breadwinner. Regardless of how the residential family unit may be composed, minimally, the male head is charged with the responsibility of providing for its security and material needs. His status as head is vested with the authority to speak for or represent the family as a unit in the public domain. Within the domestic domain, the head may delegate authority to various others. Nevertheless, he has the authority to manage the finances of the household, to settle internal disputes, and to make all important decisions affecting the affairs of the family. In effect, the head of the household is a "petit patriarch." Informants generally agreed, however, that the status of head, and the authority that his status enjoined, may be diminished or enhanced by his age, his education, and the income he derives from his work.

It is not entirely clear from the responses of informants which one of these factors—i.e., age, education, or income—is the most important with respect to the status of head and whether other factors might also be important. Putting this problem aside for a moment, it must be noted that there is a significant relationship between the income of heads and whether or not their households form single or multiple income units. Almost 81 percent of the multiple income households sampled, compared to 22 percent of the single income households, have heads who report earning no more than three minimum salaries/month. Heads who reported earning more than this are equally divided among multiple and single income households.[11]

Moreover, as we have seen in chapter 4, the composition or size of the household, and therefore the number of economically active persons it contains, is significantly related to the age of the head of the household. Thus, it is not surprising that the age of the household head is also significantly ($P < .001$) related to whether the household forms a single or a multiple income unit. Seventy-three percent of the single income households, compared to only 32 percent of the multiple income households, are headed by individuals under the age of forty. In effect, the relationship between age and the formation of multiple income units is largely an artifact of the domestic cycle. However, it remains to be considered whether or not the status that heads derive by virtue of their age is in any sense affected by their contribution to household income.

Concerning education: although the formation of multiple income units is less significantly related (P < .05) to the education of household heads, the heads of single income households are more likely to have completed a secondary education than heads of multiple income households. Again, we must ask: to what extent is the status of household heads altered by the proportion of income that they contribute to the support of the household?

To begin, among the single income households included in the study, the economic division of labor is relatively simple and it typically corresponded to and reinforced the family authority structure that most informants considered to be both ideal and traditional. In almost all of these households the only person who was gainfully employed was the husband/father. As noted above, the heads of these households were in most cases relatively young and less than 40 percent of them had a secondary education. The wives of these household heads were generally no better educated than their husbands. All of these households included some children (only four of them contained more than three) and most of the children were either pre-school or of primary school age. The occupation of the women in this type of household is generally that of homemaker. Thus, the authority vested in household heads is reinforced by their role as breadwinners and, apart perhaps from factors to which we were not privy, their authority appears to be neither modified nor compromised by the age, gender, education, or income of others within the household. Still, it must be noted that within single income households it is possible for one or another of these factors to place the status identity of head in dispute.

For example, six of the single income households included in the study were formed by extended families. Three of these presented no exception to the authority structure described above. The remaining three, however, are illuminating with regard to the status of head. One concerns the household of Antônio Garcia, a sawmill worker. Antônio lives with his wife and two young sons in one side of a duplex provided by Serraria Paranaense. The other side of the duplex is occupied by his widowed mother. Antônio's father had been an employee of the sawmill and when he died the company allowed his widow to retain, rent free, the apartment she had occupied with her husband. Despite her separate residence, Antônio considered his mother a part of his household. Conversely, his mother considered Antônio to be the head of her household. As an explanation of this she related: "A family needs a male head. Antônio takes care of me. He buys most of my food and medicine and he gives me whatever I need." In this instance, gender, gainful employment, and economic support took precedence over age in assuming the position of head.

A very similar situation existed in the case of Francisco Corrêa, a sawmill worker at Serraria Amazonense. Francisco's four brothers are married and they live widely scattered (one lived in Brasília and another in São Paulo). His three sisters have formed consensual unions and live with their amásios (lovers) in different parts of Manaus. Francisco is single and lives at home with his widowed mother and two pre-school nephews. Except for her small pension, the household derives its support from Francisco. However, Francisco's mother noted that the house, which her husband built, now belongs to her. She stated: "I am the head of the household." Francisco, on the other hand, asserted: "But I am the male head of the household." Clearly, in this case, the nominal status of headship is a matter of small dispute. Because of his gender, his gainful employment, and the support he provides, Antônio claims the status of head and, in fact, he makes most of the decisions. However, because of her age, her proprietorship of the home, and perhaps also because Antônio is not married, his mother claims the status of head.

A final case involves the household of Manoel, described in the previous section. Manoel, it will be recalled, rented out his own home in order to take up residence with his widowed mother. Because of her age, her maternal status, and her proprietorship of the home, Manoel introduced his mother as head of the household. His mother, however, rejected this presentation and stated: "No, Manoel is now the male head of the household. He makes the decisions for us." Manoel's wife agreed. However, despite his gender, his gainful employment, his support of the family, his role as decision-maker and, in this case, despite even his superior education, Manoel felt that his mother's parental status and proprietorship of the house gave her prior claim to headship.

These cases illustrate the fact that the status of headship becomes increasingly ambiguous as the social roles that attach to age, gender, parenting, proprietorship, and material support no longer converge in the traditional occupant of this position. Typically, in the single income household, these roles converge in the status of head and the exceptions are, indeed, exceptions. In multiple income households, status identities and roles are considerably more complex.

The number of economically active persons contained in multiple income households is neither related to the income nor the sector of employment of household heads. It may be recalled from the previous chapter that the number of economically active persons is largely a function of family size and this, in turn, is primarily related to the age of household heads and to the family's location in the domestic cycle. Given the low level of wages that prevail in Manaus, even those members of

Table 22. Kinship Status of Economically Active Members of Multiple Income Households by Sector of their Employment

Sector of Employment

(Row Pct.) (Col. Pct.) Domestic Status	Hegemonic		Traditional		White Collar		Self-Employed		Total	
	N	%	N	%	N	%	N	%	Total	%
Nominal Head	6	(11.1) (14.3)	20	(37.0) (58.8)	10	(18.5) (18.9)	18	(33.3) (36.0)	54	(100) (30.2)
Wife of Head	6	(23.1) (14.3)	1	(3.8) (2.9)	12	(46.2) (22.6)	7	(26.9) (14.0)	26	(100) (14.5)
Son	11	(22.0) (26.2)	10	(20.0) (29.4)	15	(30.0) (28.3)	14	(28.0) (28.0)	50	(100) (27.9)
Daughter	14	(47.7) (33.3)	0	— —	11	(36.7) (20.8)	5	(16.6) (10.0)	30	(100) (16.8)
Affine or Collateral	5	(26.3) (11.9)	3	(15.8) (8.8)	5	(36.3) (9.4)	6	(31.6) (12.0)	19	(100) (10.6)
Total	42	(23.5)	34	(19.0)	53	(29.6)	50	(27.9)	179	(100)

P<.001

working-class families who are attending secondary school will work if they possibly can. This, of course, directly affects status identities within the household. First evidence of this may be gleaned from Table 22 which summarizes the kinship status of the economically active members of multiple income households by their sector of employment.[12]

As shown in Table 22, there exists a significant difference in the kinship status of the economically active members of these households by the sector of their employment. The nominal heads of these households (i.e., those individuals who presented themselves or were presented as heads) are overwhelmingly concentrated in the *lower status sectors* of the economy (i.e. the traditional and informal sectors). If employed, the wives and daughters of household heads tend to work in the *higher status sectors* (i.e., the white collar and hegemonic sectors). Although their sons are more evenly distributed by sector of employment, more than half (52 percent) of those who work are similarly employed in the white collar and hegemonic sectors. This also tends to be the case with individuals related to heads as affines (usually a son- or daughter-in-law) or collaterals (generally younger siblings).

Since Table 22 concerns the entire sample of active workers in multiple income households, it does not reveal the status complexities that gainful employment in different sectors of the economy might enjoin within particular households. In dealing with this problem, it will suffice to consider five status dimensions relating to the authority structure of families and households: i.e., kinship, gender, education, occupation, and income. The analysis begins with Table 23, which relates the educational status of economically active household members relative to that of the heads of their respective households

.As shown in Table 23, relative to the heads of their respective households, the educational status of the gainfully employed members differs significantly according to the kinship status of the individual. In general, the educational status of wives is equal to or lower than that of their husbands. The overwhelming majority of the working sons and daughters in these households have an educational status higher than that of their fathers. Of the economically active collaterals and affines, the educational status of more than half is no higher than that of the heads of their respective households. In reference to these data, it may be recalled from chapter 3 that education is a significant factor with respect to the sector in which individuals are employed. Thus, it is not surprising to find that the occupational status of these workers relative to the heads of their respective households is also significantly related to the economic sector in which they are employed. The data in this regard are presented in Table 24.[14]

Table 23. Multiple Income Households: Educational Status of Economically Active Members Relative to the Heads of their Respective Households

Educational Status Relative to Head

(Row Pct.) (Col. Pct.) Kinship Status	Higher N	Higher %	Equal to or Lower[13] N	Equal to or Lower[13] %	Total	%
Wives	8	(30.8) (11.3)	18	(69.2) (33.3)	26	(100) (20.8)
Sons	32	(64.0) (45.0)	18	(36.0) (33.3)	50	(100) (40.0)
Daughters	23	(76.7) (32.4)	7	(23.3) (13.0)	30	(100) (24.0)
Collaterals/ Affines	8	(42.1) (11.3)	11	(57.9) (20.4)	19	(100) (15.2)
Total	71	(56.8)	54	(43.2)	125	(100)

P < .01

Table 24. Multiple Income Households: Sector of Employment of Economically Active Members and Occupational Status Relative to the Heads of their Respective Households

Occupational Status Relative to Head of Household

(Row Pct.) (Col. Pct.) Sector of Employment	Higher N	Higher %	Equal to or Lower N	Equal to or Lower %	Total	%
Hegemonic	26	(72.2) (38.2)	10	(27.8) (17.5)	36	(100) (28.8)
Traditional	5	(38.5) (7.4)	8	(61.5) (14.0)	13	(100) (10.4)
White Collar	33	(71.7) (48.5)	13	(28.3) (22.8)	46	(100) (36.8)
Self-Employed	4	(13.3) (5.9)	26	(86.7) (46.6)	30	(100) (24.0)
Total	68	(54.4)	57	(45.6)	125	(100)

P < .001

Approximately 72 percent of those employed in the hegemonic and white collar sectors have an occupational status higher than that of their respective heads. The occupational status of those employed in the traditional and informal sectors, for the most part, is equal to that of their respective heads or lower.[15] In other words, there is a substantial relationship between the kinship status of these workers, the educational and occupational status they have vis-à-vis the heads of their respective households (and we might add vis-à-vis one another), and their sector of employment.

However, as Table 25 suggests, the income status of workers vis-à-vis the heads of their respective households is a somewhat different and more complicated matter. Among workers located in multiple income households, 125 in all, only 22 percent have an income higher than that of the household head and, for the most part, these individuals may be counted among the category of sons. The income status of these household members relative to one another and to the heads of households seems to engage a complex set of factors.

Table 25. Multiple Income Households: Income and Kinship Status of Economically Active Members Relative to the Heads of their Respective Households

Income Status Relative to Head

(Row Pct.) (Col. Pct.) Kinship Status	Higher N	Higher %	Equal to or Lower N	Equal to or Lower %	Total	%
Wives	1	(3.8) (3.7)	25	(96.2) (25.5)	26	(100) (20.8)
Sons	16	(32.0) (59.3)	34	(68.0) (34.7)	50	(100) (40.0)
Daughters	6	(20.0) (22.2)	24	(80.0) (24.5)	30	(100) (24.0)
Collaterals/ Affines	4	(21.0) (14.8)	15	(79.0) (15.3)	19	(100) (15.2)
Total	27	(21.6)	98	(78.4)	125	(100)

$P < .05$

The income of these workers is not unrelated to their education, their occupational status, their sector of employment, and to considerations of gender. For example, if one combines education and income and considers the status of these individuals relative to heads, the results are as reported in Table 26. While 57 percent of the economically active in these households have an educational status higher than that of their respective heads, only 24 percent of this group also enjoys a higher income status. This select group, however, comprises 63 percent of those with a higher income status. At the same time, almost 56 percent of those individuals whose educational status is equal to or lower than that of the heads of their respective households also have a lower income status. As Table 27 discloses, a very similar pattern emerges when one combines the income and occupational status of these individuals relative to the heads of their households.

Table 26. Multiple Income Households: Educational and Income Status of Economically Active Members Relative to the Heads of their Respective Households

Educational Status Relative to Head

(Row Pct.)
(Col. Pct.)

Income Status Relative to Head	*Higher*		*Equal or Lower*			
	N	*%*	*N*	*%*	*Total*	*%*
Higher	17	(63.0)	10	(37.0)	27	(100)
		(23.9)		(18.5)		(21.6)
Equal	34	(70.8)	14	(29.2)	48	(100)
		(47.8)		(29.9)		(38.4)
Lower	20	(40.0)	30	(60.0)	50	(100)
		(28.2)		(55.6)		(40.0)
Total	71	(56.8)	54	(43.2)	125	(100)

$P < .01$

In other words, within these families it is not always the case that individuals who enjoy an educational and occupational status higher than that of the heads of their households also command a higher level of income. How is this to be explained? In part, it is related to the depressed wage structure that pervades large sectors of the working class in Manaus. This wage structure tends to diminish the economic value of the educational achievement and occupational experience of a great many individuals. Equally significant is the fact that these differences in income status within households are very much related to the inequalities in income that exist between males and females even within this depressed wage structure.

Table 27. Multiple Income Households: Occupational and Income Status of Economically Active Members Relative to the Heads of their Respective Households

(Row Pct.)
(Col. Pct.)

Occupational Status Relative to Head

Relative to Head	Higher N	%	Equal or Lower N	%	Total	%
Higher	18	(66.6) (26.5)	9	(33.3) (15.8)	27	(100) (21.6)
Equal	19	(39.6) (27.9)	29	(60.4) (50.9)	48	(100) (38.4)
Lower	31	(62.0) (45.6)	19	(38.0) (33.3)	50	(100) (40.0)
Total	68	(54.4)	57	(45.6)	125	(100)

P < .05

At this point, recall that there exists a substantial relationship between the kinship status of these workers, the educational and occupational status they have vis-à-vis the heads of their households, and their sector of employment. The working wives and daughters in these households, even more than the sons, are concentrated in the hegemonic and white collar sectors. It is precisely these sectors in which are concentrated 78 percent of the 50 workers whose income status is lower than that of the heads of their respective households.[16] The extent to which gender affects the status differential of these individuals vis-à-vis household heads is shown in Table 28. Of the 27 workers who have achieved a level of income higher than that of the heads of their respective households, more than 70 percent are males. Although no significant differences exist in the educational and occupational status of economically active females relative to the heads of their households, almost 48 percent of these women earn less income.

**Table 28. Multiple Income Households: Income Status of
Economically Active Males and Females Relative to
the Heads of their Respective Households**

Income Status Relative to Head
(Row Pct.)
(Col. Pct.)

Gender	Higher N	%	Equal N	%	Lower N	%	Total	%
Males	19	(30.6)	23	(37.1)	20	(32.3)	62	(100)
		(70.4)		(47.9)		(40.0)		(49.6)
Females	8	(12.7)	25	(39.7)	30	(47.6)	63	(100)
		(29.6)		(52.1)		(60.0)		(50.4)
Total	27	(21.6)	48	(38.4)	50	(40.0)	125	(100)

$P < .05$

Nearly 73 percent of the multiple income households included in this study contain individuals working in two or more sectors of the urban economy. The economic division of labor enjoined by this employment engages a complex pattern of status differentials involving gender, kinship, education, occupation, sector of employment, and income. Independent of whether or not these households are formed by nuclear or extended families, all of these factors assume some degree of significance in differentiating their economically active members from one another. To somewhat simplify the complexity of the previous discussion, Table 29 presents a summary of the kinship and objective status relationships within these households on three status dimensions relative to the respective heads of these family units.

The details of Table 29 need not be reiterated. What emerges from its inspection is a pattern of status relationships very different from that of single income households. In terms of percentages, the working wives in these households have a status equal or superior to that of their husbands on all but the dimension of income. However, on all three dimensions, relative to their fathers, a larger percentage of the sons and daughters of these women enjoy a higher status than their mothers. This also tends to be the case with respect to collaterals and affines; relative to the head of the household, a larger percentage of collaterals and affines enjoy a more favorable status than the dona da casa. Thus, these households contain wives, adult children, affines, and collaterals whose education, occupational experiences, and income affords them, *at least in theory,* the

Table 29. Multiple Income Households: Kinship and the Objective Status of Economically Active Members Relative to the Heads of their Respective Households on Three Dimensions of Status

Status Dimensions

Economically Active	N	Education			Occupation			Income		
		% Higher	Equal	Lower	% Higher	Equal	Lower	% Higher	Equal	Lower
Wives	26	30.8	57.7	11.5	42.3	34.6	23.1	3.8	42.3	53.8
Sons	50	64.0	28.0	8.0	58.0	32.0	10.0	32.0	38.0	30.0
Daughters	30	76.7	23.3	—	66.6	30.0	3.3	20.0	36.7	43.3
Colaterals/ Affines										
Males	12	33.3	50.0	16.6	33.3	41.7	25.0	25.0	33.3	41.7
Females	7	57.1	42.9	—	57.1	14.3	28.6	14.2	42.9	42.9
Total	125	56.8	36.0	7.2	54.4	32.0	13.6	21.6	38.4	40.0

resources and therefore the opportunity, to exercise a considerable degree of independence vis-à-vis the traditional structure of family authority. It remains to be considered the extent to which these new status identities have brought with them an increased sense of individual autonomy within the domain of domestic relations.

The Domain of Domestic Relations

The domain of domestic relations in Brazilian society, and most certainly in Manaus, tends to be private and remains relatively closed to all but members of the family and perhaps a few very close friends. Informants who freely responded to questions relating to work, income, household economy, religion, politics, and life in the community, did not readily engage in discussions concerning their personal relationships with spouses, parents, or children. When such relationships became the focus of questions, informants tended to respond in generalities or they related details that usually placed these relationships in their most favorable light. Thus, short of a prolonged and intensive involvement with particular families, the domain of domestic relations is difficult to penetrate.

Accordingly, the analysis that follows is based on recorded observations and interviews with members of approximately 20 families that we visited often and came to know rather well. The analysis also draws upon information that emerged from discursive discussions with various informants in households that we came to know primarily in terms of the family histories that we recorded. And finally, the analysis is contextualized by information obtained in interview sessions with three parish priests, two ministers, various church volunteers, two primary school teachers, and the social service director of the community center in Costa da Silva, one of the neighborhoods in Bairro Raiz. The analysis proceeds with the presentation of cases that have been selected for purposes of illustrating in broad outline how the economic division of labor and related factors seem to have affected family relationships and the authority structure of a select sample of multiple income households. The first sketch concerns the family of Eloy Ferreira.

Eloy Ferreira, fifty-one years of age, is employed in the white collar sector. He is a bookkeeper in the Secretaria da Fazenda (department of internal revenue) for the state of Amazonas. Born in the state of Maranhão, Eloy began work with FUNAI (The Indian Protection Service) when he was seventeen years of age. He later worked as a carpenter with a construction firm in Goiás. In 1945, he accepted a job with

Cruzeiro do Sul, an airline company, and was sent to Manaus. Three years later he was laid off and "joined the military police in order to study." He remained in the service for fourteen years. During this time he completed a secondary education at Dom Pedro Segundo, a private high school in Manaus. In 1962, soon after Eloy married his current wife, he passed an examination for an appointment in the Secretaria da Fazenda. At this time, he also held a job for four years teaching mathematics at Dom Pedro.[17] Because of promotions, earned, he emphasized, by passing examinations, Eloy is paid ten minimum salaries.

Eloy owns and occupies a very modest but well constructed house in Costa da Silva, a public housing conjunto. He heads a family consisting of his wife, Maria, five sons, three daughters, an unemployed son-in-law who is looking for work, and a nephew (on his wife's side) from the interior who is living with them while attending high school in Manaus.[18] Eloy's wife, whom he met while on assignment in the interior, has completed only four years of education. His oldest son, Melquíades, graduated from the University of Amazonas with a degree in electrical engineering. His second son, Gilberto, is a university graduate with a degree in administration. His third son, Reginaldo, studies economics at the university. João, his fourth son, is also enrolled in the university. The youngest son, named after President Lyndon B. Johnson, is an international medalist who expects to receive an athletic scholarship from an American university upon the completion of secondary school in Manaus. The oldest daughter is also an athlete. Still enrolled in secondary school, she trains with a view toward national and international competition. The two youngest daughters are enrolled in primary school.

Eloy's sons and daughters by his second wife are not married and all live at home. The three eldest sons have a superior educational status. The two eldest are gainfully employed and both have an occupational status equal or superior to that of Eloy. Their economic status is also equal or superior to that of Eloy. The oldest son, Melquíades, is the managing director of a small electrical equipment company. He reports earning ten minimum salaries. Gilberto is a 2nd Lieutenant in the army, a supply officer, and reports earning 10.5 minimum salaries. Notwithstanding the family's superior income, the educational achievement of Eloy's three oldest sons, or the occupation of Eloy himself, this family is generally known but not acknowledged as being in any way special by its neighbors.

Despite the economic independence and status achievements of his sons, Eloy is indeed the authority figure and head of this household. Taking care to make this known, Eloy stated: "Those who work and live at home must contribute to the family budget. Melquíades and Gilberto give a fixed proportion, usually 25 percent, of what they earn. They sometimes contribute more but I do not expect it." Eloy, with his wife's assistance, manages the family budget. "I do most of the grocery shopping because for this big house I must purchase large quantities of food at one time, at bulk rate prices. My wife tells me what the house needs and I get it."

As a further elaboration upon his status, Eloy stated: "A man cannot help himself or his family without a professional mentality. A husband and a wife have to know and understand each other in order to educate their children. You have to give advice and orientation. If I disagree with a son, I must do so with justification and not hitting him. The children have to be free but they need an orientation, love, and fraternity from the parents. You have to treat them as human beings and not dogs—as many people do out there. I grew up like this—being hit by parents. They were rigorous and could not allow a son or daughter to make mistakes. Today, things are different. Today, we must reason with our children."

From visits and discussions with various members of the family, it became evident that Eloy commands admiration for his accomplishments and respect for his values. His sons and daughters consider him a model to emulate. They attribute their educational efforts to his motivation and encouragement. And, as Melquíades stated: "We defer to his wisdom." Eloy's status has been enhanced by the moral and material support he has given his children. In effect, he retains the status of a "petit" but kindly patriarch and he plays that role accordingly.

Although Eloy claims the status of head and assumes the traditional rights and responsibilities which that status enjoins, this is not typically the case among multiple income households. More typical is the family of Erasmo de Souza, a sixty-two year old sawmill worker with Serraria Amazonense. Erasmo is the nominal head of a household that includes his wife, Raimunda, three daughters (ages 25, 23, and 22), and four sons (ages 19, 17, 15, and 12). All three of the daughters have completed their secondary education. Two of them work, both in the electronics industry, and each earns monthly one minimum salary. The oldest son, who completed only seven years of school, works at Serraria Amazonense and earns one minimum salary. His second son takes high school courses at night. During the day, he works as an office boy in a shoe store and also earns one minimum salary. The two remaining children are in primary school. Erasmo's wife, with six years of education, is in charge of the laundry service in one of the better hotels in Manaus and she too earns one minimum salary.

Erasmo and his wife were born and raised in the interior of Amazonas. They married in 1955. In the interior, Erasmo worked in agriculture, fished, collected balata gum, and subsequently worked with his brother-in-law, selling fish, food, and nuts along the river. In 1958, the family moved to Manaus. Erasmo worked two years as a carpenter and then took employment at the sawmill. When he came to Manaus at the age of thirty, Erasmo had only four years of schooling. He stated: "Because of my children, I wanted more education." By attending school at night, he finally completed secondary school with a teaching certificate at the age of sixty-two. However, he has not attempted to use this hard-earned certification to improve his occupation or his income. He continues to work at the sawmill, earning a monthly income of 1.5 minimum salaries.

In short, Erasmo has an education superior to that of his wife, equal to that of his three daughters, and superior to that of his gainfully employed sons. His occupational status is comparable to that of his wife and one of his sons; it is inferior to that of his two gainfully employed daughters and his second son. His income status is only slightly above that of the other economically active members of the household. In this context, Erasmo claims and is accorded the status of family head.

Commenting on his headship, Erasmo related: "My wife and I share the expenses of the household. Sometimes the children contribute a little but they do not help much. They are different from the children in the interior and more like the children in Manaus. They have their own expenses. They live their own lives. If we do not like what they do with their lives, we can say so, but they do it anyway. That is the way things are now. Everything has changed since I was a boy. Then, we listened more to our parents. My father was my father and I had to admire him. But in the interior we did not have our own work before having a family—sometimes not even then—and little money exchanged hands. We needed one another. Today, we have more work and more money but the family moves in all directions. It is different but I think we are still a family."

One aspect of the change that is occurring in domestic relations as a result of urban-industrial developments and the economic division of labor that it has brought to many households is exemplified in the case of Luís Viana and his wife, Francisca. Married for eleven years, they occupy a two-bedroom house, a very modest structure which they rent near Costa da Silva. The household is comprised of Luís, his wife, two daughters of pre-school age, and a maid. Luís, thirty years of age, is a migrant from Acre. He has three years of education. He came to Manaus with his widowed mother at the age of twelve. With her help, and with money earned from various jobs, he purchased a car with which he operates a taxi service. He reports an average income of five minimum salaries.

Francisca, his wife, is twenty-seven years of age. She was born in the interior of Amazonas. Her father left her mother when she was a baby. She stated: "When I was three years of age, I was sort of kidnapped from my mother by an aunt who gave me to a couple who carried me to Ceará. When I was twelve, because of the drought, they returned to Manaus. Through my aunt, I found my mother in Manaus and I ran away from the couple that raised me to live with her." In Manaus, Francisca completed a secondary education with specialization in secretarial courses. She holds two secretarial jobs, one full-time with CEPA (The State Commission for Agricultural Planning), the other part-time with a private organization (The Center for Assistance to Small Farmers). As a result of two jobs, she reports a monthly income of six minimum salaries. In terms of her education, occupation, and her income, her status is superior to that of her husband. And, from all appearances, their economic division of labor is very much related to the character of their domestic relations.

Francisca emphasized: "We are both heads of the household." He added: "We have our separate work. We keep our separate incomes but we share the expenses." "My husband," Francisca continued, "pays the rent and helps with the food. I pay the maid, the water and the electricity. With the maid, I manage the house. Because of his work, Luís is not home so much and I give more care to the children." In a subsequent interview, at her place of work, Francisca emphasized that she did not need to consult her husband with respect to her income. "I buy the things that I want—clothes, the television set, the stereo, my daughter's bed. He does with his money what he wants. He agrees with whatever I do. I can go where I want. Sometimes I go to parties with Luís and sometimes I go with friends. On weekends, I go out with the children or I visit my mother who suffers from heart problems. Sometimes on the weekend the whole family goes to the beach." In effect, Francisca considers herself sufficiently independent that she does not have to accord Luís the authority traditionally accorded the male head of the household.

The pattern of domestic relations with regard to Luís Viana's family is not very different from most of the multiple income households we encountered in which the educational, occupational, and income status of working wives was equal or superior to that of their husbands. A variation on this pattern may be illustrated by reference to the family of Antônio Pacó, fifty-one years of age, a laborer employed by DERA (The State Department of Highways).

Antônio is one of several children born to an agricultural worker in the interior of Amazonas. One by one, he and his brothers migrated to Manaus. With only four years of education, Antônio arrived in 1954 and found work in a furniture factory. In 1957, he married Emízia Barros, a high school graduate. The couple built a small house on land owned by Emízia's mother. Subsequently, they sold this house and purchased a wooden structure in Costa da Silva. Antônio, according to his wife, did not like living in the city. After his second child was born, in 1967, he quit his job in the furniture factory and took work as a mão de obra with the highway department. In conjunction with this employment, he constructed a one-room dwelling near one of the department's shelters, outside the city, where he keeps a little farm. According to Antônio, his income, including income earned from his small farm, is less than 1.5 minimum salaries.

In Manaus, Antônio's household consists of his wife, two sons, three daughters, and two nephews whom his wife took in upon the death of one of her sisters. Except for the oldest daughter, all of the children are enrolled in school. The oldest daughter, a high school graduate, is a clerk in a clothing store. Her income is one minimum salary. Antônio's wife, Emízia, is self-employed in the informal sector. Emízia and her seventeen year old son operate a luncheonette and sell beer and sandwiches out of the kitchen and courtyard of her house. On a monthly average, Emízia claims an income of three minimum salaries. Except for some produce from his "little farm" and an occasional remittance, she claims to receive little or nothing by way of support from her husband.

Out of a respect for tradition, Emízia considers her husband the head of the household. However, his status as head is mainly nominal. For the most part, Antônio lives by himself, in the dwelling he constructed outside the city. He visits the family once or twice each month. Emízia's oldest daughter, Maria, is less traditional and more emphatic about her father's status. She considers her mother to be the head of the family. Maria states: "We really do not know much about what my father does. We see him sometimes on a weekend but they (her mother and father) don't talk much. My mother makes all the decisions. I give her half of what I earn. With the rest, I buy clothes and go places with my friends. If my mother did not go to church all the time, I don't think she would need my father." We asked, does your father live with another woman? Maria responded: "No, I have never heard that. My father and mother are not separated, but mostly the family goes well without my father."

Between 1960 and 1980, the percentage of women in Manaus who were separated or divorced did not change appreciably. The proportion of married women increased but slightly, from 49.0 to 51.7 percent. However, with an increase from 8.1 to 19.8 percent, the number of families formed by consensual unions virtually exploded. Among families included in the present study, 20.7 percent were formed by consensual unions. Domestic relations in households that contain families formed in this manner are extremely variable and they also appear to be significantly affected by the economic division of labor that obtains within them. Two examples may serve to illustrate the point.

Maria da Cruz, thirty years of age, was born in Manaus. She completed eight years of education. She married at age thirteen and begin work in a clothing factory at age seventeen. She then stopped working and gave birth to two children. Soon after, she left her husband because "he found a lover." When she separated, Maria left her oldest daughter with her husband and placed the youngest in the home of her mother, herself separated from Maria's father. Maria moved in with her father. One year later, her father died and Maria inherited his house, a wooden structure in Costa da Silva. After her father's death, Maria returned to work. She worked for two years as an assembler with IGASA, an electronics firm. She then quit IGASA for a better paying job with Agá, also an electronics firm (cf. chapter 2). After five years at Agá, Maria was promoted to inspector. In 1984, she reported a monthly income of 2.5 minimum salaries.

While working at IGASA, Maria formed a consensual union and gave birth to two children. Her amásio, Demítrio de Oliveira, was born in Manaus and has had only one year of education. He holds a job as a janitor and, in his off hours, he drives a taxi which is owned by a friend. His total monthly income from this work is 1.5 minimum salaries. Thus, not only is his educational, occupational, and income status somewhat lower than that of Maria, but he lives in the house that she owns.

In the presence of Demítrio, Maria stated: "My former husband was the head of my first family. My amásio is the father of my two lovely children, but I am the head of this family. We share expenses. Every month, Demítrio gives me almost half of what he earns. The rest he keeps for himself. I give my mother a little money each month to help with the expenses for my daughter who lives with her. I think I am making a good salary at Agá. We are not rich but I have added water and electricity to my father's house. With my money, I bought a new refrigerator, a color television set, a stereo, and a fan." When asked whether or not they planned to marry, Maria responded: "No. I am only separated from my former husband. One marriage is enough. For me, it is better the way it is now."

In this and subsequent discussions with Maria and Demítrio, one senses that although this arrangement has persisted for almost ten years, it remains one of mutual convenience. Should Maria become dissatisfied with her relationship with her amásio, she controls the resources with which to terminate it. In effect, the authority structure that exists in households of this type is not only a function of the status claims that attach to education, occupation, income, and proprietorship, it is also related to whether or not the individuals involved feel that the relationship might be sustained. As evidence of this, consider the case of Linda Figueiredo, fifty-five years of age and a *parteira* (midwife).

Linda Figueiredo was born in Acre and carried to Manaus by her parents in 1931. She finished eight years of school and was seventeen when she married Marcos Figueiredo, a vendor in the informal sector. Over the years, Marcos accumulated capital and became a relatively successful comerciante. Subsequently, through SHAM, they purchased a very nice home in Costa da Silva. At age thirty-two, Linda took a job as a ward attendant in the State Mental Hospital. She worked there for only two years but during that time she completed a training course for midwives. In 1963, her husband died. Linda sold his business and went to work as a parteira in the State Maternity Hospital. After taking additional courses and with twenty years of service at the hospital, she achieved the status of *estatutária*, making her employment permanent until retirement. At the hospital, Linda works twenty-four hours/week and earns 1.5 minimum salaries. Because of her hours, Linda is also employed by a private hospital where she earns another 1.5 minimum salaries. Besides this, Linda reports earning an average of two additional salaries delivering babies nights and weekends. Thus, her total income is approximately five minimum salaries.

Living in Linda's home are her ninety-two year old mother, her eighteen year old son, a nephew by a deceased sister, her amásio, Júlio Gomes, and her amásio's son. In 1979, Linda formed a consensual union with Júlio Gomes, who is forty-nine years old. Although born and raised in Manaus, Júlio has only four years of education. He is employed as a truck driver in the Industrial District and reports earning two minimum salaries monthly. The attachment between Júlio and Linda has not resulted in marriage because Júlio is married and only separated from his wife. Regarding Júlio's marital status, Linda emphasized: "Júlio's wife left him for another man and a divorce in this country is too much trouble to obtain."

It became obvious from several visits to this household that the relationship between Júlio and Linda is considered by them to be permanent. Together, they have an extremely active social life. On one occasion, while having a beer with the two of them, Linda stated: "I love to live. I like parties, pools, soccer, movies, night clubs. In our free time, Júlio and I participate in everything. If we have no place to go we have a party at our house. We always have something to do." Despite her proprietorship of a well furnished home, her somewhat superior educational and occupational status, and despite the economic independence that she derives from her work, Linda considers her amásio to be the family head. When she stated this in an interview, he laughed. "In truth," he said, "this family has two heads. It is a very democratic family. We don't keep separate books. We share the good times, the bad times, the expenses, and together we make the decisions. If you could know us better, you would learn that my wife is a very strong person—very political." Because of their relationship, Linda has accorded her amásio the status of head. However, he acknowledges her independence and the fact that he does not, or cannot, exercise the authority that the status traditionally enjoins.

Among the multiple income households included in the study, perhaps the most extreme example of how the economic division of labor might affect the authority structure of the family is the case of Francisco Pinto, sixty years of age. Born in Manaus, Francisco has four years of education. As a foundry worker, he earns two minimum salaries. His wife, Lusia, is fifty-four years of age. She has never attended school and she is not gainfully employed. In addition, Francisco's household includes his only child, Eliana, her husband, Gilberto, and two young grandchildren. Eliana, twenty-six years of age, has a high school education, and works as an accountant in a large furniture store where she is paid three minimum salaries. In 1979, Eliana married Gilberto and they moved in with her parents.

Gilberto came to Manaus from Acre on an army transfer in 1974. While in the army and stationed in Manaus, he completed a secondary school education with courses in accounting. After his discharge, he worked four years as an accountant in a bank. At the bank, he was paid two minimum salaries. In 1983, he took a position as an accountant in the credit department with Jota, one of the two electronics firms included in the study. Gilberto earns five minimum salaries. Thus, the educational, occupational and income status of Gilberto and his wife, separately or combined, are quite superior to that of Gilberto's father-in-law.

By tradition, Gilberto's father-in-law is head of the household. He is not only Eliana's father but he owns the home in which she and her husband live. However, Gilberto and Eliana do not even nominally accord him that status. Gilberto emphatically asserted: "I am now the head of this family. When I was first married and worked in the bank, that was not so much case. But now I am the head."

When asked what had brought about this change, Gilberto related: "This house is not what it once was. With my money and money earned by my wife, we have rebuilt this house with brick. It is much larger. It now has four bedrooms, a living room, and two inside bathrooms. It has all new furniture. We made a wall around the yard. My father-in-law contributed a little work but not much." "But," he was asked, "does not your father-in-law make any decisions?" Gilberto responded: "He makes decisions for himself and my mother-in-law. He gives me and my wife whatever money he wants to give. I pay all the expenses, the water, the electricity, the food, everything. It is only fair. My mother-in-law takes care of the children while we work and my father-in-law is free to keep whatever he earns to spend on her and himself. This way the whole family lives better." When interviewed separately, Francisco related: "This house is in my name but, in truth, it belongs more to my daughter and her husband. He has become the head of the family."

Perhaps it is the case that some fragments of the parentela persist or have been reconstituted within a substantial number (approximately 30–40 percent) of urban, working-class households in Manaus. However, judging from the households under discussion, among these families kinship ties are infrequently maintained across extensive genealogical distances. Also, the strength of these ties varies considerably but, most generally, it tends to be rooted primarily in the relationships that exist between parents and children and among siblings. The network of kinship emerging from these primary relationships is not often extended to include relatives who are distant from them. Most informants knew of aunts, uncles, or cousins living in Manaus or elsewhere, but unless they lived in or close to the neighborhood, many informants were extremely vague as to the names of these relatives, where they lived, whom they lived with or married, whether they had children and how many, or what they did for work.

Depending upon the strength of these kinship ties were the manifold favors that attached to them. Such favors could involve financial assistance in the form of small loans but usually assistance did not take the form of monetary transfers. Most generally it involved helping someone find employment. However, quite frequently assistance came in the form of providing temporary housing for migrant siblings or in-laws seeking to establish themselves in Manaus, or of taking in a grandchild or a nephew from the country who wished to attend school in the city, or of providing a temporary home for a newly married son or daughter. Not infrequently, assistance entailed taking in an elderly or widowed parent. Whatever the case, from these various efforts to help there emerges a substantial number of households containing some form of extended family. The majority of these, however, appear to be constituted by temporary arrangements.

Little evidence emerged in our research to suggest that these extended families were constructed for the purpose of aggregating income in order to cope with the harsh economic circumstances of working-class life in Manaus. Nor did we find much evidence to suggest that the formation of these family units represented a calculated strategy with which to pursue the mobility aspirations that many workers entertained. In other words, while these extended families were often functional in providing assistance of some economic value, their formation did not appear to be economically determined. If in some subjective sense the opposite is the case, when compared to nuclear families, the strategy is certainly not very effective. Thus, it seems more accurate to consider the formation of these units as an artifact of the deeply rooted Brazilian cultural tradition that close kin should help one another with personal problems, particularly with personal problems arising out of such difficult circumstances as old age, the death of a spouse, a badly treated child, the need for temporary housing or for a place to stay while attending school in the city, or the search for employment. The frequency and severity of these kinds of problems, it seems, increases with urban-industrialization. Accordingly, the proportion of these extended family units, temporary and fragile as they may be, also increases.

From the point of view of domestic relations, more significant than whether or not families are nuclear or in some sense extended is the manner in which households are economically engaged. The data suggest that domestic relations within families, particularly their structure of authority, are significantly affected by their economic division of labor and the status identities that this enjoins. With some exceptions, at least in Manaus, single income households are more likely to conform to the traditional norms of family life and organization than are multiple income households. Whether headed by males who are married or who form consensual unions, or in some cases by females who are separated from their husbands, headship in single income households is generally vested with the authority to delegate or make family decisions and the exercise of that authority usually seems to command a consensus within the household.

This is less typically the case with multiple income households. These households vary tremendously in the character of their formation. In terms of kinship, age, gender, education, occupation, and income, they also vary extensively with respect to the status identities of their constituent members. Some of these households contain extended families and some do not. Because of age or gender, some members of these households are economically active and others are not. Those who are active are often engaged in very different sectors of employment. And, as we have seen, some sectors favor the employment of females rather than males. Some favor the employment of individuals of higher rather than lower educational achievement. In some sectors individuals command somewhat higher wages by virtue of their seniority; in others, their wages improve with promotions achieved by training, examinations, or educational certification. In many of these households, sons and sometimes daughters earn as much or even more than their fathers. Although wives do not do as well in this regard, they often have more education and better jobs than their husbands.

Because of these and related circumstances, multiple income households enjoin a multiplicity of status identities and the claims that attach to these identities, judging from the data, have a significant impact on the domain of domestic relations. In some of these households the status of male headship has been enhanced. In others, it has become little more than a nominal entitlement. By virtue of their gainful employment, particularly if their occupation involves higher levels of education, wives and children have achieved a considerable degree of independence from the authority traditionally exercised by those to whom they accord the nominal status of family head. Increasingly, wives and adult children command their own resources and independently make decisions for themselves. In most cases, they share in the expenses of their respective households but, whether variable or fixed, their contributions are often considered voluntary.

The loss of status among male family heads in multiple income households is a source of widespread complaint among middle-aged and elderly males. Some informants attributed to it an increase in the level of alcoholism.[19] Among interviewees, priests, ministers, and social service workers, saliently and quite emphatically considered the "weakening of the the family structure" to be one of the most serious and negative aspects of economic development within the Zona Franca. As one priest asserted: "With the money they now earn, women and children have become liberated and this has created a great many problems in Manaus. Men cannot hold up their heads at home. Families are broken by separation. For lack of supervision, young children are becoming delinquent. The consumption of drugs by young adults is so bad that in some neighborhoods even I, a priest, dare not walk at night. We are losing respect for authority." He added: "*É uma loucura.* (It makes for madness)." Needless to say, this may be an exaggeration but, nonetheless, it expresses the belief held by many in Manaus that family relationships have changed because of urban-industrial developments.

However, I am prompted by historical sources to ask whether or not family relationships have really changed and, if so, how much? The reader may recall from chapter 1 that the family structure among Caboclos reflected the conditions and restraints of their physical isolation, their pre-industrial mode of production, and their dependence on the aviamento system. Wagley (1953: 145–86) tells us that in Itá, people of all social classes shared the Brazilian ideal of the parentela, the large, patriarchally united, extended family. However, most homes in Itá contained but a nuclear family and although the man was ideally the absolute head of the household, because of his work as a collector, women in fact assumed a significant position of authority and influence. Moreover, consensual unions were common and it was not uncommon for men to "walk out" of unions that had been civilly contracted or "sanctified" by the Church.

There is little evidence from Manaus to suggest that the Brazilian ideal of the parentela has changed. There is considerable evidence to suggest that the realization of this ideal is every bit as difficult to áchieve in the urban-industrial economy of the Zona Franca as it was in the traditional extractive economy of the Caboclo. The patriarch in Brazil, after all, is one within the household who commands the resources with which to exercise authority and thereby validate the status that others accord him. In both the traditional and new urban-industrial economies, it seems that individuals within households assume status identities somewhat relative to the resources that their economic roles command and they more or less conduct themselves accordingly. Behind these status identities and claims, however, there continues to exist a sense of obligation to assist, if at all possible, kin who are closely related.

As seen in previous chapters, the industrialization that followed upon the creation of the Zona Franca engaged a processes of developmental change that has extensively transformed the economic foundations of working-class life in Manaus. Having considered how this has affected the income and occupational careers of individual workers, the economy of their households, and the domestic organization of their families, it remains to assess how it has also affected the social and cultural milieux of the city and neighborhoods in which these workers and their families live.

CHAPTER 6

Manaus in Transition: Bairros and Vizinhanças

The principal focus of this chapter is the relationship between work and social life in the city and in the bairros and *vizinhanças* (neighborhoods) formed by working-class families. Accordingly, the chapter begins with a very general description of the material and cultural impact of the Zona Franca on the urban milieu in Manaus. It then moves to a series of sections in which focus is given to the social and cultural life characteristic of the neighborhoods in which lived a substantial majority of the working-class families that were previously considered in relationship to the labor processes that exist in different sectors of employment. For purposes of comparison, the chapter concludes with a brief description of social life in Parque Solimões, a housing conjunto occupied by middle-class families and walled off for reasons of security from the working-class neighborhoods that surround it.

Material Dimensions of Urbanization

The contemporary transformation of social and cultural life in Manaus has engaged processes of change very different from those that were associated with the development that the city experienced during the rubber boom. When its economy was based primarily on the extraction of rubber, Manaus began to consolidate itself as a relatively modern urban center. It was then that the city first created a system of public utilities, including electrification, the treatment of water, and the connection of homes to a public sanitation network. It was then that it paved virtually all of its streets and provided public transportation with the use of electric cars. It was also then that Manaus expanded its public services, built medical facilities and, for the first time, opened itself to what might be called cosmopolitan cultural influences with the con-

191

struction of a university and the famous Teatro Amazonas.

Many of these early developments were designed to accommodate the economic and political elites, who extracted far more wealth from the region than they ever returned to its working-class people by way of beneficial improvements in the physical and social ambiance of urban life. Still, one needs to acknowledge that the improvements in urban life associated with the rubber boom more or less kept pace with the growth in urban population. That this was possible was due primarily to the fact that the demographic impact of the rubber boom was of a very different character from that resulting from the industrialization of the Zona Franca. The migratory flow stimulated by the extraction of rubber was mainly directed toward the seringais, the rubber fields in the interior, and not the city itself.[1] The opposite has been the case with the Free Trade Zone.

The Free Trade Zone stimulated a rapid influx of commercial and industrial enterprises, consulting firms, research institutes, public officials, entrepreneurs seeking investment opportunities, tourists seeking free trade bargains, and migrants seeking jobs, education, or health services. Moreover, all these firms, institutions, and people begin to arrive at a time when Manaus existed in a virtual state of urban decay. For more than fifty years after the collapse of the rubber economy the city stagnated. During this period, the city's streets deteriorated. The uncompleted sanitation system went to rot. The port facilities and many public buildings fell into disrepair. Medical facilities became grossly obsolete. The water and electrical plants aged to the point of almost complete breakdown. Because of the deficiency of electrical power, the city's relatively clean system of public transportation, based on the use of electric cars, was replaced by an inadequate fleet of malodorous gasoline and diesel buses.[2] In short, by 1960, Manaus was quite unprepared to cope with the growth that had fallen upon it.[3]

Spatially, the magnitude of urban growth is nothing less than staggering. Consider that in 1902 Manaus was a small port city of 50,000 people living in four or five bairros situated at the river's margin, within an area of approximately twenty square blocks. By 1984, it had become a metropolitan center of close to a million people living in fifty or more bairros sprawled over an area of almost ninety-five square kilometers.[4] More than half of this spatial expansion and ninety percent of the growth in population occurred within a period of less than twenty years. Concurrent with this growth, the population density of over half of the previously existing bairros more than doubled.

Some of the bairros that existed before 1967, Compensa for example, were already impacted favelas. Among those that were not, the process of favelization engulfed whatever patches of vacant land that could be invaded by families in need of housing. The process of favelization was not simply due to the influx of new migrants seeking opportunities. It also resulted from the displacement of population from old neighborhoods by the renovation of the port, the construction of new public facilities, and from the spread of commercial and industrial enterprises, particularly along the margins of the river where land values skyrocketed.[5] Despite the fact that between 1960 and 1980 the number of privately owned domiciles in Manaus increased from 30,979 to 118,375, there existed a housing crisis of major proportions and it stimulated both urban sprawl and favelization.

Today, favelization is most evident in the older and more centralized bairros of the city, bairros in which population densities have risen with the formation of what might be called "pocket slums." Most of these small favelas are located in the wet and unsanitary margins of igarapés and along the many natural drainage basins that traverse these areas. However, favelization is also evident in newly formed bairros, including some that contain public housing schemes. In fact, wherever population densities have risen as a consequence of the crowded construction of low cost housing on divided lots acquired by purchase from proprietors who have become small-scale land speculators, or by purchase from proprietors who have divided and sold portions of small lots because they are in need of quick money, favelization is in evidence.[6] Indeed, there now exist very few bairros that do not contain one or more of these small favelas.

In an attempt to stem the tide of favelization, the state and federal governments have plunged into the construction of public housing schemes. Some of the older of these schemes have been nicely improved by their proprietors and by the subsequent extension of public services.[7] Others, because of the continual influx of population, the sale and division of lots, and the construction of very low cost housing, have deteriorated. A few of these housing conjuntos, Costa da Silva for example, reveal a modicum of community organization. Most lack any form of organization other than that provided by the public housing agency that happened to be responsible for their initial construction and settlement.

An example of the latter is Cidade Nova, the newest, the very largest, and certainly one of the most esthetically depressing of these public housing projects. Located in a relatively isolated area of cleared forest, some eight or more kilometers distant from the center of the city, Cidade Nova's construction began in 1983.[8] When we visited the project for the purpose of collecting data in 1984, more than 5,000 units were already occupied. Planners estimated that by 1986 an additional

10,000 units would be constructed for distribution. All of these units conformed to a uniform model. Each house, built with brick, provided a family (regardless of its size) with approximately 600 square feet or less of living space. Each unit was electrified and contained running water from a system of artesian wells and was also connected to a septic system. At the time of research, some of these newly constructed homes had already been modified or extended by additions constructed of wood. In some cases these additions were constructed to amplify the living quarters of large families. Others had been extended to incorporate small-scale retail enterprises.

Cidade Nova is a massive sprawl of these small houses. The settlement is divided into a dozen or more sections. Each section contains a government office charged with the responsibility of its management, including the facilitation of property transfers and the collection of utility and house payments. All of these sections are serviced by public buses that connect them to the central city. Thus, the streets are paved. However, on the exposed, sunbaked tropical soil of the area, there exists little evidence of plant life, no landscaping and, in some sections, new house lots are already scarred by erosion. At the entrance to Cidade Nova, located a considerable distance from the highway leading to the city, there exists a complex of small shops, a supermarket, churches, and a new public school. According to the authorities, most of the inhabitants of this particular development are either recent migrants or families who have moved themselves out of favelas. Despite the location of Cidade Nova, the economic life of most of its inhabitants is dependent upon work in distant parts of the city. For those who work in the city or in its Industrial Park, transportation to and from work is one or two hours by bus, depending upon traffic.

In addition to BNH (Banco Nacional Habitação), several agencies are involved (e.g., Amazon-Lar, Cohab-Am, Promorar, SHAM, etc.) in the management or construction of these public housing schemes. The policies of these agencies contribute directly to the stratification of working-class populations. Promorar's federally financed housing program, for example, is designed to remove families from the worse favelas in the city. Preference is given to families with incomes of less than three minimum salaries. SHAM, on the other hand, manages the affairs of seven conjuntos that cater primarily to working-class families whose total income is at least three minimum salaries. Whatever the criteria applied to applicants, the waiting lists for housing in these schemes are long. The Director of SHAM, for example, indicated that his agency alone had a backlog of more than 40,000 applicants.

Industrialization has, however, indirectly brought some improvements to the physical ambience of life in Manaus. It has necessitated, for example, the renovation of many public facilities, including the port, the construction of electrical plants in order to meet the energy requirements of new industries and commercial enterprises, the construction and renovation of water treatment facilities and, in order to service the increased traffic of goods and people, the construction of new transportation arteries. Despite the negative impact of some of these improvements on land values and the distribution of population, they have not been without some benefit to the population in general. In 1960, only 37 percent of the privately owned homes in Manaus were electrified; the number has now reached approximately 90 percent. Similarly, as compared to 35 percent in 1960, close to 70 percent of the homes in Manaus are now connected to the city's potable water network.[9]

Sanitation, however, remains a serious problem. Although the sanitation network has been partially renovated and greatly expanded, it has not been able to accommodate the growth in population. Approximately 16 percent of the 30,979 domiciles that existed in 1960 were connected to the public sanitation system. In 1980, only 15 percent of the city's 118,375 domiciles were similarly connected to the system. Even if financial resources were available, the system could not be extended to the drainage areas in which many of the favelas have formed. These areas aside, it is clear that financial resources have not been sufficient for developments in the sanitation system to keep pace with the growth in population. Families not connected to the sanitation network may install septic systems of dubious quality, if they can afford the expense. Those who cannot generally build out-houses over pits or, alternatively, they dump their sewage directly into the natural courses of drainage over which many of them live.[10] Related to sanitation are serious problems affecting the removal of *lixo* or garbage. Relative to its growth in population, the city had fewer vehicles with which to remove garbage in 1980 than it possessed in 1960.[11] Even in the central city garbage can remain in the streets, attracting vermin and rodents, sometimes for days before it is removed.

As a result of poor housing and the lack of significant improvements in sanitation, there persists in Manaus a serious problem of public health. In spite of vaccination programs, the construction of ambulatory clinics in many bairros, the provision of various types of medical assistance by employers in both the public and private sectors, and the organization of a medical school at the University of Amazonas, there has been no substantial improvement in the availability of health services relative to the increase in population. Most of the major medical facilities existing in the city were constructed prior to 1966, before the Zona Franca came into being. They have not been greatly expanded. In 1978, for example, the city counted approximately the same number of hospital beds, doctors, and auxiliary medical workers as it had in 1970. Accordingly, during this period the general death rate declined but slightly (from 11.1 to 9.08). The rate of infant mortality dropped from 52.5/1,000 in 1970 to 37.7 in 1975. It then begin to rise, reaching 46.8/1,000 in 1978.[12] Parasitic infections, related to poor sanitary conditions and contaminated water, remain the principal cause of death.[13]

Institutional Changes and Popular Culture

Many of the problems resulting from urban-industrial growth in Manaus relate more to the cultural than to the physical ambiance of life. One of the most critical of these problems concerns education. It may be recalled that many of the assemblage industries that now form the hegemonic sector (e.g., Jota and Agá) prefer to recruit workers who have completed a secondary education, as do employers in the commercial and public sectors. To the extent possible, they refrain from hiring individuals who have not completed at least a primary school education.[14] These recruitment preferences have generated an increased demand for educational services. How well have the state and federal governments responded to this demand?[15]

At the level of adult education, there exists the federally funded literacy program administered by MOBRAL (Movimento Brasileiro de Alfabetização). In 1970, only 5,063 students were enrolled in this program in Manaus. The following year, the number increased to 9,660. Between 1972 and 1978, MOBRAL substantially augmented its *convênios* or contracts and the number of adults enrolled in the program reached an annual average of more than 45,000. Despite these efforts, less than half of the adults who enrolled in this program in Manaus were subsequently deemed *alfabetizado* (i.e., literate).

All over Brazil, and certainly in Manaus, the investment of the federal and state governments in education at the primary and secondary levels has kept pace neither with the growth in population nor with the increased demand for more facilities of better quality.[16] In Manaus, between 1970 and 1978, enrollment at the primary school level increased from 22,717 to 125,775 (a relative increase of 454 percent).[17] However, because the teaching staff at this level was augmented by only 256 percent, the student-teacher ratio deteriorated. Although the number of rooms available in primary schools increased from 351 to 1400, the limitations of space were such that the system could operate only by allocating students to one of two separately scheduled daily sessions.

During the period under discussion, the situation at the secondary level improved more than at the primary level. Secondary school enrollment increased by only 156 percent (from 9,152 to 23,415). With the addition of 13 secondary schools, the number of classrooms increased by 220 percent. The student-teacher ratio remained approximately the same in 1978 as it was in 1970 (roughly 20 students per teacher). Still, either because of poor primary school preparation, financial circumstances, or the location of schools, a substantial proportion of the population between 14 and 18 years of age could not avail themselves of a secondary school education.

The most significant improvement in the educational system has come with the reorganization of the University of Amazonas and its entry into the federal university system. In addition to its long established faculty of law, the university now has professional programs in medicine, dentistry, engineering, and library science. It also offers postgraduate degrees in the biological sciences. In order to centralize its activities, all of which were previously conducted in a number of old, widely dispersed buildings in the center of the city, a new campus has been constructed.[18]

Between 1970 and 1978, the number of students enrolled at the university grew from 3,093 to 5,865.[19] The number receiving degrees increased from 279 to 493. Although the addition of faculty has more or less kept pace with the growth in enrollment, it has been extremely difficult for the university to recruit and retain more than a few faculty with doctoral degrees. Unless they are native to the region, as soon as they have completed their doctoral programs young faculty members look for employment elsewhere in Brazil. According to informants, the flight of "intellectuals" from Manaus is related, inter alia, to the city's cultural impoverishment, the unattractive working conditions that exist at the university, and to the professional isolation that one suffers as a result of regional location in the Amazon.

With reference to education, one needs to underscore the organization, mainly by the federal government, of various research institutes. The most influential of these are EMBRAPA (Empresa Brasileira de Pesquisa Agropecuária) and INPA (Instituto Nacional de Pesquisa da Amazônia). EMBRAPA, nationally organized under the Ministry of Agriculture, engages approximately 200 research scientists in Manaus. INPA, organized under CNPq (Centro Nacional de Pesquisa), is a research organization of international repute. It superintends the work of more than 300 research scientists, many from Europe and the United States. In association with various universities, including the University of Amazonas, INPA offers graduate courses and directs dissertation research mainly in the biological sciences.

The only other cultural institutions of note that exist in Manaus include libraries, newspapers, museums, cinemas, a zoo maintained by the military, radio and television stations, and what CODEMA calls "cultural associations." By CODEAMA's count, there are approximately 15 libraries in Manaus. Eight of these are federally administered (six at the university, one at EMBRAPA, and one at INPA), one is administered by the state, and six are private. The city contains six relatively small museums. Only one is an art museum. Although highly publicized, the Museu do Indio and the Museu do Instituto Geográfico e Histórico do Amazonas are not terribly impressive establishments even by local standards. It is noteworthy that the notoriety of all these museums has been significantly eclipsed by the construction of a new center in which is displayed the full range of products that are now produced in the Industrial District. This "showcase of industry" and the Teatro Amazonas were the only two cultural institutions considered worthy of mention by most of the workers included in the study.

Print media production in Manaus involves the publication of four dailies, one of which includes the state's official gazette. Of the three regular newspapers, only one represents an investment that followed upon the creation of the Zona Franca. Other than these dailies, there exist various weekly or monthly newssheets that are published for special distribution by unions, industrial firms, professional associations, and the like. There exists only one literary review, published annually by the State Academy of Letters. Of the remaining half dozen or more journals, most are the special publications of state or federal agencies, business associations, or cultural associations. Except for the daily newspapers, none of the print media have a popular distribution. As for cultural associations, only eight are listed by CODEAMA. Included among these are such organizations as the Institute of Geography and History, the Cultural Foundation of Amazonas, the Cultural Institute of Brazil and the United States (mainly offering language instruction), the Franco-Brazilian Cultural Association (also offering language instruction), and the Medical Association of Amazonas. Except for those that offer foreign language instruction and the Medical Association, none of these cultural organizations report a membership in excess of one hundred. Clearly, these associations have very little impact on "popular culture" in Manaus.

With respect to popular culture, most significant have been developments relating to the non-print media, particularly television. All four of the local television stations came into being with the Zona Franca. All but the educational network (Televisão Educativa do Amazonas), which is owned and operated by the state, are private and each is affiliated with one of the three major national networks. Based on observational data, television viewing is by far the most significant source of leisure in working-class households. A survey taken during a ten-day period in Costa da Silva revealed that over 90 percent of the households there were tuned into television between the hours of six and ten P.M.

Before 1967, Manaus had two cinemas. By 1978, it had six, located in or close to the center of the city. They vary considerably in their quality and seating capacity. Their price of admission is not high relative to working-class incomes and their evening programs are generally well attended, particularly on weekends. Nevertheless, perhaps because of television, the demand for film in Manaus seems not to have been sufficient to stimulate investment in cinemas relative to the growth in the city's overall population.[20]

Outside the home, apart from museums and the cinemas, provision for leisure or recreation is more or less confined to bars, discothèques, sports clubs, community centers, and public parks, or it involves church-related programs organized for particular interest groups. The best club facilities now available to working-class families are those extended to workers employed by some of the firms that form the hegemonic sector. Most of these are located in the Industrial District and they are not easily reached by public transportation. The old and well established sports clubs in the city (e.g., Ideal, Rio Negro, Nacional, or Olympico) continue to cater to *as famílias de alta-renda* (the families of high income). With but few exceptions, community centers exist only in some of the public housing schemes, where they receive financial support from the state. The recreational facilities associated with the schools are mostly play areas for young children. Manaus contains approximately forty *praças* or public parks. As noted in one report, "most of these (praças) do not present dimensions compatible with their functions and few possess features of special attraction."[21] As for *balneários* or bathing areas, there are two: Praia da Ponta Negra and Boa Vista. The former is twenty kilometers from the city and the latter is no less than thirty. Both are now connected to the city by bus service. Both these parks provide attractive facilities and while they are quite crowded on weekends, they are more extensively used by teenagers and young adults than by older members of the community.

Perhaps the most distinguishing cultural feature of Manaus is the city's matrix, or principal commercial center. With the creation of the Zona Franca and the construction of what is perhaps the very best international airport in all of Brazil, Manaus' commercial district, an area of not more than twenty square blocks, displays the features of a large bazaar. Most of the city's banks (approximately forty), hotels (now in excess of thirty), and retail sales outlets are located here. Throughout the week and even on Saturdays, the commercial district is absolutely congested with tourists, local shoppers looking for bargains, and with merchants and street hawkers. The traffic of Manauaras (local people) in this area cannot be approximated. With regard to tourists, not to mention those who arrive by boat, the annual flow through the international airport has increased by more than 500 percent. In 1983, the international airport registered well in excess of 300,000 disembarkations.[22]

As a result of urban-industrialization, the dimensions of change in Manaus are most graphic with respect to the explosive growth of its low income population. Because of this growth, the city contains twice the number of bairros occupying more than twice the urban space as in 1960. Even with the economic growth, there appears to be as much, if not more, poverty than previously existed. Certainly there exists a serious lack of adequate housing for large segments of the working class. As a result, almost none of the city's bairros have escaped the process of favelization. In conjunction with this economic transition, the state and federal governments have been unwilling or unable to sustain a proportionate level of development with respect to the pavement of streets, the extension of various sanitation services, and the provision of medical facilities. Accordingly, improvements in public health have not kept pace with growth in population and, as a consequence, both the rate of infant mortality and the death rate due to parasitic diseases remain almost as high as they were before.

Significant improvement in certain of the city's cultural institutions is also lacking. The primary and secondary systems of education remain critically deficient in terms of the location of schools, the availability of classrooms, and the quality of instruction. Although substantial improvements have been made with regard to higher education, the requirements of university admission continue to be based on vestibular examinations which discriminate against the majority of working-class families. Unlike many middle- and upper-class families, most working-class families can neither give their children the benefit of private education nor can they assume the cost of the special tutoring that many students obtain by way of preparing for the vestibular examinations. In addition, because they need to work and provide the family with income, young adults in working-class families cannot attend the university on a full-time basis and it is a requirement of the federal system that university students fit into a full-time schedule of courses. Thus, while developments in higher education may have somewhat enriched the city's cultural milieu, this has benefited mainly the middle and upper classes.

Apart from all of this, popular culture in Manaus is largely energized by commercial enterprises. These involve television, sport clubs which are commercially sponsored, sporting events, and the night life that centers on bars, discothèques, cinemas, and the like.[23] The annual folklore festival and carnival are similarly commercialized by sponsors. Certain religious festivals, particularly St. John's celebrations, are also becoming occasions of commercial sponsorship and advertisement. In fact, in some neighborhoods it was observed that even the festivals in celebration of parish saints have become the major occasion for raising parish funds by employing, on commission, various forms of commercial entertainment.

In short, the Zona Franca has served to transform a stagnating economy based primarily on the small-scale extraction of rubber and the collection of forest products into a dynamic economy precariously based on government subsidies, assemblage industries, and external markets. In the process of this transformation, Manaus has acquired most of the characteristics and problems associated with urban-industrial growth throughout much of Brazil and Latin America. In almost every area affecting the quality of life, the growth in population has dramatically outpaced the provision of human needs. Wages are low, the cost of living is high, public housing and services are inadequate, and because large segments of the working-class live at poverty's edge, favelization is widespread. At the same time, most of the city's cultural institutions are extensively commercialized and, thus, class based.

The working-class families under consideration are very much a part of this urban milieu but, in many respects, it did not seem to be much a part of them. That is to say, while they lived and worked in the city and were very much affected by developments in its economy, the city's cultural institutions did not seem to deeply touch their lives or shape their social consciousness. Indeed, apart from work, perhaps school, shopping, an occasional sporting event, or a rare evening at the cinema, social life for these working-class families was largely confined to the bairros in which they lived. Even here social life revolved mainly in and around whatever family, workmates, or former schoolmates lived nearby, in the bairro or vizinhança (neighborhood).

Bairros and Vizinhanças

Because of the rapidity and extent of urban growth, most bairros in Manaus, and perhaps most neighborhoods, are not formed by stable intergenerational populations that, over time, have developed a notable sense of traditional communal identity and organization. For the most part, bairros are little more than locational units on maps drawn by the city government. Indeed, except for the police station, the passage of garbage collection units, and the presence in some areas of street cleaners, the institutions of city government are virtually invisible in Manaus.[24] The state and federal governments not only dominate the media but they also dominate the vast array of agencies that intersect the lives of Manauaras with respect to health, education, welfare, jobs, unemployment benefits, and the like. Thus, from the point of view of informants, the only social image that the bairro seemed to invoke is locational; it is simply that section of the city in which they happened to live.

The image of the vizinhança or neighborhood assumes more complex dimensions. Sometimes informants make locational reference to the vizinhança, in which case it comprises the cluster of houses surrounding one's own. At other times, the reference is more social than locational, in which case the vizinhança is that group of people with whom one neighbors. It is often the case that these two referents do not correspond. Not infrequently the residents of nearby houses remain strangers and they do not engage one another as neighbors. Moreover, when making reference to the people with whom one neighbors, different members of the same household have different cognitive maps of their neighborhood. For some, neighbors may live next door or across the street. For others, the neighborhood includes people several streets removed from the one in which one lives. In short, while the bairro is strictly a locational unit of habitation for most informants, the neighborhood is a unit of social interaction and its locational referent may vary considerably for different members of the same household. Sometimes the neighborhood as a locational unit corresponds to the vizinhança as a unit of social interaction. This tends to be the case for Marapatá.[25]

Marapatá

Almost all of the families of sawmill workers in the employ of Serraria Paranaense lived at Enseada do Marapatá. The families of most of the remaining employees of this firm live in Educandos. Also living in Educandos, in neighborhoods not far from the place of their employment, are the families of the majority of workers employed by Serraria Amazonese. Marapatá and Educandos are markedly different in their physical, demographic, and cultural characteristics.

Marapatá is not an urban bairro. Its population consists entirely of the twenty-five or more families (the number fluctuates somewhat) that contain workers who are employed by Serraria Paranaense and who occupy company housing. In fact, employment at the company's mill is virtually the only condition of their residence. Thus, Marapatá has no form of municipal organization. Its "public" administration is entirely vested in the "patrão" of the sawmill, Senhor Schmidt. He provides the settlement with all of its essential services and with what little local governance it possesses. Its governance consists only of an implicit understanding between workers and the patrão that individuals and families who live at Marapatá conduct their affairs without nuisance to others and that they maintain the properties in which they are housed. Services include the provision of potable water, electricity, tools and supplies with which families can maintain their dwellings and, barring emergencies, transportation to shops in Educandos on Saturday afternoons. Also included is a classroom where children are given primary school instruction (by a non-resident teacher in the employ of the state). In effect, Marapatá is best described as a company compound. However, the compound does not have a store from which the workers are sold provisions by their employer.

Marapatá is situated in an forested area separated from the eastern bairros of Manaus by a military airfield (Areoporto de Ponta Pelada) and the Industrial Park. Two highways provide access to the area. One passes by the military airport and connects Marapatá with the urban bairro of Educandos, a distance of some ten kilometers. The other, a much longer route, passes through the Industrial Park and its closest link with Manaus is through Bairro Raiz. There are no public buses that pass beyond the airport and none operate through the Industrial Park. Thus, except for transportation provided by the patrão, or by one of the two resident families who own automobiles, the population at Marapatá lives in relative isolation from Manaus and its easternmost bairros.

The rhythm of social life at Marapatá is tuned to the work schedule of the mill. Except for lunch, adult males spend virtually all of their daylight hours at work. During the dark evenings of the workweek, they have little to do but remain at home, watching television with their families or visiting with a friend or a neighbor. If they drink socially and quite heavily, as some of them do, they tend to confine their drinking to the weekend, which begins at noon on Saturday. Whatever else they may do on the weekend, Saturday afternoon is the time during which they must avail themselves of transportation to Educandos in order to purchase their week's supply of food and other necessities.

Workers may make this weekly trip to Educandos with or without their wives and/or children. If they go to "the city" with their families, they generally return in the late afternoon or early evening. If they go only in the company of fellow workers, they may spend most of the evening hours visiting bars in Educandos. For some of these workers, these drinking bouts will be interrupted by a short night's sleep when they return to Marapatá. They will then continue to drink during games of dominoes until early Sunday afternoon. Drunk or sober, on Sunday afternoon these particular workers will return to their respective homes and generally remain there, relaxing or watching television, until they retire.

Workers who return early from their shopping trip to Educandos tend to remain at home with their families or visit with relatives or neighbors. In the evening, they relax in front of the television. Sunday morning, these workers and various members of their families may join one another in a game of soccer or volleyball. Alternatively, they may take walks with their families, supervise children at play, go fishing, or simply visit. Sunday afternoon and evening at Marapatá is a period during which almost everyone remains at home, resting or watching television. Except for a few children, very little movement can be observed out-of-doors. It is as if the entire community is preparing itself for another week of work.

During the year, there are only three occasions when virtually everyone living in this close community comes together as a group. On Christmas and New Year's Day, the patrão sponsors a "small party" for the entire community. Gifts are presented to children, food and drink are provided, and everyone attends. The third communal celebration falls in June when, on the feast of St. John's, when the workers themselves organize "a little festival."

Apart from the weekly shopping trip to Educandos, the community at Marapatá has virtually no connection with urban life in Manaus. None of the associations (e.g., neighborhood associations, community centers, youth clubs, religious organizations, etc.) that one might encounter in an urban neighborhood are to be found there. Other than the firm that employs them, the teacher who offers some of their children classes, and the labor union to which the workers belong, no organization based in Manaus has representation in the community. All of the community's inhabitants declare themselves Catholic but there is no church at the mill and, except for an occasional visit by a priest (three or four times each year), there is no schedule of public religious services. Similarly, all of the workers interviewed claimed membership in the union but the sindicato has never formed a meeting at Marapatá and only one of the many informants interviewed there had ever attended a meeting of the sindicato at its headquarters in the Industrial District.

Despite the spatial separation of houses in two clusters at Marapatá, most inhabitants view the settlement as forming a single neighborhood within which everyone knows everyone else. Internally, however, the neighborhood is structured by a minor but generally acknowledged division between the twenty-two families whose regional origin is Paraná and the three Amazonense families of Caboclo origin. For the most part, social encounters between members of these ethnic-like categories tend to be confined to the workplace and sharing a few drinks while shopping in Educandos.

More significant than this division, however, is the extent to which the neighborhood is internally structured by kinship networks that have been reinforced by the company's recruitment procedures. These are further interlaced by friendship networks which have been formed as a consequence of prolonged service with the same employer and are reinforced by the relative isolation of these families from the city. Given the homogeneity of status, occupation, and ethno-regional origin of this population, except for age and sex, the only social differentiation of any significance within the community is with reference to friendship networks and kinship.

As suggested, kinship and friendship networks in the neighborhood are not mutually exclusive. Kinship relationships are pervasive. Well over half the workers who were randomly selected for initial in-depth interviews turned out to be related to one another as fathers and sons, brothers, brothers-in-law, or as uncles and nephews. Although the design of the research did not provide for the systematic collection of genealogical data, a cautious estimate would suggest that two-thirds or more of the children in these twenty-two families count one another as siblings or cousins. Still, informants draw a distinction between friends and relatives. As often as not, they listed as "friends" individuals who are not counted among their relatives. Because these networks are not co-extensive, patterns of mutual assistance, borrowing or loaning money or items of food, and the like, cross the boundaries of kinship. While such exchanges are common, according to informants, they tend to be much more frequent among close kin (e.g., parents and children or siblings) than among friends who do not share a bond of kinship.

Emerging from the matrices of these structures is a multiplicity of social circles within which individuals in the community tend to engage in somewhat different forms of social activity. Those who engage in weekly drinking bouts, for example, appear to form two relatively exclusive friendship circles. It is also the case that the participants in these two groups are among those workers who have very few, if any, relatives in the community. Similarly, most of the workers whose families join for a game of soccer on Sunday morning are related to one another.

The intensity and peculiarity of visiting patterns with respect to households also appears to coincide somewhat with the extension of kinship and the differentiation of families.

Social life in the community at Marapatá centers on family, kin, and workmates who are friends. Except for Parananenses and Caboclos, individuals in the community are socially stratified only by age, sex, and kinship status. Differences of education, income, and family wealth are minimal. To the extent that differences in wealth exist, they are reflected in the possession of an automobile and perhaps a telephone. Such differences are not a function of occupation or even of seniority at work, but rather they relate to family size and the number of gainfully employed workers the household happens to contain. Outside the mill, social encounters are somewhat more intense among kin than non-kin but these boundaries are not sharply drawn while at leisure. Within the household, unoccupied time is largely consumed by television. Outside the household, unoccupied time is consumed mostly by shopping in Educandos or, at Marapatá, by soccer, volleyball, drinking, or visiting with workmates and relatives.

Educandos

By way of contrast to Marapatá, Educandos is in every sense an urban bairro. From across Igarapé de Educandos, the bairro faces the commercial center of Manaus. In the early 1900s, this area existed completely outside of the city. Its settlement was significantly affected by its locational features. Because it could be easily accessed by the river transportation system, the area became a favorable site for the establishment of industries tied to the extraction of forest products. By the 1940s, with a new church and elementary schools, Educandos was generally recognized as a well integrated "industrial suburb" (Benchimol 1977: 76–77). Among its industries the bairro included sawmills, a rubber mill, and a plant for processing Brazil nuts. In 1941, Panair do Brasil (a subsidiary of Pan American) located its airport on the eastern edge of the bairro and, in cooperation with the Rubber Development Corporation (an agency of the U.S. Government), Panair constructed a paved road through the bairro, connecting it and the airport more directly to the central city.

With these developments, Educandos emerged as one of the most industrialized bairros in Manaus. Its residential population became overwhelmingly composed of working-class families dependent upon employment in the traditional industrial sector. As the population increased, the community acquired a thriving commercial district of its own. This commercial district is distinguished not so much by its small-scale retail outlets as by its large number of night spots and drinking establishments. Because of the latter, Educandos acquired a reputation as a troublesome working-class bairro, a nightly hangout for prostitutes, rowdy drinkers, petty thieves and, more recently, drug peddlers.

By 1978, Educandos contained more than 4,400 domiciles and a population in excess of 25,000. One of the smallest of the city's bairros in total area (75 hectares), it ranked among the five most densely populated. Of its urban space, 25 percent was occupied by thoroughfares, 20 percent by commercial enterprises, 5 percent by industry, and 5 percent by public institutions (mainly churches and schools). Considering that only 35 percent of the area is available and/or suitable for housing, the residential density of Educandos is in excess of 900 inhabitants/hectare. Thus, it is not surprising that there exists today in Educandos a large number of excessively crowded neighborhoods with almost impassable streets, poorly constructed homes, and inadequate public sanitation. It is estimated that more than 7,000 of the bairro's inhabitants are gainfully employed. A substantial but unknown percentage of this number work in industries located close to the neighborhoods in which they live.[26] This is certainly the case for those workers who are employed in the wood-processing industry.[27]

The urban scene in Educandos reveals a multiplicity of institutions, organizations, and associations that are completely lacking at Marapatá. Most visible are those of public administration and security, primary schools, and churches of various denominations. Among the voluntary associations are organized groups for children, teenagers, mothers, the elderly, recreational groups, and a few neighborhood councils. Informant data suggest that most of these voluntary organizations and associations struggle to maintain a membership. Many of them are frequently formed out of a burst of interest on the part of a small group of people; they persist for a brief time and then disappear for lack of continued leadership or interest on the part of their participants.

Participation in church-related groups is a case in point. Most of the families studied in Educandos considered themselves to be moderately-to-fervently religious. Still, very few in these families gave evidence of identifying with a local church, parish, or spiritist group. The periodic observation of religious celebrations in Catholic as well as Protestant churches revealed that it was mainly elderly women and school children who participated. Except for the celebration of weddings, baptisms, funerals, parish festivals (which assume a carnival-like atmosphere), and Christmas, the participation of adult males in these services rarely reaches a level of ten percent of those in attendance. None of the men who were interviewed in Educandos could provide the name of the priest or local minister for churches located in or close to the neighborhoods in which they lived.

It is not known how many neighborhoods in Educandos contain neighborhood associations. The existence of only one could be authenticated among the five neighborhoods in which informants were distributed. Although a few informants had heard that some neighborhoods had organizations of this type, none knew whether or not an association existed in their own neighborhood. In fact, except for limited church participation and perhaps membership in a soccer group, it is not an exaggeration to state that voluntary associations scarcely touched the social life of adults in these working-class families. Although the children in these families might be involved in youth groups at school or the church, except for a few mothers (usually elderly women in their fifties and sixties), the parents almost never assisted in the organization or supervision of such groups.

In large part, the social life of the sawmill workers living in Educandos is circumscribed by work schedules and conditions that do not differ appreciably from those that exist at Marapatá. However, once they leave their work, they immediately enter and move about in a distinctly urban milieu. There is, as Roberto DaMatta (1985) would describe it, a life in the streets. This is certainly evident as workers proceed home from their places of employment. Unlike the workers at Marapatá, those in Educandos visit shops, stop at bars, or catch a bus to the central city. At one time or another, some of them do all of these things. Generally, however, most walk from Serraria Amazonense to their separate neighborhoods in small groups and, almost as a matter of routine, they will interrupt their journey home by spending an hour or two at one of a half dozen or more of the bars close to the mill. Invariably, the conversation attending these diversions centers on work, football, women, inflation, the cost of living, political corruption, and sometimes personal problems. When the mill closes and pay envelopes are received at Saturday noon, many of these bar groups collect for the remainder of the afternoon and some party well into the evening. In fact, some of these workers will rejoin their friends and workmates on Sunday, either at home or in a neighborhood bar.[28]

This pattern of behavior is not so evident among the workers from Paraná who live in Educandos with their families at the depósito of Serraria Paranaense. At the end of the workday, most of these workers generally go directly to their homes. The few that do not may gather, but only briefly, at a bar across from the depósito. Also, considerably less drinking was observed among these workers on the weekends than among their fellow workers at Marapatá or among other sawmill workers in Educandos. When asked to explain this, one housewife stated: "Here at the depósito we live under the eyes of the patrão and his son. It is a good thing because the men are not always drunk and life for the family is much better. At Marapatá one does not often see the patrão on the weekend and there is not much to do but drink and watch television. Here, we sometimes go to church, the cinema, or visit the shops (in downtown Manaus)."

Within the neighborhoods of Educandos, communal life for the older members of these families centers primarily on relationships among relatives and workmates who live nearby. That of the younger members, particularly if they have grown up in the neighborhood, tends to be more oriented to former schoolmates than workmates. Because of the urban character and complexity of these neighborhoods, however, there are important differences. The movement of population in and out of these neighborhoods is such that neighbors often remain anonymous or relative strangers to one another. Social encounters with these individuals tend to be fragmented, brief, and almost always in the street. As numerous informants stated when asked about their relationship to neighbors: "I do not know my neighbors well." "I almost never visit with them." "My relationship is good morning, good afternoon, or good evening." Or, "We talk only in passing." Even if neighbors are long standing and relatively well known to one another, unless they are close friends, neighboring is typically done in the street (in front of the home, at the market, or perhaps a bar). Close friends may visit one another's homes with some degree of regularity but, in Educandos, these are more often workmates who live in the neighborhood. Alternatively, they are older women who may be involved in some church-related activity.

Relations based on kinship, as previously noted, are pervasive among the families at Marapatá. This is somewhat less the case in Educandos. Approximately 70 percent of the workers interviewed at Serraria Amazonense have consanguineal or affinal relatives living in Educandos. However, these families are considerably more scattered and it is exceptional for more than one or two of them to live nearby, in the same neighborhood. Visiting patterns among kin, however, tend to center on families living "nearby." Still, even among these propinquitous households, social relationships are neither as frequent nor as intense as they are at Marapatá. This is particularly the case among the younger members of these families who report briefly visiting the nearby home of an uncle, a grandparent, or even a sibling, perhaps once a week. Visited much less often, or not at all, are kin living in more distant neighborhoods.

Propinquity is not the only factor affecting the character of these relationships. Among the families at Marapatá, everyone who is gainfully employed works at the sawmill. This is not the case in Educandos where even various members of the same household are much more likely to be occupationally diversified. They are employed in different sectors of the economy and they work in different parts of the city. As a consequence, they are connected to social networks that do not often intersect. In the context of these networks, and according to the interests that they share with workmates or former schoolmates, members of the same household, not to mention those of different households, are not drawn into intense relationships with one another. They of course come together in the home, but outside the home, according to their different interests and social networks, they tend to go their separate ways.

Still, it should be emphasized that relationships within the family remain the mainstay of social life in Educandos. Apart from the time they spend at work, the workers at Serraria Amazonense spend more time at home with their families than they spend in the streets, socializing with workmates and neighbors. However, social encounters with kin who do not live nearby are much less frequent. Such encounters often occur by chance. Otherwise, they involve scheduled celebrations (e.g., a baptism, perhaps the birthday of a parent, or Christmas) or they are provoked by a family crisis (e.g., an illness or a death).

Raiz[29]

In 1978, Raiz contained approximately 3,900 households with a population in excess of 22,000. In total area, the bairro is somewhat larger than Educandos. And, with approximately 460 residents/hectare, it is less densely populated than Educandos.[30] Perhaps because of its location, away from the river, Raiz contains virtually no industry. The bairro is connected to the central city, a distance of approximately six kilometers, by two thoroughfares that pass through the most densely populated of the city's eastern bairros. Both these thoroughfares are well serviced by the public transportation system and residents enjoy rather easy access to downtown Manaus and, from there, to virtually all parts of the city.

Whether because of its lack of industry, its location and easy access to the center of the city, or for some other reason, it is also the case that Raiz does not contain a large commercial district of its own. There is but one small district in which there exists a significant concentration of retail outlets, mostly supermarkets, pharmacies, and luncheonettes where one can eat as well as drink beer and cachaça. There are only two or three major nightspots in the entire bairro and these are mainly hangouts for teenagers or unmarried adults. Raiz has no public parks, no private schools, no secondary schools, and its only primary school is shared with a neighboring bairro.

Within the boundaries of Raiz there exist two Catholic churches, Cristo-Rei and Nossa Senhora do Carmo. Each is located in a different neighborhood, a very short walk from one another, and both are served by the same *padre* or priest. There also exist three Protestant churches. One is a newly constructed and relatively large Methodist church with a rapidly growing congregation. The Methodist church is situated next-door to Nossa Senhora do Carmo. A short walk from these, on the edge of a favela, is a small and somewhat older church of the Baptist congregation. The Baptist congregation is not large but its members are active proselytizers and the congregation is growing. The third Protestant church is a relatively new one constructed by the Adventists, close to Cristo-Rei. The Adventist congregation remains small but because of its proselytizing, it too is growing. All of these churches feature organized youth groups, classes for religious instruction, altar societies, bible groups, mothers' groups, and the like.

Reflecting the history of its residential settlement, the social composition of the population in Raiz is considerably more heterogeneous than that of Educandos. In the 1950s much of what is now Raiz was *mata* or jungle. The urban population from the easternmost bairro of Manaus, Cachoeirinha, began to spill into these vacant lands. By the end of the decade, the settlement of Raiz was well underway. However, what most stimulated the influx of population into Raiz was the decision taken by the federal and state governments in 1965 to renovate and extend Manaus' port facilities in conjunction with the impending creation of the Zona Franca. In order to implement this project, it became necessary to eliminate the so-called *Cidade Flutuante*, the previously mentioned favela that had grown on the Rio Negro, next to the main port.

To advance the project, with assistance from the Federal Government, the Governor of Amazonas formed public agencies (e.g., Cooperativa de Habitação do Amazonas–COHAB-AM and Sociedade de Habitação do Estado do Amazonas–SHAM) and charged them with the responsibility of constructing *conjuntos* of low-cost public housing to which the inhabitants of the "floating city" and other favelas could be removed. All of these conjuntos were to be constructed in what were then considered peripheral areas. It was decided to locate the first of these conjuntos, Costa da Silva, in Raiz.[31] Not quite according to plan, Costa da Silva was constructed in two phases. In the first phase, COHAB built approximately 90 houses along a bluff overlooking the rest of the neighborhood. Subsequently, SHAM built an additional 381 houses in the low-lying area that existed below the bluff and which, for lack of drainage, became virtually a swamp whenever it rained.[32]

Many of the houses built in the first phase of construction were sold to families selected by lot from the "floating city." By the time the second phase of construction was completed, however, the "floating city" had been eliminated and all of its inhabitants removed. Accordingly, a good number of houses built during the second phase of construction were sold to working-class families selected by lot from among SHAM's general pool of applicants for placement in public housing schemes. Unlike those families that moved to Costa da Silva from the "floating city," one of Manaus' poorest favelas, those drawn from the general pool of applicants for public housing were considerably more diversified in their economic status. Thus, from the beginning, the settlement of Costa da Silva enjoined some degree of social stratification in its construction and occupation.

In the early 1970s another housing conjunto, Jardim Brasil, was also constructed in Raiz. Jardim Brasil is located on the southern boarder of the bairro, approximately eight blocks removed from Costa da Silva and across the street from Nossa Senhora do Carmo and the Methodist Church. It forms a somewhat different working-class neighborhood from Costa da Silva. Unlike the latter, Jardim Brasil is not comprised of separately constructed houses. Instead, it was designed as a rather unattractive complex of fourteen, four-storied, tightly compacted, concrete block buildings containing 450 low-cost, two- and three-bedroom apartments. Originally, Jardim Brasil was not a public enterprise. Its construction was initiated by a private firm which sold apartments to buyers with sufficient capital to negotiate mortgage loans. Accordingly, Jardim Brasil came to be occupied by a somewhat higher strata of working-class families. Subsequently, however, the firm that constructed and managed the conjunto declared bankruptcy and the Banco Nacional de Habitação assumed responsibility for outstanding mortgages and the conjunto, in effect, became a public housing scheme under the organizational supervision of COHAB.[33]

During the early period of its settlement, the construction of housing in Raiz was not limited to these developments. Even before these housing schemes were initiated, large portions of Raiz consisted of privately owned land. In time, almost all of this land was divided and sold for the construction of homes. In addition, the bairro also contained tracts of public land that were invaded by families who constructed houses without title. Most of these homes are among the poorest in the bairro. This is certainly the case for those that form a cluster of neighborhoods strung north to south, along and over the entire drainage basin that divides Raiz on its western border from the neighboring bairro of Cachoeirinha. The appearance of the neighborhoods in this drainage area is such that one would think that the "Cidade Flutuante" was not eliminated but only pushed back from the Rio Negro, into Igarapé da Cachoeirinha, the upland tributary of Igarapé de Educandos. For convenience, we shall identify this nameless section of Raiz as Novo Santo. Consider, first, the living conditions and the social and cultural life of families living in this section of the bairro.

Novo Santo

Novo Santo is a densely impacted favela. Most of the homes in the neighborhood are of makeshift construction and many are so badly built that during the rainy season various household contents are rearranged in order to protect them from the elements and pans have to be put out to catch the water. The majority of these houses are built on stilts over the swampland formed by the slow running water course that carries sewage through the badly polluted drainage. Adding to the pollution, all of these dwellings have attached outhouses which dump into the water beneath them. The streets, if indeed they can be called streets, are formed by a shaky network of stilted plank walkways on which young children play dangerously over the water. At night, these plank walkways are dimly lit by low wattage bulbs socketed in wires strung on makeshift poles. On both sides of the drainage, the walkways are connected by planks to streets that parallel the banks of the drainage system. The streets also are poorly lit, unpaved, and often almost impassable because of the mud formed by rain or by the waste material that flows into them from the houses constructed along and above them.

Novo Santo is where the poorest segment of Raiz's working-class population lives. Although half of the ten families investigated in this neighborhood formed multiple income households, seven of the ten reported earning two minimum salaries or less and none earned more than four. Moreover, four of these ten families lived in houses for which they paid rent to "slumlords" who also lived in the favela. Adding to this impoverishment, there existed few social amenities in the favela. There were no neighborhood associations, no clubs, in fact, no semblance of communal organization. The only recreational facilities consisted of the drinking establishments that were situated outside the neighborhood, in Avenida Costa da Silva. In the stilted network of walkways there are no places where more than two or three adults can conveniently gather for conversation and, except along the banks of the drainage, there are no streets in which children can play.

The lack of community organization, voluntary associations, recreational facilities, and the like, appears to be of little consequence to the people living in Novo Santo. Most of them do not command the minimal resources that they felt were necessary to be active without embarrassment in the affairs of even church-related groups that might ask them for small donations of food or money. Consequently, except for the prayer groups to which a few of the women and one or two of the men belonged, according to informants in and outside of the neighborhood, the members of these households are rarely involved in organized groups or functions.

A characteristic feature of Novo Santo is that when a family takes possession (by purchase or invasion) of land on which two or more cabanas or small houses can be constructed, a pocket settlement of related families will usually emerge. Approximately half of the families sampled formed what might be called small extended family clusters. In light of these family clusters and the lack of opportunity for "street life," it is not surprising that informants in Novo Santo tended to divide the people living there into two categories: relatives and strangers. Neighbors who are not relatives are not only thought of as strangers but it is generally the case that they are indeed strangers. Because of the movement of people into and out of the community, the non-kin among one's neighbors are not often sufficiently well-known to be counted among friends. As a matter of fact, when members of these households were asked to identify their five closest friends, either they listed members of the immediate family, or relatives living nearby, or they listed workmates and almost none of these workmates lived in the neighborhood. The children of neighbors who are strangers may play or go to school with one another, but these school friendships do not seem to join their parents in visiting relationships or reciprocal exchanges. On the contrary, several informants cited the behavior of children in this very congested area as a major source of the conflict and bickering that seemed to characterize relationships among neighbors who were not kin.

Thus, the social lives of these workers and their families do not extend much beyond the home. The married adults in these households spend most of their free time at home, watching television, or visiting with relatives if they live nearby. Those who are not married may interrupt this routine by having a few beers with friends or workmates outside the immediate neighborhood. Alternatively, they may visit the parks and walk the streets in downtown Manaus, or attend a "little party" with a girlfriend or a boyfriend. They do not frequent the cinemas. A few mentioned an occasional, one-day, excursion to the beach at Ponta Negra. They seldom read or buy newspapers. And, unless they visit relatives in the interior, they do not travel outside the city. What they know of other parts of Brazil is mostly what they see on television. During the July holiday, they remain close to home and, if possible, they will spend their vacation time working in order to earn a little extra income with which to buy clothing, repair the house, or pay off the debts they acquire when they have to buy food or clothing on credit.

All of this is perhaps best illustrated by the comments of informants. Maria Duarte, an electronics worker, lives in a small, poorly constructed, three-room house, with her parents, two sisters, and two brothers. She and her parents work and the family income is three minimum salaries. She stated: "My married brother lives in the house in back and we are like one family. My two grandmothers live in Manaus but not nearby. I see them only once or twice a year. I have many aunts and uncles scattered all over the city. I do not know most of their names, what they do, or where they live. Except for my brother, we visit with my grandmothers and a few relatives mainly when we come together for a little celebration at Christmas."

When asked about her friends and neighbors, she stated: "My mother participates in everything at church but we have almost nothing to do with neighbors. We stay away from them because they are only trouble. My friends are all at work. None of them live in the neighborhood. Sometimes I go to bars with my friends or we have a little party somewhere. Mostly everyone stays at home and watches television." Entering the discussion, her mother stated: "I go to the church every week but none of the family goes." Her husband added: "We all go to midnight mass on Christmas Eve. God does not need to see me at church and I have no money to give to the priest. I have no time for the neighbors. They are people I do not know."

Similarly, Santos Lima Gomes lives in a two-room cabana, constructed on his mother's "property," with his common-law wife and son. He earns one minimum salary at Agá. Except for one table, two hammocks, and five wooden boxes, the house contains no furniture. Three of the boxes serve as chairs. On the fourth is a color television unit. The fifth serves as a cabinet for a stereophonic unit. Santos Lima stated: "My house is surrounded by relatives. My mother and three sisters live in front. My brother and his wife live to the side and on the other side I have a sister who lives with her husband. In back, of course, is a sewer. I have many aunts, uncles, and cousins in Manaus. I am told that some live on a hill somewhere but I have never been there. My neighborhood is my family. The rest are strangers. My life here is very simple. I work all day and after work, if I have money, I drink with a few friends at the bar in Avenida Costa da Silva. On Saturday and sometimes on Sunday, I stay at the bar all day and get drunk. I come home quietly and do not bother anybody. My mother wants me to join the Baptist church but I drink too much for those people." And what about your wife? What does she do? His wife, Maria, smiled: "I stay home, wash, clean, watch television, and visit with my sisters-in-law. Sometimes I go to the bar with my husband."

Except for the little money he earns (less than one minimum salary) repairing television units, Roberto Dias has been unemployed since losing his job at Agá. His wife earns one minimum salary from her work at Jota. Together with their four children they occupy a two-room cabana in Novo Santo. Roberto stated: "My mother lives in the next bairro and I visit with her every week. My wife has a brother, a sister, and an aunt in Manaus. We sometimes see them at Christmas. Recently my wife converted to the Jehovah Witness church and she goes there with the children but I have not made up my mind about this." When asked what they do together with their neighbors, Roberto's wife responded: "We do not have enough money to do anything. We cannot even fix the roof of this ugly house to keep out the rain. The neighbors here are not very friendly. They are mostly strangers with us. We only see them bickering with one another because of the kids. We stay at home and they stay at home. There is no visiting except with my friends at work and at the church. My husband mostly visits his mother. We have no money to do anything or go anywhere with the children."

Jardim Brasil

Living conditions in Jardim Brasil are somewhat different and immeasurably better than those that exist in Novo Santo. Physically, the conjunto is formed by the parallel arrangement of fourteen, block-constructed, four-storied apartment buildings. The area occupied by these buildings is fenced off from adjacent neighborhoods and the traffic of Avenida Costa da Silva. Access to the conjunto is loosely controlled by a privately employed security force. The alleys separating the apartment blocks are all paved but their construction is far too narrow and too obstructed to allow for the passage of automobiles or even motorcycles. The only internal street runs north to south, perpendicular to the apartment blocks and parallel to the line of their construction. At the midpoint of the complex, this street is broken by the location of a building that provides a meeting place for the association of *moradores* (proprietors). To assist in the financing of a few neighborhood festivities, the association commissions out of this building a small lunch counter where children can buy sweets and soft drinks and adults can buy beer and cachaça. The conjunto has no pool, recreational facilities, playground equipment, or designated play areas for children. Children play in the street or in the alleys between the buildings. Still, unlike the children in Novo Santo, they do not play dangerously on stilted walkways or in unpaved streets muddied by rain and sewage.

Judging from the households included in the sample and from informant interviews, perhaps 60 percent or more of the families living in Jardim Brasil form multiple income households. Two-thirds of the families surveyed reported earning five minimum salaries per month or less. The vast majority own or are paying mortgages on their apartments.

Almost all of the apartments in the conjunto open noisily on one another across deeply shaded alleys. The apartments are small relative to the size of most families (some contain as many as fifteen people) and crowded by television units, stereophonic equipment, and other household furnishings. In general, the families who live in these apartments do not like them and they complain endlessly about living conditions in the conjunto. As one informant emphasized: "These apartments were made for lower class people. Mine is one of the worse in Manaus. We live here because we have to and when I have enough money, I plan to sell this apartment and build a house of my own. There is no room for the kids in these apartments. They have to play below, in the alleyways or in the streets and we do not see the things they do there."

There appears to be a considerable amount of turnover in the apartment units at Jardim Brasil. Walking through the conjunto, one can always spot several units advertised for sale or rent and there always seems to be a family moving in or out of one block or another. When they marry, the children within these households move out as soon as they can find a place in which to live because the apartments are too small for extended family units. And when they move out, even if it were their choice, most could not afford to rent or buy an apartment in the conjunto. Consequently, neighbors in the conjunto are almost always non-kin and often they are complete strangers.

Luiz Ferreira Lima, for example, describes the situation in his section of the block. "I have lived here," he stated, "for five years. I hardly know the people who live on my floor. The apartment across has been rented twice and I have never seen this new neighbor. The one across is a man and his wife but we do not know their names. The one on the other side was recently sold. I have seen the people who live there but we do not know them even in passing." Or, in the case of Evandro Motta who has lived with his parents in Jardim Brasil for almost fifteen years: "The conjunto is like a bee's nest. I know many people in the building but also I do not know them. I have only one friend who lives here. We went to school together. Most of my friends are schoolmates and workmates and they do not live here."

Thus, outside the immediate household, not many families can count relatives who live in Jardim Brasil. They know most of their neighbors casually or not at all. And, because of the physical construction of the apartment blocks, the neighbors with whom families are most familiar are not those who occupy adjacent apartments but rather those who live a few feet away, on the same level and directly across the alley from their own apartment. Most neighboring occurs not in the narrow hallways or stairways that connect floors in separate sections of the same block but among members of households that face one another across the alley. Conversations among these neighbors are conducted from little balconies that protrude from each apartment unit. Weather permitting, the doors to these balconies remain open throughout the day and from their vantage point one can see and hear almost everything that transpires in the living room across. Hence, families living across the alley become more acquainted with one another's affairs than those who occupy adjacent apartments on the same floor of the building. It is on these balconies that the women hang their wash and members of the household go to "take air" or view a small section of the sky above or the alleyway below. It is also from these balconies that women discuss television programs and family problems of mutual interest, and men converse about the weather, their jobs, politics, the soccer game they are watching, or arrange to meet one another for a drink at a nearby bar.

For the most part, the social life of young adults living in these apartments draws them out of the house and outside the conjunto. Their friends are mostly old schoolmates and workmates who live in other neighborhoods of Raiz or in neighboring bairros. As one young informant stated: "There is nothing for us to do here in the conjunto. The apartments are too small for parties and if you should have one with friends there would be too much gossip." Hence, young adults spend much of their free time away from Jardim Brasil. They frequent the bars, the "discos," the cinema. They attend parties and, if they have access to a car, they spend Sunday at the beach. Some who work for the hegemonic firms, particularly those who are not married, make use of the clubs and recreational facilities that their employers provide.

Concerning the neighborhood as a community, it evinces but a modicum of organization. There is a neighborhood association, which is presumably formed by proprietors who meet and elect its officers. In effect, it is comprised of a very small group of "regulars," mostly original proprietors who have lived in the conjunto for many years and who expressly shared an interest in maintaining the conjunto's physical ambiance. The activities of this small group elicit very little interest from most moradores. Among the informants interviewed, not a single one had ever attended a meeting of the association. No one in their families could name a single one of the association's officers or describe how their infrequent meetings were normally conducted. All that was known of the association was the fact that it sells food and drinks and holds raffles in order to raise money with which to organize an occasional weekend dance with the use of sound equipment. The association's major community event, however, is the celebration of the Festival of St. John's. For this occasion, the moradores are asked to participate by contributing a little food and money. Lights are strung, professional musicians are hired, and late into the night there is much dancing, eating, and drinking by all who attend.

Nossa Senhora do Carmo, the parish church that is located close to Novo Santo and directly across the street from Jardim Brasil, assumes no direct role in organization of either of these neighborhoods. Conversely, not many people from these neighborhoods assume a role in the organization of church celebrations or parish affairs. Two masses are offered on Sunday, one in the morning and one in the evening. Because of baptisms and the relatives that attend them, the church is generally filled on Sunday morning. Even then, 90 percent of the attendance is comprised of women and children. In the evening, the congregation is quite small. The mass celebrated on Christmas Eve, which is usually followed by a family dinner, is the only occasion on which a substantial number of men claim to attend church with their wives and children.

Apart from Christmas Eve, there are only two festive occasions based at Nossa Senhora that draw many participants from their homes in the surrounding neighborhoods. One of these, held in July, is the annual celebration of the feast of Nossa Senhora. The other, usually held in November, is arraial. The feast of Nossa Senhora begins with a procession that assumes all of the characteristics of a small parade. In 1984, the procession was led by a van with loudspeakers over which hymns were played and a few prayers were said. It departed from the church and followed a relatively short route of approximately twelve blocks. Following the van was a file of perhaps 400 parishioners, a great many of whom were children dressed in school uniforms. The members of the church youth group wore white tee-shirts with a picture of Christ emblazoned over the heart. Some of the women in the parade wore white dresses decorated with red sodality emblems. In the middle of the procession was a flatbed truck which carried an icon of Nossa Senhora do Carmo. The icon was decorated with ribbons and flowers and surrounded by six young girls dressed in white and wearing a pair of angel's wings. The end of the procession was brought up by a small uniformed band of the local fire brigade. The parade terminated at the church where an altar was decorated on a flatbed truck for the celebration of an outdoor mass. The altar was parked in front of a store that separated the courtyard of Nossa Senhora from that of the new Methodist Church. Less than half of the participants in the parade remained for the celebration of mass. During the mass, a few street vendors, including a nephew of the priest, hawked food and trinkets among the celebrants.

At the conclusion of the mass, a few women presented cakes and food to the priest. These gifts were used mainly for the entertainment of guests whom he invited into his home. There were not many invited guests, only the five or six parishioners who had helped Father Fernando with the organization of the festival. During the course of this little repast, Father Fernando somewhat bitterly expressed his disappointment with the festivities. He claimed that the Protestant churches in Raiz were distracting hiɔ congregation and he was quite perplexed to explain it.[34] He also complained that his parishioners in Manaus, unlike those he had served as a young priest in the state of Alagoas, " . . . know so little about Nossa Senhora do Carmo that they do not show much interest in celebrating her feastday."

The second festival that engages some degree of communal participation is arraial. The arraial, however, is fundamentally secular and only indirectly serves a religious function. It is best described as a small carnival-like affair that the parish organizes each year for the purpose of raising funds with which to repair and maintain the church and provide some support for parish programs. Arraial assumes a somewhat different character in different parishes but its observance is widespread in Brazil. In Raiz, because Father Fernando serves as the pastor for two adjacent neighborhood parishes (Nossa Senhora do Carmo and Cristo-Rei), both parishes join in the organization of arraial.

The carnival itself takes place in the more spacious churchyard at Cristo-Rei, in the neighborhood of Costa da Silva. Preparation for the carnival begins with the organization of volunteers. Among them, women from the *irmandades* or sodalities solicit gifts of food and money from parishioners. Not many men volunteer their time to the festival. A few build booths but most of the work involved in decorating the churchyard and the booths is done by members of the youth group. The carnival itself begins late Friday afternoon and closes at midnight. The affair continues Saturday afternoon and evening. Cakes and clothing are raffled, food and soft drinks are sold, and various games of chance are played. A few mechanical rides, including a ferris wheel, are hired on a commission basis for the purpose of drawing attendance as well as raising additional income. Relative to the population of Raiz, the number who attended this affair was not very impressive. Certainly at any given time not more than fifty-to-sixty people could be counted in the churchyard and usually the majority of these were children and teenagers living not in Jardim Brasil or Novo Santo but Costa da Silva. In fact, the entire festival appeared to draw most of its support from Costa da Silva and not from the neighborhoods surrounding Nossa Senhora do Carmo.[35]

Other than Father Fernando and those of his relatives who live with him (e.g., his mother, two young brothers, two sisters, a brother-in-law, and the latter's two children), the church activists in the parish of Nossa Senhora do Carmo include mainly an irmandade, an altar society comprised of elderly women, and the youth group. The overall membership of both is small and that of the youth group is constantly changing. Within the irmandade there is a core of perhaps a dozen women who assist the priest in various parish functions, including liturgical services, decorating the altar, visiting the sick, prayer meetings, and organizing the church's two major events, the celebration in honor of the patroness Nossa Senhora and arraial.

The youth group is comprised of fifteen to twenty teenagers, perhaps a dozen of whom seem to meet with some regularity, two or three times a month. For the most part, the youth group attempts to attract membership by seeking to organize educational and recreational activities (liturgical discussions, games, field trips, and the like). Apart from this, various members of the group make themselves available to assist Father Fernando in whatever task for which he might need assistance. Each Saturday morning, for example, they round up younger children and together they wash the floor of the church and sweep clean the churchyard. They run errands. They organize and conduct the children's choir at the children's mass. In all of these activities, less than a third of the youth group's membership comes from the neighborhoods of Jardim Brasil and Novo Santo.

It is noteworthy in this regard that two ex-members of the youth group, separately interviewed in Novo Santo, indicated that they had left the group "because it had nothing really important to do." When asked to explain this, both emphasized that there existed much poverty and a great many problems in the area about which Father Fernando needed to speak out in public if the people were to be helped. However, they noted: "Father Fernando has no consciousness of these things. He does not want to discuss them. He does not want the youth group to become involved with these problems. He is concerned only with sin and cleaning the church."

And indeed, the observations of these two youths were not inaccurate. Neither Nossa Senhora do Carmo nor Cristo-Rei provide a base for the formation of political ideas or the organization of political activity. Despite the fact that Father Fernando is of humble peasant origins and from the politically conscious Northeast of Brazil, he was in no sense a political activist and he emphatically expressed no interest in assisting in the mobilization of a politically active church in the midst of these working-class neighborhoods. In numerous interviews and discussions, it became quite clear that while this friendly and cooperative priest was sensitive to the suffering of workers and the harsh living conditions that existed in the various neighborhoods of his parish, and while he was privately contemptuous of the affluence that existed in different sectors of Manauara and Brazilian society, he was very much disinclined to view all of this in terms of secular ideologies.

Brazilian politicians, in his view, were simply the product of a sinful and corrupt society. They, like so many others, had fallen away from God. The role of the church was to bring them back, to somehow restore a morally acceptable political order by confronting the problem of sin rather than assisting in the construction of a political economy in which everyone could be equally sinful. Thus, Father Fernando was not supportive of liberation theology. Nor was he supportive of a politically active clergy or of church-related movements such as the Comunidades de Base. "Thank God," he stated, "these things (i.e., Comunidades de Base) are not felt in Manaus except among one or two parishes that have foreign clergy." It is not known how widely Father Fernando's views were shared by his parishioners. However, practically every informant queried in the neighborhoods associated with Father Fernando's two parishes indicated that except for spiritual guidance, the church contributed absolutely nothing materially or politically by way of assisting working-class people.

Despite Father Fernando's unwillingness to openly assume a political posture in relationship to his moral and religious convictions, under certain circumstances he could be shrewdly political because of these convictions. For example, when boisterous neighbors, mostly non-practicing Catholics living in a pocket favela behind the church, secured a writ from the public authorities to open the churchyard in order to give them more direct access to the cabanas in which they lived, Father Fernando protested. Without a word of notice to anyone, he simply disappeared from the parish. From whatever hideout to which he retreated, during the second week of his absence he let it be known through his family that he would not return to the church until the public authorities withdrew their order to open the churchyard and "make of this holy ground a public street in which the sinful could noisily interrupt church services by their drunken behavior and foul language." Upon hearing this, a few parishioners reported Father Fernando's absence to the prelacy and indicated he would not return to his priestly duties until the writ was withdrawn by the public authorities. Shortly thereafter, the writ was withdrawn and Father Fernando reappeared.

Costa da Silva

Costa da Silva forms the most stable and perhaps the best organized working-class neighborhood in Bairro Raiz. One basis for this assessment concerns the proprietorship of homes. No less than 28 of the 38 families surveyed in Costa da Silva were the original proprietors of the houses they occupied. Moreover, each of these 28 families had lived in the neighborhood 14 years or longer. Of the remaining ten families surveyed, only three were renting. Apropos the stability of Costa da Silva's population, one informant emphasized: "This conjunto has become one of the best for workers in the city. People who have come here, particularly from the 'floating city,' do not want to live elsewhere. They have had the same neighbors since the conjunto was built."

The character of Costa da Silva can only be understood in relationship to the social origins of its resident population and the manner in which the neighborhood was formed. As previously noted, this particular neighborhood was constructed as a public housing scheme for the purpose of relocating families displaced by the renovation of Manaus' port facilities. The construction of the scheme was mandated by the state government and assigned to the Department of Roads and Public Works. Its settlement and subsequent organization as a neighborhood community were eventually assigned to SHAM. In all, SHAM financed the sale of 471 single-family homes in Costa da Silva.[36] With the demolition of the "floating city," the neighborhood's domiciles were rapidly built, sold, and occupied. As early as 1969, the population of Costa da

Silva more or less stabilized at its current level of approximately 2,700 inhabitants.

Although much of the older generation now living in Costa da Silva came from a reputedly poor favela, this should not be allowed to disguise critical features relating to their social and cultural origins. Based on data reported in SHAM's 1976–77 survey of the public housing schemes under its supervision, 71.3 percent of the 471 household heads living in Costa da Silva were born in the state of Amazonas. Of this group, 61 percent were Manauaras (born in Manaus) and distinctly urban in their social and cultural origins. Moreover, of those originating outside of Manaus, either in the interior of Amazonas (131) or elsewhere in Brazil (135), no less than 59 percent had lived in the city 15 years or longer and, thus, their movement to the city predated by several years the creation of the Zona Franca. Moreover, of these migrants, only 17 percent (a total of 32) reported working in agriculture prior to their arrival in Manaus. Most of the remainder came to Manaus as wage workers of various types (51 percent), students (24 percent), comerciantes (16 percent), public functionaries (7 percent), or they were on military assignment (5 percent). As near as can be determined, not more than 5 percent of these household heads were identified by SHAM as "analfabeto" or illiterate. Finally, most of these household heads (353 or 75 percent) were married (65 percent religiously and civilly, 28 percent civilly, and 7 percent religiously). Of the remainder (118), 11 percent were widowed, nine percent were single, three percent were separated or divorced, and only three percent were living "amasiado" (in a consensual union).

SHAM did not note the specific occupations of these 471 household heads. However, it was reported that 59 (13 percent) were retired and only 33 (7 percent) were unemployed. Of the 379 who were gainfully employed, 72 percent worked for wages and 28 percent were self-employed. Of the latter, 45 percent were registered with INPS (Instituto Nacional da Previdência Social). With regard to wage workers, almost 56 percent of them had been working for the same employer six years or longer and only 27 percent had changed employers during the three-year period preceding their interview. As far as income is concerned, 184 or 39 percent of these household heads reported a family income that placed them in the lowest of the four income categories differentiated by SHAM (i.e., reporting an income of Cr$4,000/month or less). Of the remaining 287, only 35 percent reported family incomes in excess of the second these income categories (i.e., in excess of Cr$8,000/month).[37]

The point to be made in light of these data is that compared to the families that we encountered at Marapatá, Educandos, and other neighborhoods in Raiz, those selected by SHAM for settlement in Costa da Silva were in many ways better positioned to take advantage of whatever opportunities the Zona Franca might offer for economic mobility. That this was indeed the case may be further substantiated by the income status and occupational structure of the households surveyed in 1984. Consider first the income status of these families by neighborhood as reported in Table 30.

Table 30. Distribution of Households by Family Income and Neighborhoods in Raiz

Neighborhoods

Family Income (Min. Sal.)	Costa da Silva		Jardim Brasil/ Novo Santo		Marapatá/ Educandos		Total
	N	%	N	%	N	%	
3 or <	5	13.2	8	44.4	13	59.1	26
4 to 5	11	28.9	5	27.8	5	22.7	21
6 or >	22	57.9	5	27.8	4	18.2	31
Total	38		18		22		78

P < .01

As Table 30 shows, the percentage of households sampled in Costa da Silva and reporting incomes in excess of six minimum salaries is all of twice that which we encountered in other neighborhoods of Raiz, and more than three times that of households surveyed in Marapatá and Educandos. Moreover, independent of whether these households are representative of the neighborhoods in question, and observational data would suggest that they are, it is clear that the economic status of families in these neighborhoods is very much a function of the character of their labor market participation. Two factors are relevant in this regard: one has to do with the number of economically active persons/household and the other concerns the economic sector in which these persons are employed.

Regarding the first of these factors, 90 percent of the households sampled in Costa da Silva are formed by multiple income families. This was the case for only 72 percent of the households drawn from other neighborhoods of Raiz and 46 percent of those investigated in Marapatá and Educandos. Related to this, it is also significant that 65 percent of the multiple income households in Costa da Silva contained *three or more* economically active persons whereas 60 percent of those in the other neighborhoods contained no more than two. As to sector of employment, data relating the percentage distribution in different neighborhoods of households that contained one or more economically active persons in particular sectors of the economy are summarized in Table 31.

Table 31. Percentage of Households Containing Economically Active Persons in Various Sectors of Employment by Neighborhood

Households with Economically Active Persons

Neighbor-hoods	Households N	White Collar % of N	Hegemonic % of N	Traditional % of N	Self-Employed % of N
Costa da Silva	38	63.2	55.3	28.9	50.0
Other Raiz	18	27.8	77.8	22.2	33.3
Educandos/ Marapatá	22	18.2	9.1	90.9	18.2
Total	78	42.3	47.4	47.4	37.2

As Table 31 reveals, almost two-thirds of the households in Costa da Silva contained at least one person working in the white collar sector. Half or more of these households also contained one or more workers who were either self-employed or employed in the hegemonic industrial sector. Only 28.9 percent contained workers employed in the traditional industrial sector and, we may add, most of these workers were older members of the family who were close to retirement age. Among the families living in Jardim Brasil and Novo Santos, most economically active members held low-paying jobs in the hegemonic industries. Only a few of these households contained economically active persons who had found their way into the white collar sector. And, as might be expected, very few households in Marapatá and Educandos contained economically active workers engaged outside of the traditional industrial sector.

Most of the families that moved into Costa da Silva as the Zona Franca was being organized, including those who were displaced from the "floating city," were families that were predominantly urban, literate, and in command of relatively stable employment. They were also families who encouraged the education of their children up through the secondary level. Accordingly, these families more or less typified a segment of the working class in Manaus that was in a somewhat more favorable position to take advantage of whatever opportunities for upward mobility the Zona Franca might provide. That they have taken advantage of these opportunities is evidenced by their occupations, incomes, housing, and consumption patterns.

As originally contracted by SHAM, the homes in Costa da Silva were of modest but relatively solid construction. All of them were brick-made and sold unfinished to their proprietors. Most were built contiguous to one another in a rectangular complex of streets fronted by Avenida Tefé, one of the two major transportation arteries in Raiz. Two simple patterns of construction were followed. One provided a bedroom, a living room, a small dining area, a kitchen, inside bath facilities, a patio area separated from the street by a small wall, and a small amount of empty yard space in the rear. The other followed a similar line of construction except that the houses were built on slightly larger lots and they contained two bedrooms.

Since their original construction, virtually all of these houses have been in someway enlarged or substantially improved by their proprietors. Some have been extended in the rear by the addition of a bedroom. In most cases patios have been covered, tiled, and protected by decorative iron grating to form a sitting area outside the living room. In some cases proprietors have made even more substantial improvements by the addition of a second story that allows the entire first floor to be used as a living and dining area or for other purposes. These larger and more substantial houses now comprise approximately 20 percent of the homes in the conjunto and they clearly reflect the upward economic mobility of its resident families.

However, apart from having to finish the houses they purchased through SHAM, the families who moved to Costa da Silva were confronted by numerous problems. For one thing, the public authorities procrastinated in clearing much of the area of brush. They also procrastinated in providing the conjunto with adequate sewage and drainage. Because of these delays, for several years the low lying section of the neighborhood remained a virtual swamp during the rainy season. In addition to this, potable water presented a problem for the residents. During the early phase of construction, drinking water was pumped from a deep well into a central tank fed by gravity to individual homes. The tank's capacity was insufficient for the number of homes that were eventually built. Thus, whenever the tank ran dry, residents had to carry and then boil their water supply from shallow wells dug in the basin and contaminated by surface runoff. From time to time, even these wells ran dry and water had to be obtained from delivery trucks parked in Avenida Tefé. Added to these difficulties were sanitation problems. Until sewer lines were finally extended to the area, septic tanks in the lower sections of the neighborhood overflowed during the rainy season and spread a stench over the entire community. And, as the streets were not paved, during the rainy season it was often the case that garbage could not be collected and the neighborhood became infested with rats.

As evidenced by the newspapers of the period, the existence of these problems provoked meetings among some of the moradores who organized members of the community in public protest. Notwithstanding their protests, it was not until the mid-seventies that most of these problems were finally solved.[38] However, from the experience of these protests, an Association of Moradores was organized by SHAM to formalize discussions with the residents. For a time, this seems to have provided the neighborhood with a measure of corporate organization.

Concerning the neighborhood's commercial development, small-scale enterprises began to appear in the early seventies when a section of land was set aside by SHAM for the construction of licensed market stalls. By the time of research in 1984, the marketplace included the registration of 40 stalls selling fresh meat, fish, fruits, vegetables, rice, spices, dry goods, and various other items on a daily basis (from 7 A.M. to approximately midday), excepting Sundays.[39] Not all of the proprietors of these little enterprises live in the neighborhood. Some come from other neighborhoods and bairros. Moreover, commercial development has not been confined to the marketplace. Outside the marketplace, there existed in 1984 no less than 58 commercial establishments of varying size and capitalization. Included among these were two drugstores, sixteen bars or drinking establishments (most of which provided seating for no more than five or six people), six dress shops, four hairdressers, two photoprocessers, three meat markets, several shops selling sweets, snacks, and soft drinks, and shops specializing in the repair of watches, televisions, automobiles, or furniture. Almost all of these enterprises were attached to homes that had been modified by their resident families for commercial purposes and less than half of them operated under license from the public authorities.[40]

The cultural development of the neighborhood has taken a variety of forms. In 1969, the Adventists elected to locate in Costa da Silva the first of two churches that they eventually were to build in Bairro Raiz. A small school, used mainly for religious instruction, was constructed behind the church. A public primary school, shared with nearby neighborhoods, was constructed in 1972. About the same time, following numerous complaints about rowdyism by the moradores, the authorities provided the neighborhood with police protection in the form of a subdelegacia (local police station). A small medical clinic soon followed.[41] Then in 1976, again in response to petitions signed by the moradores, the state government opened a social center (Centro Social Urbano André Araújo), the first to be built in the public housing schemes under SHAM's supervision.

In cooperation with SETRAS (Secretaria de Estado de Trabalho e Serviços Sociais), the Social Center was assigned a full-time director and sufficient annual funds with which to recruit two part-time local assistants to help organize programs with a view toward "improving the social, economic, educational, cultural, political, religious, and recreative life of the neighborhood's inhabitants." Featured among these programs are a crèche to assist working mothers in the care of their children, an office for the issuance of work cards, and an extensive but unfulfilled schedule of educational activities. The children enrolled in the crèche (approximately 70 up to the age of six years) are given daily snacks and lunches. Regarding educational activities, interested mothers are offered instruction in nutrition, health, sewing, cooking, and home management, and the elderly are invited to take instruction in arts and crafts.

With respect to leisure, the Center promotes a club for mother's and a separate club for the elderly. It provides both indoor and outdoor game facilities. It promotes recreational groups for school-aged children and teenagers. It sponsors dances and organizes festivals in celebration of its own anniversary, Carnival, Mother's Day, Father's Day, and Children's Day. As for religion, after it opened, the Center provided the priest at Nossa Senhora do Carmo a room in which to celebrate Sunday mass. Complaining that these facilities were too secular, the priest subsequently persuaded the prelacy to obtain land on which a church could be built in the neighborhood. A parish group was organized to raise funds and assist in the construction of a modest church. Thus, the parish of Cristo-Rei was established.[42] Independent of Cristo-Rei, however, the Social Center continues to sponsor festivals in celebration of the Feast of São João, Christmas, and Easter.

In the area of political development, as established by SHAM, the Association of Moradores with its elected Council and the Director of the Social Center were to form various commissions (recreative, religious, educational, etc.) to allocate to different programs the funds that the Center received annually from SETRAS. However, for reasons discussed in a later context, this has not happened. Moreover, except for its own election (which seems to engender little or no interest on the part of residents), the Association of Moradores and its officers play no role vis-à-vis local, state, or national politics. In all these arenas, the Association neither assumes a political posture nor vents whatever political views its members might hold. In the local political arena, it appears that issues resulting in some sort of action on the part of residents vis-à-vis public authorities are seldom channeled through the Association of Moradores. More often than not, political action in the neighborhood takes the form of a spontaneous and unorganized demonstration. If such a demonstration draws the attention of the news media, it increases the probability that the public authorities will do something to solve the problem.

The Social Center's program in political education, particularly with reference to the nation, is confined to symbolic and ceremonial expressions of patriotic values. For example, in cooperation with the Council of Moradores, the Center allocates funds with which to organize festivals in celebration of the *Descobermento do Brasil* (the discovery of Brazil), Tiradentes (a celebration in memory of an eighteenth-century political martyr executed by the Portuguese), Semana da Asa (Air Force Week), Dia da Bandeira Nacional (flag day), and Semana da Pátria (Independence Week). The most significant of these celebrations is Semana da Pátria and at the Center this particular holiday is an occasion for a parade and the organization of soccer and volleyball tournaments involving teams from other neighborhoods and bairros.

Below the surface of its organization by SHAM and its funding by SETRAS, as a neighborhood community Costa da Silva features the strong disinclination of working-class families in Manaus to involve themselves in corporately organized groups or associations. Developments relating to the Social Center and the Association of Moradores are nicely illustrative of the point.

To begin, the facilities of the Social Center are available to all the residents of Costa da Silva and the Center's director is required to maintain a rough record of their use. On average, approximately 3,000 admissions/month are recorded. Well over half of these admissions are attributed to the morning daycare services which the Center freely provides for working mothers. Most of the rest are accounted for by a gymnastics group organized for girls between the ages of seven and sixteen. In effect, the crèche is the major activity of the Center and it is perhaps the major source of community interest in the Center.

Apart from the crèche, the Social Center and its programs command very little community interest or support. Consider, for example, the Club for the Elderly. It has 62 signatures on its manifest (four of whom are men). A weekly meeting—usually but not always a luncheon meeting—is scheduled. "If a luncheon meeting is scheduled," stated the Director, "perhaps 30 of the members will come. However, most of them will stay only long enough to collect a lunch box and carry it to their homes. The Mother's Club has virtually disbanded itself. It survives only among a dozen elderly women who volunteer to help me and my assistant with the crèche." The Director's view that the Social Center simply does not provide a focus of community interest or a source of community organization was substantiated by the opinion of almost everyone whom we interviewed in the neighborhood.

Much the same is true with respect to the Association of Moradores and its elected Council. Graça Barros, Director of the Social Center, stated: "Everything I promote here I am supposed to discuss with the Council of Moradores. This is impossible. The Council is no longer structured—no longer organized. The Association no longer exists. I do not know why it is disorganized but we (SETRAS) are worried about this. We have tried to reactivate it, to hold elections, but there is no interest."

Problems relating to the Association were pursued further with Sr. Roberto, President of the Council until 1982. Senhor Roberto did not know who had succeeded him in office. Reflecting upon his own experiences as Council President, he stated: "It was a continual struggle keeping the Council alive. Each street is supposed to elect a representative. This never happened. It was difficult to get even those few who were elected to make meetings. When the Social Center was new, there was much interest for a time but it soon passed. I do not know for certain why there is no participation. I think the struggle for survival is what keeps people away. The moradores have to work too hard to stay alive and when they are not at work, they want to drink with their friends or stay home and watch television. Unless there is a crisis in the neighborhood, they show no interest in its problems." Indeed, none of the moradores in the thirty-eight families interviewed had ever been involved in the Association of Moradores. None of them knew whether or not the Council was alive and active, or who had been elected to succeed Sr. Roberto as its President.

Apart from the Social Center and the Association of Moradores, the only other institutions that might conceivably impart to Costa da Silva some sense of corporate organization are the *Delegacia* (police), the Adventist church, and Cristo-Rei. As for the Delegacia, the police are neither from the neighborhood nor are they considered a source of community organization. As several informants emphasized, in Costa da Silva there has always been a very uneasy relationship between the residents and the police. Indeed, during the course of research, an incident erupted between police officers who were drinking and a comerciante which resulted in a discharge of guns and a wounded teenager. The incident was followed by a large but spontaneous demonstration involving approximately 400 residents, including children. Having drawn the attention of the news media, a petition was circulated requesting that the Governor remove the involved officers from the community. As one informant stated: "The people at the Delegacia are uneducated, impertinent, and ill-bred. They have shot a guy in the leg. They also have shot a girl's foot. This was the third incident involving them. We have always had trouble with the Delegacia in this place and the (state) police are not respected."[43]

The churches in Costa da Silva are organizations that do command respect. Nevertheless, they socially engage relatively few people and they appear to exert very little influence on the social life of the neighborhood. The Adventist church has a small and active congregation. However, the congregation is largely comprised of families who have more recently migrated to Manaus from the interior and very few of these families live in Costa da Silva. The Adventists are active proselytizers but they have had little success in recruiting members from the more urbanized population of Costa da Silva. The pastor attributed this lack of success to the local population's addiction to "the venal pleasures of alcohol, tobacco, and sex." He suggested that it might also have something to do with the influence of Catholicism. While the Adventist pastor may have correctly assessed the local population's interest in "venal pleasures," data suggest that he perhaps misinterpreted the influence of Catholicism.

Informants recalled that the construction of Cristo-Rei was a neighborhood project that engaged a large number of families in support of church activities. They also recalled that the priest who preceded Father Fernando maintained a variety of parish programs at Cristo-Rei (e.g., Christian Family Movement, special instruction for children, a club for teenagers, special services for different groups, etc.) in addition to performing his duties at Nossa Senhora do Carmo. Thus, for a time after its construction, Cristo-Rei is reputed to have been a center of activity for many families in the neighborhood. However, following the arrival of Father Fernando, interest in these programs, particularly those involving adults, declined. Some informants consider this change due to the personality of the priest, suggesting that he gets on better with young children than with adults. Others attribute the change to the increase of population in Raiz that followed upon the creation of the Industrial Park. They suggest that as the population of the bairro increased, Father Fernando simply could not manage the affairs of two parishes. Accordingly, he devoted most of his attention to Nossa Senhora do Carmo and left the affairs of Cristo-Rei largely in the hands of volunteers who could not sustain community involvement.

By 1984, Cristo-Rei appeared to exert very little influence in the social and religious life of Costa da Silva's Catholic population. For example, while 92 percent of the workers interviewed in the neighborhood identified themselves as Catholic, 59 percent of those identifying themselves as such did not know, could not name, and had never spoken to the parish priest. Only 36 percent, mostly women and young adults, claimed to attend church regularly on Sundays. Apart from occasionally attending mass, respectively, 91 percent of the males and 77 percent of the females interviewed reported that they did not participate in any church-related group or function. Related to this, 57 percent of the Catholic households researched did not have anyone, not even among the children, who was in any way involved in a church-related group or program. Asked to explain this lack of church influence, one of the most knowledgeable members of the parish stated: "In Brazil, the Church does much work together with the community but this does not happen here in Manaus. There are no base communities in Manaus. Father Fernando is a good man but he is not concerned with our problems. The church in Manaus is outside our reality."[44]

Although the stability of its population has not resulted in much by way of corporate communal organization, how has it affected social life within the neighborhood in other respects? When queried about their views of the neighborhood, most informants gave focus to its social ambiance. They noted, for example, that their neighbors are pleasant; that they are quiet; that they stay at home and do not bother others; that they mind their own business and are not troublesome. Very few informants mentioned doing things with or for their neighbors. When asked to name their four or five best friends, the overwhelming majority of informants named members of the household or kin who lived nearby. Fifty-five percent of the lists compiled in this manner failed to include the name of a single neighbor who was not a kinsman of the informant queried. Among informants, it was generally the young adults who included a neighbor or two among their close friends and in most instances these "friends" were either former schoolmates, current workmates, or persons they were dating.

Regarding the level of family income, housing, and related patterns of consumption, Costa da Silva is a stable and marginally affluent working-class neighborhood. The affluence of the neighborhood is related to the urban origin of its working-class families, their level of education, the number of economically active workers they contain, and the tendency of these workers to be employed in other than the traditional sector of the economy. The stability of the neighborhood's population is also related to these factors. However, the stability and relative affluence of its working-class population have not contributed to the corporate organization of the neighborhood. As far as the organization of the community is concerned, Costa da Silva does not differ very much from Marapatá, Educandos, Novo Santo, and Jardim Brasil.

To the extent that any of these neighborhoods are corporately organized, the source of their organization is external—the patrão in the case of Marapatá, COHAB in the case of Jardim Brasil, and SHAM in the case of Costa da Silva. Independent of their social origins, their level of education, their sector of employment, or their economic well-being, working-class families in all of these neighborhoods generally revealed a strong disinclination to involve themselves in organized groups or associations. Accordingly, they do not extend a great deal of support to neighborhood associations, church organizations, labor unions, or political parties. The only significant exceptions to this seem to involve a few elderly women in Educandos and Raiz who were very religiously inclined and young adults, mainly males, who belonged to athletic clubs.

Beyond the modicum of communal organization that derives from external sources, social life in these communities is fundamentally rooted in family values. Thus, it is centered in the household and in the relationships that obtain between parents and their children and among siblings. Where need exists and time, propinquity, or resources allow, these relationships may be narrowly extended to include other kin. Outside this network, and apart from work, social life is largely confined to the streets.[45] In the streets, except as workmates or former schoolmates who live nearby are involved, social relationships among neighbors amount to little more than pleasant visitations in passing or, for various reasons, they are distant to the point of indifference and sometimes hostility. Accordingly, what most significantly differentiates social life in these various working-class neighborhoods is the extent to which kin are joined in their employment and in their residentiality—as at Marapatá and in Educandos—or the extent to which family and kin aggregate in poverty—as tends to be the case in the favela of Novo Santo.

A Middle-Class Neighborhood

Situated in the midst of working-class neighborhoods in Raiz is Parque Solimões, a privately developed housing conjunto specifically designed for individuals or families whose incomes and occupations placed them well within the middle class in Manaus. Parque Solimões is the least affluent of two middle-class housing conjuntos developed in the late 1970s and early 1980s by a private company, Coencil, which was organized by a Brazilian engineer from the Central South who married into a well-to-do Manauara family. The concept that gave form to Parque Solimões is one that expresses the paradox of middle- and upper-class existence in the midst of Brazil's impoverished masses. In effect, the material possessions that symbolically identify the privileged few who belong to the middle and upper classes simultaneously engender a deeply felt fear that these possessions make of them a target of *malandros* (i.e., hooligans, thieves, and the like). The sense of insecurity arising from this fear, particularly in cities like São Paulo, has driven large segments of the middle and upper classes into garrison-like villas and apartment buildings within which life and property are felt to be protected. With industrialization, the process is now being repeated in Manaus.

Parque Solimões forms a compound walled off from the working-class neighborhoods that surrounded it. Within the compound there exist twelve nicely spaced two-storied buildings, each one of which contains twelve two- or three-bedroom apartment units. Centered in the compound is a club that provides the residents a private bar, light food services, a swimming pool, a playground, and an enclosed court which is used for soccer and volleyball. The residents of Parque Solimões pay condominium fees to a manager selected from among their group. The manager, in turn, employs various personnel, including street cleaners and an armed security force that controls access to the compound day and night. The people who live outside the compound consider Parque Solimões to be a place for the rich. The validity of this perception is relative. The truly rich in Manaus live neither in Parque Solimões nor Bairro Raiz. Nevertheless, in the context of Raiz, the residents of Parque Solimões are thought to be *famílias de classe superior.* Thus, for comparative purposes, it is instructive to briefly consider how this small middle-class section of Raiz lived.

Unlike the family heads discussed in previous chapters, those who owned or rented apartments in Parque Solimões were occupationally connected to the upper strata of the white collar world. If gainfully employed at all, the women in these households were similarly connected. Many of the men and women in these households had attended or graduated from college. Some were young professionals—barristers, dentists, and doctors. A few had advanced degrees and were employed as specialists or research scientists by the federal or state governments. Most were middle-level managers, sales representatives, insurance adjustors, personnel officers, chief accountants, design engineers, and the like. Some were Manauaras who had made their way into the middle class as a result of business or political connections. A substantial number, however, were individuals who had been transferred to Manaus from other parts of Brazil by government agencies or private firms. Virtually all of these transfers looked forward to the day when they could return to their places of origin, mainly cities in the Central South.

On the whole, the families who lived in Parque Solimões were relatively young. They were small (usually having no more than three children), nucleated, and they were upwardly mobile. They transported their school-aged children to private primary and secondary schools, none of which were located in Raiz. Almost none of these families were related to one another. Those that had come to Manaus from other parts of Brazil usually saw their relatives only when they traveled during their annual vacation periods in January or July. Otherwise, they maintained contact with relatives by mail or telephone. Those who were Manauara maintained closer contact with kin, mostly parents and siblings, who lived elsewhere in the city. This was particularly evident on weekends when Manauara families living in the compound often received relatives who, as guests, were allowed to use the facilities of the club and pool.

Typically, the families in Parque Solimões were not joiners. With the exception of a few businessmen who belonged to service clubs and professionals who claimed membership in professional associations, they did not belong to political parties, engage in the work of sindicatos, become active in voluntary associations, or participate in church-related groups. Outside the compound, their social life involved private parties, eating out, night clubs, the beach, and the cinema. On vacation, they traveled outside the region. Within the compound, where they spent most of their leisure hours, their social life centered on their families, the club, and the pool. The women who were not employed spent a great deal of their time sunbathing, supervising their young children at the pool, shopping, transporting their older children to school, or running errands. Their husbands, of course, had variable work schedules that took them to different parts of the city. Still, when they returned home, usually in the late afternoon, they generally joined neighbors for a beer or two by the pool. In the evening, depending upon the schedule of television programs, some played soccer or volleyball. During the workweek, the tempo of this type of activity was moderate and it generally terminated early, usually before nine o'clock.

The weekends, however, were a different matter. Beginning Friday evening, partying was almost continuous at the club. The men mostly drank, joked with one another, and engaged in casual conversation. Inevitably, during the course of these conversations they revealed their social origins and their education. They discussed their work, the economy, and argued their political views. They argued also about soccer, automobiles, clothing styles, films, and television programs. In short, they chatted about anything and everything that happened to come to mind. Given the time they spent drinking and talking, conversations often turned completely nonsensical. In the event that one became bored with it all, he retired to his apartment, rested an hour or two, and then returned. Having missed nothing while absent, he would take up pretty much where he had left off. When not preparing meals or doing chores, the women participated in all of this. As everyone knew everyone else, individuals frequently changed tables and, accordingly, shifted from one topic of discussion to another. Regarding the purchase of drinks, in order that reciprocity remained balanced, a tab was formally kept at the bar. Sometimes on Sundays the party was enriched by the addition of guests, perhaps music, and a barbecue or *churrasco* for which everyone shared the cost.

Many of the families who were living at Parque Solimões did not participate in these affairs. Included among the non-participants were mainly the families of Manauaras whose principal networks were outside the neighborhood. Within the compound these families generally remained at home. If they partied at all, they partied privately at home with relatives, friends, and associates who did not live in Parque Solimões. Although these residents recognized and politely greeted their neighbors, they did not associate with them. Still, these families were joined by those who networked within the compound in the exhibition of distinctively middle-class consumption values.

For example, almost all of the families living in Parque Solimões owned automobiles that they, or someone they hired, washed at least once each week. Their apartments featured air conditioners, color television units, VCRs, stereophonic units, and the like. Their kitchens generally displayed the full range of electric appliances. They employed maids to cook, clean, and mind their children. Their women spent a great deal of time applying lotions with which they sunned themselves. They had their hair, fingernails, and toenails done weekly. They were extremely sensitive to fashions. They frequently dined out, went to nightclubs, and patronized the cinema. They gave or attended parties with friends and work associates. They sponsored rather elaborate parties in celebration of their children's birthdays. And when they vacationed, they usually traveled out of the region. Very few of them regularly attended religious services and, if they did, they did not go to the neighborhood churches.[46]

People living in the working-class neighborhoods of Raiz caught only glimpses of how the inhabitants of Parque Solimões lived. Otherwise, they heard tell of it from domestics, watchmen, and the like. Thus, some working-class informants considered the conjunto to be occupied mostly by people who lived well because they were *estrangeiros* or foreigners. Most informants, however, believed that the residents of Parque Solimões lived a rich and comfortable life because they were "very intelligent and well educated, politically connected, and highly positioned in the economy." This was not generally a cause for working-class resentment; rather, it was a source of envy. Accordingly, the residents of Parque Solimões disclosed a standard of living that was held in esteem by most working-class families in Costa da Silva and Jardim Brasil and it structured the mobility aspirations that they expressed either for themselves or their children. As for the families in Novo Santo, they considered the life lived by the residents of Parque Solimões to be quite beyond their hopes and aspirations. For them, Parque Solimões existed as a constant reminder of the *miséria* (misery or poverty) that they associated with working-class status not only in the Zona Franca but all over Brazil.

CHAPTER 7

Manaus: A Theoretical View of a Microcosm

Manaus is a microcosmic case of urban-industrial development in Brazil. It is, however, rather unusual in several important respects. Its peculiarity derives partly from the Amazonian location of the city, the demography of its hinterland, and the cultural formation of its working-class populations. Given the location of the city in relationship to factor and product markets, the low density of the regional population, and the traditional association of the city's economy with the extraction and trade of tropical forest resources, Manaus is not where one might expect to find an export-driven industrial economy based on the assemblage of such consumer durables as television units, VCRs, radios, tape recorders, watches, and the like. And yet, as a result of a massive complex of federal and state programs, this is precisely the type of economy that now exists in Manaus. Finally, the peculiarity of the case is further accentuated in that there exists no other export-processing zone of this type in Brazil.[1]

It is because of these peculiarities that Manaus presents itself as a fascinating case for the study of urban-industrial development. Rooted as they are in the cultural history of the Amazon, one cannot help but wonder how various segments of the city's population have been affected by developmental forces externally anchored in the corporate interests of capitalist firms and enterprises, and in the national interest of the federal government. Thus, in the preceding chapters, I have undertaken to report the results of research, the substantive purpose of which was to determine the economic, social, and cultural impact of urban-industrial development on a sample of working-class families. The investigation proceeded mainly in the form of an anthropological case study. However, the design of the study also had in view some important issues arising out of theoretical discussions concerning the nature and consequences of urban-based development projects of the type under consideration.

As related in the Introduction, two problems of political economy have engaged considerable theoretical discussion among students of development. One has to do with the role and significance of capitalism for promoting developmental change. The other concerns the economic, social, and cultural consequences of urban-based industrial development for working-class populations. Modernization theorists, so-called dependency theorists, and various Marxist scholars approach these problems from markedly different perspectives. Despite their differences, however, scholars of all three theoretical persuasions tend to converge on some aspects of the marginalization thesis; specifically, they tend to agree that dependent capitalist industrialization has as one of its major consequences the exclusion of some, if not most, of the working-class population from the presumed economic, social, and cultural benefits of economic change. In consequence of this convergence, the marginality thesis seemed to provide a point of departure from which to interrogate further, and perhaps more empirically, the conceptual adequacy and heuristic value of these three paradigms for purposes of comparative research.

Fundamentally, the marginality thesis treats as problematic the relationship of various segments of the working class to whatever impulses for change that might arise out of capitalist-inspired development processes. Can the exclusion of various working-class elements from the benefits of such change be attributed to the persistence of traditional institutions and values? If so, the marginality of working-class elements is but the expression of already existing inequalities and social divisions which perhaps have only deepened as a consequence of new forms of capitalist development. Or, alternatively, is marginality the expression of inequalities and social divisions arising out of such development? Whatever the case, the social exclusion of working-class elements from the benefits of capitalist development entails an analysis of the extent to which the working-class population is internally differentiated and socially stratified as a consequence of processes like those involved in the industrialization of Manaus.

In constructing the collection and analysis of data with reference to these issues, a loosely interpreted "modes of production" approach was judged most appropriate. The reasons for this decision are not theoretically complicated. For one thing, the economistic proclivities of the approach are more or less congruent with the prevailing tendency in the literature to conceptualize developmental change in economic terms.[2] In addition, by underscoring the centrality of the labor process in the production and reproduction of social life, the paradigm requires that we pay attention to the cultural historical context in which specific developmental changes emerge. Accordingly, it was assumed that there exists a determinate relationship between the work that individuals must do in order to make a living and the social lives they live in order to work. Thus, I expected to find that the labor processes engaged by firms and enterprises in different economic sectors would significantly affect the economic status of workers employed in those sectors, the economy of their households, the organization of their families and, more generally, the kind of social life they could create for themselves and for others in the community and in the larger society.

In concluding, the discussion of the theoretical issues with which we have been concerned may proceed more meaningfully if it is preceded by a succinct summary of the substantive findings that are deemed most relevant to their consideration. Apropos the approach adopted throughout the investigation, it seems logical to begin the summary with data concerning the historicity of particular modes of production in the Amazon region.

Modes of Production in the Amazon

Although the capitalist mode of production constituted the major focus of Marx's economic anthropology, the expression "mode of production" did not assume the position of a critical or well-defined concept in his theoretical framework. Current fascination with the concept has been attributed to the influence of French Marxists, Althusser/Balibar (1970) and Godelier (1977), whose concern was to draw from classical Marxism a framework in terms of which the paradoxical combination of pre-capitalist and capitalist modes of production within a particular social formation could be explained without adopting dualistic conceptions of society or the economy similar to those employed by modernization theorists. Thus, for Marx's sketchy outline of historical stages, Althusser and Balibar, Godlier, and others substituted a structural methodology that gave focus to the "articulation" of different modes of production.[3]

Turning to the case at hand, it needs to be emphasized that the process of economic development in Amazonas did not begin with the creation of the Free Trade Zone and the industrialization of Manaus. As related in chapter 1, prior to the creation of the Free Trade Zone in 1967, Manaus had existed for almost 300 years as an administrative center and a port of trade. During this time, the social and cultural character of the city, including the size and composition of its population, varied more or less with the character and scale of extractive economies that succeeded one another as the region was more fully explored and the marketing of its various resources became profitable.

Historical data reveal that these extractive economies gave shape to a social formation within which mercantilist firms, engaged mainly in the export of primary materials to external markets, assumed hegemony over petty commodity producers, many of whom combined a subsistence mode of production with the collection and trade of forest products. By the time the rubber economy reached its peak of development, these different modes of production had become institutionally joined within the framework of the aviamento system of credit. The reader may recall from chapter 1 that this system of credit essentially involved a network of exchange relationships extending from import-export companies to trading posts run by seringalistas who leased or claimed estates in the uplands along the rivers, to small-scale entrepreneurs or comerciantes who plied the rivers for trade, and from these to Caboclos whose nucleated families engaged in subsistence activities while their menfolk spent much of the year collecting rubber and other forest products to be exchanged for necessities that they could not produce for themselves.

Fundamentally, the aviamento system was formed by a complex of dependency relationships based on credit arrangements and, in its most exploitative dimensions, the system involved virtually all categories of workers in some form of debt peonage. However, it is precisely these credit arrangements that seem to have provided a base for articulating cultural values associated with perhaps the most deeply entrenched of all systems of dependency in Brazil: i.e., *a família*. By force of circumstance, workers in the interior did not command collateral with which they could secure the credit they needed to provision themselves and their families while collecting forest products. In extending credit to workers in the form of provisions, creditors secured these loans mainly by the confidence they derived from their personal acquaintance with the workers involved, and from the knowledge that these workers and their families understood well the extent to which their future support depended upon honoring the obligations that attached to their debts. In effect, the extent to which debtors and creditors could personalize their relationships, perhaps by formally establishing a *compadrio* or familistic bond with one another, creditors could augment the social collateral they needed to secure loans and workers, assured of credit, could obtain the wherewithal they needed to support themselves and their households.[4]

The aviamento system of exchange thereby joined employers and employees as creditors and debtors in a complex structure of dependency relationships. However, notwithstanding the fact that at bottom these relationships often assumed the economic character of debt peonage, to function well, the system had to be culturally grounded in something other than economic exchanges.[5] The system functioned best, so it seems, when it was embedded in a more extensive network of social relationships reinforced by patronal cultural values of the type that are commonly associated with the Brazilian parentela.

By joining employers and employees as creditors and debtors within an extended network of dependency relationships, the aviamento system of credit served to conjoin elements of the domestic, petty commodity, and mercantilist capitalist modes of production within a relatively integrated extractive economy. The integration of these different modes of production, however, was both facilitated and reinforced by the fact that the dependency relationships they enjoined were themselves embedded within a more extensive, and less economic, network of compadrio relationships reinforced by patronal cultural values. In the political frame of this social formation, compadrio relationships served the organization of cliques or *panelas*. At the higher political levels, these cliques nested within an oligarchic structure that mediated and more or less controlled whatever power might be locally exercised by the very limited bureaucratic apparatus of the national state.[6]

The decline of the rubber economy seems to have had a contradictory effect within this social formation. On the one hand, it deepened the poverty that engulfed most of the population of the region and, thereby, weakened the regional and national play of local oligarchical power. On the other hand, it increased the dependency of working-class populations upon those local entrepreneurs whose enterprises survived the stagnation that ensued. This may help explain why particularistic values and a patronal pattern of organization has persisted among the locally owned, family-managed, industrial and commercial enterprises described in chapter 2.

With the creation of the Free Trade Zone and the industrialization of Manaus, the social formation that came into being with the aviamento system and the collection and trade of forest products gave way to one in which the capitalist production of consumer goods by national and multinational firms assumed a hegemonic position relative to traditional mercantilist interests, petty commodity producers, and the like. The hegemony of these exogenous firms is substantiated by the position they occupy in the urban economy as a consequence of the capital they control, the employment they provide, the fiscal incentives they receive from the federal government, and the investment of public funds in infrastructural projects that is made on their behalf.

The articulation of modes of production within the social formation that has emerged as a consequence of this change is no longer based on the aviamento system of credit and the patronal values it enjoined. Rather, it is now the direct result of the state's industrialization project and the market organization of social and cultural life that has followed upon the implementation of that project.

Stated more concretely, based on the employment data presented in chapters 1 and 2, the growth and economic well-being of most peripheral enterprises (e.g., food processors, construction firms, sawmills, wholesale and retail commercial establishments, law firms, realtors, etc.) is increasingly dependent upon the economic well-being of the new industrial enterprises that have been established in Manaus. At the same time, the economic well-being of these hegemonic enterprises is in part related to the cost benefits that these firms and their employees derive from doing business with the more peripheral, locally organized enterprises. The latter, in effect, are low cost suppliers to the hegemonic industries as well as the workers they employ. As an example, consider the petty commodity production of the self-employed workers included in the study. Most of these workers and their small-scale enterprises depend for their profits on the expenditure of workers who, because of the low wages they receive in the hegemonic industrial sector, shop assiduously for low cost goods and services in the informal sector. The low level of wages paid these workers is determined, in the first instance, by the federal government's regional calibration of the minimum wage structure. However, this calibration is itself depressed by the low cost of goods and services that petty commodity producers make available. The market mechanism and the government thus serve to integrate different modes of production in Manaus and, at the same time, they protect the wage monopoly that prevails among the national and multinational capitalist enterprises that dominate the local economy.

The Marginalization of Producers

As previously noted, a modes of production approach features the analytic centrality of the labor process for comprehending the economic, social, and cultural life of workers. In conformity with their somewhat different modes of production, it was assumed that firms operating in the hegemonic and peripheral sectors of the economy would reveal corresponding differences in their labor processes; i.e., they would recruit, appropriate, and value labor differently. It followed from this assumption that one might expect workers to be socially differentiated and economically stratified according to the labor processes that generally exist in different sectors of the economy. Ultimately at issue here is the extent to which the working-class population in Manaus is becoming internally stratified and whether this is a consequence of the articulation of different modes of production within a particular social formation.

The case studies presented in chapter 2 demonstrate unquestionably that the processes by which labor is recruited, organized, used, and valued differs substantially from one sector of the Manauara economy to another and that, in some degree, this is related to the modes of production that prevail in these various sectors. The findings in this regard may be briefly summarized as follows:

1. The commoditization of labor is most fully developed in the hegemonic industrial sector where the organization of work tasks has been thoroughly rationalized. To minimize the possibility of any social interruption of tight assemblage schedules, the firms that operate in this sector seek to depersonalize the work situation. This is accomplished by the use of presumably universalistic criteria in the recruitment of workers, the mechanical organization of work tasks and the evaluation of workers, the exclusion of individual merit considerations in the payment of wages, and by supervisors who are generally encouraged to assume an impersonal, authoritarian posture in their relationship with workers. In effect, firms in this sector give focus to the employment not of persons but of units of labor power compliant with the organization of production. The labor power of such individuals is fully commoditized; it is retained or released as production schedules are rationally adjusted to market assessments or to the availability of unit components. Thus, other than the economic value of their labor, workers in this sector are accorded little social recognition by their supervisors or by the firms that employ them.

2. Surviving more than half a century of relative stagnation, many of the locally capitalized, family-managed, industrial enterprises that gave contour to the mercantilist economy of the past have been significantly revitalized by the creation of the Free Trade Zone and its industrial development. Although many of these enterprises have been mechanized according to more contemporary standards, workers are neither closely supervised nor systematically evaluated for their output. The labor processes within these enterprises conform in large part to the substantive rationalities by which their proprietors elect to operate. To a degree depending largely upon the proprietors involved, these substantive rationalities incorporate traditional values supportive of a patronal mode of organization. Accordingly, employers are concerned to recruit workers who are known to themselves or other workers to be of good character, reliable, and willing to give "a day's labor for a day's pay" without the need for close supervision. Thus, workers are often valued

as much for their character and their social connections with other workers, overseers, or proprietors, as they are economically valued for their labor. In this manner, workers in this sector are not fully commoditized for their labor; they retain some sense of individual identity with their supervisors and employers.

3. The expanded commercial and public sectors in Manaus include such a heterogeneous mixture of firms and enterprises that it becomes a bit hazardous to generalize about the labor process in reference to white collar work. Nevertheless, whether it is in a department of government, a branch of a nationally-based bank or commercial enterprise, or a small, locally-owned hotel or department store, the white collar work provided by enterprises of this type discloses some common features in respect to the recruitment, appropriation, and the valuation of workers. Employers in this very complex sector of productive activity generally consider that most of the work their firms provide requires more by way of "intelligence" or "mental capacity," or "formal education," than mechanical skills or physical stamina. Accordingly, white collar workers are usually recruited with reference to a combination of personal qualifications involving, inter alia, their age, sex, physical appearance, training, level of educational achievement, communication skills, and previous experience.

Despite the consideration given to the character and personal attributes of the prospective employee, in a bureaucratically determined and controlled fashion, and according to some or all of these criteria, individual white collar workers assume different levels of commodity value. Except within family-owned establishments in the commercial sector, promotions are possible and they are usually based on systematic evaluations of work performance and the acquisition of more specialized education, training, or creditable experience. However, these conditionalities aside, within the workplace, individual white collar workers are often given a great deal of preferential treatment by their superiors on the basis of their personalities or their family and social connections.

4. The labor process of self-employed workers is embedded in the interstices of the economy—i.e., in those spaces left open by firms to individuals and households generally because the markets in which they operate are too small to conform to economies of scale. Such spaces are extremely variable and, consequently, work in this sector is also variable. What most distinguishes the labor process of self-employed workers is their autonomy. These workers do not present their labor power in exchange for wages in the market. Rather, they market products that they have made or purchased wholesale, or they contract jobs for which they do work or provide a service under their

own supervision. They do not take orders, submit to authority, or worry about relationships with bosses. Their workmates, if they have any, are typically spouses, siblings, or children. Thus, if they pay wages, they usually pay them by way of a gratuity to a member of the family.

The Social Differentiation of Workers

With reference to these labor processes, firms and enterprises tend to "rationalize" their demand for particular types of workers. Firms operating in the hegemonic and more peripheral sectors of the economy are differentially selective of the kinds of workers they seek to employ. As a consequence, workers are socially typed or categorically identified in terms of characteristics presumably related to their ability to perform particular kinds of work. As reported in chapter 3, the findings in this regard may be briefly summarized as follows:

1. Employment opportunities in the new hegemonic industrial sector significantly favor workers whose social origins are urban rather than rural, who are under the age of thirty, and who have completed at least eight years of formal education. With respect to assemblage operations and office work in this sector, employment opportunities are far better for women than for men.

2. By virtue of their limited access to other sectors of employment, workers in the traditional industrial sector are predominantly males of very limited formal education (usually less than four years) and, not surprisingly, the overwhelming majority of them are migrants from areas that are characteristically rural.

3. Employment opportunities in the public, commercial, and service sectors of the new industrial economy substantially favor relatively young workers whose social origins are more urban than rural and who have completed, or who are in the process of completing, a secondary level of education. It is also the case that employment opportunities in this sector seem to be significantly more accessible to women than they are to men.

4. Self-employed workers are as likely to have been born and raised in Manaus as they are to be counted among migrants from rural areas. As is the case with workers in the traditional industrial sector, self-employed workers tend to be older males with little formal education. However, what most distinguishes the identity of the workers we encountered in this sector is their self-assertive claim of being independent types who preferred to work on their own terms. That they could work autonomously mattered more to them than the type of work they performed.

5. The recruitment criteria by which wage workers were socially differentiated and categorically typed with reference to particular sectors of production were not generally considered by the workers themselves to have significantly affected their employment, or to be particularly relevant to their prospects for promotion. And yet, it is clear from the data collected that the opposite was in fact the case.

The Economic Stratification of Workers

The status identities accorded workers as a consequence of their discriminate recruitment by firms and enterprises in effect segments the urban labor market in relationship to the labor processes that prevail in various sectors of the economy. To what extent does this segmentation enjoin a differential command of material resources and, thereby, fashion a system of status inequalities among workers? The data presented in chapter 3 are generally supportive of the following conclusions in this regard:

1. Relative to their parents, more than two-thirds of the workers included in the study have experienced upward social mobility in terms of their education and occupations. It is also the case that more than two-thirds of these upwardly mobile workers are employed in the hegemonic and white collar sectors. However, the educational and occupational mobility of workers has not been matched by any substantial improvement of their economic circumstances. Nearly 60 percent of the workers interviewed reported wages no better than the wages earned by one or both of their parents. What is perhaps even more significant is the fact that of the few workers who considered themselves economically better off than their parents, more than half are employed in the traditional industrial and informal sectors. Thus, while dependent capitalist development in Manaus may have contributed something to the educational and occupational mobility of workers, it has not substantially improved their economic status relative to that of their parents.

2. Consistent with the above is the income distribution of workers by sector of employment. The status inequalities among workers as a consequence of their individual incomes are not terribly large but they are significant and, to the extent that they do exist, they are related to the labor processes that exist in different sectors of employment. Noteworthy in this regard is the fact that as far as wages are concerned, workers in the traditional industrial and informal sectors seem to do somewhat better than workers in the hegemonic industrial sector. The possibility of earning wages in excess of four minimum salaries/month

is considerably better for white collar workers than it is for workers in other sectors. However, despite the potential for improving one's economic status by performing white collar work, the percentage of workers earning but one minimum salary/month is as high among white collar workers in Manaus as it is for any other group.

3. Regarding the income status of workers, gender is a critical factor affecting the differences that exist with reference to the sector of employment. In all sectors of the economy the incomes of women are generally lower than those of their male counterparts. When gender is factored out, the income status of workers employed in different sectors of the economy virtually disappears. To state the matter differently, the recruitment preference for female workers among firms operating in the hegemonic and white collar sectors has the general effect of depressing the income status of almost all workers employed in these sectors and this is a source of considerable complaint among males. It is not that males working in these sectors think that women ought to receive wages equal to their male counterparts; rather, they believe that because females are willing to work for lower wages, they invite the firms operating in these sectors to discriminate against the employment of males.

The Alienation of Workers

In concluding chapter 3, voice was given to the views of individual workers with respect to their work and the lives they were living, or wanted to live, at home with their families, in their neighborhoods, or in the larger society. These qualitative data reveal the extent to which various categories of workers seemed alienated in the sense that they construed the demands of their work as time spent away from doing the things they would prefer to do, or as time spent apart from being with people they would much prefer to be with. These subjective feelings of separation or exclusion from important areas of social life varied more or less according to the sector of employment and may be briefly summarized as follows:

1. The deepest and most widespread expressions of alienation were encountered among workers in the hegemonic industrial sector. Most of the workers interviewed from this sector felt that their work afforded them more prestige than they might derive from self-employment or work in the traditional industrial sector. However, except for those classified as técnicos, very few of these workers indicated that their work provided them with an encompassing sense of worth. Many of them felt that their work did not measure up to their personal qualifi-

cations, that they were held in very low regard by their employers, and that they had no possibility of a future with the firms that employed them. Males particularly felt that their employers much preferred female workers because of their docility. Apart from all of this, most of the workers interviewed in this category, males as well as females, considered that their work seriously intruded upon their social life; that it separated them from the community; and that it gave them very little time to be family and friends.

2. Expressions of alienation among white collar workers typically depended not so much upon the nature of their work as upon the character of their employer. For example, as much as they worked in order to live, most of those who worked for government, particularly the federal government, derived a great deal of self-esteem from their employment. They enjoyed their work and the people with whom they worked. This was much less the case among teachers and medical workers employed by the state of Amazonas. Still, even these types seemed to derive from their employment a status identity esteemed by their families and friends. However, at the bottom of the white collar sector there exists a veritable army of workers—bank clerks, telephone operators, hotel desk clerks, store clerks, and the like—who were found to be as deeply alienated by their work and by their employers as were those who worked in the hegemonic industrial sector.

3. For the majority of self-employed workers interviewed, their self-employment involved an exercise of choice influenced by considerations of income, or taken for reasons of personal ambition, the desire to be one's own boss, or perhaps because it afforded them the opportunity to work with relatives or friends. Whatever the case for rejecting wage-employment in favor of self-employment, many of these workers painfully related that the satisfaction and self-esteem that they derived from the nature and circumstances of their work were not generally shared by many of their relatives and friends. Apart from this feeling that meaningful others depreciated their work, expressions of alienation were relatively absent from the comments of these workers. In fact, most felt their social and cultural lives to be enriched by their autonomy and the type of work in which they were engaged.

4. The sawmill workers included in the study must be counted among those who expressed the least amount of social alienation. Most acknowledged that workers in other industries did not hold sawmill work in high regard because the work is difficult, dirty, and sometimes dangerous. However, they themselves expressed a profound sense of satisfaction with this work, their employers, and with the conditions of their employment. Most of these workers knew, and were known, by

their employers. Most counted at least some of their relatives and neighborhood friends among their workmates. In fact, as previously emphasized, so much did these workers construct their social lives in terms of their jobs and, to an almost equal degree, their jobs in terms of their social lives, that they tended to collect in occupational neighborhoods or communities.

Within the social formation that now exists in the Free Trade Zone, workers are increasingly differentiated and socially typed by firms and enterprises in relationship to the labor processes that characterize different sectors of employment. However, the status identities associated with these labor processes enjoin incongruous cultural values. Specifically, work in different sectors of the economy is differentially esteemed. Workers and their families generally accord more prestige value to white collar work than work in any other sector. This is followed by the social prestige assigned work, respectively, in the hegemonic industrial, traditional industrial, and informal sectors. However, the social evaluation of work by workers and their families does not match the economic evaluation of work by employers. Thus, the status inequalities that exist among different categories of workers do not ordain a corresponding command of resources. Thus, workers of unequal occupational status enjoy very little differential economic empowerment.

Because of this incongruity of values, independent of their occupational or educational mobility, it is difficult for individual workers in the higher status sectors of employment to muster the resources needed to validate status claims commensurate with the prestige their work brings to them. As a crude example, a typical worker in the wood processing industry will command perhaps more income with which to entertain or help a friend than will a more highly educated worker employed in the more prestigious hegemonic industrial sector. Or, despite the expectations that might attach to differences in their prestige, the lower status sawmill worker can afford to be more generous and helpful with friends than the higher status electronics worker. Clearly, this inability to validate status claims commensurate with one's work and occupational identity is not unrelated to the sense of alienation expressed by various workers, particularly by workers employed in the white collar and hegemonic sectors.

The Marginalization of Producers

What conclusions can be drawn concerning the marginalization of workers in relationship to the labor processes that now exist in different sectors of the Manauara economy? There are several. They may be stated as follows:

1. We could produce no substantial evidence to the effect that any particular segment of the urban population—whether it be migrants or non-migrants, persons of rural origin, individuals with much or little formal education, or whether females or males—is categorically marginalized in the sense of being excluded from any or all forms of employment. Nor could evidence be found with which to conclude that there existed in Manaus a reserve surplus of workers forced to make a living as best they could in the so-called informal sector. Indeed, almost to a person, the workers who operated small-scale enterprises in this sector did so not because they were unemployed but because they wanted to be self-employed.

2. Dependent capitalist development in Manaus has not resulted in the formation of a dual economy. If for no reason other reason, the availability of the cheap goods and services produced in the informal sector is as necessary to the low wages paid workers in other sectors of the economy as the payment of low wages in these sectors is necessary in order that workers do business in the informal sector.

3. Despite their articulation, the modes of production that prevail in various sectors of the economy enjoin labor processes with reference to which firms and enterprises are differentially selective in their recruitment of workers. The result of this process of social differentiation is that workers disclosing unacceptable characteristics tend to be *marginalized as producers. However, as producers, such individuals are not excluded from the economy in some general or absolute sense; rather, they are more or less excluded from specific sectors of production.*

4. Workers themselves tend to acquiesce in many of the values by which the managers and/or proprietors of firms and enterprises rationalize and articulate their recruitment preferences in relationship to the labor processes that exist in various sectors of the economy. That is to say, in much the same way as these managers and supervisors consider work in some sectors more prestigious, in a similar fashion so also do workers and their families tend to esteem work in different sectors of employment. Thus, workers tend to socially stratify one another with reference to work and sectors of employment in terms of the same social values used by firms to rationalize their recruitment preferences. Workers thereby reinforce the very processes by which they are selectively excluded from specific types of productive activity.

5. Because the values with which work is socially acknowledged differ substantially from the market values by which work is economically rewarded, the inequalities that exist among workers as a result of

their work and sector of employment are more social or ideational than than are material. Independent of their sector of employment, over half (53 percent) the workers interviewed were paid but the minimum wage and more than four-fifths (83 percent) earned three minimum salaries/month or less. Thus, the stratification of workers by sector of employment does not relate to any truly significant access or control of resources. Often this makes it difficult for individual workers, particularly those who enjoy somewhat higher status than others, to validate the status claims that attach to their work. *However, the subjective sense of alienation associated with this disjunction of social and economic values, appropriately considered, is a dimension of the marginalization of workers not as producers, but as consumers.*

The Marginalization of Consumers

The social formation that has emerged in conjunction with the industrialization of Manaus is one within which workers, as producers, have been significantly more *proactive* than *reactive*. That is to say, despite whatever alienation individual workers expressed as a consequence of their particular circumstances, almost without exception, they were found to be supportive of the Free Trade Zone and of the consumption values upon which its industrial growth is based. Specifically, they not only welcomed the employment with which industrial development has provided them but, in addition, many of them considered it an opportunity to acquire some of the luxury goods that, before the Free Trade Zone, only upper-class Brazilians could acquire.

Workers disadvantaged or oppressed by the circumstances of their employment, or by whatever difficulties developments in the Free Trade Zone posed with respect to the material circumstances of living in Manaus, were more inclined to consider these as personal or family problems than problems of milieu. Thus, their response to these problems was generally proactive in the sense that they did not take issue with the limitations imposed upon their ability to give material expression to the consumption values they had internalized. For example, they did not join labor organizations and give collective voice to a militant demand for more economic empowerment. Nor did they curtail their wants in order to conserve their limited purchasing power. To the contrary, their response has been to devise ways of securing the income with which to satisfy as many of their wants as possible without compromising too many of their needs.

In a social formation of the type that now exists in Manaus, one within which the production of luxury goods and consumer durables is hegemonic to the production of wage goods, the consumption behavior of individuals has increasingly become the cultural measure of their marginalization or social exclusion. In this context, the social exclusion of particular types of workers from specific sectors of productive activity is one thing; their consumption behavior is quite another. Furthermore, the relationship between the two is somewhat problematic. When controlled for gender, as far as income is concerned, the capacity of individual workers to consume varies in terms of their sector of employment but the differences in this respect are not terribly significant. However, the consumption behavior of workers is not always determined by their individual incomes. Their purchases are often affected not only by what they earn but also by what they can obtain by pooling resources with their parents, siblings, or other kin. For these reasons, it was deemed most appropriate to consider whatever relationship might exist between production and consumption not in terms of the behavior of individual workers but, instead, with reference to the economy of households. The data in this regard are presented in chapter 4 and they are generally supportive of the following conclusions:

The Income Productivity of Households

1. The fundamental stratagem by which the low income productivity of workers is reconciled with their desire to acquire various kinds of luxury goods is familistic and it unfolds mainly within the household as a unit of consumption. On the production side, it involves a multiple income strategy in terms of which all members of the unit are encouraged to become economically active as soon as they are able. As related in chapter 4, this multiple income strategy bears no relationship to the nuclear or extended composition of families, to the rural-urban origins of household heads, nor to their sector of employment. It varies significantly only in relationship to the size or composition of households and this is largely a function of the domestic cycle and the age of household heads.

2. Reflecting the relatively low level of wages paid most categories of workers in Manaus, the per capita income of households is more significantly affected by their size or composition than by the number, or the sector of employment, of their economically active members. The opposite is the case with respect to total income. The total income of households was found to be related to both the number and the sector of employment of their economically active members. Moreover, the

total income of households is much more determinative of their consumption behavior than is their per capita income.

3. Regarding the relationship of total household income to sector of employment, the overwhelming majority of white collar and hegemonic industrial workers in the samples drawn were found living in multiple income households reporting six minimum salaries or more/month. The overwhelming majority of workers encountered in the traditional industrial and informal sectors were found living in multiple income households reporting five minimum salaries or less. Thus, while the income difference among individual workers in different sectors of employment are not terribly significant, those between households vary substantially according to the sector in which their economically active members are employed.[7]

The Consumption of Households

1. Approximately two-thirds of the households included in the study were owned by the families that occupied them. Although the proprietorship of homes was found to be related to factors other than the income of families and the sector of employment of their economically active family members, the quality of houses was found to be significantly related to the latter. More than 80 percent of the white collar workers interviewed lived in brick-constructed homes containing five or more rooms as well as indoor sanitation facilities. Almost invariably, the poorest homes were those occupied by single income families whose economically active member was employed in the hegemonic industrial sector.

2. Secondary data indicate that families earning up to five minimum salaries/month in Manaus spend, on average, slightly more than half their incomes for food. An additional 30 percent is spent for related necessities. Among the households under study, little variation was found that could be attributed to family income and sector of employment with regard to the types of food served at family meals and the reported frequency with which they were served on a daily, weekly, or monthly basis.

3. The purchase of luxury items—especially color television units, stereophonic sound equipment, tape recorders, telephones, and the like—is most significantly related to total household income and to the sector of employment of family members. With respect to these goods, the penetration of the consumer economy begins most markedly with multiple income families who report earning between four and five min-

imum salaries (70 percent of the households at or above this level of income, for example, contained color television units). The order in which families are excluded from the purchase of such luxuries varies according to the number of family members who are engaged, respectively, in the traditional industrial, informal, hegemonic industrial, and white collar sectors. For example, as related in chapter 4, more than 72 percent of the white collar workers lived in multiple income households containing a color television unit as compared to 67 percent of the hegemonic industrial workers, 58 percent of those who were self-employed, and 41 percent of those working in the traditional industrial sector. The purchase of most other consumer durables discloses a similar pattern in relationship to household income and sector of employment.

The marginalization of workers as producers is very different from their marginalization as consumers and it important that these two types of social exclusion not be confounded. The marginalization of specific categories of producers is largely a function of the labor processes characteristic of firms and enterprises. Although the low commodity value of labor connected to these processes in Manaus affects the purchasing power of individual workers and cannot be ignored, generally, individual workers are not the effective consumers of television sets and the like. More typically, the real consumers of these products are the families of workers or the households in which they live. Thus, except perhaps for single income households or households in which a worker lives alone, the marginalization of workers as consumers is more critically affected by the total income of their respective households than the commodity value of the work they individually perform.

Critical to the consumption of households are the income strategies with which workers and their families seek to augment their acquisition of the things they want as well as the things they need. Given the low commodity value of labor in Manaus, however, the income generating potential of families is largely a function of the composition of their households, the number of economically active persons they contain, and the sector in which these persons are employed. The composition of households is very much related to the age of household heads and to factors, cultural as well as economic, affecting the domestic cycle and the organization of domestic groups.

The Domestic Organization of Households

The income productivity and consumption of households is very much related to the organization of domestic groups. However, the nature of this relationship is not a simple matter to discern. For example, as reported in chapter 5, approximately 61 percent of the households in Manaus are occupied by nuclear families and the vast majority of the remainder contain some form of extended family. Based on the work of Rosen (1982), it would seem reasonable to assume that the organization of extended family households constitutes a multiple income strategy by which upwardly mobile lower strata families seek to improve their economic circumstances. However, one could just as reasonably suggest that such households constitute a survival strategy by which lower strata families seek to cope with harsh economic conditions. To further complicate the problem, it is also conceivable that the formation of such households has very little to do with economic forces as such. The question is: how do the income strategies of households affect the organization of families? Without further recapitulation of what is at issue, the data presented in chapter 5 favor the following conclusions:

1. Whether the household is occupied by a nuclear or an extended family bore no significant relationship to the size or demographic composition of households, nor to the age, migratory status, level of education, income, or sector of employment of household heads.

2. There appears to be a significant relationship between family type (nuclear or extended) and whether or not households form single or multiple income units. However, the economic determination of this relationship is problematic. While 83 percent of the extended families included in the study formed multiple income households, 53 percent of the multiple income households contained nuclear families. Moreover, if only multiple income households are considered, there exists no significant difference between nuclear and extended families in respect to the number of persons economically active in these families.

3. Similarly, no substantial difference was found to exist between either the per capita or the total incomes of nuclear and extended families. Thus, if extended families constitute a strategy with which low strata households seek to enhance their mobility by increasing their incomes, at least in Manaus, the strategy does not seem to work. By the same force of logic, because no significant difference exists between these types of families among the lowest income households, it is unreasonable to conclude that the extended family constitutes a survival strategy taken in response to the harsh economic circumstances that prevail in Manaus.

4. Independent of occupation, economic circumstances, or sector of employment, the nuclear family household is the cultural preference among workers in Manaus. In-depth case studies reveal that the formation of extended family households has little to do with income considerations as such. In most cases, extended family households were formed

in response to problems emerging out of the urban context: e.g., problems related to migration, housing, the search for employment, or the desire to pursue an education available only in the city. In some cases, extended families were formed because of domestic problems: e.g., taking in aging parents, leaving a drunken husband, or providing a temporary home for an unmarried mother.

5. The social boundaries of extended family units are very narrowly drawn. They center mainly on the nuclear family, on the relationship between parents, their children and grandchildren, and siblings. Beyond this, they include only persons who are married to or living with a son, a daughter, or a sibling. Seemingly, they involve relationships rooted in the mutual affection that members of the nuclear family have for one another. However, to the extent that these individuals are joined within a household, more often than not, the household economy involves a multiplicity of economically active workers.

6. What most differentiates single and multiple income households formed by nuclear or extended families is their economic division of labor and the impact of this on the relationships that exist among family members. Extended or not, in single income households the social roles that attach to age, gender, parenting, proprietorship, and material support converge on the traditional head of the household, typically a male in the role of husband and/or father. This not the case with multiple income households.

7. As related in chapter 5, almost 73 percent of the multiple income households included in the study contained economically active workers employed in different sectors of the economy. The economic division of labor associated with this engages a complex pattern of status differentials involving gender, kinship, education, occupation, sector of employment, and income. Independent of whether these households are formed by nuclear or extended families, all of these factors assume some degree of significance with respect to family relations. Briefly, the working wives in these households enjoy a status equal or superior to that of their husbands in all but the dimension of income. Relative to their fathers, the sons and daughters of these women enjoy a higher status than that of their mothers. Even on the dimension of income, the majority of these sons and daughters have a status equal or superior to that of their fathers.

8. Based on in-depth case studies, as a consequence of the above developments, the status of headship in most multiple income households is often little more than a nominal entitlement. The wives and adult children in these households were often found to command their own resources and make decisions for themselves.

In sum, the multiple income stratagem by which working-class families seek to cope with or improve their economic circumstances in relationship to the consumption economy that now exists in Manaus is one that has little to do with the formation of nuclear or extended family households. However, in those households where a multiple income stratagem exists, it has had a significant impact on the authority structures that typically characterize status relationships involving husbands, wives, adult children and siblings, not to mention other relatives. The loss of status so often experienced by the male heads of multiple income households is thought by some—e.g., priests, social workers, and teachers—to have seriously weakened the family and undermined the respect for authority that previously existed. Such informants attribute to this a plethora of social problems (e.g., alcoholism among adult males, the rowdy behavior of children, the delinquency and sexual promiscuity of teenagers, etc.) and they consider it one of the most negative aspects of the changes that have resulted from urban growth and industrialization.

Marginalization and Community Life

How has all of this affected the community life of workers and their families? Without retracing the data reported in the previous chapter regarding the impact of industrialization on the physical and cultural ambiance of the city, the response to this question may be stated as follows:

1. Almost none of the workers interviewed, and very few members of their households, reported any type of associational involvement. None were in any sense active in the affairs of a labor organization. None belonged to a political organization or party. None were active in civic organizations or neighborhood associations of any type. No one in these households belonged to a base community and, in fact, no one knew if such groups even existed in Manaus. Except for the few individuals who claimed membership in a church-related group or a pick-up athletic team of one type or another, independent of their occupation or sector of employment, the associational involvement of these workers and their families was virtually non-existent.

2. To the extent these workers and their families participated in the life of the city, they did so primarily in their jobs and as the consumers of goods and services that were either marketed in the private sector, or made freely available to them in the public sector.

3. For most of them, popular culture involved consuming commer-

cially packaged forms of entertainment sold at bars, discothèques, music shops, cinemas, and eating establishments located either in the central city or in their respective neighborhoods.

4. Social life within the neighborhoods studied was centered mainly in the household. The daily rhythm of activity was largely modulated by the status identities of household members, the division of family labor, the work schedules of those who were economically active, and the personal interests according to which various members elected to spend their free time. It was observed that much, if not most, of the free time available to individuals of all ages and occupations was consumed by television.

5. Except for school children and young adults, and other than in the neighborhoods where workmates lived close to one another (e.g., Marapatá and Educandos), neighboring among non-kin was found to be quite limited and largely confined to chance meetings in the street or at nearby drinking establishments.

6. Because of the rapidity and character of urban growth, the working-class neighborhoods in which data were collected were found not to be populated by families that, over time, had developed a strong sense of communal identity or an interest in communal organization. A modicum of communal organization was found to exist only in the public housing schemes and in these, even with the assistance of trained social workers, neighborhood associations could hardly be kept organized.

7. The physical quality of living conditions within neighborhoods is significantly related to the income status of the working-class households they contain and this is very much a function of the number and sector of employment of the economically active persons who live in these households.

8. Independent of their income status, or the sector of employment of their economically active members, in fact independent of the education or social origins of their respective heads, these working-class families expressed little interest in wanting to become engaged in a social life that might extend their commitments beyond their families to include more than perhaps a few close friends in the neighborhood, usually workmates or former schoolmates. Despite their consciousness of problems, almost none of the informants in these working-class households expressed any interest in becoming organizationally involved in the affairs of the neighborhood or the political life of the larger society.

In view of these observations, the exclusion or marginalization of workers from the political and social life of their respective neighborhoods, the city, or the larger society, appears to be somewhat of a spurious issue. To state the matter more concretely, because of their economic circumstances, these working-class families did not give a damn about politics or politicians, local or national. Nor did they consider themselves to be in any way excluded from the social relationships they most valued (i.e., with family and a few friends), or excluded from membership in any association of interest. However, they did consider themselves marginalized. Because of what they believed to be unreasonably low wages and unreasonably inflated prices, they could not buy the things they wanted most (e.g., telephones, air conditioners, and automobiles), or afford better houses in physically more attractive neighborhoods (e.g., Parque Solimões), or visit the places in Brazil they most wanted most to see (i.e., Rio). Thus, to the extent that these working-class families were in some way excluded from living the social life they culturally preferred to live, it was because of the limitations imposed on their ability to consume as a consequence of their work.

These substantive findings concerning the industrialization of Manaus and the marginalization of workers invite considerations of a more general nature with respect to macrotheories of dependent capitalist development and the social and cultural formation of working-class populations.

Empirical Construction of Marginality

It is not necessary here to review the many schools of thought that have contributed to the theoretical construction of the marginality thesis.[8] As it entered the context of the present study, the concept did not derive its intellectual force from what is often labeled "marginality theory." Rather, its introduction came about by way of relating the conceptual construction and organization of the project in Manaus to more general theoretical discussions concerning the nature and consequences of dependent capitalist development in Brazil and other Latin American nations.

At the risk of being unconscionably repetitive, in the context of these theoretical discussions, marginality is not a theory or a paradigm with which to explain development. More properly, it is a condition of underdevelopment presumably resulting from the expansion of a particular type of economy: i.e., dependent capitalism. Accordingly, marginality simply refers to the exclusion of working-class populations from full participation in the economy and their exclusion from full participation in the social, cultural, and political life of the society. This exclusion is typically construed as a general or undifferentiated condition. In terms of the modernization paradigm, this condition comes about because of the persistence of traditional institutions and values alongside the introduction of the more formally rationalized institutions and values that presumably accompany capitalist development. From the point of view of dependency and related neo-Marxist approaches, marginality more or less follows upon the introduction of capital-intensive or technologically sophisticated labor processes which have the effect of creating a surplus army of underemployed and unemployed workers who cannot gain access to the benefits that are usually attributed to capitalist development by those who are ideologically inclined to favor this type of economy.

In spite of the ideological proclivities and conceptual terminologies that distinguish these various approaches, the logic of their construction suggests that capitalist development, dependent or otherwise, engages processes that occasion the differentiation and stratification of the workers vis-à-vis one another as well as other social classes. The case of Manaus suggests the need for some refinement, and perhaps even a synthesis, of these macrotheories in order to better understand the social formation of working-class populations in the context of developmental change.

There is simply no basis on which to conclude that dependent capitalist development has resulted in the formation of a reserve army of surplus labor in Manaus. Even with the tremendous growth in population that has come with industrialization, there exists little evidence that substantial numbers of the population were underemployed or looking for work. Although the number of self-employed workers has increased since the creation of the Free Trade Zone, their proportion among the economically active has declined substantially. And, as previously noted, all but one or two of the self-employed workers included in the present study had refused or given up wage employment because they preferred to work for themselves.

An additional consideration in this regard concerns the hypothetical marginalization of unskilled labor as a result of the technological sophistication of capital-intensive industries. Even if generally valid, this proposition is certainly not applicable to the assemblage industries that have become hegemonic in Manaus. Despite their presumed technological sophistication, most of the workers employed in this sector are fundamentally unskilled and whatever training they need is generally acquired in a very brief period of observation. Indeed, given the extent to which they employ assembly workers in the routine performance of very simple tasks, it seems a distortion to describe these industries as capital-intensive. Considerations such as these render somewhat problematic the view that all forms of dependent capitalist development engage technologies and labor processes that tend to marginalize and relegate to the informal sector large numbers of unskilled workers.

Somewhat less problematic is the view issuing from the modernization paradigm that attributes the marginalization of working-class elements to the persistence of traditional institutions and values alongside the introduction of presumably more modern institutions and values. The case of Manaus lends some degree of support to this thesis. However, to the extent that the modernization paradigm employs a dualistic conception of the economy, not to mention a unilinear conception of change (a point to be discussed in a later context), it remains untenable.

It is certainly the case that the firms in what we have identified as the hegemonic and traditional industrial sectors differ in their labor processes. Characteristically, the latter tend to enjoin values and relationships that, at least locally, have in some sense acquired the force of tradition. Although the persistence of these values can be taken as evidence of their traditionality, this is neither an explanation of their persistence or their functionality. Moreover, in what sense are the labor processes characteristic of the firms and enterprises that primarily engage white collar workers traditional, or for that matter modern? And what analytic value can be derived from considering the petty commodity production of self-employed workers any less contemporary than the production of wage workers employed in the electronics industry?

The social differentiation of workers resulting from the labor processes that exist in various sectors of the Manauara economy can no more be attributed to the mode of production characteristic of enterprises that have locally acquired the force of tradition than it can to the mode of production characteristic of national and multinational based enterprises. The social differentiation of workers previously described is a function of the *articulation* or integration of different modes of production and not the result of the traditionality of one or another. However, this is not to deny the authentic historicity of the modes of production that have come into relationship in Manaus. Indeed, by virtue of their historicity, these modes of production are as much cultural as they are economic in their determination.

To illustrate the point: we have seen that firms operating in the hegemonic industrial sector have a preference for workers of a type that is different from that which sawmills and other locally based industrial enterprises seek to employ. Objectively, and for the most part, these recruitment preferences appear to have very little to do with economic considerations directly affecting the labor process.

Most of the production work available in the hegemonic and traditional industrial sectors requires very little education or technical training to be efficiently performed. Related to this, the previous experience of workers counts for naught in terms of wages because the minimal salary is virtually standard for all new employees. And, quite apart from the performance of workers, there exists in both sectors almost no opportunity for promotion.

It follows, then, that the recruitment preferences associated with the different labor processes that exist in these industrial sectors has little, if anything, to do with the economy of firms: i.e., with their capitalization, product orientation, technology, or market position. What, then, might account for the differences in their recruitment preferences? Fundamentally, they are a product of the substantive rationalities with which these firms configure their labor processes and, for the most part, these substantive rationalities are culturally formed. They involve, on the one hand, the formal rationality that hegemonic industrial firms consider substantive to the efficient organization of production. And, on the other hand, they involve the particularistic or patronal values that local entrepreneurs consider substantive to the rational organization of their particular enterprises.

To state these problems more succinctly: the modernization paradigm gives somewhat imprecise focus to the influence of cultural factors that generally impinge upon the organization of enterprises and the circumstances of workers. As a rule, those who employ the paradigm oversimplify or ignore the determinative consequences of the economic forces that attach to the productive activities in which different types of enterprises and different categories of workers are engaged. Characteristically, these economic forces and their organizational expressions are the foci of the modes of production approach. However, those who subscribe to this approach tend to be overly economistic in interpreting or explaining the behavior of firms and the workers they engage. Accordingly, these macrotheories often confound or ignore variables that are critical to the ethnological configuration of substantive cases.

The empirical construction of economic marginality in Manaus is considerably more complex than is suggested by these macrotheories. Although related, the marginalization of workers as producers and workers as consumers are quite different phenomena and they engage very different institutional forces. The social exclusion or marginalization of workers with respect to productive activities is *not* a general condition associated with the technological sophistication of firms, resulting in widespread unemployment and the formation of a dual economy. In the case of workers as producers, the condition is not general but sectionally specific. It is mainly associated with labor processes and the behavior of firms; and, as suggested, these processes are not entirely or even primarily economic in their determination. In the case of workers as consumers, the condition is more general than specific and it has to do not so much with the economic value of individual labor, which is significantly influenced by the government, as with the income productivity and management of households.

There is also a psychocultural dimension of marginality, a dimension that derives its force from the social value of labor. Specific categories of workers (mostly those employed in the white collar and hegemonic industrial sectors) generally acquiesce in the cultural values according to which firms hold particular types of work in esteem. Other categories of workers (especially self-employed workers) do not concur in these values. At the same time, the social esteem in which firms and workers hold different types of work does not necessarily correspond to the market value of labor, a value that in the case of Manaus is not so much determined by supply and demand as it is politically determined.

When viewed in this perspective, the social formation that now exists in Manaus as a result of dependent capitalist development is one within which workers are increasingly differentiated and *socially* stratified with reference to their work. However, the differential status attaching to the occupational achievements of individual workers does not confer upon them the economic empowerment to acquire those luxury goods with which middle- and upper-class Brazilians (e.g., Brazilians such as those living in Parque Solimões) communicate and/or validate their status identities. In fact, the capacity of workers to acquire such goods seems to vary more according to circumstances affecting the size and composition of their particular households, and the extent and manner in which members of their families are economically active, than it depends upon their individual occupational achievements. Thus, in relationship to dependent capitalist development, workers in Manaus do not form a culturally coherent and socially integrated economic class.

It was suggested in the Introduction that to advance the discussion joined by contradictory studies relating to the dependent-development-marginality thesis, it may be helpful to lay aside assumptions concerning the nature of marginality in *theoretically constructed* social formations in favor of an "ethnological" point of view. The latter would give focus to the social and cultural differentiation of working-class elements in relationship to the processes of change occurring within a *real* social formation. Having done this, what are we to make of the modernization, dependency, and modes of production paradigms? Against the background of this case study, this author is very much inclined to agree with Roxborough's (1988) recent suggestion that when stripped to their core propositions, these paradigms do not assume quite the antagonistic contours vis-à-vis one another that they have acquired in contentious theoretical discussions.

The modernization paradigm, for example, underscores the ascendency of cultural systems that link the increased capacity for control with the formal rationality of human action.[9] Apropos this linkage, whether human action has to do with the control of material resources, people, technologies, markets, or physical environments, it has to be determined (1) whether calculated strategies confront, use, or modify cultural practices antecedent to their adoption, and (2) which of these strategies are *substantively rational* for what categories of actors. It is difficult to imagine how these determinations can be made without paying serious attention to the different processes by which producers, non-producers, and the means of production are actually brought into some kind of arrangement, and how this affects the overall structure of social formations. At their core, this is what the modes of production and various other neo-Marxist approaches are all about.

In view of this convergence, it seems that little can be gained by construing these approaches as antagonistic. It would perhaps be more productive if we were to move beyond these approaches and, in their synthesis, once again relocate studies of "development" within more general theoretical frameworks related to social and cultural change. At the same time, we need to pay much closer attention to the comparison of the microcontexts in which the more global processes of change are locally structured. In bringing this work to an end, I should like to elaborate this suggested shift in theoretical focus by briefly drawing attention once again to historical developments in the Amazon and describing how they seem to have affected the process, and thus the pattern, of those more current developments to which we have attributed the formation of working-class culture in Manaus.

Global Processes, Microcontexts, and Patterns of Change

As previously noted, economic development in the Amazon did not begin with the industrialization of Manaus. It began with a succession of extractive economies the development of which, until recent times, assumed the the character of an *intransitive* process of change.[10] The organization of extractive enterprises, even during the boom in rubber, generally conformed to a pattern of capital investment that was neither centrally planned nor coordinated at either the local or the national levels. Whatever planning was involved, it originated in the private sector among entrepreneurial groups whose interests in the export of primary materials to external markets did not collectively include a concern for developing the economy of the region. The capital with which these groups organized their enterprises was largely exogenous to the region. Since little manufacturing industry was locally involved, most of the capital accumulated by these entrepreneurial groups was in one way or another exported from the region. In effect, with respect to the development of these extractive economies, the state was a bystander and not a major actor in the process of economic change.[11]

This mode of developmental change stands in sharp contrast to the manner in which the federal government proceeded to centrally plan and construct an industrial pole in Manaus. With the creation of the Free Trade Zone, the superintendency of SUFRAMA, the use of public funds for infrastructural projects and with the provision of fiscal incentives to those firms and enterprises it has selectively favored, the state, not a particular government, became a major actor in the process of economic change. Thus, the industrialization of Manaus has proceeded predominantly in a *transitive* mode.

That the process of economic change shifted from an intransitive to a predominantly transitive mode in this regard is not surprising. Given the intransitive mode by which extractive enterprises emerged, given also their associated labor processes, their dependency on exogenous sources of capital, and their disengagement from a complete cycle of capital accumulation, after the rubber boom, the Amazon Valley contained little by way of population, capital, or national political influence. Consequently, substantial industrial development in Manaus, or anywhere else in the Amazon, could not possibly proceed in the same mode that had given rise to the region's extractive economies. If consequential industrialization were to occur at all, a transitive process of change had to be engaged. More specifically, it required a state-led political project in which public funds and large amounts of exogenous capital could be enlisted.

However, even in a transitive mode, industrial development could not proceed completely independent of the ethnohistorical factors arising out of the intransitive process that gave shape to the region's extractive economies. As we have seen, the state-led industrialization of Manaus necessitated the continued economic play of mercantilist entrepreneurial interests. These local entrepreneurs would individually respond to market opportunities and, without centralized planning or coordination, they would organize new enterprises or expand old ones in terms of the rationalities to which they were accustomed.

Additionally, because of the local factors, it was not feasible for the state to include in its development project the establishment of just any type of industry. Whatever the industry it contemplated establishing, its profitability could not depend upon a regional market comprised of less than seven million, mostly impoverished, consumers. Thus, it had to be responsive to external markets. Related to this, because of location, transportational costs would vary rather significantly according to the bulk of the product. For these and other reasons, it made some economic sense for the state to selectively promote the establishment of assemblage industries of the type previously described. Still, given its location in relationship to capital and product markets in general, why would the government want to establish an industrial pole in Manaus in the first place?[12]

Whatever the answer to the above question, the industrial development of Manaus has engaged a predominantly transitive process in which the state has become the most significant actor. This has not reordered the relationship between the state and Brazilian society. That was accomplished by the military in 1964. O'Donnell (1973), among others (Cardoso 1973, Erickson 1977, Evans 1979), has cogently described how Brazil's development model enjoined the military imposition of an authoritarian regime capable of constraining, almost to the point of absolute control, the economic and political aspirations of the impoverished popular sectors. The Free Trade Zone was but one regional project under the national development policy of the military and its supportive elites. Although this regional project did not alter the relationship that the military created between the state and Brazilian society, it did substantially restructure the relationship that previously existed between the state and local society. With industrialization, the state became the ultimate patrão in Manaus. With this change, a substantial segment of the working-class population has become a mass of faceless units of labor employed by the divisions of national and multinational enterprises, and increasingly dependent upon exogenous political forces for their economic well-being.

In conclusion, development in the Amazon has engaged two very different processes of change. Whether considered from the macro-perspective of the whole society or with reference to smaller units of analysis, the case of Manaus reveals that as economic changes are involved, these two processes are perhaps best thought of as standing in a dialectical-historical relationship. The case further reveals that the determination and consequences of these global processes for the social formation of working-class populations cannot be altogether understood without paying close attention to the ethnohistorical contexts in which economic changes unfold; nor can they be understood apart from the realization that the modernization, dependency, and modes-of-production approaches to the study of change are, in their core propositions, a necessary complement to their investigation.

Notes

Introduction.

1. As translated from "Zona Franca—Desenvolvimento (en novas bases) para a Amazônia Ocidental," *Interior* (janeiro/fevereiro de 1982), p. 4.

2. On a more personal note, this review of the literature was initiated during the final two years of my administrative duties as a departmental chairperson. When these were concluded in 1980, I was given a sabbatical leave and I returned to Brazil where I spent most of the year studying Portuguese, working in libraries, and collecting secondary data in São Paulo, Rio, Belém, and Manaus.

3. To cite but a few examples, see Meggers (1971); Gómez-Pompa et al. (1972); Denevan (1973); Hanbury-Tenison (1973); Sioli (1973); Reis (1974); Goodland and Irwin (1975); Katzman (1975, 1977); Cardoso and Müller (1977); Davis (1977); Moran (1977, 1981); Ianni (1978); Bunker (1979, 1980, 1981, 1985); Mahar (1979); Ferreira (1980); Pinto (1980); Foweraker (1981); Hecht (1980); Sautchuk et al. (1980); and Mougeot and Aragón, eds. (1983).

4. See, for example, Wagley, ed. (1974); Moran (1974, 1977, 1981); Cardoso and Müller (1977); Davis (1977); Schmink (1977); Ianni (1978, 1979); Bunker (1979, 1980, 1981, 1985); Sawyer (1979); Hecht (1980); and Foweraker (1981).

5. In this regard, the reader might want to consult Cardoso (1960, 1962); Lopes (1964); Reis (1964); Pereira (1965); L. Martins (1966); Leeds (1969); Rodrigues (1970); Erickson et al. (1974); Berlinck (1975); Erickson and Peppe (1976); Leeds and Leeds (1976); Perlman (1976); Wells (1976); Erickson (1977); Kowarick (1977); Carmargo, et al. (1978); Villalobos et al. (1978); Rosen (1982); and Krischke, ed. (1984).

6. See Mougeot (1980) and the collection of papers edited by Mougeot and Aragón (1983).

7. Among the best of these works are those reported by Tastivin (1943);

Meggers (1950); Wagley (1953); Watson (1953); Galvão (1955, 1959); Condurú (1974); Moran (1974); Reis (1974); Anderson (1976); Miller 1976); Ross (1978); Ianni (1978); Bunker (1979, 1981, 1985); Santos (1979); and Sawyer (1979). In general, Caboclos are descendants of Indians and Luso-Brasilians who in varying numbers at different times moved into the region in search of a livelihood. The literature to which I refer here generally excludes anthropological studies that have given exclusive focus to indigenous Indian populations.

8. See, for example, Foster-Carter (1976); Cardoso (1977); Chilcote (1974, 1981, 1984); Chilcote and Johnson, eds. (1983); Bunker (1985: 20–58); Chilcote and Edelstein (1986); Valenzuela and Valenzuela (1981); and de Janvry (1985). The de Janvry piece is particularly illuminating in its summary comparison of theories of development.

9. It appears to me somewhat ironic that while these studies question the validity of the marginalization thesis in relationship to dependent industrial development, studies carried out in the hegemonic economies of advanced industrial societies seem to accomplish the opposite. Braverman's (1974) "degradation of work" hypothesis in reference to monopoly capitalism could be construed as a version of the marginalization thesis. Another version has been put forth by Friedman (1977), who contends that a "center" and a dependent "periphery" emerge even within advanced capitalist economies. Friedman concludes that the principles of uneven development that operate on a national scale also operate on a world scale. Similarly Edwards (1979) has presented an analysis of "core" and "peripheral" modes of production in the American economy and concludes that the development of monopoly capitalism has so "marginalized" and factionalized the working class that it is unable to challenge the capitalist hegemony in American society.

10. It seems that the marginality thesis simply will not go away. In economics and economic anthropology, the concept has emerged again in researches relating to the "formal" and "informal" sectors. See, for example, Hart (1973); Souza and Tokman (1976); Moser (1978, 1984); Portes and Walton (1981); Despres (1987, 1988); Peattie (1987); and Lomnitz (1988).

11. Dissatisfied with various macrotheoretical constructions concerning working-class populations, including the marginality thesis, Zaluar (pp. 33–64) argues that the concept of "classes populares" resolves the problem of categorizing the working-class populations while facilitating paying much needed analytical attention to the fact that such populations are quite heterogeneous in their social, economic, and political circumstances. Although I will argue in this work that the marginality concept retains some, if not much, analytic value, I would have little quarrel with the position taken by Zaluar.

12. In addition to Zaluar (1985), recommended among studies of this type are: Bonilla (1964); Miller (1965); Chaplin (1970); Greaves (1972); Peppe (1977); Spalding, Jr. (1977); Goldschmidt (1978); Nash (1979); Taussig (1980); Salaff (1981); and Fausto Neto (1982).

13. The size of this household sample was strictly a function of the time available for the collection of field data.

Chapter 1.

1. The aviamento system has been described in considerable detail by Wagley (1953: 81–100) and others (see e.g., Cardoso and Müller 1977: 31–32; Bunker 1985: 65–72). Various features of the system have been analyzed in some detail by Sawyer (1979).

2. The word 'formation' has a double meaning. On the one hand, it refers to a state of being at a given historical moment—what anthropologists sometimes call the 'ethnographic present.' On the other hand, 'formation' can imply a process of change and, thus, a comparison of historical moments. The cultural formations to be briefly described here are models abstracted from the literature relating to Amazonian populations engaged in aviamento.

3. In the Amazon, the appellation Caboclo is generally applied to a person of inferior status and, thus, it is rarely used for purposes of self-identity. Caboclo culture has been profiled in a substantial number of studies (e.g., Tastevin 1943; Meggers 1950; Wagley 1953; Watson 1953; Galvão 1955, 1959; Condurú 1974; Moran 1974; Reis 1974; Anderson 1976; Miller 1976; Ross 1978; Santos 1979; Sawyer 1979; Bunker 1981, 1985: 58–76). As Wagley (1953: 35) has noted, the leading student of Amazon colonial history is Artur Cezar Ferreira Reis (1942). More recently, however, the history of Caboclo culture has been succinctly summarized by Moran (1974), Ross (1978), Sawyer (1979: 5–45), and Bunker (1985: 58–76).

4. See also Bunker (1985: 58–65).

5. This estimate is based on the total population reported for the Northern Region, plus the population of the states of Mato Grosso, Goias, and Maranhão, minus the urban population reported for this total area.

6. For a brief description of these cults, collectively known as *Batuque* in Belém, see Moran (1974: 153–54).

7. One exception to this statement may be the Círio (procession) de Nazareth, celebrated each year on the second Sunday of October in honor of Our Lady of Nazareth, the patroness of Belém. Hundreds of thousands of people attend this festival from localities in the Lower Amazon and, indeed, many come from the Northeast and other regions of Brazil.

8. For an analysis of cooperative work groups in Brazil, see J.V. Freitas Marcondes (1948: 374–84).1

9. Minas Gerais is an exception to this pattern of urbanization. In Minas,

urban settlements generally preceded the organization of rural enterprises.

10. The culture described by Freyre for these cidades is wonderfully embellished by Jorge Amado (1962) in his celebrated novel, *Gabriela.*

11. In Brazilian politics, this pattern of local control is often referred to as *coronelism,* a name deriving from the fact that in many municípios the local landowner or political leader was often a person of military rank in the local militia of the area. Afterwards, the great landowners were called "colonels."

12. Concerning the power and ideology of contemporary political elites in Brazil, see McDonough (1981).

13. Source materials in this regard are scattered and difficult to gather. Ernesto Cruz (n.d.) has compiled historical materials for Belém. Benchimol (1947) presented an M.A. thesis relating the history of Manaus, portions of which have been updated and summarized in a more recent work (Benchimol 1977). Much of Benchimol's summary is itself based on earlier works by Miranda (1908), Mata (1916), Bitencourt (1925), Reis (1931, 1935), and Monteiro (1946).

14. As quoted by Reis (1935) and cited by Benchimol (1977: 72), and translated by the author.

15. These figures are based on data reported in Anuário Estatístico do Brasil, FIBGE, 1983, pp. 76–79.

16. In 1890, the Federal Government commissioned a young army officer, Cândido Mariano da Silva Rondon, to carry out military and scientific expeditions in the Amazon. These expeditions were conducted over a twenty-five year period and they received considerable publicity. Whatever else Rondon accomplished, he instilled in the Brazilian military a tradition of concern for the security and economic potential of the region (Davis 1977: 1–3).

17. Much of the material presented here has been abstracted from various sources, including: Katzman (1975, 1977); Davis (1977); Cardoso and Müller (1977); Mahar (1979); Skillings and Tcheyan (1979); and publications issued by the *Superintendency for the Development of Amazonia* (SUDAM 1973, 1974). Regarding federal development agencies operating in the Amazon, material relating to the legislation by which these were established, their authority, organization, fiscalization, objectives and functions are best summarized by Cardoso and Müller (1977: 109–38) and Mahar (1979: 1–34).

18. For purposes of analysis, it is not necessary to detail here the modification in development plans that followed upon *Operation Amazônia* and the Castelo Branco government. These changes have been succintly summarized and analyzed by Mahar (1979: 10–34). In effect, SUDAM's role in development action was somewhat lessened by the *Programa de Integração Nacional* (PIN, 1970), the Programa de Redistribuição de Terras (PROTERRA, 1971), the creation or reorganization of such sectorial agencies as *Empresa Brasileira de Turisimo* (EMBRATUR), *Instituto Nacional de Colonização e Reforma Agrária*

(INCRA), the *Superintendência da Zona Franca de Manaus* (SUFRAMA), and the *Companhia de Pesquisa de Recursos Minerais* (CPRM). See also Cardoso and Müeller (1977: 109–38).

19. Project Radam involved an infra-red, aerial-photographic and mapping survey of the entire Amazon Basin and was carried out mainly by the Aero Service Division of Litton Industries in the United States in association with LASA, Brazil's leading civil engineering firm. See Davis (1977: 62–65 and 89–99). Also see 'Project Radam Maps the Unknown in Brazil,' *Engineering and Mining Journal* (November 1975: 165–8). The results of this project indicated that the Amazon Basin contained one of the most valuable and diverse mineral profiles in the world.

20. Carajás is a huge mineral extraction project currently under development in Pará. The Brazilian government has estimated that Carajás will eventually involve private investments totaling approximately U.S. $61 billion. Similarly, the Jari Project (which has been judged a failure) also has received world attention. As originally developed, it involved a land concession of 38,000 km² in Pará and Amapá to a group of companies held by the American industrialist Daniel Keith Ludwig, principally for the cultivation of timber and the production of cellulose. Despite Ludwig's personal investment of almost U.S. $1 billion, concessions made to him and his group of companies have been considered a national scandal by many Brazilians. See, for example, Filha (1980: 7–40) for criticism of the Jari Project. Today the project has been assumed by the Brazilian government and is managed by Brazilian companies.

21. These priorities have not been significantly altered by more recent development plans. For example, under SUDAM's PDAM III (*III Plano de Desenvolvimento da Amazônia 1980–85*), a total of Cr$735,856.8 millions (1979 prices) was projected for project disbursement. Of this amount, 57.6 percent was to be allocated as follows: projects relating to agroindustrial development (12.9 percent), manufacturing industry (15.5 percent), energy (12.0 percent), and transportation (17.2 percent). Of the remaining 42.4 percent, 19.4 percent was to be allocated to health and sanitation, 7.9 percent to housing, and 6.2 percent to education and professional training. See SUDAM (1982: 67).

22. It should be noted in this context that between 1965 and 1977, 80 percent of the development funds disbursed by SUDAM were allocated to projects in the eastern Amazon. For an analysis of this intra-regional distortation, see Salazar (1981).

23. Local economists often refer to the new industries in Manaus as capital-intensive. I consider this concept to be extremely misleading. In theory, capital-intensive industries are those in which the cost of capital figures more significantly than the cost of labor in the unit cost of production. I have never seen data to this effect with respect to the industries implanted in Manaus. However, most of these industries are assemblage in type and they are extremely dependent upon the use of unskilled labor and therefore wages are low.

24. The bias in favor of so-called capital-intensive industries of the type described here is further amplified by SUFRAMA's annual allocation of import quotas. Between 1979 and 1983, relative to commercial and service establishments, industries in Manaus have received between 74 and 84 percent of the import quotas established for the ZFM and the lion's share of this has gone to capital-intensive industries dependent for their production upon the foreign import of components. See SUFRAMA (1983: 9). Also see Mahar (1979: 63–79 and 142–51) on foreign and domestic trade.

25. The sense of this dependency was particularly evident in 1984 when talk emerged in certain circles of the Federal government concerning the possibility of creating a second free trade zone at Foz do Iguaçu in the state of Paraná, near the massive Itaipu hydroelectric dam on the border of Paraguay. The thought of industry leaving Manaus for this more favorable location struck fear of another prolonged period of stagnation among commercial and political elites in the state of Amazonas. It was immediately evident to all concerned that the ZFM could not be sustained in competition against a parallel program of this type.

26. Sena Filho (1983: 27–53) relates despovoamento to survival strategies associated with the processes of dependent development.

27. In a study made by Tupiassú and Jatene (1978) and cited by Mougeot and Aragón (1983: 12) for the period 1967–72, a significant increase in the concentration of land is reported for all states and territories of the Northern Region. Martins (1980: 87) reports that in 1975–76, no less than 60 percent of all land disputes in Brazil, and 90 percent of the deaths resulting from such disputes, occured in Amazonia. See also Ianni (1979) and Martins (1981).

28. Bentes' report is mainly demographic and it excludes the analysis of a great deal of non-demographic data that was collected during the course of his research.

29. The calculations reported in Table 3 were computed from Table 18, as published by IBGE, Censo Demográfico de 1960, VII Receseamento Geral, Vol. l, Parte 2, pp. 120–21, and Censo Demográfico de 1980, IX Recenseamento Geral, Vol. l, Tomo 5, No. 4, Tables 1.7 and 1.25, pp. 29–34 and 225–31. In making these calculations, it was assumed for 1960 that the distribution of economically active population by economic sector in Manaus was generally proportionate to the município's share of the economically active urban population for Amazonas. Judging from the 1980 census, this assumption may somewhat underestimate the number employed in Manaus for the public administration and defense sectors of the economy but not enough to distort the overall picture drawn by Table 3.

30. The calculations reported in Table 4 were computed from Table 13, IBGE, Censo Demográfico de 1960, VII Recenseamento Geral do Brasil, Vol. 1, Parte 2, pp. 180–81, and Table 1.8, Censo Demográfico de 1980, IX Recensea-

mento Geral do Brasil, Vol. 1, Tomo 5, No. 4, pp. 35–36. In making these caculations, it was assumed that the distribution of the economically active population by occupational position and economic sector in Manaus was generally proportionate to the município's share of the economically active urban population for Amazonas. The only check I was able to make concerning the validity of this assumption is based on a study of 5,336 household heads living in seven public housing schemes and conducted in 1978 by SHAM (Sociedade de Habitação do Estado Do Amazonas). No employers lived in these public housing schemes. However, the distribution of wage and self-employed workers in these households closely approximates that reported in Table 4. Autonomous workers, according to IBGE, are individuals who are self-employed or who employ only family. Except for some independent professionals who might be included in this category, most autonomous workers are engaged in the so-called informal sector of the economy. The informal sector will be given more detailed consideration in a later context.

31. This particular datum raises a number of theoretical problems that have been addressed elsewhere. See Despres (1987: 67–88; 1988a; 1988b).

32. By the labor process, I am simply referring to the coordinated set of activities and relationships involved in the production of goods and services.

Chapter 2.

1. FAMASA is an affiliate of Sharp do Brasil and, thus, directly tied to the electronics industry. As of 1982, even the packaging material used in the shipment of finished products originated outside of Amazonas.

2. CODEMA: unpublished report. In 1982, the electronics industry accounted for 29 percent of the total value of imports by the state of Amazonas from the rest of Brazil.

3. Export data were not available for 1982, but in 1980, these three states received 87 percent of the total value of goods exported from Amazonas to the national market. CODEMA: unpublished report.

4. Tourists arrive by air and by ship. In 1982, according to SUFRAMA (1983: 21) almost 306 million domestic passengers disembarked at Manaus' international airport " . . . because of interest in the region and in order to buy foreign goods and goods produced in the ZFM." Informants at SUFRAMA estimate that approximately 1500 additional passengers arrive each week by ship.

5. The electronics sector in Manaus accounted for approximately 15 percent of SUFRAMA's fixed investment in infrastructural development. Within the Industrial Park, however, the electronics sector absorbed almost 29 percent of SUFRAMA's fixed investment in infrastructural development. As of 1983,

SUFRAMA's fixed investment in infrastructural industrial development was reported to be U.S. $155 millions (1972 rate of exchange). Because of the fluctuation in the value of the cruzeiro in the international market, the usual procedure is to report dollar values at the rate of exchange in 1972 when one U.S. 1$ was valued at Cr$ 1,000. Unless otherwise indicated, this procedure will be used throughout the text. The reader needs to be informed that the purchasing power of the cruzeiro in 1984 was generally less than half its purchasing power in 1972.

6. These multinational affiliates represent a fixed infrastructural investment by SUFRAMA of U.S. $23 millions (SUFRAMA 1983: 31–54). The capital investment of the firms themselves, in plant and machinery, could not be obtained.

7. For example, Evadin Componentes Da Amazônia, with 55 employees, makes small motors and coils for Evadin Indústrias Amazônia.

8. The rationale for this selection was to determine if the national origin of these affiliates significantly affected their managerial styles, benefit structures, and relationships with workers. For purposes of anonymity, these firms will be respectively identified by the Portuguese letters (H) and (J). The research included the administration of a comprehensive interview schedule with the personnel directors, extended tours of production facilities, and in-depth interviews with a sample of workers drawn from these and eight additional firms. Workers were interviewed in their homes and not at their place of work.

9. Between 1982 and 1984, because of the recession in Brazil, the number of workers employed by these firms fell off 25 percent. At the time of research, both firms projected a recovery in employment in 1985 as a result of plans to add new product lines.

10. This datum was confirmed by independent sources as well as observation. Indeed, administrators at Jota could not participate in this research until they were authorized to do so from São Paulo.

11. Indeed, Agá's Director of Industrial Relations indicated that because of serious locational disadvantages the firm would probably not continue its operations in Manaus if the fiscal incentives of the Zona Franca were terminated or substantially diminished.

12. Some electronics firms reserve the classification "qualified worker" for technicians and consider montadoras as "un-qualified." Whatever the case, assembly workers are the lowest level personnel in the organizational structure of these firms and are not differentiated from janitors, sweepers, cleaning women, and the like. Technicians, including inspectors, are one grade higher and sometimes occupy the position of sub-department or group "chefe" and oversee the work of 20–40 workers.

13. In Brazil the minimum salary is established by federal legislation and was being adjusted twice each year relative to the cost of living in different

regions of the country. At the time of research, the minimum salary in Manaus was Cr$97,000/month. Because of biannual adjustments for inflation, the number of minimum salaries earned is used as a standard of comparison rather than the amount of cruzeiros. At 1982 rates of exchange, because of inflation, the dollar equivalent of one minimum salary at the official rate of exchange fell from approximately U.S. $59.00 to U.S. $34.00 within a period of less than six months.

14. The recreational facilities and programs at Jota are considerably more elaborate than those currently provided by Agá. Interview data, however, suggest that because of the character and schedule of events, transportation problems, and family commitments, the majority of workers at both firms do not avail themselves of these facilities. This is particularly the case with female employees.

15. Among the workers interviewed, there exists no consensus about the differential quality of care at private and public clinics.

16. This situation has changed significantly.

17. At the time of research, the metallurgical union in Manaus was engaged in an internal factional dispute that was of some concern to the electronics firms because it posed the possibility of a much closer alliance between the newly elected officers of the metallurgical union in Manaus and their more militant counterparts in São Paulo. The anxiety generated by the dispute was further heightened by the fact that 1984 happened to be an election year and it had become increasingly evident that the next government would be formed by Tancredo Neves and the PMDB (*Partido do Movimento Democrático Social*). The PMDB has been considered to be much more responsive to the interests of workers than the ruling PDS (*Partido Democrático Social*), the party that had controlled the Brazilian government since the military coup of 1964.

18. Agá's director of industrial relations is from Minas Gerais. He was educated in São Paulo and spent several years abroad. Jota's director of industrial relations was born and educated in São Paulo and was subsequently sent abroad for training "in the home company."

19. To illustrate his point, the director noted: "Jota recently had three production units that we wanted to unify. It involved transferring workers from one unit to another. The workers had to be transferred or fired. They held a meeting and some refused to be transferred to similar work without raises. They were fired immediately and replaced."

20. CIPA committees are elected by workers and, by law, are charged with the responsibility of seeing to it that employers comply with federally prescribed safety regulations.

21. Because capital did not own the means of production (chiefly labor) and the mode of production was essentially pre-industrial, and also because capital exacted surplus value through a system of debt peonage rather than the pay-

ment of wages, Bunker (1985: 65–72) argues that the extractive economy in the Amazon was profoundly non-capitalist. This position seems to unduly restrict the application of the capitalist model to its industrial forms to the exclusion of mercantilism. Clearly, the type of mercantilism that existed in the Amazon virtually precluded the possibility of an industrial transformation independent of external sources of capital.

22. Timber cutting in the várzea tends to be seasonal in that trees are generally felled when flood waters recede and are left there to be floated to collection points when the várzea is flooded. Even today, holding ponds at sawmills are often depleted when logs cannot be floated out of the várzea for delivery to Manaus.

23. The number of serrarias (54) given for Manaus in 1972 by Bruce (1976) does not square with the estimates I was given in interviews with two prominent sawmill owners in 1984. Both owners and the President of *Sindicato dos Trabalhadores de Madeira* contended that approximately 15 serrarias existed in Manaus in 1984 and that the number did not exceed 100 for the entire State of Amazonas. However, these informants did not count small, backyard, family enterprises operating with a saw attached to a gasoline engine and cutting boards, not logs, mainly for sale in the informal sector. It is not known if these were included in Bruce's figure: whatever the case, the number of serrarias in Manaus fell off considerably between 1972 and 1984.

24. It is locally reputed that the laminated woods produced in Manaus are not highly bonded because of the low quality and moisture content of the wood used.

25. The inclusion of a fábrica de compensado in the field research might have been instructive. However, this was precluded because of the limits of time and financing. However, concurrent with my fieldwork, a study of female participation in the labor force of a large compensado was in the process of being completed by Edila Arnaud Ferreira Moura, a professor of sociology at the University of Amazonas, and she kindly made available to me a preliminary report of her data.

26. These names, of course, are fictitious.

27. Figures were not made available for the losses incurred in the processing of wood. However, most serrarias in Manaus, including Serraria Amazonense and Serraria Paranaense, do not conserve sawdust and wood scraps for the production of by-products and the yard manager estimated up to fifty percent of the delivered value of logs may be lost by decomposition in the holding pond, by sawing and planing, and by discarding boards unfit for sale.

28. Probationary status means that the worker's work card is either withheld or not issued. The length of this probationary period is supposed to be fixed by law for particular categories of workers but it is often made indeterminate by unscrupulous employers in order to avoid paying benefits. Such employers know that workers who are badly in need of employment will not push the matter to an

official complaint. According to workers, neither of these serrarias engaged in this unscrupulous practice but they knew of others that did.

29. At the sawmill, there is at least one case of an elderly widow of a former employee who has been allowed to retain her "home" since her husband's death several years past.

30. I should note that the initial selection of workers in this sector included at least two of the following types: office secretaries, office workers, telephone operators, nurses, store clerks, bank clerks, bookkeepers, and primary school teachers. The sample was expanded as we encountered white collar workers among the households included in the study. I should also note here that an in-depth study of a selection of firms in this sector was quite beyond the possible scope of my preliminary research.

31. As originally introduced by Hart (1973) in his anthropological studies of Accra, the informal sector concept was employed simply to present an ethnographic description of the range of income opportunities available to the urban poor. The subsequent application of the concept by the ILO and others to the analysis of development and underdevelopment has engendered a great deal of theoretical debate (see Bromley 1978; Moser 1978, 1984; Peattie 1987). This is not the place to engage these discussions. Here, it suffices to note that according to one's particular macrotheoretical orientation, dependent structural linkages between the informal and formal sectors are shaped by the commingling of petty commodity and capitalist modes of production or, alternatively, they result from the wage and labor strategies of capitalist enterprises which seek to lower costs by maintaining a reserve army of surplus labor (see e.g., Frank 1970; Roberts 1978: 159–77; Souza and Tokman 1976; Portes and Walton 1981: 67–106). In view of these theoretical discussions, it seemed to me that a study of working-class developments in Manaus could not proceed without including a selected sample of self-employed workers and their families. To proceed otherwise would be to exclude from purview what much of the literature portrayed as containing the poorest elements of the urban working class. With reference to Brazil, the informal sector concept has been applied by Alessio (1970), Merrik (1976), Tolsa (1976 and 1978), Prandi (1980), Jelin (1980), and Vianna (1980). Clearly, as revealed in these studies, the flow of goods and services through the informal sector is very much related to the demand created for these goods and services by wage workers as well as firms operating in the formal sector.

Chapter 3.

1. "Selectivity" in this and similar contexts implies that either employers prefer to hire individuals disclosing specified social characteristics, in this case urban or rural origins; or, alternatively, individuals having these characteristics

tend to find employment in one sector rather than another independent of whether or not this is their preference.

2. It was my general impression that the hiring preference of many employers in the white collar sector favored males rather than females. However, I do not have substantial data to conclude that this is the case.

3. By categorical status differentiation I refer to the tendency of firms and enterprises to ascribe social differences to persons on on the basis of categorical attributes such as gender or social origins and and to do so independently of their individual qualifications. An example of this is the view held by hegemonic firms that women are more adaptive to tedious work tasks than are men.

4. Actually, only two workers reported less than one minimum salary.

5. It may be noted that the income distribution reported here for self-employed workers did not include data that were collected in a special study of comerciantes. Had the income data for twenty comerciantes been included, the number of self-employed workers earning three-to-four minimum salaries would have increased from 20.8 to 28.9 percent and the percentage reporting five minimum salaries or more would have remained the same.

6. For example, only two self-employed workers reported earning more than six minimum salaries and none reported more than eight. In the white collar sector, this level of monthly income was matched or exceeded only by workers in the state or federal services, mainly accountants, communications specialists, statisticians, and the like.

7. Some but not much. In this sector, 52 percent of those with a secondary education earned only one minimum salary/month. The comparable figure for the white collar sector is 43 percent.

8. It needs to be emphasized that this summary of data presents patterns that are more or less typical. I do not wish to imply that the parents of workers always migrated together or that both were employed when they arrived in Manaus. If both were employed, the male is taken as a referent for purposes of this analysis.

9. Whenever informants expressed no knowledge of the income status of their parents, the cases were omitted for purposes of this analysis. It should be noted that even if the information reported by informants in regard to parental income was not verifiable, and thus may not be objectively accurate, it nevertheless reflects their subjective perception of how much their income status has improved relative to that of their parents.

10. Self-employed workers, of course, are excluded.

11. Several of the electronics workers interviewed indicated that they wanted to work in the hegemonic industries only long enough to accumulate sufficient capital by way of wages or indemnification funds to buy the equip-

ment they needed to set-up shop as television and radio repairmen in their neighborhoods, or to buy a car with which they would establish a taxi service, or to purchase inventory for a small shop or street stand.

12. I appropriated the term "living work" from Marx but my conceptualization and use of it are very different (see Marx 1967: 173–192).

13. This particular case will be discussed in a later context where it will be noted that Linda inherited a very nice home as well as a pension from her deceased husband. Her elderly mother lives with her and also receives a small pension. In addition, her "amasiado" works and receives four minimum salaries.

14. This statement requires two caveats. Among electronics workers, generally those who were classified as "técnicos," like many white collar workers, derived a profound sense of status from their work. They, however, are a very small minority of the workers in this sector. Also, it should be noted that among the informants drawn from this sector, men were much more inclined than women to discuss in considerable detail their social lives in relationship to their work. Except for those with a higher level of education, female informants were a bit more cautious in discussing relationships at work. Female workers appeared to be more fearful of losing their jobs than did their male counterparts. Oftentimes in the interview situation, it was their husbands or other members of the household who encouraged them to be more open in discussing these matters.

15. For example, 60 percent of the sawmill workers interviewed had worked in excess of ten years for the same firm. Sixty-five percent of these workers, compared to 25 and 18 percent of white collar and hegemonic industrial workers, counted one or more relatives among their workmates. And 55 percent, as compared to 40 and 18 percent of white collar and hegemonic industrial workers, counted one or more of their workmates among their closest friends.

16. The most recent example of this is the settlement that has been established at Enseada do Marapatá, where the proprietor of Serraria Paranaense has housed many of the families he moved with the company from Paraná. These industrial neighborhoods will be considered in more detail in a later context.

17. Only one comerciante was included in my household sample of 45 self-employed workers. As a consequence, a special but more limited study was made of 22 comerciantes. The research gave focus almost exclusively to the economic and organizational dimensions of their enterprises. Whereas the monthly income of the 45 self-employed workers interviewed averaged 1.85 minimum salaries, that of comerciantes averaged 5.8 minimum salaries, an amount in excess of that earned by most white collar workers in the public sector.

Chapter 4.

1. As simple and straightforward as this question appears, it is one fraught with theoretical and methodological difficulties. Nancy Folbre (1986: 245–55) has recently pointed out that despite their very different perspectives, both neoclassical and Marxian economic theory converge on the view that the household forms an "almost wholly cooperative, altruistic unit." Needless to say, anthropologists tend to share this view of the household. As Folbre notes, this idyllic view of the household has been seriously questioned by a growing body of feminist research.

2. Cf. Introduction, pp. 8–9.

3. The overall distribution of these households in terms of size does not differ significantly from that reported for the 5,336 families that resided in the seven public housing conjuntos managed by SHAN (1978: 116). Because these conjuntos are occupied almost exclusively by working-class families, I consider them rather typical of the population under investigation. Thus, whenever the data are comparable, I used SHAN's survey of these conjuntos to evaluate the representativeness of the households included in the present study.

4. The households included in the sample averaged 6.24 persons/household. The division between small and large households is taken to be five, a breakpoint that falls closer to the median (5.27).

5. Only five of the eighty-eight households included in the study were headed by women and all five were either widowed or separated.

6. Almost 31 percent of these informants had siblings living in the neighborhood and 51 percent had siblings living elsewhere in Manaus.

7. In its survey of public housing conjuntos, SHAN does not provide data relating the organization of family units. However, in 1980, IBGE reported that 60.7 percent of the family units in Manaus were "nuclear" and 39.3 percent were "extended" or "composite."

8. An approximation of the representativeness of the sample of households included in this study can be gleaned from a comparison of the distribution of household incomes reported in Table 11 with that based on an analysis of the large random sample of households that Bentes (1983) drew from Bairro Raiz. Twenty-seven percent of the households in Bente's sample, compared to 33 percent in the author's sample, reported incomes of three minimum salaries or less. At the other end of the distribution, the author's sample contained six percent fewer households reporting incomes in excess of six minimum salaries or more. Thus, in terms of household income, the author's sample seems somewhat biased toward lower working-class households.

9. As reported by *A Noticia* (Sept. 19, 1984), one of the newspapers in Manaus, between 1980 and 1984 the number of commercial establishments in

the state of Amazonas declined by more than half as a result of the recession.

10. As reported in *A Noticia* (Oct. 4, 1984). According to the report in *A Noticia*, households earning up to 5.25 minimum salaries tend to spend 100 percent of their earnings and households falling in this category most directly influence the composition of consumer prices in Manaus.

11. Other hard liquors (e.g., whiskey, gin, vodka, and wines) are readily available but they are expensive, and only two of the highest income households reported purchasing these kinds of beverages for holidays or family celebrations.

12. All but one of these were occupied by employees of Serraria Paranaense.

13. Based on interviews with housing authorities, it seems that among low income groups, particularly among those who have access to public housing, the cost of owning a house in Manaus is not much more than the cost of renting from what might be described as the typical "slumlord." In 1980, approximately 82 percent of those paying monthly rent in Manaus paid less than one minimum salary, a level of payment comparable to 70 percent of those who were buying homes. See Censo Demográfico-Famílias e Domicílios, IBGE, 1980, pp. 88–89.

14. It may be noted that these relationships obtain at a statistically significant level (P <.001). If the homes of workers at Serraria Paranaense, all of which were constructed of wood by their employer, are excluded, the probability of the relationship drops to the .02 level of significance.

15. In assessing space, it was not possible to take physical measurements. Only rooms were counted. Space divided by curtains or impermanent decorative furniture such as moveable cabinets or room dividers was not counted as separate rooms.

16. By no means can these families be counted among the poorest in Manaus. The quality of their housing, however, is not much better than that reported for 35,069 domiciles occupied by families earning two minimum salaries or less/month. In 1980, these domiciles represented 26.6 percent of all the households in Manaus. See Censo Demográfico-Famílias e Domicílios, IBGE, 1980, pp. 52–53.

17. It may be noted that only three households contained a deep-freeze unit in addition to a refrigerator and in each case this represented a capital investment for a self-employed worker. One stored and sold frozen meats from the freezer and two sold ice cream bars. Similarly with washing machines. Only five households contained a washing machine. Four of these were used in conjunction with a "biscate"; i.e., the "dona da casa" took in wash as a source of income. The other was located in a multiple income household in which both the husband and wife worked as accountants and reported a combined income of 11 minimum salaries/month.

18. All three of the households without a television unit had access to one owned by a relative living in the neighborhood.

19. It should be noted that seven of the upper income households contained two color televisions. Three upper and three middle income households contained both color and black and white units and two lower income households contained two black and white units.

20. It was observed that stereophonic equipment is extensively used for playing records and tapes in middle- and upper-middle-class households in Manaus. Even in these households, however, the playing of stereophonic units takes second place to watching television.

21. It is noteworthy that while 77 percent of the households inventoried contained at least one electric fan, only six households, all upper income, had an air conditioning unit. Less than 22 percent of the households had one or more bicycles. All of these were purchased for use by children and 66 percent of these were located in upper income households.

22. It should be noted that with the creation of a Honda factory for the assemblage of motorcycles in Manaus, young male workers were increasingly looking toward the purchase of a motorcycle rather than the more expensive automobile. However, despite its cost, the automobile remained the preferred status symbol.

23. It may be noted that all but three of these households were multiple income units and white collar workers comprised 62 percent of the economically active persons within these units.

24. These lower income households may be counted among the 65 percent of all households in Manaus that reported earning five minimum salaries or less in 1980.

Chapter 5.

1. Although implicit in the work of Marx (see e.g., *The Grundrisse*, as translated by David McLellan, 1971: 17–46), the insertion of the household in the productive structure of society begin to receive more empirical focus with the work of such social historians as E. P. Thompson (1963). In anthropology, the work of Claude Meillassoux (1981) has been theoretically influential with regard to household studies. For Brazil, see Bilac (1978); Macedo (1979); Schmink (1979); Banck (1980); Durham (1980); Jelin (1980); Vianna (1980); and Fausto Neto (1982); Merrick and Schmink (1983); Barbosa (1984); Augel (1984).

2. I attempt to avoid assumptions concerning decision-making strategies within households. Whether a consensus existed with reference to such strate-

and thus no effort was make to gather systematic data in this regard.

3. In Manaus between 1960 and 1980, the number of married couples reporting both a civil and a religious union declined from 51 to 46 percent. The number reporting a religious marriage declined from 21 to 8 percent. The number reporting a civil marriage increased from 19 to 27 percent.

4. The evidence provided for this by Rosen consists of data derived from verbal responses to a survey instrument administered to the wives and most of the husbands of 816 families, randomly selected in five communities centering on the state of São Paulo. The communities themselves were selected with reference to a rural-urban-industrial continuum, the city of São Paulo representing the most industrialized of the communities. Rosen's conclusions with respect to the strength of the parentela is largely based on a statistical analysis of the responses obtained from women to attitudinal questions. Although Rosen reports a significant relationship between the strength of the parentela as measured by these variables and industrialization, the relationship with social class is even more significant.

5. The best description available in the literature remains that of Wagley (1963: 184–204).

6. The extensive collection of kinship data was clearly beyond the scope and outside the focus of the author's research.

7. A household contains a nuclear family if it includes the head of a household with children, married or not, or a married couple without children.

8. This is not an entirely satisfactory criterion for the presence or absence of a modified parentela because residentiality is a sufficient but not a necessary condition for the existence of such a unit. However, this is the only measure we have available from IBGE with which to draw comparisons.

9. IBGE defines a domicile occupied by a composite family when the household contains a non-relative, excluding domestics. The problem is that the non-relative may be attached to a household that includes either a nuclear or an extended family. Thus, this category cannot be disaggregated for comparative purposes. The author's sample included four households of this type (4.5 percent) and they were classified on the basis of the principal family unit. In all four cases the arrangement was temporary and the non-relative was a close friend of the family, a migrant in the process of relocating in Manaus. One had found employment and was preparing to move at the time of interview.

10. For conceptual reasons, this comparison also demands caution. As defined by Leis Municipais (31 August 1960), urban areas in Brazil are defined as administrative and not populational units. Urban areas include sites of Municípios, villages that function as administrative sites of Districts, and "isolated" urban areas delimited by municipal authorities. All areas falling outside these administrative units are defined as rural. In effect, many areas classified

as urban are very small and relatively isolated centers of population.

11. This difference between the sampled households exceeds the .02 level of significance. It may be noted that the distribution of multiple and single income households by the sector of employment of household heads does not reach a level of significance.

12. To contextualize Table 22 for the reader: 48.8 percent of the 62 multiple income households in the sample contained two economically active workers; 24.2 percent contained three; 14.5 percent contained four; and 14.5 percent contained five or more.

13. The categories "equal to" and "lower" had to be collapsed to meet the requirements of X^2 analysis. The educational status of only nine individuals was lower than that of their respective household head.

14. For purposes of this analysis, from low to high, the occupational status of individuals was classified as follows: helper or mão de obra, operator, technician (including inspector) or office worker, functionary (e.g., accountant, school teacher, nurse), and supervisor. This ranking was based on interviews with personnel officers of four firms, one bank, and two government offices. In the informal sector, unless special skills were clearly involved (e.g., television repair, mechanic, beautician, watch repair, etc.) individuals were given the status of helper.

15. These categories "equal to" and "lower" were collapsed to meet the requirements of X^2 analysis. Seventeen individuals, fourteen self-employed, fell into the lower status category.

16. Without presenting another table, it may be noted that the distribution of these workers by sector of employment and their income status relative to that of their respective household heads reaches the .05 level of significance.

17. The significance of this point is that despite his age, Eloy remains a "student" and he considers himself an "intellectual." He is an avid reader of economic, political, and historical texts. An active Mason, he participates in a small study group which convenes once or twice a month at the Mason Hall.

18. The unemployed son-in-law is the ex-husband of a daughter who issued from a consensual union that Eloy formed when he first came to Manaus. Thirty-eight years of age, the son-in-law is more a guest than a member of the household.

19. We observed that the consumption of alcohol is quite high among male workers, particularly those employed in the traditional industrial sector. However, we have no data with which to assess the belief that alcoholism is any higher now than it has ever been or that the consumption of alcohol is related to a loss of status by male heads of households.

Chapter 6.

1. Prior to the rubber boom, in 1872, Manaus contained 50.9 percent of the state's population. Between 1872 and 1900, while the population of the state increased by more than 70 percent, the number residing in Manaus declined to 20.1 percent of the total. See Table 2 (chapter 1).

2. In this particular context the increase of vehicular traffic should be noted. The city's paved streets, particularly in the central district, have become absolutely congested with motor vehicles. In the three year period 1975–78, the number of privately registered automobiles alone showed a relative increase of almost 50 percent, from approximately eighteen to more than twenty-six thousand and, except for the recession years of 1980–82, this rate of growth appears to have been sustained despite the lack of substantial improvement in city streets.

3. Some idea of the magnitude of these problems can be gleaned from a rather comprehensive study that was made in the mid-seventies, less than ten years after the creation of the Zona Franca. The study was commissioned by SUFRAMA and carried out by the Division of Urban Planning of the Prefeitura Municipal. Known as PDLI Manaus, this report was circulated among various authorities but never published. It contained estimates of population growth up to 1993, when the fiscal incentives for the Zona Franca are supposed to terminate. The report outlined in considerable detail the problems that the city would face as a consequence of industrialization and urban growth and it made specific recommendations as to what steps might be taken to alleviate these problems. A xeroxed copy of this report was made available to the author. To my knowledge, there does not exist a follow-up study with respect to the specific steps that might have been taken to implement this plan. It is my general impression that much of what was accomplished in this regard—e.g., the reconstruction of port facilities, highway construction, the construction of hotels to cope with the influx of tourists, the renovation of public buildings, etc.—contributed more to the commercial and industrial development of the city than to the solution of problems related to housing, sanitation, health, education, and recreation, in short, to the general welfare of the lower income strata of the population.

4. The Cadastro Imobiliário de Manaus, made in 1978, listed thirty-seven bairros in the city (see Bentes 1983: 11–12). The 1983 edition of the Planta da Cidade de Manaus includes what appear to be approximately fifteen additional bairros. All of these are located in what were peripheral areas and some, like Cidade Nova and São José, are large public housing schemes which, as of this writing, may or may not have been officially recognized as bairros.

5. In 1965, for example, Manaus' famous "floating city," really a favela constructed over the river and occupied by more than 2,000 people, was demolished in order to make way for the renovation of port facilities. Much of this population was removed to public housing projects which, in the process of construction, were no better served by public services than the floating city itself.

6. The Director of SHAM (Sociedade de Habitação do Estado do Amazonas) related that house and land speculation had become such a serious problem in public housing schemes that every new applicant has to be checked to determine whether or not the individual has already purchased and sold land and/or a house in one or another of these conjuntos. He stated: "If there were enough houses we would close our eyes to this kind of thing, but there are not enough houses and we have to deal with these people in a very objective way." In effect, housing problems have added a new dimension to the informal economy.

7. This is particularly the case with respect to those that were constructed in the period 1967–78, when more than 21,000 homes and apartments were built and sold in approximately thirty projects of this type. In 1984 the construction of public housing continued at a furious pace.

8. Informants claimed that this particular housing scheme was promoted by a former state governor for the purpose of profiting from the sale of land that he owned to the state.

9. Data of this type can be gleaned from a variety of sources. Particularly useful are the Anuários Estatísticos published by CODEAMA (Comissão de Desenvolvimento do Estado do Amazonas).

10. In many bairros it is not uncommon to smell or encounter fecal material draining along the streets.

11. In 1984 the distribution of filth on city streets was such that numerous informants, particularly among managers and government employees who had been transferred from other cities in Brazil, likened Manaus to "uma meda de adubo" (a pile of shit).

12. At the time of research, data collected by CODEAMA for subsequent years, including 1979, remained to be processed. Most of these data were in such a crude state of analysis that they could not be compared to the period 1970–78.

13. Beginning in 1975, the rate of parasitic infections showed an increase in every year for which data were available. By 1978, almost 32 percent of all registered deaths were attributed to parasitic diseases. Despite the morbidity and the fatalities attributed to parasitic diseases, an informant at the medical school claimed that the government appeared more interested in spending money on cardiovascular technology than on the treatment and prevention of parasitic diseases.

14. The educational system in Brazil is structured a bit differently from that of the United States. The introductory unit, called the "preliminar," is pre-primary. Primary school, called the "primeiro grau," consists of two four-year divisions, the primário and the ginásio. The segundo grau, sometimes called the "científico," extends three years and is roughly equivalent to high school. The third year of the segundo grau, called the pré-vestibular, is preparatory to tak-

ing the nationally administered university entrance examinations. Without passing these, an individual cannot enter the tuition-free federal or, in some cases, state university systems.

15. In Brazil, local government is not significantly involved in education. From top to bottom, the system is under federal regulation and, except for those that are private, schools and universities are administered by either the federal or state governments.

16. Related to this is the fact that teacher training is woefully inadequate. Moreover, the salaries and working conditions of teachers are so poor that they are a constant source of grievance and turnover in the profession.

17. According to data issued by the Department of Urban Planning, in 1973, 37 percent of the population between 7 and 14 years, and 48 percent of that between 15 and 18 years, were not attending school. It was speculated that the reason for this was the concentration of schools in the older bairros of the city and insufficient construction of schools in the peripheral areas.

18. In 1984, when the first phase of construction was completed, the humanities and social science divisions were moved to the new campus. The campus is a good fifteen kilometers from the center of the city and students and faculty alike complained bitterly that it was inadequately serviced by the public transportation system.

19. Perhaps because of industrialization, the percentage increase of students enrolled in the physical sciences was three times that of students in the humanities and social sciences.

20. With the restoration of the Teatro Amazonas, there now exists one playhouse in Manaus but this does not appear to be a focus of much popular interest.

21. Report of the Commission on Urban Planning.

22. Related to this "movimento," a majority of the younger workers who were interviewed, particularly among the women, indicated that they preferred to spend their leisure hours perambulating the commercial district.

23. To this, according to newspapers and knowledgeable informants, has been added a rapidly expanding underground economy in the sale of drugs.

24. It may be of interest to note that almost none of the persons interviewed in these households acknowledged the existence of the "prefeitura" or city government in the sense of identifying its functions and works. For most, it was indistinguishable from the state government.

25. Fifty-seven of the eighty-eight families included in the study lived in one of three neighborhoods in Bairro Raiz. In order to facilitate the collection of data with respect to communal life, an effort was made to locate workers and households in a single bairro and, further, to minimize as much as possible their distribution among various neighborhoods within the bairro. It was impos-

sible to locate sawmill workers in Raiz. Half of these families lived at Enseada do Marapatá and almost all of the rest in Bairro Educandos. Half of the families of autonomous workers lived in Raiz; the remainder were distributed among six different bairros in which we could make only superficial observations with respect to community life. Thus, the analysis here is largely based on data collected with reference to Raiz, Educandos, and Enseada do Marapatá.

26. This estimate is based on projections made by Manaus' Department of Urban Planning.

27. Jute processing firms are located nearby, in two neighboring bairros and, in addition to sawmills, are a major source of employment for residents of Educandos.

28. These drinking sessions posed somewhat of a problem with respect to obtaining interviews from these workers. Some interviews had to be postponed until late Sunday afternoon or evening when informants had sobered enough to respond to questions. This happened only once at Marapatá.

29. As previously noted, fifty-seven of the eighty-eight families included in the study lived in one of three neighborhoods in Bairro Raiz. Thus, these neighborhoods became the major focus of research for the purpose of collecting observational and other data relating to the social and cultural life of working class families at home, in the neighborhood, and in the larger urban milieu.

30. However, with the construction of the Industrial Park some four kilometers to the southeast, Raiz has continued to grow. In 1984, public officials and informed residents estimated the bairro's population to be considerably in excess of 30,000 inhabitants.

31. By the end of 1977, SHAM had constructed and assumed responsibility for the organization of seven conjuntos containing a total of 5,698 housing units of varying quality. Costa da Silva was the fifth largest of these conjuntos and provided housing for 471, representing a total population of approximately 2,700 inhabitants.

32. Even today drainage remains a problem in this section of the conjunto.

33. From its inception, the financial arrangements relating to the purchase of these apartments has remained in a state of complete confusion. In many cases, the original proprietors of these apartments sold them with unpaid mortgages to subsequent buyers who did not understand that they were receiving property without clear title. Some of these buyers have been harassed for payments that they do not think they owe. Some have felt compelled to remit these payments and some have refused to do so. More than 2,000 of Raiz's inhabitants live in Jardim Brasil.

34. It is noteworthy in this regard that while Father Fernando concluded these festivities with the celebration of an outdoor mass, next-door the Baptist Church was filled with participants in its Sunday evening services.

35. Father Fernando indicated that the total income derived from arraial had never exceeded U.S. $700 or 800, including money contributions.

36. In addition to the collection of a considerable variety of observational data, thirty-eight of these homes were selected for in-depth study. A more specialized study was also made of twenty-three small-scale enterprises in the neighborhood. All of these data were further supplemented by the systematic interview data that SHAM collected in its survey of household heads living in the community in 1978.

37. Because of inflation and re-evaluations of the cruzeiro, it is difficult to convert these data into current values or minimum salaries. In July of 1977 the official rate of exchange was Cr$14.26 to U.S. $1.00. This would suggest that in 1984 values, approximately 35 percent of these households reported incomes in excess of five minimum salaries.

38. In fact, as of 1984, almost half of the streets in the lower section of the neighborhood were still without pavement.

39. The marketplace remains unpaved. All but a dozen or more stalls are relatively small, perhaps 25–30 sq. ft. in size, and poorly constructed. Those selling large quantities of meat and fish are relatively large and considerably more substantial in their construction. For the most part, these particular vendors are retail sales agents employed by large-scale distributors. Most stalls have very limited space for storage and, except for those selling dry goods, their inventories are replenished by wholesale deliveries several times each week. Some vendors have only tables or trays on which they display vegetables, toys, clothing, or other items.

40. The registered enterprises included the bars, drugstores, meat shops, three dress shops, and two hairdressers.

41. By 1984, the medical clinic had been moved to a neighboring bairro.

42. As previously noted, even today Cristo-Rei shares its priest with Nossa Senhora do Carmo.

43. The Delegacia in Costa da Silva is staffed by policemen in the employ of the state. Residents seem to have more respect for federal police and generally call them when problems arise.

44. Interviews with diocesan leaders attached to the prelacy revealed that the prelacy in Manaus has been dominated by a long line of conservative bishops, and thus, parish priests, even when liberal, have been very reluctant to actively engage themselves in programs that might polititically ignite working class populations. Indeed, there are few politically active priests in Manaus and to my knowledge, all of them are foreigners who belong to missionary orders and much of their political effort is directed toward assisting Indian populations in the interior.

45. Again, one is reminded of Roberto DaMatta's (1985: 25–54) perceptive analysis of these contrastive social domains in Brazilian culture.

46. It is often the case that middle- and upper-class families in Manaus attend church at the "matrix" or cathedral.

Chapter 7.

1. This type of export-driven industrialization is more typically associated with development in Puerto Rico, the Dominican Republic, the Mexican board-er area, and countries located along the Pacific rim. See Fernandez (1973) and NACLA (1975) for a discussion relating to Mexico and Latin America. For the Pacific Rim see, for example, AMPO (1977), Lim (1980), Salaff (1981), and Gold (1986).

2. Apropos this point, John W. Bennett (1988: 10) states: "The fundamen-tal rhetoric of development—even in the fields of 'social development,' such as education, migration, and labor—is economic: the costs and gains of proposed changes are measured by monetary values." A review of a random selection of articles appearing in any one of the major journals reporting studies of develop-ment would provide substantial support of Bennett's contention in this regard.

3. Putting aside the controversy that this approach has generated among Marxist savants [see, e.g., Hindess and Hirst (1977), Foster-Carter (1978), Goodfriend (1979), Soiffer and Howe (1982), Hart (1983), and Prattis (1987)], as I interpret Balibar (1970: 199–208), a mode of production is a process by which producers (i.e., workers), non-producers (i.e., entrepreneurs), and the means of production (i.e., technology) are brought into some form of relation-ship. Social formations generally contain an articulation of different modes of production in terms of which one mode tends to be hegemonic in determining the overall structure of the formation.

4. For an analysis of the extension of compadrio relationships between individuals of different economic and social position in the Amazon, see Wagley (1953: 156–59). For discussion of the Brazilian tendency to personalize *o mundo* (the world) by transforming impersonal, but important, secondary relationships into close personal or familistic ties, see Maeyama (1975), particularly pp. 92–3.

5. Under the frontier circumstances that existed in the rubber fields, credit arrangements could not be comfortably secured by legally enforceable paper agreements or contracts.

6. The role of the state in this and the subsequent Amazonian social for-mation will be discussed in a later context.

7. This is not as paradoxical as it may seem when it is considered that the recruitment preferences of firms in the hegemonic and white collar sectors is

for young men and women who are more likely to be unmarried and living with their parents.

8. Such a review has been nicely done by Janice E. Perlman (1976: 91–131). Also see Zaluar (1985: 33–63).

9. Rational in this context, notes Roxborough (p. 756), means "calculable."

10. For the distinction drawn here between intransitive and transitive processes of change, I am indebted to H.W. Arndt (1981: 457–66). In this short but insightful article, Arndt traces two channels through which the concept of economic development entered common usage. One leads directly to Marx's *Capital* where, Arndt argues, the notion of development derives from the intransitive verb; accordingly, development is conceived as an historical, dialectical process in which the forces of production progressively evolve or unfold in the society as a whole. The other conception, associated with the transitive verb, Arndt traces to the British historians of Empire who conceived of development as an activity of government or private enterprise. Arndt seems to construe this distinction as involving two opposing theoretical views of development. I find these terms useful but, the reader may note, I have take liberty with Arndt's use of the terms. In what follows, I view the distinction as involving two empirical alternatives: i.e., development can be predominantly one or the other of these processes of change, and each has a different empirical character and consequences.

11. The most recent phase in the development of extractive enterprises, particularly as it relates to the mining of minerals, is of the opposite character. It involves a great deal of planning on the part of the state, state-led enterprises, and multinational firms and, as in the case of Carajas, it involves a great deal of industrial processing (see Companhia Vale do Rio Doce, 1981).

12. This question cannot be answered definitively from the primary and secondary data collected. If I had to hazard a response, the project seems to have been motivated, at least in part, by the political desire to concentrate sufficient employment opportunities in a network of urban places to effect a redistribution of population from the interior, thereby clearing the way for the development not of people but of natural resources by agro-industrial firms, mining interests, and large-scale forest projects like Jari. See, e.g., Cardoso and Müller (1977), Ianni (1978), and Garrido (1980).

Bibliography

Althusser, Louis and Etienne Balibar
1970   Reading Capital. New York: Pantheon.

Amado, Jorge
1962   Gabriela, Clove and Cinnamon. Translated from the Portuguese by
            James L. Taylor and William Grossman. New York: Alfred K.
            Knopf.

AMPO
1977   Free trade zones and industrialization of Asia. AMPO: Japan-Asia
            Quarterly Review 8: 4 and 9: 1–2.

Anderson, Robin A.
1976   Following Curupira: Colonization and Migration in Pará, 1758–1930.
            Unpublished Ph.D. dissertation, University of California, Davis.

Araújo, André Vidal de
1974   Sociologia de Manaus: Aspectos de Sua Aculturação. Manaus:
            Edições Fundação Cultural do Amazonas.

Arndt, H.W.
1981   Economic development: a semantic history. Economic Develop-
            ment and Cultural Change 29(3): 457–66.

Augel, Johannes
1984   The contribution of public goods to household reproduction: case
            study from Brazil. In Joan Smith, Immanuel Wallerstein, and Hans-
            Dieter Evers, eds., Households and the World-Economy. Beverly
            Hills, CA.: Sage Publications.

Balibar, E.
1970   The basic concepts of historical materialism. In L. Althusser and E.
            Balibar, eds., Reading Capital. New York: Pantheon, pp. 199–208.

Banck, Geert, A.
1980   Survival strategies of low-income urban households in Brazil. Urban Anthropology 9: 227–42.

Barbosa, Eva Machado
1984   Household economy and financial capital; the case of passbook savings in Brazil. In Joan Smith, Immanuel Wallerstein, and Hans-Dieter Evers, eds., Households and the World-Economy. Beverly Hills, CA.: Sage Publications.

Benchimol, Samuel
1947   Manaos: The Growth of a City in the Amazon Valley. Unpublished M.A. thesis, Miami University, Oxford, Ohio.
1977   Amazônia Um Pouco-Antes e Além-Depois. Manaus, Brasil: Editora Umberto Calderaro.

Bennett, John W.
1988   Anthropology and development: the ambiguous engagement. In John W. Bennett and John R. Bowen, eds., Production and Autonomy—Anthropological Studies and Critiques of Development. Society for Economic Anthropology Monograph No. 5. New York: University Press of America, pp. 1–30.

Bentes, Rosalvo Machado
1983   A Zona Franca o e Processo Migratorio para Manaus. Unpublished M.A. thesis, Universidade Federal do Pará, Brasil.

Berlinck, Manoel T.
1973   A Vida como ela é. Campinas.
1975   Marginalidade Social e Relações de Classes en São Paulo. Petrópolis, Brasil: Editora Vozes.

Bilac, Elizabete D.
1978   Famílias de Trabalhadores: Estratégias de Sobrevivência. São Paulo: Símbolo.

Bittencourt, Agnello
1925   Chorographia do Amazonas. Manaus: n.p.

Bonilla, Frank
        1964 The urban worker. In John J. Johnson, eds., Continuity and Change in Latin America. Stanford: Stanford University Press, pp. 186–205.

Braverman, Harry
1974   Labor and Monopoly Capital: The Degradation of Work in the 20th Century. New York: Monthly Review Press.

Bromley, Ray
1978   Introduction—to the urban informal sector: why is it worth dis-
            cussing? World Development 6(9/10): 1033–39.

Bruce, Richard W.
1976   Produção e Distribuição de Madeira Amazônica. Rio: IBDF.

Bunker, Stephen G.
1979   Power structures and exchange between government agencies in
            the expansion of the agricultural sector. Studies in Comparative
            International Development 14 (1): 56–76.
1980   Forces of destruction in Amazonia. Environment 22 (Sept.): 14–20,
            34–43.
1981   The impact of deforestation on peasant communities in the Médio
            Amazonas of Brazil. Studies in Third World Societies 13: 45–60.
1985   Underdeveloping the Amazon. Urbana: University of Illinois Press.

Burawoy, Michael
1979   The anthropology of industrial work. In Annual Reviews of Anthro-
            pology 8: 231–66.

Camargo, Cândido Procópio Ferreira de, et al.
1978   São Paulo: Growth and Poverty. London: The Bowerdean Press in
            association with The Catholic Institute for International Relations.

Cardoso, Fernando H.
1960   Proletariado e Mudança Social. Sociologia, Vol. XXI, No. 1, São
            Paulo.
1962   Proletariado no Brasil: situação e comportamento social. Revista
            Brasiliense, No. 41, pp. 98–122.
1973   Associated-dependent development: theoretical and practical impli-
            cations. In Alfred Stephan, ed., Authoritarian Brazil. New Haven:
            Yale University Press, pp. 142–78.
1975   Autoritarismo e democratização. Rio: Paz e Terra.
1977   The consumption of dependency theory in the United States. Latin
            American Research Review 13, No. 3, pp. 7–24.

Cardoso, Fernando H. and G. Müller
1977   Amazônia: Expansão do Capitalismo. São Paulo: Editora
            Brasiliense.

Castro, Edna Maria Ramos de, Maria Lúcia Sá, Edila Arnaud Ferreira Moura,
Ernesto Renan Freitas Pinto, and Marilene Corrêa da Silva
1984   A Utilização do Trabalho Feminino nas Indústria de Belém e Man-
            aus. Manaus: Preliminary manuscript. Cited with permission of the
            authors.

Chaplin, David
1970   Industrialization and labor in Peru. In Arthur J. Field, ed., City and

Country in the Third World. Cambridge, Mass.: Schenkman, pp. 165–200.

Chilcote, Ronald H.
1974   A critical synthesis of dependency theory. Latin American Perspectives 1, Vol. 1, pp. 4–29.
1981   Issues of theory in dependency and Marxism. Latin American Perspectives 8: 3–16.
1984   Theories of Development and Underdevelopment. Boulder, Co.: Westview Press.

Chilcote, Ronald H. and Dale L. Johnson, eds.
1983   Theories of Development—Mode of Production or Dependency? Beverly Hills, Calif.: Sage Publications.

Chilcote, Ronald H. and Joel C. Edelstein
1986   Latin America—Capitalist and Socialist Perspectives of Development and Underdevelopment. Boulder, Co.: Westview Press.

Companhia Vale do Rio Doce
1981   Eastern Amazon—Preliminary Development Plan, Vols. I and II.

Condurú, Jose Maria Pinheiro
1974   Agriculture in the Brazilian Amazon. In Charles Wagley, ed., Man in The Amazon. Gainesville: University of Florida Press, pp. 230–42.

Cruz, Ernesto
n.d.   Bélem. Rio: Livraria José Olimpio Editora.

da Cunha, Euclydes
1913   A Margem da História. Porto Alegre: Livraria Chardron de Lelo e Irmão.

DaMatta, Roberto
1985   A Casa & A Rua—Espaço, cidadania, mulher e morte no Brasil. São Paulo: Brasiliense.

Davis, Shelton H.
1977   Victims of the Miracle: Development and the Indians of Brazil. London: Cambridge University Press.

de Janvry, Alain
1985   Social disarticulation in Latin American history. In Kwan S. Kim and David F. Ruccio, eds., Debt and Development in Latin America. Notre Dame: University of Notre Dame Press, pp. 32–73.

Denevan, W.
1973   Development and the imminent demise of the Amazon rainforest. The Professional Geographer, 25, No. 2, pp. 130–35.

Despres, Leo A.
1987   Urban-industrial development and the marginality of workers in Manaus: some theoretical implications. In Werner von der Ohe, Kulturanthropologie. Berlin: Duncker & Humblot, pp. 67–88.
1988a   Dependent development and the marginality thesis: a case study from Manaus. In John W. Bennett and John R. Bowen, eds., Production and Autonomy—Anthropological Studies and Critiques of Development. Society for Economic Anthropology Monograph No. 5. New York: University Press of America, pp. 293–310.
1988b   Macrotheories, microcontexts, and the informal sector: case studies of self-employment in three Brazilian cities. Notre Dame, In.: Working Paper 110, Kellogg Institute for International Studies.

Diégues, Manuel Jr.
1960   Regiões Culturais do Brasil. Rio: Centro Brasileiro de Pesquisas Educacionais.

Durham, Eunice Ribeiro
1980   A família operária: consciência e ideologia. Dados 23: 201–13.

Edwards, Richard
1979   Contested Terrain: The Transformation of the Workplace in the Twentieth Century. New York: Basic Books.

Epstein, D. G.
1972   The genesis and function of squatter settlements in Brasília. In Thomas Weaver and D. White, eds., The Anthropology of Urban Environments. Boulder, Co.: SAA Monograph No. 11, pp. 51–8.
1973   Brasília, Plan and Reality: A Study of Planned and Spontaneous Urban Development. Berkeley: University of California Press.

Erickson, Kenneth P.
1977   The Brazilian Corporative State and Working-Class Politics. Berkeley: University of California Press.

Erickson, Kenneth P., Patrick V. Peppe, and Hobart A. Spalding, Jr.
1974   Research on the urban working class and organized labor in Argentina, Brazil, and Chile: what is left to be done? Latin American Research Review, IX, pp. 115–42.

Erickson, Kenneth P. and Patrick V. Peppe.
1976   Dependent capitalist development, U.S. foreign policy, and the reapression of the working class in Chile and Brazil. Latin American Perspectives, Vol. III, pp. 19–44.

Evans, Peter B.
1979   Dependent Development: The Alliance of Multinational, State, and Local Capital in Brazil. Princeton: Princeton University Press.

Faria, Vilmar E.
1978   Occupational Marginality, Employment and Poverty in Urban
            Brazil. Unpublished Ph.D. dissertation, Harvard University.

Fausto Neto, Ana Maria Q.
1982   Família Operária e Reprodução da Força de Trabalho. Petrópolis,
            Brasil: Vozes.

Fernandez, Raul A.
1973   The border industrial program of the United States-Mexican Bor-
            der. The Review of Radical Political Economics 5: 37–52.

Ferreira, Barros
1980   Amazônia Arrasada. São Paulo, Brasil: Editora Referência Ltda.

Filha, Irene Garrido
1980   O Projeto Jari e os Capitais Estrangeiros na Amazônia. Petrópolis:
            Vozes.

Flynn, Peter
1978   Brazil—A Political Analysis. Boulder, Co.: Westview Press.

Folbre, Nancy
1986   Hearts and spades: paradigms of household economics. World
            Development 14: 245–55.

Foster-Carter, Aidan
1976   From Rostow to Gunder Frank: conflicting paradigms in the analy-
            sis of underdevelopment. World Development 4: 167–80.
1978   The "mode of production" controversy. New Left Review 107: 44–77.

Foweraker, Joe W.
1981   The Struggle for Land. New York: Cambridge University Press.

Frank, Andre Gunder
1970   Latin America: Underdevelopment or Revolution? New York:
            Monthly Review Press.

Freyre, Gilberto
1963   The Mansions and The Shanties. Translated from the Portuguese
            and edited by Harriet de Onís. New York: Alfred A. Knopf. First
            published as Sobrados e Mucambos. Rio, 1936.

Friedman, Andres
1977   Industry and Labour: Class Struggles at Work and Monopoly Capi-
            talism. London: Macmillan.

Furtado, Celso
1968   The Economic Growth of Brazil. English-language edition, translat-
            ed by Ricardo W. de Aguiar and Eric Charles Drysdale. Berkeley:
            University of California Press.

Galvão, Eduardo
1952   The Religion of an Amazon Community. Ph.D. dissertation,
          Columbia University. Subsequently published under the title Santos
          e Visagens: Um Estudo da Vida Religiosa de Itá, Amazonas.
1955   Santos e Visagens: Um Estudo da Vida Religiosa de Itá, Amazonas.
          São Paulo, Brasil: Companhia Editora Nacional.
1959   Aculturação Indigena no Rio Negro. Belém: Boletim Museu
          Paraense Emilio Goeldi, No. 8.

Godlier, Maurice
1977   The concept of 'social and economic formation': the Inca example. In
          Maurice Godlier, Perspectives in Marxist Anthropology. Translated
          by Robert Brain. Cambridge: Cambridge University Press, pp. 63–69.

Gold, Thomas B.
1986   State and Society in the Taiwan Miracle. New York: M. E. Sharpe, Inc.

Goldschmidt, Walter
1978   As You Sow: Three Studies in the Social Consequences of Agribusi-
          ness. Montclair, N.J.: Allanheld, Osmun.

Gómez-Pompa, A., C. Vásquez-Yanes, and S. Guevara
1972   The tropical rainforest: a non-renewable resource. Science, 177: 762–65.

Goodfriend, Douglas E.
1979   Plus ça change, plus c'est la même chose: the dilemma of the
          French structural Marxists. In Stanley Diamond, ed., Toward a
          Marxist Anthropology—Problems and Perspectives. The Hague:
          Mouton, pp. 93–124.

Goodland, R. J. A. and H. S. Irwin
1975   Amazon Jungle: Green Hell to Red Desert? Amsterdam: North Hol-
          land.

Greaves, Thomas C.
1972   The Andean rural proletarians. Anthropological Quarterly, Vol. 45
          (2); 65–83.

Hanbury-Tenison, Robin
1973   A Question of Survival for the Indians of Brazil. New York: Scribner
          & Sons.

Hart, Keith
1973   Informal income opportunities and urban employment in Ghana.
          The Journal of Modern African Studies 11: 61–89.
1983   The contribution of Marxism to economic anthropology. In Sutti
          Ortiz, ed., Economic Anthropology—Topics and Theories. Society
          for Economic Anthropology Monograph No. 1. New York: Universi-
          ty Press of America, pp. 105–144.

Hecht, Susanna B.
1980   Deforestation in the Amazon Basin: magnitude, dynamics and soil resource effects. Studies in Third World Societies 13: 61–108.

Henfrey, Colin
1981   Ideological, theoretical, or Marxist practice? Dependency, modes of production, and class analysis of Latin America. Latin American Perspectives 8: 17–54.

Hindess, Barry and Paul Hirst
1977   Mode of Production and Social Formation. Atlantic Highlands: Humanities Press.

Ianni, Octavio
1978   A Luta Pela Terra. Petrópolis, Brasil: Editora Vozes.
1979   Colonização e Contra-Reforma Agrária na Amazônia. Petrópolis, Brasil: Editoria Vozes.

IBGE   Fundação Instituto Brasileiro de Geografia e Estatística
1960   Censo Demográfico. VII Receseamento Geral, Vol. 1, Parte 2. Acre, Amazonas, and Pará.
1980   Censo Demográfico. IX Recenseamento Geral, Vol. 1, Parte 5, Amazonas Mão-de-Obra.
1980   Censo Demográfico. IX Recenseamento Geral, Vol. 1, Part 6, Amazonas Famílias e Domicílios.
1980   Anuário Estatístico do Brasil.
1983   Anuário Estatístico do Brasil.

Interior
1982   Zona Franca—Desenvolvimento (en novas bases) para a Amazônia Ocidental.

Jelin, Elizabeth
1980   A baiana na força de trabalho: atividade doméstica, produção simples e trabalho assalariado em Salvador. In Angela Ramalho Vianna, et al., Bahia de Todos os Pobres. Caderno CEBRAP No. 34, Petrópolis, Brasil: Editora Vozes, pp. 167–84.

Katzman, Martin T.
1975   The Brazilian frontier in comparative perspective. Comparative Studies in Society and History 17: 266–85.
1976   Paradoxes of Amazonian development in a 'resource starved' world. Journal of Developing Areas 10: 445–60.
1977   Cities and Frontiers in Brazil: Regional Dimensions of Economic Development. Cambridge: Harvard U. Press.

Kowarick, Lúncio
1977   Capitalismo e Marginalidade na América Latina. Rio: Paz e Terra.

Krischke, Paulo, ed.

1984   Terra de Habitação vs. Terra de Espoliação. São Paulo, Brasil: Cortez.

Leeds, Anthony
1969   The significant variables determining the character of squatter settlements. América Latina 12: 44–86.
1974   Housing-settlement types, arrangements for living, proletarianization and the social structure of the city. In W. Cornelius and F. Trueblood, eds., Latin American Urban Research, Vol. 4. Beverly Hills, CA.: Sage Publications, pp. 67–99.

Leeds, Anthony and Elizabeth
1970   Brazil and the myth of urban rurality: urban experience, work, and values in 'squatments' of Rio de Janeiro and Lima. In A. J. Field, ed., City and Country in the Third World: Issues in the Modernization of Latin America. Cambridge, Mass.: Schenkman, pp. 229–85.
1976   Accounting for behavioral differences: three political systems and the response of squatters in Brazil, Peru, and Chile. In John Walton and Louis Masotti, eds., The City in Comparative Perspective. New York: John Wiley, pp. 193–248.

Lim, L. Y. C.
1981   Women's work in multinational electronics factories. In R. Dauber and M. L. Cain, eds., Women and Technological Change in Developing Countries. Boulder, Co.: Westview Press, pp. 181–90.

Lomnitz, Larissa Adler
1988   Informal exchange networks in formal systems: a theoretical model. American Anthropologist 90 (1): 42–55.

Lopes, Juarez Rubens Brandão
1964   Sociedade Industrial no Brasil. São Paulo, Brasil: Dífusão Européia do Livro.

McDonough, Peter
1981   Power and Ideology in Brazil. Princeton: Princeton University Press.

Macedo, Carmen Cinira
1979   A Reprodução de Desigualdade: O Projecto de Vida Familiar de um Grupo Operária. São Paulo: Hucitec.

Maeyama, Takashi
1975   Familization of the Unfamiliar World (The Família, Networks, and Groups in a Brazilian City). Unpublished Ph.D. dissertation, Cornell University.

Mahar, Dennis J.
1979   Frontier Development Policy in Brazil: A Study of Amazonia. New York: Praeger.

Marcondes, Freitas J. V.
1948   Mutirão or mutual aid. Rural Sociology 13: 374–84.

Martins, Jose de Souza
1980   Expropriação & Violência—A Questão Política no Campo. São Paulo: Hucitec.
1981   Os Camponeses e a Política no Brasil. Petrópolis, Brasil: Vozes.

Martins, Luciano
1966   Industrialização, Burguesia Nacional e Desenvolvimento: (Introdução à Crise Brasileira. Rio de Janeiro: Editora Saga.

Marx, Karl
1967   Capital. First published and edited by Frederick Engels in 1867. Unabridged Vol. 1, translated from the Third German Edition by Samuel Moore and Edward Aveling. New York: International Publishers.
1977   The Grundrisse. Edited and translated by David McLellan. New York: Harper Torchbooks.

Mata, Alfredo Augusto da
1916   Geographia e Topographia Médica de Manaus. Manaus: n.p.

Meggers, Betty J.
1950   Caboclo life in the mouth of the Amazon. The Anthropological Quarterly 23: 14–28.
1971   Amazonia: Man and Culture in a Counterfeit Paradise. Arlington Hts., Illinois: AHM Publishing Corporation.

Meillasoux, Claude.
1981   Maidens, Meal and Money: Capitalism and the Domestic Community. Cambridge: Cambridge University Press.

Merrick, T. W.
1976   Employment and earnings in the informal sector in Brazil: the case of Belo Horizonte. Journal of Developing Areas 10: 337–54.

Merrick, Thomas W. and Marianne Schmink
1983   Households headed by women and urban poverty in Brazil. In Mayra Buvinic, Margaret A. Lycette, and William Paul McGreevey, eds., Women and Poverty in the Third World. Baltimore: Johns Hopkins Press, pp. 244–71.

Miller, Darrel L.
1976   Itá in 1974. In Charles Wagley, Amazon Town: A Study of Man in the Tropics. New York: Oxford U. Press, pp. 296–325.

Miller, Solomon
1965   Proletarianization of Indian peasants in Northern Peru. Transactions of the New York Academy of Sciences, Ser. II, 27, pp. 782–89.

Miranda, Bertino de
1908   Cidade Manaus, sua História e seus Motins Políticos. Manaus: n.p.

Monteiro, Mario Ypiranga
1946   História das Ruas de Manaus. Manaus: Jornal do Comércio, 1946.

Moran, Emilio F.
1974   The adaptive system of the Amazônian caboclo. In Charles Wagley, ed., Man in the Amazon, pp. 136–59. Gainesville: University of Florida Press.
1977   Estratégias de sobrevivência: o uso de recursos ao longo da rodovia Transamazônica. Acta Amazônica, Vol. 7, No. 3, pp. 363–80.
1981   Developing the Amazon. Bloomington: Indiana University Press.

Morse, Richard M.
1971   São Paulo: case study of a Latin American metropolis. In Francine F. Rabinovitz and Felicity M. Trueblood, eds., Latin American Urban Research, Vol. 1. Beverly Hills, Calif.: Sage Publications, pp. 151–86.

Moser, Caroline O. N.
1978   Informal sector or petty commodity production: dualism or dependence in urban development? World Development, Vol. 6, Nos. 9/10, pp. 1041–64.
1984   The informal sector reworked: viability and vulnerability in urban development. Regional Development Dialogue, Vol. 5, No. 2, pp. 135–75.

Mougeot, Luc J. A.
1980   City-Ward Migration and Migrant Retention During Frontier Development in Brazil's Northern Region. Unpublished Ph.D. dissertation, Michigan State University.
1984   Alternative migration targets and Brazilian Amazonia's closing frontiers. Centre for Development Studies Monograph Series XVIII. Norwich: Geography Books/CDS-USC.

Mougeot, Luc J. A. and Luis E. Aragón, eds.
1983   O Despovoamento do Território Amazônico: Contribuições para sua Interpretação. Belém, Brasil: Cadernos Núcleo de Altos Estudos Amazônicos, No. 6.
1983   O Despovoamento do Território Amazônico: Quatro Tendências. In Mougeot and Aragón, eds., O Despovoamento do Território Amazônico. Belém, Brasil: Cadernos Núcleo de Altos Estudos Amazônicos, No. 6, pp. 9–26.

NACLA
1975   Hit and run: U.S. runaway shops on the Mexican border. Latin America and Empire Report 9: 2–20.

Nash, June
1979   We Eat the Mines and the Mines Eat Us. New York: Columbia University Press.

O'Donnell, Guillermo A.
1973   Modernization and Bureaucratic-Authoritarianism. Berkeley, CA.: Institute of International Studies.

Oliveira, Francisco de
1972   A economia brasileira: crítica à razão dualista. Estudos CEBRAP 2: 5–82.

Peattie, L.
1987   An idea in good currency and how it grew: the informal sector. World Development, Vol. 15, No. 7, pp. 851–60.

Peppe, Patrick V.
1977   Parliamentry socialism and workers' consciousness in Chile. In June Nash, et al., Ideology and Social Change in Latin America. New York: Gordon and Breach, pp. 92–109.

Pereira, Luiz
1965   Trabalho e Desenvolvimento no Brasil. São Paulo, Brasil: Difusão Européia do Livro.

Perlman, Janice E.
1976   The Myth of Marginality: Urban Politics and Poverty in Rio de Janeiro. Berkeley: University of California Press.

Pinto, Lúcio Flávio
1980   Amazônia: No Rastro do Saque. São Paulo, Brasil: Hucitec.

Portes, Alejandro and John Walton
1981   Labor, Class, and the International System. New York: Academic Press.

Prandi, José Reginaldo
1980   Trabalhadores por conta própria em Salvador. In Angela Ramalho Vianna, et al., Bahia de Todos os Pobres. Caderno CEBRAP No. 34. Petrópolis, Brasil: Editora Vozes, pp. 129–66.

Prattis, J. Iain
1987   Alternative views of economy in economic anthropology. In John Clammer, ed., Beyond the New Economic Anthropology. New York: St. Martin's Press, pp. 8–44.

Quijano, Anibal
1974   The marginal pole of the economy and the marginalized labor force. Economy and Society 3: 393–428.

Reis, Arthur Cesar Ferreira.

1931 História do Amazonas. Manaus: n.p.
1935 Manaus e Outras Vilas. Manaus: n.p.
1942 Sintese da História do Pará. Belém: n.p.
1974 Economic history of the Brazilian Amazon. In Charles Wagley, ed., Man in the Amazon. Gainesville: University of Florida Presses, pp. 33–44.

Reis, Nélio
1964 Problemas Sociológicos do Trabalho. Rio: Freitas Bastos.

Roberts, Bryan R.
1978 Cities of Peasants—The Political Economy of Urbanization in the Third World. Beverly Hills, Calif.: Sage Publications.

Rodrigues, Leôncio Martins
1966 Conflito Industrial e Sindicalismo no Brasil. São Paulo, Brasil: Difusão Européia do Livro.
1970 Industrialização e Atitudes Operárias: Estudo de um Groupo de Trabalhadores. São Paulo, Brasil: Brasiliense.

Rosen, Bernard C.
1982 The Industrial Connection. New York: Aldine.

Ross, Eric
1978 The evolution of the Amazonian peasantry. Journal of Latin American Studies 10: 193–218.

Roxborough, Ian
1988 Modernization theory revisited. A review article. Comparative Studies in Society and History 30(4): 753–61.

Salaff, Janet W.
1981 Working Daughters of Hong Kong. London: Cambridge University Press.

Salazar, Admilton Pinheiro
1981 Perspectivas gerais e visão atual do planejamento em suas relações com a economia regional e com o desenvolvimento estadual. Revista Amazonense de Desenvolvimento 10: 73–104.

Santos, Roberto
1979 Sistema de propriedade e relações de trabalho no Meio Rural Parnese. In José Marcelino Monteiro da Costa, ed., Amazônia: Desenvolvimento e Occupação. Rio: IPEA/INPES, pp. 103–40.

Sautchuk, J., Horácio Martins de Carvalho and Sérgio Buarque de Gusmão
1980 Projeto Jari: A Invasão Americana. Brasil HOJE, Vol. 1, pp. 13–111.

Sawyer, Donald
1979 Peasants and Capitalism on an Amazon Frontier. Unpublished Ph.D. dissertation, Harvard University.

Schmink, Marianne
1977   Frontier expansion and land conflicts in the Brazilian Amazon: con-
            tradictions in policy and process. Paper presented at the meetings
            of the American Anthropological Association, Houston.
1979   Community in Ascendance: Urban Industrial Growth and House-
            hold Income Strategies in Belo Horizonte, Brazil. Unpublished
            Ph.D. dissertation, University of Texas, Austin.
1984   Household economic strategies: review and research agenda. Latin
            American Research Review, Vol. XIX, No. 3, pp. 87–101.

Sena, Maurício Filho
1983   Contribuições para uma teoria de migração para a Amazônia: notas
            de discussão. In Mougeot and Aragón, eds., O Despovoamento do
            Territorio Amazônico. Belém, Brasil: Cadernos Núcleo de Altos
            Estudos Amazônicos, No. 6, pp. 27–53.

SHAM   Sociedade de Habitação do Estado do Amazonas.
1978   Pesquisa Sócio Econômica Relaizada nos Conjuntos Habitacionais
            da SHAM Localizados em Manaus, Amazonas. Manaus: SHAM

Sioli, Harold
1973   Recent human activities in the Brazilian Amazon region and their
            ecological effects. In Betty J. Meggers, Edward S. Avensu, and W.
            Donald Duckworth, eds., Tropical Forest Ecosystems in Africa and
            South America: A Comparative View. Washington: Smithsonian, pp.
            321–34.

Skillings, R. and N. Tcheyan
1979   Economic Development Prospects of the Amazon Region of Brazil.
            Occasional Paper Series, no. 9, School of Advanced International
            Studies. Washington, D.C.: School of Advanced International Stud-
            ies, Johns Hopkins University.

Soiffer, Stephen M. and Gary N. Howe
1982   Patrons, clients and the articulation of modes of production: an
            examination of the penetration of capitalism into peripheral agricul-
            ture in Northeastern Brazil. Journal of Peasant Studies 9: 176–206.

Souza, Paulo R. and Victor E. Tokman
1976   The informal urban sector in Latin America. International Labour
            Review, Vol. 114, No. 3, pp. 355–65.

Spalding, Hobart A., Jr.
1977   Organized Labor in Latin America: Historical Case Studies of
            Urban Workers in Dependent Societies. New York: Harper & Row.

SUDAM
1973   Amazon Model of Integration. Brasília: Superintendency for the
            Development of Amazonia, Department of Documentation.

1974   Amazônia Novo Universo. Brasília: Superintendency for the Development of Amazonia, Department of Documentation.
1982   III Plano de Desenvolvimento da Amazônia 1980–85. Belém: Superindendency for the Development of Amazônia, Department of Documentation.

SUFRAMA
1983   Desenvolvimento Industrial—Perfil dos Projetos Aprovados na Amazônia Ocidental. Manaus: Superintendência da Zona Franca de Manaus, Coordenadoria de Comunicação Social.
1984   Relatório de Actividades 1983. Manaus: Superintendência da Zona Franca de Manaus, Coordenadoria da Comunicação, Social.

Tastevin, Constant
1943   The Middle Amazon: Its People and Geography. Washington, D.C.: Office of Emergency Management.

Taussig, Michael T.
1980   The Devil and Commodity Fetishism in South America. Chapel Hill: The University of North Carolina Press.

Thompson, E. P.
1963   The Making of the English Working Class. New York: Pantheon.

Tolosa, H. C.
1976   Subutilização e mobilidade de mão-de-obra urbana. In Josef Barat, ed., Política de Desenvolvimento Urbano. Rio: IPEA, pp. 68–78.
1978   Causes of urban poverty in Brazil. World Development 6(9/10): 1087–1101.

Valenzuela, J. Samuel and Arturo Valenzuela
1981   Modernization and dependency: alternative perspectives in the study of Latin American underdevelopment. In Heraldo Muñoz, ed., From Dependency to Development—Strategies to Overcome Underdevelopment and Inequality. Boulder, Co.: Westview Press, pp. 15–42.

Vianna, Angela Ramalho
1980   Estratégias de sobrevivência num bairro pobre de Salvador. In Angela Ramalho Vianna, et al., Bahia de Todos os Pobres. Caderno CEBRAP No. 34. Petrópolis, Brasil: Editora Vozes, pp. 185–214.

Villalobos, André, Eduardo Viola, J. A. Guilhon-Albuquerque, Lúcio Kowarick, and Luiz B. L. Orlandi (contributors)
1978   Classes Sociais e Trabalho Produtivo. São Paulo, Brasil: CEDEC and Paz e Terra.

Wagley, Charles
1953   Amazon Town—A Study of Man in the Tropics. New York: Macmillan.

1963   An Introduction to Brazil. New York: Columbia University Press.
1971   An Introduction to Brazil. Rev. ed. New York: Columbia University Press.

Wagley, Charles, ed.
1974   Man in the Amazon. Gainesville: University of Florida Press.

Watson, James
1953   Way station of westernization: the Brazilian Caboclo. In James Watson, et al., Brazil: Papers Presented in the Institute for Brazilian Studies. Nashville: Vanderbilt University Press, pp. 9–59.

Wells, John
1976   Subconsumo, tamanho de mercado e padrões de gastos familiares no Brasil. Estudos CEBRAP 17, pp. 5–60.

Zaluar, Alba
1985   A Máquina e a Revolta. São Paulo, Brasil: Editora Brasiliense, S.A.

Index

313